Penguin Education

Penguin Critical Anthologies
General Editor: Christopher Ricks

W. B. Yeats

Edited by William H. Pritchard

W.B.Yeats
A Critical Anthology

Edited by
William H. Pritchard
Penguin Books

Penguin Books Ltd, Harmondsworth,
Middlesex, England
Penguin Books Inc, 7110 Ambassador Road,
Baltimore, Md 21207, USA
Penguin Books Australia Ltd,
Ringwood, Victoria, Australia

First published 1972
This selection copyright ©William H. Pritchard, 1972
Introduction and notes copyright © William H. Pritchard, 1972

Made and printed in Great Britain by
Hazell Watson & Viney Ltd
Aylesbury, Bucks
Set in Monotype Bembo

Contents

6 Contents

7 Contents

Part Two Later Criticism (after 1939)

8   Contents

9 Contents

Preface

I regret that I was unable to obtain F. R. Leavis' permission to reprint either his discussion of Yeats in *New Bearings in English Poetry* or his *Scrutiny* reviews of *The Winding Stair* and of *Last Poems*. I was also unable to reprint T. S. Eliot's *Athenaeum* and *Criterion* notices of Yeats, or his pages on the poet from *After Strange Gods*.

In editing this selection I have corrected some misspellings and misprints, added some footnotes and dropped out a few when they didn't seem relevant. All footnotes not designated as by the editor are to be found in the original sources.

I should like to thank the staff of the Amherst College Library for their cooperation in the preparation of this anthology. More particular thanks go to Christopher Ricks and Lola O'Hara for various helpful suggestions, and to Stephen Gunnels, Robert-Louis Abrahamson and Marietta Pritchard.

Table of Dates

1897 *The Secret Rose* published. Visits Coole Park, collects folklore there with Lady Gregory.

1899 *The Wind Among the Reeds* wins the *Academy* prize as the best book of poetry of the year.

1900 Proposes marriage to Maud Gonne in London. Forms new order of the Golden Dawn.

1902 Founding of Irish National Theatre Society, Yeats president. *Diarmuid and Grania* written in collaboration with George Moore. *Cathleen ni Houlihan* performed in Dublin with Maud Gonne in title role.

1903 *In the Seven Woods*; *Ideas of Good and Evil* (essays). First American lecture tour (forty lectures) financial success. Maud Gonne marries John MacBride.

1904 Opening of the Abbey Theatre. *The King's Threshold* and *On Baile's Strand*.

1905 *The Shadowy Waters*.

1906 *Poems, 1899–1905*. Named director of Abbey Theatre with Lady Gregory and Synge.

1907 Yeats defends Synge at riots at opening of *Playboy of the Western World*. John Butler Yeats sails for America.

1908 *Collected Works* (8 vols.). Complete revision of early work. Meets Ezra Pound.

1909 Death of Synge.

1910 *The Green Helmet and Other Poems*.

1912 Yeats lectures at Harvard on 'The Theatre of Beauty'. *Cutting of an Agate* (essays) published in America.

1913 Pound acts as Yeats' secretary. They spend the autumn in a cottage in Sussex.

1914 *Responsibilities*. Finishes *Reveries* (first section of *Autobiographies*).

1915 Refuses offer of knighthood.

1916 Easter Rising in Dublin. Maud Gonne's husband killed. Yeats proposes marriage once more.

1917 Buys Castle at Ballylee. Proposes to Iseult Gonne (Maud's daughter). Marries Georgie Hyde-Lees on 21 October. *The Wild Swans at Coole*. Mrs Yeats' automatic writing begins on honeymoon. *Per Amica Silentia Lunae*.

1918 Restoration of Ballylee Tower.

1919 Anne Butler Yeats born. Yeats and family move into Ballylee. *The Wild Swans at Coole* published in enlarged (Macmillan) edition.

1920 American lecture tour.

1921 *Michael Robartes and the Dancer*. Michael Butler Yeats born.

1922 *The Trembling of the Veil* (second section of *Autobiography*) published. John Butler Yeats dies in New York. Irish Civil War. Yeats becomes member of Irish Senate.

1923 Nobel Prize for Poetry. Accepts in person.

1924 Working on *A Vision*.

1925 *A Vision* published.

1927 Lung congestion and influenza lead to collapse. Ordered to take complete rest.

1928 Convalesces in Cannes and Rapallo. *The Tower* published. Finishes term in Irish Senate.

1929 *A Packet for Ezra Pound*.

1931 D.Litt. degree from Oxford. Last summer visit with Lady Gregory at Coole.

1932 Lady Gregory dies. Last American tour. *Words for Music Perhaps and other poems*.

1933 *The Winding Stair*.

1934 Steinach rejuvenation operation performed; Yeats regards it as successful. *Collected Plays*.

1935 *A Full Moon in March*. Translating *Upanishads* with Swami Shri Purohit.

1936 Seriously ill. BBC lecture on 'Modern Poetry'.

1937 Four BBC broadcasts. Edits *Oxford Book of Modern Verse*. *Essays 1931–1936*. *A Vision* revised.

1938 Moves to south of France. *The Herne's Egg* and *Purgatory*. Last appearance at Abbey Theatre.

1939 Dies 28 January. Burial at Roquebrune, France. *Last Poems and Two Plays*; *On the Boiler* (prose).

1948 Body reinterred at Drumcliffe Churchyard, Sligo.

Part One Early Criticism (to 1940)

In 1900 he believed in fairies; that was bad enough; but in 1930 we are confronted with the pitiful, the deplorable spectacle of a grown man occupied with the mumbo-jumbo magic and the nonsense of India. Whether he seriously believed such stuff to be true, or merely thought it petty, or imagined it would impress the public, is immaterial. The plain fact remains that he made it the centre of his work. Gentlemen, I need say no more.

In this manner, Auden's Public Prosecutor summed up the case against the late Mr W. B. Yeats shortly after his death in 1939. Although Counsel for the Defence replied eloquently, and Auden also took the opportunity of his commemorative poem to assure Yeats that 'You were silly like us; your gift survived it all', the prosecutor was able to make the exaggerated point as firmly as he did because he spoke at the end of one tradition of response to the poet's work, the response that however great a poet Yeats was in promise or performance, he required a good deal of putting up with. D. H. Lawrence said it most succinctly: 'He seems awfully queer stuff to me now – as if he wouldn't bear touching.' Fifty-three years before Auden's Prosecutor rested his case, Gerard Manley Hopkins amusingly stated his in similar terms when, writing to Patmore, he referred to Yeats' early *Mosada*, which the poet's proud father had presented for Hopkins' admiration, as 'a strained and unworkable allegory'. Hopkins wanted to ask questions about how the young man and sphinx, situated on a rock in the sea, got there in the first place, or what they ate, and he justified this 'prosaic' criticism by asserting that 'common-sense is never out of place anywhere'. And in what was probably the most elaborate attempt by a critic during Yeats' lifetime to understand the poet's use of 'magic' as a 'feature of the rational imagination', R. P. Blackmur had also to admit that, as a tool for poetry, magic was defective insofar as it had 'no available edifice of reason reared upon it conventionally independent of its inspiration'. Hopkins' common-sense, it turned out, was still not out of place five decades after he invoked it.

Blackmur used the term 'magic' with particular reference to those later poems of Yeats, particularly from *The Tower*, which made use of the systematic explanation of human history and personality he had developed in *A Vision*. But by extending and loosening the term's sense we can see that, from the very beginning of Yeats' career, readers responded to something like the magic in or of his poems. Reviewers of the early volumes, at least through *The Wind Among the Reeds* (1899), typically expressed their admiration and delight in Yeats' poetic virtue by saying that they, mere critics, couldn't express it, that indeed it was inexpressible; so we find more than usual reliance upon phrases like 'incommunicable beauty', 'irresistible' and 'inexhaustible' metaphors, spirit that is 'insubstantial and uncapturable as a gust of the night'. A handy word in which all these terms could be summed up was, of course, Celtic, and as with Herbert Spencer's *The Unknowable*, all the different inexpressible somethings could be captured and vibrantly named by it. Lionel Johnson, perhaps remembering that he was a classicist, insisted that though Yeats wrote Celtic poetry he did it in the classical manner with an art that was full of reason; but he did not pursue these claims, and no one else recognized them, if indeed they had much existence outside Johnson's head. On the whole, reviewers of Yeats talked about his art in exactly the way he himself preferred to see it: as, in the language of his essay 'The Autumn of the Body', creating 'wavering meditative organic rhythms' which would cast out the energetic beat of daylight Victorian poetry in favour of 'disembodied ecstasy'. The more 'incalculable' his rhythms or incommunicable his beauty seemed, the better. Robert Louis Stevenson was thus in perfect phase with a larger pattern of response when he sought words 'in vain' to express his inexpressible feelings about *The Lake Isle of Innisfree*.

'Then in 1900 everybody got down off his stilts; henceforth nobody drank absinthe with his black coffee; nobody went mad; nobody committed suicide; nobody joined the Catholic church; or if they did I have forgotten.' Though it may be presumptuous to apply Yeats' fine sweep of social history to readers and critics as well as to the poets, it does seem that soon after this century began, appreciations of Yeats' work contain more sharply expressed criticisms of its excesses. William Archer, who had a good eye for excesses in general, felt compelled at least to raise the possibility that the poet might be accused of 'mannerism', though he himself does not accede to the charge. But he points, with the term 'fossilized symbolism,' to what was becoming a real sticking-point for many appreciators of Yeats: the presence of a symbolism that seemed, in Archer's word, 'fossilized', and which others characterized as arbitrary, vague or unintelligible. In the face of the Immortal Rose or the Polar Dragon, did not a reader need more help than Yeats gave him? Was the inability of these symbols to stand and reveal themselves without explanatory commentary not an indication of poetic weakness rather than necessarily of incommunicable beauty? How was one to be sure that it *was* beauty when nobody, not even the poem itself, was quite able to put it into words? And in response to the *Academy's* praise of *Ideas of Good and Evil*, Yeats' 1903 collection of his essays, A. Clutton-Brock responded by claiming that the very premises on which the Poetry of Reverie was written gave in too easily to the subconscious and the vaguely profound.

Yeats himself was soon quite willing to join his critics in pointing out, with more elegance and craftiness than they could muster, the limitations of his early verse. He did this most significantly by constantly revising that verse, up to and after collecting it in the grand edition of 1908, but also by disowning, often in a lordly manner, his own words as belonging merely to last year's language. So the richly eloquent essay 'The Autumn of the Body' was almost no sooner published than its author announced he was tired of that sort of thing. By 1914, in composing the *Reveries* section which was to become the first part of *Autobiographies*, he found on rereading his early poetry that it contained little but 'Romantic convention, unconscious drama', and proffered a sentiment with which no reader could possibly disagree: 'It is so many years before one can believe enough in what one feels even to know what the feeling is.' Even before that, particularly in the essay 'Poetry and Tradition', Yeats' emphasis has shifted from talk about style as creating disembodied essences to the notion of it as 'the playing of strength when the day's work is done' and as most importantly exploiting 'that touch of extravagance, of irony, of surprise' which catches up reader and poet into 'the freedom of self-delight'. The latter term is to occur significantly in later poems: in *Meditations in Time of Civil War* where it is 'the abounding glittering jet' that springs out of 'life's own self-delight'; in *A Prayer for My Daughter* where it is prayed that the daughter may become 'Self-delighting, self-appeasing, self-affrighting'. The play of the fountain, or of the flourishing hidden tree, is made possible by cultivating strength down there at the base, beginning to believe enough in what one feels so that, again in the language of *A Prayer for My Daughter*, 'the soul discovers radical innocence' – and 'radical' is precisely the rooted word Yeats wanted.

Predicting what the poet was going to do next on the basis of what he had just done turned out to be an increasingly hazardous occupation. In the first full-scale book on Yeats' poetry – and a good book too – Forrest Reid guessed in 1915 that his future poems would not differ much from the sort he had just published in *Responsibilities*: they would be less 'rapturous', less 'inspired' than were his earlier poems, and their beauty would lie in the 'hard, intellectual quality' of lyric. How could Reid have known or suspected that in the same year Yeats was to write *Ego Dominus Tuus*, laying out the rationale for new possibilities of inspiration in a poem whose final apostrophe defined wisdom as blindness and spoke of seeking 'an image, not a book':

I call to the mysterious one who yet
Shall walk the wet sands by the edge of the stream
And look most like me, being indeed my double,
And prove of all imaginable things
The most unlike, being my anti-self.

These words are spoken by 'Ille' (Willie, quipped Ezra Pound). Poor 'Hic', the other speaker, simply couldn't understand this kind of talk, but it's not evident that Pound himself, who had just reviewed *Responsibilities* and praised Yeats as a sort of Imagist who wrote poems with 'hardness of outline' would have had much respect for the kind of 'image' Yeats was now in search of. Like Stephen Dedalus, who walked around Joyce's novels with Michael Robartes and Fergus in his head and dreamed impossible dreams, Yeats, to avoid the 'dissipation and despair' Ille speaks of as the artist's lot, would become ever more of an impossible poet in the demands his art made on reality. Fifty-one years old, and a year later, he wrote *The Wild Swans at Coole*, a poem where passion and conquest attend upon the swans but not upon the speaker; and if Middleton Murry had been responding to that poem alone when he reviewed the volume in 1919, his judgement that the book was indeed Yeats' swan song and 'eloquent of final defeat' might have had a different ring than it now has. Murry not only ignored the stirrings in *Ego Dominus Tuus* but also the powerful way poems like the Robert Gregory epistle or *The Fisherman* made passion and conquest strongly visible. And though *Easter 1916* had not yet been published in 1919 it had been written, as had *The Second Coming* and *Prayer for My Daughter*, poems no more eloquent of final defeat than they were notable for 'hardness of outline' or imagistic self-sufficiency. Neither Murry nor Pound could make Yeats stay still.

The years 1914 to 1921 were marked by the publication of volumes as richly various as *Responsibilities, The Wild Swans at Coole* and *Michael Robartes and the Dancer,* by the first volume of autobiography, and by *Per Amica Silentia Lunae* in which the anti-self theory is expounded and the foundations for *A Vision* laid. Further marked by Yeats' final rejected proposals to both Maud Gonne and her daughter, his marriage, purchase of the tower and birth of his two children, they defy summarizing commentary. But in looking ahead to the increasingly demanding critical attention Yeats was to receive during the remaining eighteen years of his life in the twenties and thirties, it is worth pausing momentarily over the most demanding of all Yeats' critics. John Butler Yeats' letters to his son, an endlessly rereadable collection of brilliant forays in all directions, must have exhilarated the poet, yet made him feel how impossible it would be for any mere man fully to act out or on the father's advice. At one point (in 1914) J. B. Yeats pronounces that the artist is the 'antithesis of the man of action', that 'the chief thing to know and never forget is that art is dreamland' and that for a poet to meddle with ethics or think scientifically is to lose all music and cease to be a poet at all. A rather vigorous dreamland, preferably Homeric and Shakespearian – could it have been attained by the son's poem that same year which called out for the imagining of 'a man who does not exist,/A man who is but a dream' (*The Fisherman*)? But then, seven years later in one of the very last of the father's letters he speaks as if W. B. Yeats' work has been done, the swan-song sung, and as if it were all now a matter of what might have been. Yeats, his father tells him, should have wedded his wild imagination to concrete fact, should have made 'the game of life' his subject, should not have put on a 'dress coat' and shut himself in, should have – somehow – stayed with

father: 'Had you stayed with me, we would have collaborated. . . .'
Imagine the combination of feelings – guilt, annoyance, frustration,
tenderness – with which such a letter must have been received.
The sum of father's advice turns out to be that a poet must both
completely transcend and completely accept life, must dream high
while remaining wholly in touch with the smallest tick of human
feeling. Could even *Meditations in Time of Civil War*, begun in
1921, live up to John Butler Yeats' enormous expectations and
poetic demands?

His father died in 1922; two years later Yeats received the
Nobel Prize. But the question of how appropriate it was for a
poet to act and write as if all art was dreamland, or indeed whether
in fact his art behaved as if it were dreamland, provided the main
critical preoccupation for the impressive list of British and
American critics who, after the publication of *The Tower* in 1928,
addressed themselves to the significance of Yeats' work.
Interestingly enough, with the exception of Theodore Spencer's
review, they did not write in direct response to that
extraordinary volume the appearance of which Dr Leavis has
recently claimed was the occasion when the poet's greatness
became clear. The two most challenging attempts to see Yeats'
career as a whole, though it was very far from finished at the
time they were made, appeared within a year of one another in
considerations by Leavis and Edmund Wilson. While Wilson's
essay is not as critically questioning as Leavis' it provided a lucid
and somewhat reassuring discussion of *A Vision*, Yeats' attempt to
systematize dreamland. Leavis' essay on the poet from *New
Bearings in English Poetry* (1932) is admiring, almost wondering at
how it was Yeats managed to come out as well as he had, considering
the dreadful late-nineteenth century poetic tradition in which he
grew up. A few years previously, I. A. Richards had defined
Yeats' work as a 'repudiation of the most active contemporary
interests', treated the poetry rather briefly and disapprovingly as a

mode of escape ('Mr Yeats retires behind black velvet curtains') and sweepingly declared that Yeats had repudiated 'life itself, in favour of a supernatural world'. Unlike Richards, Leavis had the advantage of reading through *The Tower*, and he shows how the contending claims of nature and the supernatural animate and make poignant the life of *Sailing to Byzantium* or *The Tower* or *Among School Children*. Perhaps the most valuable feature of Leavis' essay was its firm linking of Yeats' early work with nineteenth-century English poetry. By quotation and deft commentary Leavis brought out the indebtedness of particular poems to Keats, Tennyson, William Morris and others, and demonstrated how Yeats' dream world is to be understood in relation to the Romantic tradition. Leavis' description of the 'remarkable change' shown by the poetry between *The Wind Among the Reeds* (1899) and *The Green Helmet* (1912) has become almost canonical:

It is hard to believe that the characteristic verse of the later volume comes from the same hand as that of the earlier. The new verse has no incantation, no dreamy, hypnotic rhythm; it belongs to the actual, waking world, and is in the idiom and movement of modern speech. It is spare, hard and sinewy and in tone sardonic, expressing the bitterness and disillusion of a man who has struggled and been frustrated.

Stressing the continuities between *The Tower* (1928) and its predecessors, Leavis saluted its 'ripeness in disillusion', its 'difficult and delicate sincerity, an extraordinarily subtle poise'.

Having said thus much in praise, Leavis ended his essay by some qualifying words, aimed at suggesting why Yeats' achievement was less complete than it might have been had the poetic tradition he inherited been a finer one:

What he testifies against is not the poetic tradition, but the general state of civilization and culture; a state which, he contends, makes waste inevitable for the sensitive. But he implies nothing against holding that if the poetic tradition had been different, as it might very well have been, he might have brought more of himself to expression.

At any rate

No Englishman ... could have profited by the sources of strength open to Mr Yeats as an Irishman, and no such source is open to any one now. No serious poet could propose to begin again where Mr Yeats began.

A year later, reviewing *The Winding Stair* in *Scrutiny*, Leavis used the word 'disappointing' in his opening sentence, finding that the 'proud sardonic tension' of *The Tower* had slackened, that a 'sterile bitterness' was now evident in many poems, and that the tension of the earlier volume had now relaxed into vacillation, into relative inertness. It was the 'vital tension between counter-attracting presences' that now seemed absent; while the simplifications of the Crazy Jane persona were hardly an adequate substitute. And after Yeats' death, reviewing *Last Poems*, Leavis began with 'This is a saddening volume', found only a single poem 'to add to the number of the memorable' (curiously enough it was a rather ordinary one called *Those Images*) and after recurring again with reference to Yeats' achievement, to the waste, the 'sense of a heavy price paid', he acknowledged Yeats as a major poet but ranked him below Donne, Marvell, Pope, Wordsworth, Byron, Hopkins and Eliot.

T. S. Eliot's comments on Yeats have the particular fascinations of those made by one leading poet of an era on the other. Eliot began his notice of Yeats in 1919 with an oblique review of *The Cutting of an Agate*, a collection of essays and prefaces. Titling his review, significantly, 'A Foreign Mind', Eliot set out to emphasize Yeats' uniqueness and to look askance at it: 'its author, as much in his prose as in his verse, is not "of this world" – *this* world, of course, being our visible planet with whatever our theology or myth may conceive as below or above it.' Observing, pointedly, that 'Mr Yeats' cosmos is not a French world, certainly', Eliot admitted that it was probably Irish, but at any rate that 'The difference between his world and ours is so complete as to seem almost a physiological variety, different nerves and senses'. He went on to charge Yeats with making no distinction between dream and reality and with writing in the style of Walter Pater. Seductive though that style may be, Yeats is judged sometimes incoherent as a 'philosopher of aesthetics' and Eliot sums up the case thus:

> But all of his observations are quite consistent with his personality, with his remoteness. His remoteness is not an escape from the world, for he is innocent of any world to escape from; his procedure is blameless, but he does not start where we do. His mind is, in fact, extreme in egoism, and, as often with egoism, remains a little crude. . . .

But Eliot admits that 'in verse at least' Yeats' feeling is not 'simply crudeness and egoism, but that it has a positive, individual and permanent quality'.

Fifteen years later, in *After Strange Gods*, Eliot discussed Yeats' search for a tradition, commenting on the 'somewhat artificially induced poeticality' of the early poetry which, in a memorable comparison, he said, like Swinburne's verse, 'has the effect of repeated doses of gin and water'. Yeats is admired for having outgrown the 'wrong supernatural world' of those poems, admired for having 'packed away his bibelots and resigned himself to live in an apartment furnished in the barest simplicity'. The 'austerity' of the later verse 'on the whole, should compel the admiration of the least sympathetic'; and Eliot observes, wryly, that though Mr Yeats is still perhaps a little too much weather-worn Triton among the streams, he has arrived at greatness against the greatest odds; if he has not arrived at a central and universal philosophy he has at least discarded, for the most part, the trifling and eccentric, the provincial in time and place.

These remarks set the stage for Eliot's 1935 notice in the *Criterion* coinciding with Yeats' seventieth birthday. In a markedly more generous assessment of the poet than he had hitherto given, Eliot stressed Yeats' services, as an Irish writer, to English literature:

In his *literary* nationalism, therefore, Mr Yeats has performed a great service to the English language. His poetry, in his latest and greatest period, has tended to divest itself of the more superfluous stage properties of Ireland, and is perhaps all the more Irish for being unaffectedly so. There is a rhythm, an intonation, a way of making the simplest statement in the fewest and barest words, which belong to Mr Yeats and to no one else. His influence upon English poetry has been great and beneficial. . . .

He concludes by affirming that Yeats 'has been and is the greatest poet of his time' whose extraordinary long period of development makes him 'At no time . . . less out-of-date than today, among men twenty and forty years his juniors.'

Eliot expressed his gratitude to Yeats most fully and generously in the Dublin lecture delivered after his death. Surely it is difficult to imagine Eliot sitting down for an evening with Yeats' poetry and not experiencing the most complex as well as simple kinds of dissatisfaction: perhaps the best way to think of them together is to remember that *The Waste Land* was published in the same year as *Meditations in Time of Civil War* (1922), as were *Gerontion* and *The Second Coming* (1919) or *Ash Wednesday* and *Byzantium* (1930). And the particular distinctions of R. P. Blackmur's long essay on how Yeats' poetry uses magic is that, in raising questions about Yeats as a 'modern' poet, Blackmur finds it necessary to recur to Eliot as a point of comparison, analogy, and distinguishing force.

Yeats' death in 1939 set off large numbers of attempts to see him steadily and whole but this section confines itself to two tributes from W. H. Auden. Auden has recently edited out certain of the stanzas of 'In Memory of W. B. Yeats' that are here presented: no doubt he decided it was presumptuous to speak for Time and 'pardon' Yeats for his 'views' as it already had Kipling and would Paul Claudel. But it is too bad not to have this cultural and personal touch for the way it confirms that like other readers of Yeats, Auden was unwilling quickly and painlessly to affirm the poet's greatness. Yeats was 'silly like us', but he was also very much unlike us; unlike the literary 'we' Eliot spoke to as *Athenaeum* or *Criterion* readers, unlike I. A. Richards' or Leavis' 'we' of agnostic moral men who deplore a too extensive acquaintance with Fairies and Gyres; unlike the politically sound and unsilly 'we' of Auden's enlightened humanitarianism. As the speaker in John Berryman's recent *Dream Song no. 334* declared:

Yeats knew nothing about life: it was all symbols
and Wordsworthian egotism: Yeats on Cemetery Ridge
would not have been scared, like you & me,
he would have been, before the bullet that was his,
studying the movements of the birds,
said disappointed and amazed Henry.

But Maud Gonne wrote a more simply noble epitaph in 1940: 'Spirits need no language to transmit their thought, and the Spirit of Ireland spoke through Willie Yeats, telling of unspeakable beauty and of its heroic call.' It remained to be seen how the words of this dead man would be modified in the guts of the living.

Gerard Manley Hopkins

from a letter to Coventry Patmore   7 November 1886

Then there is a young Mr Yeats who has written in a Trinity College publication some striking verses and who has been perhaps unduly pushed by the late Sir Samuel Ferguson (I do not know if you have read or heard of him: he was a learned antiquary, a Protestant but once an ally of Thomas Davis and the Young Ireland Party, but he withdrew from them and even suppressed some of his best poems for fear they, or he, should be claimed by the Nationalists of later days; for he was a poet; the *Forging of the Anchor* is, I believe, his most famous poem; he was a poet as the Irish are – to judge by the little of his I have seen – full of feeling, high thoughts, flow of verse, point, often fine imagery and other virtues, but the essential and only lasting thing left out – what I call *inscape*, that is species or individually-distinctive beauty of style: on this point I believe we quite agree, as on most: but this is a serious parenthesis). I called on his, young Yeats' father by desire lately; he is a painter; and with some emphasis of manner he presented me with *Mosada: a Dramatic Poem* by W. B. Yeats, with a portrait of the author by J. B. Yeats, himself; the young man having finely cut intellectual features and his father being a fine draughtsman. For a young man's pamphlet this was something too much; but you will understand a father's feeling. Now this *Mosada* I cannot think highly of, but I was happily not required then to praise what presumably I had not then read, and I had read and could praise another piece. It was a strained and unworkable allegory about a young man and a sphinx on a rock in the sea (how did they get there? what did they eat? and so on: people think such criticisms very prosaic; but common-sense is never out of place anywhere, neither on Parnassus nor on Tabor nor on the Mount where our Lord preached. . . .

John Todhunter

from a review of *The Wanderings of Oisin and other Poems*,
Academy, vol. 35 30 March 1889

This is a remarkable first volume; not merely full of promise in the
aggregate, but containing a few poems of distinct achievement,
which deserve a more than ephemeral recognition. Every poet must
finally be judged by the quality of his verse; and Mr Yeats' is not
the fashionable verse of the day – smooth, cultured, elegant, not
without a certain intellectual charm, but wanting in spontaneous
music. A poem with the true breath of life in it is rhythmical with an
incalculable and unexpected rhythm, following the natural ebb and
flow of the emotion. It is not too self-conscious to dare some breach
of the fashionable canon in its adventurous sallies after fuller expression. Mr Yeats' verse is of this adventurous kind, and is not
without its wood-notes wild of originality. The supercilious critic-
of-all-work could, no doubt, in the natural exercise of his functions,
easily quote from these poems lines and passages which, apart from
their context, might be made to seem ridiculous. There are even real
flaws of execution – slovenly lines, awkward and uncouth con-
structions, exuberances which are not beauties, concentrations of
expression which are crude and stiff rather than powerful. But in the
main, Mr Yeats has the true poet's instinct for imaginative diction
and musical verse, musical both in rhythm and sound. Many passages
pleasantly haunt the ear and the imagination.

There is a good deal of variety in this little volume – narrative
poems, short dramatic sketches, meditative and fanciful lyrics,
ballads, songs, and quatrains. *The Wanderings of Oisin*, which gives
its title to the book, is a long narrative poem, founded on the old
Irish tradition that the Fenian hero Oisin (the Ossian of Macpherson)
was lured away by a fair enchantress to Tir-nan-oge, the Land of
Youth; and that, having sojourned there for three hundred years, he
longed for the old human life, and returned, to find the Fenians gone
and the Christians in possession. His foot having accidentally touched
mortal soil, the enchanted steed which had carried him back vanished,
old age fell upon him, and he became the unwilling disciple of St
Patrick. Mr Yeats makes him tell St Patrick the story of his adventures

in the three islands – of the Living, of Victories, and of Forgetfulness; and the narrative is agreeably varied by good bits of dramatic dialogue between the heathen and the saint. The poem is in three parts, each in a metre appropriate to the subject – the first in free octosyllabics, the second in Keatsian decasyllabic couplets, the third in quatrains of long-lined anapaestic and dactylic verse. The first and third of these metres are managed with considerable mastery, especially the third, which is distinctly original in its music. In the Keatsian verse Mr Yeats is evidently much less at ease. There are good bits of imaginative description in all three sections, perhaps the finest being that of the enchanted heroes lying asleep in the Island of Forgetfulness with great owls sidling about their prostrate bodies and nestling in their beards and hair. Here the long, sleepy gallop of the heavy-footed anapaests is most effective. The whole poem is drenched in youthful fantasy, pleasant and winning: and the reader is borne easily along from vision to vision. . . .

Lionel Johnson

from a review of *The Countess Kathleen and Various Legends and Lyrics*, *Academy*, vol. 42 1 October 1892

Mr Yeats has published two volumes of verse: *The Wanderings of Oisin* and *The Countess Kathleen*. Doubtless it is difficult to speak with perfect security about the first books of a living writer; but I feel little diffidence in speaking of these two volumes. In the last two or three years much charming verse has been published by many writers who may make themselves distinguished names; but nothing which seems to me, in the most critical and dispassionate state of mind, equal in value to the poems of Mr Yeats. Irish of the Irish, in the themes and sentiments of his verse, he has also no lack of that wider sympathy with the world, without which the finest national verse must remain provincial. Yet, for all his interests of a general sort, his poetry has not lost one Irish grace, one Celtic delicacy, one native charm. It is easy to be fantastic, mystical, quaint, full of old-world delight in myths and legends, devoted to dreams and sentiments of a fairy antiquity; but writers of this kind are commonly successful by fits and starts, their charm is elusive and fugitive. They have the vague imagination of Welsh and Irish folk: that perpetual vision of things under enchanted lights, which makes the thought and speech of many an old peasant woman so graceful, so 'poetical'. But when they approach the art of literature, they are unequal to its demands; they cannot so master the art as to make it convey the imagination. Many and many an Irish poem, by writers quite obscure, startles us by the felicity of lines and phrases here, and by the poverty of lines and phrases there. The poet has cared more for his inward vision than for its outward expression: so something of what he feels be expressed, he is content. Others, again, have so cultivated a technical excellence as to lose the intrinsic beauty of their themes or thoughts: their work is polite and dull.

The distinction of Mr Yeats, as an Irish poet, is his ability to write Celtic poetry, with all the Celtic notes of style and imagination, in a classical manner. Like all men of the true poetical spirit, he is not overcome by the apparent antagonism of the classical and the romantic in art. Like the fine Greeks or Romans, he treats his subject according to its nature. Simple as that sounds, it is a praise not often to be bestowed. Consider the 'Attis' of Catullus: how the monstrous, barbaric frenzy of the theme is realized in verse of the strictest beauty. It is not a Latin theme, congenial to a Latin nature: it is Asiatic, insane, grotesque; its passion is abnormal and harsh. Yet the poem, while terrible in its intensity of life, is a masterpiece of severe art. It is in this spirit, if I may dare so great a comparison, that Mr Yeats has written: his poetry has plenty of imperfections, but it is not based upon a fundamental mistake; he sees very clearly where success may be found. When he takes a Celtic theme, some vast and epic legend, or some sad and lyrical fancy, he does not reflect the mere confused vastness of the one, the mere flying vagueness of the other: his art is full of reason. So he produces poems, rational and thoughtful, yet beautiful with the beauty that comes of thought about imagination. It is not the subjects alone, nor the musical skill alone, nor the dominant mood alone, but all these together that make these poems so satisfying and so haunting. They have that natural felicity which belongs to beautiful things in nature, but a felicity under the control of art. . . .

The 'legends and lyrics' of this volume are very various. There are stories from the old Irish cycles, ballads founded upon more modern

incidents, mystical love poems, and poems of imaginative beauty
upon other things than love. They conclude with a poem, in which
Mr Yeats makes his profession of faith and loyalty towards Ireland,
and justifies the tone of his poems, their 'druid' quality, their care
for an ideal beauty of love and an ideal wisdom of truth: because in
singing of these he is singing of Ireland and for Ireland.

Ah, faeries, dancing under the moon,
A Druid land, a Druid tune!
    (*To Ireland in the Coming Times*)

In these poems, the immediate charm is their haunting music, which
depends not upon any rich wealth of words, but upon a subtile
strain of music in their whole quality of thoughts and images, some
incommunicable beauty, felt in the simplest words and verses.
Collins, Blake, Coleridge, had the secret of such music; Mr Yeats
sings somewhat in their various ways, but with a certain instinct of
his own, definitely Irish. The verse is stately and solemn, without
any elaboration; the thought falls into a lofty rhythm. Or the verse
is wistful and melancholy, an aërial murmur of sad things without
any affectation.

Who dreamed that beauty passes like a dream?
For these red lips, with all their mournful pride,
Mournful that no new wonder may betide,
Troy passed away in one high funeral gleam,
    And Usna's children died.
    (*The Rose of the World*)

From verse so stately turn to this quite humble, simple poem, the
Lamentation of the Old Pensioner, merely versified from the old man's
own words.

I had a chair at every hearth,
    When no one turned to see,
With 'Look at that old fellow there,
    And who may he be?'
And therefore do I wander on,
    And the fret lies on me.

The road-side trees keep murmuring.
  Ah, wherefore murmur ye,
As in the old days long gone by,
  Green oak and poplar tree?
The well-known faces are all gone,
  And the fret lies on me.

In all the poems, even the most mystical in thought, there is a deep tone of sympathy with the world's fortunes, or with the natures of living things: a curiously tender gladness at the thought of it all. The poet finds

In all poor foolish things that live a day,
Eternal beauty wandering on her way.
    (To the Rose upon the Rood of Time)

His ballads are full of this natural sentiment, shown rather in their simple mention of facts and things, as an old poet might mention them, than in any artificial simplicity. There is humour in this verse: a sense of the human soul in all things, a fearless treatment of facts, a gentleness towards life, because it is all wonderful and nothing is despicable. And through the poems there pierces that spiritual cry, which is too rare and fine to reach ears satisfied with the gross richness of a material Muse. . . .

W. B. Yeats

from 'Nationality and Literature' 1893 (reprinted in John P. Frayne (ed.), *Uncollected Prose by W. B. Yeats*, vol. 1, 1970)

In the age of lyric poetry every kind of subtlety, obscurity, and intricate utterance prevails, for the human spirit has begun to look in upon itself with microscopic eyes and to judge of ideas and feelings apart from their effects upon action. The vast bulk of our moods and feelings are too fine, too subjective, too impalpable to find any clear expression in action or in speech tending towards action, and epic and dramatic poetry must deal with one or other of these. In a lyric age the poets no longer can take their inspiration mainly from external activities and from what are called matters of fact, for they must express every phase of human consciousness no matter how subtle,

how vague, how impalpable. With this advancing subtlety poetry
steps out of the market-place, out of the general tide of life and
becomes a mysterious cult, as it were, an almost secret religion made
by the few for the few. To express its fine shades of meaning, an
ever more elaborate language, an ever more subtle rhythm has to be
invented. The dramatic form, and the ballad and epic forms exist
still, of course, but they do so, as the lyric form existed in the age of
drama and of epic, and their whole burden is lyrical. The old simplicity has gone out of them, and an often great obscurity has come
in its stead. The form of Browning is more commonly than not
dramatic or epic, but the substance is lyrical. Another reason why the
poetry of the lyric period steps aside further and further from the
general life is, that in order to express the intricate meaning and
subtle changes of mood,[1] it is compelled to combine external objects
in ways never or seldom seen in nature. In other words, it is compelled
more and more to idealize nature. But the most obvious distinction
between the old and the new is the growing complexity of language
and thought. Compare, for instance, the description of nature in
almost any old ballad, description in which the sea is simply blue and
the grass simply green and the flowers simply sweet-smelling, with
such a description as that contained in Tennyson's famous line, 'A
roaring moon of daffodils',[2] or compare the simple thought of
Chaucer or of the ballad writers, or the writers of the miracle plays
with the elaborate thought of modern poems like *In Memoriam*, the
Paracelsus and *Sordello* of Browning; the sonnets of Rossetti, *The
Atalanta in Caledon*, [sic] or the *Tristan and Iseult* of Swinburne, or
with any of the poetry of George Meredith. The very names of these
writers and of these poems are enough to prove my case. The tree has
come to its greatest complexity of leaf and fruit and flower. And what
is true of England is true also of all the older literatures of Europe. I
need but mention to you the name of Goethe, having in my mind
more particularly his *Faust*, and of Hugo, having in my mind more
particularly his later and more oracular song. Everywhere the elaborate luxuriance of leaf and bud and flower.

1 Yeats changed this word in MS 12148 (National Library of Ireland). *United
Ireland* printing read 'word'.
2 The phrase 'in this roaring moon of daffodil' is from Tennyson's prefatory
sonnet, contributed to the first number of *The Nineteenth Century*, March 1877.

Now, I want to notice especially one peculiarity of all these poets. They more often than not go to foreign countries for their subjects; they are, in fact, citizens of the world, cosmopolitans. It is obvious that a story like that of the Siege of Troy or stories like those in Chaucer cannot be separated from the countries they happened in, and that characters like Macbeth and Lear, like Oedipus and Agamemnon, cannot be separated either from the world about them. But tell me to what nations do hatred, fear, hope, and love belong? The epic and the dramatic periods tend to be national because people understand character and incident best when embodied in life they understand and set amid the scenery they know of, and every man knows and understands his own country the best. They may now and then permit their poets to fare far afield even unto the seacoast of Bohemia,[1] but they soon call them home again. But the lyric age, upon the other hand, becomes as it advances towards an ever complete lyricism, more and more cosmopolitan; for the great passions know nothing of boundaries. As do the great beasts in the forest, they wander without let or hindrance through the universe of God.

Granted fit time and fit occasion, I could apply the same law of division and sub-division and of ever increasing complexity to human society itself – to human life itself – and show you how in the old civilizations an endless sub-division of society to trades and professions, and of human life to habits and rules, is making men every day more subtle and complex, less forcible and adaptable. The old nations are like old men and women sitting over the fire gossiping [sic] of stars and planets, talking of all things in heaven and earth and in the waters under the earth, and forgetting in a trance of subtlety the flaming heart of man.

If time and fit occasion offered, I could take you upon that path, beaten by the feet of the seers, and show you behind human society and human life the causal universe itself, 'falling', in the words of my master, William Blake, 'into division', and foretell with him 'its resurrection into unity'. But this is not fit time or fit occasion. And already the fascination of that beaten path has taken me further than I would. I wished merely to show you that the older literatures of Europe are in their golden sunset, their wise old age, that I might the better

1 Yeats refers to Shakespeare's famous solecism in *A Winter's Tale*, in which the stage direction for Act III reads 'Bohemia. A desert country near the sea.'

prove to you, in the closing parts of my lecture, that we here in Ireland who, like the Scandinavian people, are at the outset [of] a literary epoch, must learn from them but not imitate them, and by so doing we will bring new life and fresh impulse not only to ourselves but to those old literatures themselves. But are we really at the outset of a literary epoch? or are we not, perhaps, merely a little eddy cast up by the advancing tide of English literature and are we not doomed, perhaps, to its old age and coming decline? On the contrary, I affirm that we are a young nation with unexhausted material lying within us in our still unexpressed national character, about us in our scenery, and in the clearly marked outlines of our life, and behind us in our multitude of legends. Look at our literature and you will see that we are still in our epic or ballad period. All that is greatest in that literature is based upon legend – upon those tales which are made by no one man, but by the nation itself through a slow process of modification and adaption, to express its loves and its hates, its likes and its dislikes. Our best writers, De Vere, Ferguson, Allingham, Mangan, Davis, O'Grady, are all either ballad or epic writers, and all base their greatest work, if I except a song or two of Mangan's and Allingham's, upon legends and upon the fortunes of the nation. Alone, perhaps, among the nations of Europe we are in our ballad or epic age.

Robert Louis Stevenson

Letter to W. B. Yeats   14 April 1894

Vailima, Samoa

Dear Sir,

Long since when I was a boy I remember the emotions with which I repeated Swinburne's poems and ballads. Some ten years ago, a similar spell was cast upon me by Meredith's *Love in a Valley*; the stanzas beginning 'When her mother tends her' haunted me and made me drunk like wine; and I remember waking with them all the echoes of the hills about Hyères. It may interest you to hear that I have a third time fallen in slavery: this is to your poem called the *Lake Isle of Innisfree*. It is so quaint and airy, simple, artful, and

eloquent to the heart – but I seek words in vain. Enough that 'always night and day I hear lake water lapping with low sounds on the shore', and am, yours gratefully,
Robert Louis Stevenson

W. B. Yeats

'The Moods' 1895 (reprinted in *Essays and Introductions*, 1961)

Literature differs from explanatory and scientific writing in being wrought about a mood, or a community of moods, as the body is wrought about an invisible soul; and if it uses argument, theory, erudition, observation, and seems to grow hot in assertion or denial, it does so merely to make us partakers at the banquet of the moods. It seems to me that these moods are the labourers and messengers of the Ruler of All, the gods of ancient days still dwelling on their secret Olympus, the angels of more modern days ascending and descending upon their shining ladder; and that argument, theory, erudition, observation, are merely what Blake called 'little devils who fight for themselves,' illusions of our visible passing life, who must be made serve the moods, or we have no part in eternity. Everything that can be seen, touched, measured, explained, understood, argued over, is to the imaginative artist nothing more than a means, for he belongs to the invisible life, and delivers its ever new and ever ancient revelation. We hear much of his need for the restraints of reason, but the only restraint he can obey is the mysterious instinct that has made him an artist, and that teaches him to discover immortal moods in mortal desires, an undecaying hope in our trivial ambitions, a divine love in sexual passion.

Ernest Rhys

from a review of *Poems, 1895*, *Academy*, vol. 49   22 February 1896

In this thrice-taking volume, with its pale buff and gold covers of mystic design, we have the total accomplishment in poetry, so far, of Mr Yeats. It contains, he tells us, all he cares 'to preserve out of his previous volumes of verse', in some cases revised, in others re-written; and the result is as handsome an argument as a younger poet need wish to offer contemporary criticism. With it, in fact, so far as that criticism goes, Mr Yeats may be said to emerge from the coteries and to reach the centre.

In putting it together Mr Yeats has clearly subjected himself to a severer criticism than any but hypercritics else are likely to offer. Those who have learnt to know his poems in those slim earlier volumes out of which this is built, may complain, possibly, over some of his new readings of familiar passages and new versions of familiar names; as in his conversion of 'Oisin' to 'Usheen'. Again, they will miss some favourite pieces.

But, mainly, what one finds in these changes is that if Mr Yeats is growing more literary, he is, too, more severe an artist than he used to be. In making them it is clear that he has tried to heighten the imaginative truth of his poems, even at the cost of throwing away their fanciful trappings. His revision is, then, generally good, if sometimes bad.

That he should have paused to go back and review himself in this way, instead of hastening on, in the fashion of our time, to do end-less new things, says much for his artistic conscience; and it is as an artist through and through that he is likely to impress his readers in these collected poems. This alone makes him a notable appearance among the Irish poets, who have hitherto (with two or three notable exceptions) showed more fervour than poetic form, and more facility than fine art. And this, remembering that there are others working with him, may show that Irish literature, in its modern interpretation, has entered on a new phase. So far as one can see now, indeed, it is to Mr Yeats that men will point hereafter, as marking the beginning of the new period; and this volume of his may serve as a striking landmark in a remarkable movement. Modern criticism has cleared the way and prepared the audience and made the standards plain; and the new poets, if they be indeed poets born, like Mr Yeats, and not merely made, like Mr —, have an opportunity such as Keats and Shelley might have envied.

W. B. Yeats

'The Autumn of the Body' 1898 (reprinted in *Essays and Introductions*, 1961)

Our thoughts and emotions are often but spray flung up from hidden tides that follow a moon no eye can see. I remember that when I first began to write I desired to describe outward things as vividly as possible, and took pleasure, in which there was perhaps, a little discontent, in picturesque and declamatory books. And then quite suddenly I lost the desire of describing outward things, and found that I took little pleasure in a book unless it was spiritual and unemphatic. I did not then understand that the change was from beyond my own mind, but I understand now that writers are struggling all over Europe, though not often with a philosophic understanding of their struggle, against that picturesque and declamatory way of writing, against that 'externality' which a time of scientific and political thought has brought into literature. This struggle has been going on for some years, but it has only just become strong enough to draw within itself the little inner world which alone seeks more than amusement in the arts. In France, where movements are more marked, because the people are pre-eminently logical, *The Temptation of Saint Anthony*, the last great dramatic invention of the old romanticism, contrasts very plainly with *Axël*, the first great dramatic invention of the new; and Maeterlinck has followed Count Villiers de l'Isle-Adam. Flaubert wrote unforgettable descriptions of grotesque, bizarre, and beautiful scenes and persons, as they show to the ear and to the eye, and crowded them with historical and ethnographical details; but Count Villiers de l'Isle-Adam swept together, by what seemed a sudden energy, words behind which glimmered a spiritual and passionate mood, as the flame glimmers behind the dusky blue and red glass in an Eastern lamp; and created persons from whom has fallen all even of personal characteristic except a thirst for that hour when all things shall pass away like a cloud, and a pride like that of the Magi following their star over many mountains; while Maeterlinck has plucked away even this thirst and this pride and set before us faint souls, naked and pathetic shadows already half vapour and sighing to one another upon the border of the last abyss. There has been, as I think, a like change in French painting, for one sees everywhere, instead of the dramatic stories and picturesque moments of an older school, frail and tremulous bodies unfitted for the labour of life, and landscape where subtle rhythms of colour and of form have overcome the clear outline of things as we see them in the labour of life.

There has been a like change in England, but it has come more gradually and is more mixed with lesser changes than in France. The poetry which found its expression in the poems of writers like Browning and Tennyson, and even of writers who are seldom classed with them, like Swinburne, and like Shelley in his earlier years, pushed its limits as far as possible, and tried to absorb into itself the science and politics, the philosophy and morality of its time; but a new poetry, which is always contracting its limits, has grown up under the shadow of the old. Rossetti began it, but was too much of a painter in his poetry to follow it with a perfect devotion; and it became a movement when Mr Lang and Mr Gosse and Mr Dobson devoted themselves to the most condensed of lyric poems, and when Mr Bridges, a more considerable poet, elaborated a rhythm too delicate for any but an almost bodiless emotion, and repeated over and over the most ancient notes of poetry, and none but these. The poets who followed have either, like Mr Kipling, turned from serious poetry altogether, and so passed out of the processional order, or speak out of some personal or spiritual passion in words and types and metaphors that draw one's imagination as far as possible from the complexities of modern life and thought. The change has been more marked in English painting, which, when intense enough to belong to the processional order, began to cast out things, as they are seen by minds plunged in the labour of life, so much before French painting that ideal art is sometimes called English art upon the Continent.

I see, indeed, in the arts of every country those faint lights and faint colours and faint outlines and faint energies which many call 'the decadence', and which I, because I believe that the arts lie dreaming of things to come, prefer to call the autumn of the body. An Irish poet whose rhythms are like the cry of a sea-bird in autumn twilight has told its meaning in the line, 'The very sunlight's weary, and it's time to quit the plough.' Its importance is the greater because it comes to us at the moment when we are beginning to be interested in many things which positive science, the interpreter of exterior law, has always denied: communion of mind with mind in thought and without words, foreknowledge in dreams and in visions, and the coming among us of the dead, and of much else. We are, it may be, at a crowning crisis of the world, at the moment when man is about to ascend, with the wealth he has been so long gathering upon his shoulders, the stairway he has been descending from the first days. The first poets, if one may find their images in the *Kalevala*, had not Homer's preoccupation with things, and he was not so full of their excitement as Virgil. Dante added to poetry a dialectic which, although he made it serve his laborious ecstasy, was the invention of minds trained by the labour of life, by a traffic among many things, and not a spontaneous expression of an interior life; while Shakespeare shattered the symmetry of verse and of drama that he might fill them with things and their accidental relations to one another.

Each of these writers had come further down the stairway than those who had lived before him, but it was only with the modern poets, with Goethe and Wordsworth and Browning, that poetry gave up the right to consider all things in the world as a dictionary of types and symbols and began to call itself a critic of life and an interpreter of things as they are. Painting, music, science, politics, and even religion, because they have felt a growing belief that we know nothing but the fading and flowering of the world, have changed in numberless elaborate ways. Man has wooed and won the world, and has fallen weary, and not, I think, for a time, but with a weariness that will not end until the last autumn, when the stars shall be blown away like withered leaves. He grew weary when he said, 'These things that I touch and see and hear are alone real,' for he saw them without illusion at last, and found them but air and dust and moisture. And now he must be philosophical above everything, even about the arts, for he can only return the way he came, and so escape from weariness, by philosophy. The arts are, I believe, about to take upon their shoulders the burdens that have fallen from the shoulders of priests, and to lead us back upon our journey by filling our thoughts with the essences of things, and not with things. We are about to substitute once more the distillation of alchemy for the analyses of chemistry and for some other sciences; and certain of us are looking everywhere for the perfect alembic that no silver or golden drop may escape. Mr Symons has written lately on Mallarmé's method, and has quoted him as saying that we should 'abolish the pretension, aesthetically an error, despite its dominion over almost all the masterpieces, to enclose within the subtle paper other than – for example – the horror of the forest or the silent thunder in the leaves, not the intense dense wood of the trees', and as desiring to substitute for 'the old lyric afflatus or the enthusiastic personal direction of the phrase' words 'that take light from mutual reflection, like an actual trail of fire over precious stones', and 'to make an entire word hitherto unknown to the language' 'out of many vocables'. Mr Symons understands these and other sentences to mean that poetry will henceforth be a poetry of essences, separated one from another in little and intense poems. I think there will be much poetry of this kind, because of an ever more arduous search for an almost disembodied ecstasy, but I think we will not cease to write long poems, but rather that we will write them more and more as our new belief makes the world plastic under our hands again. I think that we will learn again how to describe at great length an old man wandering among enchanted islands, his return home at last, his slow-gathering vengeance, a flitting shape of a goddess, and a flight of arrows, and yet to make all of these so different things 'take light from mutual reflection, like an actual trail of fire over precious stones', and become 'an entire word', the signature or symbol of a mood of the divine imagination as imponderable as 'the horror of the forest or the silent thunder in the leaves'.

Anonymous

from 'Mr Yeats' Poems', *Academy*, vol. 56 6 May (unsigned review of *The Wind Among the Reeds* and *Poems* new edition) 1899

It is an inhuman beauty, a haunting of something remote, intangible, which the poet himself only feels, but cannot trace to its source. In proportion as he becomes, or tries to be, definite this power passes from him. It is when he is obeying the dictates of an emotion, a sentiment, as insubstantial and uncapturable as a gust of the night, that he achieves this most delicate and evanescent charm. With a true instinct of his own prevailing quality he calls this latest book *The Wind Among the Reeds*. No less frail and mysterious than such a wind is the appeal of Mr Yeats' best verse.

The very finest examples are contained in his collected *Poems* – namely, *The Lake Isle of Innisfree* and *The Man who Dreamed of Fairyland*. The first expresses in most daintily sweet verse the appeal of remembered solitary water and reedy isle to a born dreamer stranded in city streets. The second embodies in finely haunting verse Mr Yeats' most constant mood – the call upon the visionary's heart-strings of the legendary country, where is 'the light that never was on sea or land'. On the whole, it is Mr Yeats' best poem. And it should be; for he is himself 'the man that dreamed of fairyland'. All his poetry is one plaintive cry for a domain set apart from 'life's exceeding injocundity'. We are not pronouncing whether this is a wholesome or desirable frame of mind. Perhaps we have other views. We merely state the case. And since every poet is best when he expresses his dominant love, Mr Yeats is always at his best when he is dealing with the world of fays or spirits. At such times his lightness of touch is exquisite. It is hard to say where the fascination lies. It is as much in the music as the apparent words – a true test in lyrics of this kind, which are sensitive rather than intellectual. Take this quite incidental lyric from the fairy play, *The Land of Heart's Desire* – a song sung by fairies to entice a mortal girl:

The wind blows out of the gates of the day,
　The wind blows over the lonely of heart;
And the lonely of heart are withered away,
　While the fairies dance in a place apart:
Shaking their milk-white feet in a ring,
　Tossing their milk-white arms in the air;
For they hear the wind laugh and murmur and sing
　Of a land where even the old are fair,
And even the wise are merry of tongue;
　But I heard a reed of Coolaney say:
'When the wind has laughed and murmured and sung,
　The lonely of heart shall wither away.'

Could anything be more airy and delicate? In this sense Mr Yeats has always been a mystic. He has always 'dreamed of fairyland'. But in this new volume there are signs that he desires to be a mystic in a more recondite sense. The old Irish mythology, which always attracted him, he has taken up the study of in its symbolic meanings, and endeavours to import it into his verse as a vehicle for the expression of modern and personal ideas.

Frankly, we view this development with alarm. It would always be a perilous experiment, because (unlike the language of Greek or Biblical religion) Irish mythology is so unknown to English readers. But Mr Yeats' treatment of it increases the difficulty. He frequently uses this mythological imagery in a sense of his own, though in his elaborate notes he acknowledges himself doubtful about the correctness of his interpretation – that he is, in fact, guessing at the meanings of the symbols he uses. But how shall the reader follow this arbitrary use of symbolism, or be certain where the poet himself is uncertain? The only road out is the clumsy expedient of explanatory notes. This is not the true use of symbolism, and from a purely poetical standpoint is quite inartistic. It creates wanton difficulty. Mr Yeats should at any rate be clear to the few who understand the system of mythological imagery. But his arbitrary use of it often leaves even them in the dark. 'I use this to signify so and so', is the formula. But he should not 'use it to signify' anything. He should use it (if he needs it) for what it does signify; and if he is unsure what it signifies, he should not use it at all. It is wantonness to darken his poetry by employing recondite imagery, which he confesses elaborately he is doubtful about the meaning of. Frankly, there is more ingenuity than insight in much of it. . . .

W. B. Yeats

from 'The Symbolism of Poetry' 1900 (reprinted in *Essays and Introductions*, 1961)

The purpose of rhythm, it has always seemed to me, is to prolong the moment of contemplation, the moment when we are both asleep and awake, which is the one moment of creation, by hushing us with an alluring monotony, while it holds us waking by variety, to keep us in that state of perhaps real trance, in which the mind liberated from the pressure of the will is unfolded in symbols. If certain sensitive persons listen persistently to the ticking of a watch, or gaze persistently on the monotonous flashing of a light, they fall into the hypnotic trance; and rhythm is but the ticking of a watch made softer, that one must needs listen, and various, that one may not be swept beyond memory or grow weary of listening; while the patterns of the artist are but the monotonous flash woven to take the eyes in a subtler enchantment. I have heard in meditation voices that were forgotten the moment they had spoken; and I have been swept, when in more profound meditation, beyond all memory but of those things that came from beyond the threshold of waking life. I was writing once at a very symbolical and abstract poem, when my pen fell on the ground; and as I stooped to pick it up, I remembered some fantastic adventure that yet did not seem fantastic, and then another like adventure, and when I asked myself when these things had happened, I found that I was remembering my dreams for many nights. I tried to remember what I had done the day before, and then what I had done that morning; but all my waking life had perished from me, and it was only after a struggle that I came to remember it again, and as I did so that more powerful and startling life perished in its turn. Had my pen not fallen on the ground and so made me turn from the images that I was weaving into verse, I would never have known that meditation had become trance, for I would have been like one who does not know that he is passing through a wood because his eyes are on the pathway. So I think that in the making and in the understanding of a work of art, and the more easily if it is full of patterns and symbols and music, we are lured to the threshold of sleep, and it may be far beyond it, without knowing that we have ever set our feet upon the steps of horn or of ivory.

If people were to accept the theory that poetry moves us because of its symbolism, what change should one look for in the manner of our poetry? A return to the way of our fathers, a casting out of descriptions of nature for the sake of nature, of the moral law for the sake of the moral law, a casting out of all anecdotes and of that brooding over scientific opinion that so often extinguished the central flame in Tennyson, and of that vehemence that would make us do or not do certain things; or, in other words, we should come to understand that the beryl stone was enchanted by our fathers that it might unfold the pictures in its heart, and not to mirror our own excited faces, or the boughs waving outside the window. With this change of substance, this return to imagination, this understanding that the laws of art, which are the hidden laws of the world, can alone bind the imagination, would come a change of style, and we would cast out of serious poetry those energetic rhythms, as of a man running, which are the invention of the will with its eyes always on something to be done or undone; and we would seek out those wavering, meditative, organic rhythms, which are the embodiment of the imagination, that neither desires nor hates, because it has done with time, and only wishes to gaze upon some reality, some beauty; nor would it be any longer possible for any-body to deny the importance of form, in all its kinds, for although you can expound an opinion, or describe a thing, when your words are not quite well chosen, you cannot give a body to something that moves beyond the senses, unless your words are as subtle, as complex, as full of mysterious life, as the body of a flower or of a woman. The form of sincere poetry, unlike the form of the 'popular poetry', may indeed be sometimes obscure, or ungrammatical as in some of the best of the *Songs of Innocence and Experience*, but it must have the per-fections that escape analysis, the subtleties that have a new meaning every day, and it must have all this whether it be but a little song made out of a moment of dreamy indolence, or some great epic made out of the dreams of one poet and of a hundred generations whose hands were never weary of the sword.

William Archer

from 'William Butler Yeats', *Poets of the Younger Generation* 1902

Since the foregoing pages were written, Mr Yeats has published two books: *The Wind Among the Reeds*, a collection of lyrics, and *The Shadowy Waters*, a poem in dramatic form. In these his peculiar gifts of imagination and of utterance are seen at their best. He extracts from a simple and rather limited vocabulary effects of the rarest delicacy and distinction. There is a certain appearance of mannerism, no doubt, in Mr Yeats's individuality. One can scarcely turn a page of these books without coming upon the epithets 'dim', 'glimmering', 'wandering', 'pearl-pale', 'dove-grey', 'dew-dropping', and the like. His imagery is built up out of a very few simple elements, which he combines and re-combines unweariedly. The materials he employs, in short, are those of primitive folk-poetry; but he touches them to new and often marvellous beauty. What in our haste we take for mannerism may be more justly denominated style, the inevitable accent of his genius. . . .

One other word, and I have done. It appears from the notes to *The Wind in the Reeds*, rather than from the poems themselves, that Mr Yeats is becoming more and more addicted to a petrified, fossilized symbolism, a system of hieroglyphs which may have had some inherent significance for their inventors, but which have now become matters of research, of speculation, of convention. I cannot but regard this tendency as ominous. His art cannot gain and may very easily lose by it. A conventional symbol may be of the greatest interest to the anthropologist or the antiquary; for the poet it can have no value. If a symbol does not spring spontaneously from his own imagination and express an analogy borne in upon his own spiritual perception, he may treasure it in his mental museum, but he ought not to let such a piece of inert matter cumber the seed-plot of his poetry.

Fiona Macleod (William Sharp)

from 'The Later Work of Mr W. B. Yeats', *North American Review*, vol. 175   October 1902

Mr Yeats is assuredly of that small band of poets and dreamers who write from no other impulse than because they see and dream in a reality so vivid that it is called imagination. With him the imagination is in truth the second-sight of the mind. Thus it is that he lives with symbols, as unimaginative natures live with facts.

A symbolist stands in some danger here. The obvious peril is a confusion of the spiritual beauty behind the symbol with the arbitrary expression of that spiritual beauty through that particular symbol. There are blind alleys and lost roads in symbolism, and few of those who follow that loveliest trail into 'the undiscovered Edens' of Beauty but sometimes lose themselves, and go after shadows, and idly name the stars, and inhabit planets with their own desires, putting their vain dreams upon these unheeding children of eternity.

Perhaps a truer wisdom is that which would see the symbols in the facts, and the facts translated from their material body to their spiritual significance. It is the constant reminder of the man who breaks stones to the man who measures the stars, that he concerns himself with remote unrealities; but the star-gazer is also apt to forget that without broken stones no road would be paven. And I cannot but think that Mr Yeats is a star-gazer too reluctant to listen to the plaint of those who break stones or are spiritually dumb hewers of wood and drawers of water. He does not always sing of things of beauty and mystery as the things of beauty and mystery are best sung, so that the least may understand; but rather as those priests of Isis who, when bidden to chant the Sun-Hymn to the people, sang, beautifully, incomprehensible algebraical formulae.

The Powers whose name and shape no living creature knows
Have pulled the Immortal Rose:
And though the Seven Lights bowed in their dance and wept,
The Polar Dragon slept,
His heavy rings uncoiled from glimmering deep to deep:
When will he wake from sleep?
    (*The Poet Pleads with the Elemental Powers*)

Or again:

We who still labour by the cromlech on the shore,
The grey cairn on the hill, when day sinks drowned in dew,
Being weary of the world's empires, bow down to you,
Master of the still stars and of the flaming door.
    (*The Valley of the Black Pig*)

Or that strange poem of love with its fantastic dream-beauty, beginning:

Do you not hear me calling, white deer with no horns?
I have been changed to a hound with one red ear.
　　(He Mourns for the Change That has Come Upon him)

To some there is no need to explain 'the white deer with no horns', 'the hound with one red ear', 'the boar without bristles, out of the West': to some the symbols of the 'Polar Dragon' and the 'Immortal Rose' stand evident. But these must be few: and though in a sense all excelling poetry is mystical, in the wider and not less true sense it should be as water is, or as air is, or as flame is. For it too is an elemental, being in the spiritual life what wind is in the natural life.

When the reader, unfamiliar with 'the signature of symbol', shall read these and kindred lines, will he not feel that this young priest of the Sun should translate to a more human key his too transcendental vision? What, he will ask, is the Immortal Rose, and what the Polar Dragon? Who is the guardian of the flaming door, and of what is it the portal? If a Gael, he may have heard of the white fawn that is Love, of the white hound that is Death. Is it this symbol that lives anew in the hound with one red ear, in the white deer without horns?

For all who may not be able readily to follow his honey of old wisdom, Mr Yeats has added notes. It would be more exact to say that one-half of the book comprises the prose equivalent of the verse. If all notes afforded reading such as one may read here! Mr Yeats turns round mentally and shows us the other side, where the roots grow and the fibres fill with sap, and how they grow to that blossom we have already seen, and what the sap is. In their kind, these notes have something of the charm of the poems to which they stand interpreter. Yet they should be superfluous. It is not their presence that one objects to, but their need. Poetry is an art which should be as rigorously aloof from the explicative as the art of painting is, or as sculpture is, or music. When Mr Yeats gives us work on a larger scale, with a great sweep, he will, let us hope, remember that every purely esoteric symbol is a vague image – and vagueness is the inevitable defect against which the symbolist has to contend.

Francis Thompson

from 'Fiona Macleod on Mr W. B. Yeats', *Academy*, vol. 163
25 October 1902 (reprinted in Rev. Terence L. Connolly (ed.),
Literary Criticisms by Francis Thompson, 1948)

Mr Yeats' latest poems do, as she says, display the dawning of a new
motive; but of new music we are not so sure.[1] There are poems in
the older volumes which seem to us to have all the quality of the
latest ones. The new motive is the uncontrolled set of his poetry
towards that mysticism to which it always, consciously or unconsciously, tended. It has its dangers, which Fiona Macleod clearly sees
and indicates. The greatest lies in his research of symbolism. For it is
more than a use of symbolism; we would go further than Fiona
Macleod, and call it an actual abuse of symbolism. Symbolism is
used (to our mind) where not only was its employment unneeded,
but the meaning could more beautifully have been given without it.
This, however, is a temporary phase, we believe, which will rectify
itself. In Mr Yeats' discovery of a novel power (since symbolism is no
less), he has come to love and use it for the mere delight in using it;
as a young artist revels in technique for the sake of technique. The
painter presently learns to handle technique severely as a means to an
end; and the like sobering will come about in Mr Yeats' handling of
symbolism. Yet we cannot quite sign to Fiona Macleod's dictum that
'the things of beauty and mystery are best sung, so that the least
may understand'. If it were always possible, then it were indeed best
so. But the highest 'things of beauty and mystery' cannot be sung
so that they may be understanded of the least. Where, else, were the
mystery?

But in the bulk of Mr Yeats' work, even of this latest work, there
seems to us nothing beyond the proper and beautiful indefiniteness
of remote suggestion. Such is that exquisite poem which Fiona
Macleod quotes:

Had I the heaven's embroidered cloths,
   Enwrought with golden and silver light;

1 In 1902 Fiona Macleod had not been identified as William Sharp, thus
Thompson uses 'she'. [Ed.]

The blue and the dim and the dark cloths
  Of night and light and the half light;
I would spread the cloths under your feet;
  But I, being poor, have only my dreams;
I have spread my dreams under your feet,
  Tread softly because you tread on my dreams.
  (*He Wishes for the Cloths of Heaven*)

There is a poem by an older Irish writer, which ends with one fine line:

Dance light, for my heart it lies under your feet, love!

If Mr Yeats ever saw the poem, then with the skill of a consummate artist he has ennobled the line into a thing of perfect beauty, which is rightfully his own. His highest work, like this poem, stirs echoes in the imagination which reverberate to the dimmest verges of consciousness. It is this unique power of subtly remote suggestion which makes him typically the poet of what we understand by Celtic spirituality. The words seem to awaken a series of answering harmonics, which are lost at last on the other side this life. Whether Fiona Macleod's final conjecture be correct, that Mr Yeats may yet work out a new and spiritual drama, ranging under no existing precedents, is another matter. To us, as to her, it seems impossible at present that his genius should fit the stage. He has declared his conviction that such a drama must revert to the Shakespearean stage, and shake off the trammels of scenery. Wagner's conception of a new drama went the other way, demanding the last perfection of scenery and mechanical device. Yet we strongly incline to it, that in this matter Mr Yeats is right. Nothing would drag us to see *The Tempest* mounted with even Bayreuthian completion. But is spirituality possible short of a Greek or lyric drama? And after all, Mr Yeats' ethereal gift seems to us to have no rightful connection with passion at all, save the clear passion of yearning for the infinitely far, and regret for the unknown, which is plaintive in all his verse.

Arthur Bingham Walkley

from 'The State Called Reverie', *Academy*, vol. 64 13 June 1903
(review of *Ideas of Good and Evil*)

[Yeats] lures us away from the impetus towards action, and the desire
of life, to watch with him the wraiths rising slowly from the abyss.
And these wraiths carry to him the immortal legacies of dead songs
and hidden symbols, all the sorrowful inheritance of an elder faith.
For to this author a legend is the surviving soul of a lost poetry, into
which are woven one knows not what despairing messages. It is in
itself the universal tie linking man with man across the accidental
barriers of time. For a legend is the supreme confession of a race,
haunting its children until they have become dulled to all save
external voices. Moreover, it is generally the confession, not of
attainment but of infinite desire, not of gladness and success but
rather of sorrow and despair. In the following exquisite passage the
author seeks to explain this persistent melancholy:

Life was so weighed down by the emptiness of the great
forests and by the mystery of all things, and by the
greatness of its own desires, and, as I think, by the
loneliness of much beauty; and seemed so little and so
fragile and so brief, that nothing could be more sweet in the
memory than a tale that ended in death and parting, and
than a wild and beautiful lamentation. Men did not mourn
merely because their beloved was married to another, or
because learning was bitter in the mouth, for such
mourning believes that life might be happy were it
different, and is, therefore, the less mourning; but because
they had been born and must die with their great thirst
unslaked. And so it is that all the august, sorrowful
persons of literature, Cassandra and Helen and Deirdre, and
Lear and Tristan, have come out of legends, and are,
indeed, but the images of primitive imagination mirrored in
the little looking-glass of the modern and classic
imagination.

This seems to us to convey the artistic inspiration of *Ideas of Good and Evil* (Bullen). It is in harmony with the message of Maeterlinck which would bid us abandon the logical triumphs of the intelligence in order to absorb the pervading consciousness around us. For ever pervading the little external circumstances of the individual life, the petty triumphs and defeats, the transitory loves and hates, is the totality of what the world has hoped and dreamed and feared. There is the inspiration, there the common inheritance from which we turn aside avid of the immediate barter. 'Those who are subject', quotes Mr Yeats from Shelley's fragment upon life, 'to the state called reverie, feel as if their nature were resolved into the surrounding universe or as if the surrounding universe were resolved into their being.' It is to the reverie as opposed to the rhetoric of drama that these new poets would guide us.

It is not a revolution that they demand, but rather a reversion to the old simplicity and the submission of a more acutely sensitive consciousness to influences brooding ever near us. And the expression of this poetry will be neither optimism nor pessimism in the accepted sense. It will be the expression of one who having found joy in the mysterious beauty, is yet penetrated by the knowledge that it must remain for ever elusive. And because the source of joy is remote from external things and can be neither acknowledged nor defended by the human reason, this poetry will draw nearer and nearer to the shadowy creations of legends and further and further away from the practical bargains and contracts of life.

A. Clutton-Brock

from a reply to 'The State Called Reverie', *Academy*, vol. 64
20 June 1903

Sir,

In the Academy for June 13 there was an article on this subject provoked by Mr W. B. Yeats' book, *Ideas of Good and Evil*, the writer of which agrees with Mr Yeats that reverie is the begetter both of wisdom and of good art. Anyone who has read Mr Yeats' works knows that by reverie he means the surrender of the mind to the subconsciousness uncontrolled by reason or the will, and the writer shows throughout his article that he means this by it also. . . .

It is contended that the mind, by being thus thrown open to this uncontrolled influence, will acquire a mysterious wisdom beyond the reach of reason, and that it is a worthy task for a poet to describe the sensations and experiences of his subconsciousness thus uncontrolled. Now no one can deny that the subconsciousness of a poet must be richly stocked; that music and vivid images must exist in it before they can become part of his natural language. It is the subconsciousness that supplies him with the machinery of his art. The conscious exercise of the will or the reason will inspire him with the magic of words or of allusive phrases. It is certain also that a man whose subconsciousness is acutely sensitive to external influences, will be richer in experience and therefore wiser, if wise at all, than a man who takes in nothing except by conscious effort. But that is not to say that the habit of uncontrolled reverie is valuable for the practice either of life or art; or that the mere processes of a mind in uncontrolled reverie are fit subjects for poetry. . . .

Unreasoning thought is the chief symptom of hypochondria. It is also the note of much of the poetry of reverie, which sees an immense significance in mere mental sensations, and reasons perversely about them. For instance, beautiful things fill the poet with sadness, not because there is anything essentially sad in beauty, but by the mere reaction of delight into pain.

But the poet will not exercise his reason about that sadness. He will not see that it is a mere mental sensation. Associating it with beauty, he comes to think of it as beautiful in itself, and gives himself up to the luxury of grief about nothing. If he is able to express that grief beautifully, and in terms of beautiful things, he persuades himself and many others that there is some profound poetic significance in a process that is wholly physical. Looking to reverie for new poetic material, he gets from it what is material really only for the flattest prose.

Eugenia Brooks Frothingham

from 'An Irish Poet and his Works', *Critic*   January 1904

A nostalgia for unseen and immortal loveliness is the dominating
note of this poetry, and it is in the work of William B. Yeats that the
tendency finds its most vital and beautiful expression. 'How', he
asks, 'can one be interested in the rising and setting of the sun, and
in the work that men do under the sun, when the mistress that one
loves is hidden behind the gates of death; and it may be behind a
thousand gates besides – gate beyond gate.'

At their own confessing, this little community 'follows after
shadows', believing them to be more immortal than substance. Theirs
is a poetry of symbols, and they share the danger common to all
symbolists, which is that of emphasizing the arbitrary and material
form of the symbol at the expense of its spiritual significance. This
fault leads to a dry and distressing confusion. A symbolic formula
that is to them laden with suggestions of beauty and spirtuality,
becomes to those unfamiliar with 'the signature of symbol' a meaningless category of fantastic and often absurd images. There is no
better example of this danger than in the verse of Mr Yeats, in which
Mongan mourns for the change that has come upon him and his
beloved and longs for the end of the world:

Do you not hear me calling, white deer with
No horns! I have been changed to a hound
With one red ear; – I have been in the
Path of stones and the wood of thorns, –
For somebody hid hatred, and hope and
Desire and fear – under my feet that they
Follow you night and day. A man with
A hazel wand came without sound. He
Changed me suddenly; I was looking another
Way: and now my calling is but the calling
Of a hound; and Time and Birth and Change are
Hurrying by. I would that the boar without bristles
Had come out from the West – and had rooted

Sun and moon and stars out of the sky – and
Lay in darkness, grunting, and turning to his rest.
> *(He Mourns for the Change that has Come Upon Him and his
> Beloved and Longs For the End of the World)*

To the happy few initiated into the mysteries of Irish mythology
these lines may contain suggestions of the mystic and the beautiful,
but to the rest of us they present a stupefying array of unrelated
images. Convinced that no one would dare to appear so meaningless
unless meaning a great deal, we ask ourselves feverishly why the
hound should have a red ear, and if he calls to the white deer because
of it, or because somebody has hid hatred and hope and desire and
fear under his feet; and why the man with the hazel wand should
have changed him; and what 'Time' and 'Change' and 'Birth' have
to do with any of it; and last of all, why the red hound should have
wanted this particular, bristleless boar to come out of the West. In
the excessive revival of Irish mythology the writers of this group are
in danger of localizing their work by rendering it unintelligible to
the great reading public.

W. B. Yeats

from 'Poetry and Tradition' 1907 (reprinted in *Essays and
Introductions*, 1961)

In life courtesy and self-possession, and in the arts style, are the sensible impressions of the free mind, for both arise out of a deliberate
shaping of all things, and from never being swept away, whatever
the emotion, into confusion or dullness. The Japanese have num-
bered with heroic things courtesy at all times whatsoever, and
though a writer, who has to withdraw so much of his thought out of
his life that he may learn his craft, may find many his betters in daily
courtesy, he should never be without style, which is but high breed-
ing in words and in argument. He is indeed the creator of the standards of manners in their subtlety, for he alone can know the ancient
records and be like some mystic courtier who has stolen the keys from

the girdle of Time, and can wander where it please him amid the splendours of ancient Courts.

Sometimes, it may be, he is permitted the licence of cap and bell, or even the madman's bunch of straws, but he never forgets or leaves at home the seal and the signature. He has at all times the freedom of the well-bred, and being bred to the tact of words can take what theme he pleases, unlike the linen-drapers, who are rightly compelled to be very strict in their conversation. Who should be free if he were not? for none other has a continual deliberate self-delighting happiness – style, 'the only thing that is immortal in literature', as Sainte-Beuve has said, a still unexpended energy, after all that the argument or the story needs, a still unbroken pleasure after the immediate end has been accomplished – and builds this up into a most personal and wilful fire, transfiguring words and sounds and events. It is the playing of strength when the day's work is done, a secret between a craftsman and his craft, and is so inseparate in his nature that he has it most of all amid overwhelming emotion, and in the face of death. Shakespeare's persons, when the last darkness has gathered about them, speak out of an ecstasy that is one-half the self-surrender of sorrow, and one-half the last playing and mockery of the victorious sword before the defeated world.

It is in the arrangement of events as in the words, and in that touch of extravagance, of irony, of surprise, which is set there after the desire of logic has been satisfied and all that is merely necessary established, and that leaves one, not in the circling necessity, but caught up into the freedom of self-delight: it is, as it were, the foam upon the cup, the long pheasant's feather on the horse's head, the spread peacock over the pasty. If it be very conscious, very deliberate, as it may be in comedy, for comedy is more personal than tragedy, we call it fantasy, perhaps even mischievous fantasy, recognizing how disturbing it is to all that drag a ball at the ankle. This joy, because it must be always making and mastering, remains in the hands and in the tongue of the artist, but with his eyes he enters upon a submissive, sorrowful contemplation of the great irremediable things, and he is known from other men by making all he handles like himself, and yet by the unlikeness to himself of all that comes before him in a pure contemplation. It may have been his enemy or his love or his cause that set him dreaming, and certainly the phoenix can but open her young wings in a flaming nest; but all hate and hope vanishes in the dream, and if his mistress brag of the song or his enemy fear it, it is not that either has its praise or blame, but that the twigs of the holy nest are not easily set afire. The verses may make his mistress famous as Helen or give a victory to his cause, not because he has been either's servant, but because men delight to honour and to remember all that have served contemplation. It had been easier to fight, to die even, for Charles' house with Marvell's poem in the memory,[1] but there is no zeal of service that had not been an impurity in the pure soil where the marvel grew. Timon of Athens contemplates his own end, and orders his tomb by the beached verge of the salt flood, and Cleopatra sets the asp to her bosom, and their words move us because their sorrow is not their own at tomb or asp, but for all men's fate. That shaping joy has kept the sorrow pure, as it had kept it were the emotion love or hate, for the nobleness of the arts is in the mingling of contraries, the extremity of sorrow, the extremity of joy, perfection of personality, the perfection of its surrender, overflowing turbulent energy, and marmorean stillness; and its red rose opens at the meeting of the two beams of the cross, and at the trysting-place of mortal and immortal, time and eternity. No new man has ever plucked that rose, or found that trysting-place, for he could but come to the understanding of himself, to the mastery of unlocking words, after long frequenting of the great Masters, hardly without ancestral memory of the like. Even knowledge is not enough, for the 'recklessness' Castiglione thought necessary in good manners is necessary in this likewise, and if a man has it not he will be gloomy, and had better to his marketing again.

Darrell Figgis

from 'Mr W. B. Yeats' Poetry', *Studies and Appreciations* 1912

The Wind Among the Reeds is not only the hour of Mr Yeats' purest and truest success: it is, indeed, the limit of progress in that direction. The thing he sought for from the first, he achieves here: and thereby closes that path for himself, under the peril of mere repetition. For

1 *An Horatian Ode', upon Cromwell's Return from Ireland.* [Ed.]

this mute sincerity has not alone its very severe limitations, its even unpoetic limitations, but it has no less its extreme perils. It has been hinted that he never supports his muse by rhetoric. In fact, he sets his face very deliberately against rhetoric. Yet it would be interesting to ask what this rhetoric is that incurs his artistic anger. Often there is the uncomfortable feeling that, in a kind of special pleading justifiable in an artist, he identifies the colour of tone or the magnificence of speech with rhetoric. But if the colour or the magnificence be authentic, that is if they arise from true moods of colour and magnificence purely conceived, it would be a violation of all meaning to speak of the result as rhetoric. Similarly, muteness is not always sincere; and in so far as it is not sincere, it is rhetorical. One may lean on a simple device of words not less than on a pompous device of words.

It is this that is the peril he has incurred in the continual chastening of his verse. He has chastened out one kind of rhetoric; but he has almost chastened himself into another. In one of his early poems the phrase 'rim of the world' struck us as a failure to express his idea and a dependence on a manner of speech; and more than once, when his meaning has demanded some subtle and ritual word, he has turned aside and used 'druid'. To be sure, this is in his early work. Yet in the maturity and fullness of *The Wind Among the Reeds*, pure and haunting though the poems be, it is not altogether a happy spectacle to see a poet compelled to elucidate his poems by an appendix of notes, like any learned professor.

It is, however, *The Wind Among the Reeds* that comes as a test. Its very success makes it its own limit of progress. If its manner be not wide enough to embrace all that is proper to the understanding of its vision, by reason of an overchastening, it yet, and even thereby, stands up on the borders of possibility to point a danger beyond. Its muteness may be sincere: it may have spoken its vision in a sincere economy of simple words: but, since processes will continue themselves if made a law of the mind, how will a further refinement bear any poetic vision at all? We have seen, in the two examples quoted earlier, how Mr Yeats came to purge imperfection into perfection of simplicity. Over against these let a later example be set, and it will be seen that the purging process continues, but that it is poetic vision that has been lost, not imperfection.

The fascination of what's difficult
Has dried the sap out of my veins, and rent
Spontaneous joy and natural content
Out of my heart. There's something ails our colt
That must, as if it had not holy blood,
Nor on Olympus leaped from cloud to cloud,
Shivered under the lash, strain, sweat, and jolt
As though it dragged road metal. My curse on plays
That have to be set up in fifty ways,
On the day's war with every knave or dolt,
Theatre business, management of men.
I swear before the dawn comes round again
I'll find the stable and pull out the bolt.
   (*The Fascination of What's Difficult*)

Like most things said in verse, it tells its concern wiselier far than lies in the possibility of prose; and one need only read it carefully for a sufficient commentary on what has been said. It is indeed true that 'the fascination of what's difficult has dried the sap out of his veins': it has dried the poetry out of his verse. His 'craft of verse' has become a craft for its own sake. The expression takes a value from its own skill, and not because it expresses anything. And that is a form of rhetoric. It was not so in *The Wind Among the Reeds*. There the poet's vision was foremost: as it should be, for a poet without a vision is no poet at all, but a clever, or an otherwise than clever, versifier. It is not his technique that saves a poet from sterility, but his vision.

Ezra Pound

'The Later Yeats', *Poetry*   May 1914 (review of *Responsibilities*, reprinted in *Literary Essays of Ezra Pound*, 1954 copyright 1918, 1920, 1933 by Ezra Pound. Reprinted by permission of New Directions Publishing Corporation)

I live, so far as possible, among that more intelligently active segment of the race which is concerned with today and tomorrow; and, in consequence of this, whenever I mention Mr Yeats I am apt to be assailed with questions: 'Will Mr Yeats do anything more?', 'Is Yeats in the movement?', 'How *can* the chap go on writing this sort of thing?'

And to these inquiries I can only say that Mr Yeats' vitality is quite unimpaired, and that I dare say he'll do a good deal; and that up to date no one has shown any disposition to supersede him as the best poet in England, or any likelihood of doing so for some time; and that after all Mr Yeats has brought a new music upon the harp, and that one man seldom leads two movements to triumph, and that it is quite enough that he should have brought in the sound of keening and the skirl of the Irish ballads, and driven out the sentimental cadence with memories of *The County of Mayo* and *The Coolun*; and that the production of good poetry is a very slow matter, and that, as touching the greatest of dead poets, many of them could easily have left that *magnam partem*, which keeps them with us, upon a single quire of foolscap or at most upon two; and that there is no need for a poet to repair each morning of his life to the *Piazza dei Signori* to turn a new sort of somersault; and that Mr Yeats is so assuredly an immortal that there is no need for him to recast his style to suit our winds of doctrine; and that, all these things being so, there is nevertheless a manifestly new note in his later work that they might do worse than attend to.

'Is Mr Yeats an Imagiste?' No, Mr Yeats is a Symbolist, but he has written *des Images* as have many good poets before him; so that is nothing against him, and he has nothing against them (*les Imagistes*), at least so far as I know – except what he calls 'their devil's metres'.

He has written *des Images* in such poems as *Braseal and the Fisherman*; beginning, 'Though you hide in the ebb and flow of the pale tide when the moon has set'; and he has driven out the inversion and written with prose directness in such lyrics as, 'I heard the old men say everything alters'; and these things are not subject to a changing of the fashions. What I mean by the new note – you could hardly call it a change of style – was apparent four years ago in his *No Second Troy*, beginning, 'Why should I blame her', and ending –

Beauty like a tightened bow, a kind
That is not natural in an age like this,
Being high and solitary and most stern?

Why, what could she have done being what she is?
Was there another Troy for her to burn?

I am not sure that it becomes apparent in partial quotation, but with the appearance of *The Green Helmet and Other Poems* one felt that the minor note – I use the word strictly in the musical sense – had gone or was going out of his poetry; that he was at such a cross roads as we find in

Voi che intendendo il terzo ciel movete.[1]

And since that time one has felt his work becoming gaunter, seeking greater hardness of outline. I do not say that this is demonstrable by any particular passage. *Romantic Ireland's Dead and Gone*[2] is no better than Red Hanrahan's song about Ireland, but it is harder. Mr Yeats appears to have seen with the outer eye in *To a Child Dancing on the Shore* (the first poem, not the one printed in this issue). The hardness can perhaps be more easily noted in *The Magi.*

Such poems as *When Helen Lived* and *The Realists* serve at least to show that the tongue has not lost its cunning. On the other hand, it is impossible to take any interest in a poem like *The Two Kings* – one might as well read the *Idylls* of another. *The Grey Rock* is, I admit, obscure, but it outweighs this by a curious nobility, a nobility which is, to me at least, the very core of Mr Yeats' production , the constant element of his writing.

In support of my prediction, or of my theories, regarding his change of manner, real or intended, we have at least two pronounce-ments of the poet himself, the first in *A Coat*, and the second, less formal, in the speech made at the Blunt presentation. The verses, *A Coat*, should satisfy those who have complained of Mr Yeats' four and forty followers, that they would 'rather read their Yeats in the original'. Mr Yeats had indicated the feeling once before with

Tell me, do the wolf-dogs praise their fleas?[3]

1 'Ye who by understanding move the third heaven'; from an early poem of Dante's addressed to the angelic order of Principalities who control this 'third heaven'. *Paradiso*, 8, 36 (trans. John D. Sinclair). [Ed.]
2 *September 1913.* [Ed.]
3 The line reads, 'But was there ever dog that praised his fleas?' [Ed.]

which is direct enough in all conscience, and free of the 'glamour'. I've not a word against the glamour as it appears in Yeats' early poems, but we have had so many other pseudo-glamours and glamourlets and mists and fogs since the nineties that one is about ready for hard light.

And this quality of hard light is precisely what one finds in the beginning of his *The Magi*:

Now as at all times I can see in the mind's eye,
In their stiff, painted clothes, the pale unsatisfied ones
Appear and disappear in the blue depth of the sky
With all their ancient faces like rain-beaten stones,
And all their helms of silver hovering side by side.

Of course a passage like that, a passage of *imagisme*, may occur in a poem not otherwise *imagiste*, in the same way that a lyrical passage may occur in a narrative, or in some poem not otherwise lyrical. There have always been two sorts of poetry which are, for me at least, the most 'poetic'; they are firstly, the sort of poetry which seems to be music just forcing itself into articulate speech, and secondly, that sort of poetry which seems as if sculpture or painting were just forced or forcing itself into words. The gulf between evocation and description, in this latter case, is the unbridgeable difference between genius and talent. It is perhaps the highest function of art that it should fill the mind with a noble profusion of sounds and images, that it should furnish the life of the mind with such accompaniment and surrounding. At any rate Mr Yeats' work has done this in the past and still continues to do so. The present volume contains the new metrical version of *The Hour Glass*, *The Grey Rock*, *The Two Kings*, and over thirty new lyrics, some of which have appeared in these pages, or appear in this issue. In the poems on the Irish gallery we find this author certainly at *prise* with things as they are and no longer romantically Celtic, so that a lot of his admirers will be rather displeased with the book. That is always a gain for a poet, for his admirers nearly always want him to 'stay put', and they resent any signs of stirring, of new curiosity or of intellectual uneasiness. I have said that *The Grey Rock* was obscure; perhaps I should not have said so, but I think it demands unusually close attention. It is as obscure, at least, as *Sordello*, but I can not close without registering my admiration for it all the same.

John Butler Yeats

from a letter to W. B. Yeats   22 June 1914

. . . It seems to me that the modern movement is towards a creating of art out of some *single* emotion – which of course is an impossibility. Art achieves its triumphs great and small by involving the universality of the feelings – love by itself is lust, that is primitive animalism, and anger what is it but homicide? Art lifts us out of the sphere of mere bestiality, art is a musician and touches every chord in the human harp – in other words a single feeling becomes a mood, and the artist is a man with a natural tendency to thus convert every single feeling into a mood – he is a moody man. Browning was not a great poet because he tended away from the true mood of the whole man into the false mood of the idea; certainly he did not linger in the bestial sphere, yet reading him I am not a free man, he shackles me all the time with logic and philosophy and opinion – he binds me to the ground with thorns not of the flesh.

I have again been reading Homer – under his spell I follow this and that desire in untrammelled flight. He talks constantly of the winds as separate personalities. The South wind and the East wind working together and yet each separately like two dogs chasing a hare. My emotions aroused by him are like these winds, only there are thousands of them all working together and yet separately in a riot of enjoyment, and the poor hare they chase is precisely that single emotion that dared to start up and lead its single existence – like a cry of quarrelling from some distempered servant that at dead of night rouses the whole household, even to the head of the household in his tasselled nightcap. . . .

John Butler Yeats

from a letter to W. B. Yeats   18 August 1914

My dear Willie,

There is one thing never to be forgotten. *That the poet is the antithesis of the man of action.* Even though the hero is always a poet. When Achilles 'sulked' in his tent it was because the poet had driven out into exile the hero – the man of action. When Byron to satisfy his vanity or to put himself right with his contemporaries turned hero, it was because the man of action prompted and reinforced by ignoble or it may be noble motives (it is difficult to credit him with anything noble) had driven out the poet (to his own and the world's loss).

It would be a fine poetical invention to write a description of Achilles when he was 'sulking'. The beloved Patroclus with affection without a thought of self, caressing his master and listening to his complaints – the story-tellers drawing near to relate the achievements of other heroes, yet flattering him in their professional way – and when he thought of Briseis the musicians would have their chance and show their skill. Suddenly Patroclus is killed, and Hector insolently assumes his arms which had been Achilles' arms. Then the primitive man awakes – now the primitive man is either hero or poet according as he has or has not his enemy in sight and has or has not weapons to his hand. A poet indeed is a hero behind the bars, imprisoned either by circumstances too strong for him or by his own thoughts. At first Achilles was imprisoned by his own thoughts – his desire for revenge on Agamemnon and on the Greeks, who on his absenting himself from the fight would be conquered – also he would escape Fate and live long though it be ingloriously – his pride took this ignoble form – and he became *his own prisoner*. Then grief mastered him. A *single feeling*, and as is the wont with a single feeling it turned him again into a man of action. Yet in a rich and abundant nature a single feeling in time takes to itself other feelings, and the poet of many feelings resumes the sovereign power, and the man of action departs however reluctantly. The politic leader of the Grecian hosts took the chance which offered and Achilles was never again the poet. Achilles imprisoned by his own thoughts is as modern as Hamlet. At the last he is the primitive man – acting too quickly for the single feeling to become the multitudinous.

John Butler Yeats

Letter to W. B. Yeats   21 December 1914

The chief thing to know and never forget is that art is dreamland and that the moment a poet meddles with ethics and the moral uplift or thinking scientifically, he leaves dreamland, loses all his music and ceases to be a poet. Meredith is musical while he stays in dreamland – Browning also. When they turn away from it to discuss actual life as they constantly do, their lines grown harsh – they cease to sing. Shakespeare never quitted his dreams. The scene where Hubert talks with Arthur about the putting out of his eyes is all a dream[1] – in actual life such conversation would have been impossible. We all live when at our best, that is when we are most ourselves, in dreamland. A man with his wife or child and loving them, a man in grief and yielding to it, girls and boys dancing together, children at play – it is all dreams, dreams, dreams. A student over his books, soldiers at the war, friends talking together – it is still dreamland – actual life on a far away horizon which becomes more and more distant. When the essential sap of life is arrested by anger or hatred we suddenly are aware of the actual, and music dies out of our hearts and voices – the *anger subtly present* in ethical thought – as it is also in most kinds of argument; how many poems has it laid low? . . .

The poet is a magician – his vocation to incessantly evoke dreams and do his work so well, because of natural gifts and acquired skill, that his dreams shall have a potency to defeat the actual at every point. Yet here is a curious thing, the poet and we his dupes know that they are only dreams – otherwise we lose them. With our eyes open, using our will and powers of selection, we, together in friendship and brotherly love, create this dreamland. Pronounce it to be actual life and you summon logic and mechanical sense and reason and all the other powers of prose to find yourself hailed back to the prison house, and dreamland vanishes – a shrieking ghost.

1 In *King John*, IV, 1. [Ed.]

W. B. Yeats

from *Reveries Over Childhood and Youth* 1914 (reprinted in *Autobiographies*, 1955)

Some one at the Young Ireland Society gave me a newspaper that I might read some article or letter. I began idly reading verses describing the shore of Ireland as seen by a returning, dying emigrant. My eyes filled with tears and yet I knew the verses were badly written – vague, abstract words such as one finds in a newspaper. I looked at the end and saw the name of some political exile who had died but a few days after his return to Ireland. They had moved me because they contained the actual thoughts of a man at a passionate moment of life, and when I met my father I was full of the discovery. We should write out our own thoughts in as nearly as possible the language we thought them in, as though in a letter to an intimate friend. We should not disguise them in any way; for our lives give them force as the lives of people in plays give force to their words. Personal utterance, which had almost ceased in English literature, could be as fine an escape from rhetoric and abstraction as drama itself. But my father would hear of nothing but drama; personal utterance was only egotism. I know it was not, but as yet did not know how to explain the difference. I tried from that on to write out of my emotions exactly as they came to me in life, not changing them to make them more beautiful. 'If I can be sincere and make my language natural, and without becoming discursive, like a novelist, and so indiscreet and prosaic,' I said to myself, 'I shall, if good luck or bad luck make my life interesting, be a great poet; for it will be no longer a matter of literature at all.' Yet when I re-read those early poems which gave me so much trouble, I find little but romantic convention, unconscious drama. It is so many years before one can believe enough in what one feels even to know what the feeling is.

Forrest Reid

from *W. B. Yeats: A Critical Study*   1915

Mr Yeats' characteristic rhythms approach to the rhythms of nature. They are wavering, passionate, deliberately uncertain; now lingering, dying like faint echoes, now rich and full and triumphant as the breaking of the sea. Sometimes a poem opens out slowly, with a sort of spreading, increasing movement that breaks at last into a proud lonely magnificence of phrasing, as in the concluding lines of *The Rose of the World*:

Bow down, archangels, in your dim abode:
Before you were, or any hearts to beat,
Weary and kind one lingered by His seat;
He made the world to be a grassy road
Before her wandering feet.

Here, no doubt, much depends upon the solemn grandeur of a single phrase, which recalls the splendour of Milton's

Where the bright Seraphim in burning row. . . .
    (At a Solemn Music)

This particular quality in Mr Yeats's poetry, and in his prose also, is the more remarkable when we learn that he has no ear for music apart from words. That he has given, on the other hand, a closer study to the connection between poetry and music than most poets have, is apparent from his writings and from experiments prolonged over years. 'I wrote,' he says, 'and still speak the verses that begin "Autumn is over" to some traditional air, though I could not tell that air or any other on another's lips. . . . When, however, the rhythm is more personal than it is in these simple verses, the tune will always be original and personal, alike in the poet and in the reader who has the right ear; and these tunes will now and again have great beauty.' And he continues, 'I am certain all poets, even all delighted readers of poetry, speak certain kinds of poetry to distinct and simple tunes, though the speaker may be deaf to ordinary music'; adding that 'different tunes will fit different speakers or different moods.'
    The tunes will, I think, vary, certainly, with different readers, but

not nearly so much, and if really distinct tunes hardly at all, with different moods, particularly as they themselves help to create the mood. Poe's Annabel Lee, for instance, is to my sense written to so definite and elaborate a tune that it would be quite impossible to vary it. In Annabel Lee, indeed, I find the tune too pronounced, exercising a sort of tyranny over the meaning of the words, over the substance of the poem, throwing it, just as a composer's setting of any lyric invariably does, too much into the background. I prefer the less emphatic tunes of Mr Yeats, which are written more in monotone, and with a greater subtlety and expressiveness. If I might put it in this way, I should say that the tune of Annabel Lee is external, is not inevitable, while Mr Yeats' tunes are internal, are an integral part of the poem, tune and substance melting together so that the form and the sense are one.

Despite the subtlety of his rhythms, Mr Yeats has perhaps sacrificed less to rhythm than any other poet has. The metre is never helped out by superfluous adjectives, his poetic style is in this respect as austere as the baldest prose style. A poet like Swinburne – I cannot help returning to him because his art affords such a complete contrast to that of Mr Yeats – has a little list of words that come and go for no other purpose than to help out the lines to their allotted length, or to supply a rhyme. Vaguely poetic in sound, they have no particular meaning as they are applied. The most they do is not to get in the way of the sense, and repeated from poem to poem they become at last tedious in the extreme. Like coins whose inscriptions have become effaced by constant handling, it seems as if they must be remelted and recast before they can ever again be used. The art of Mr Yeats is innocent of any such labour-saving expedients. In the phrase of Monsieur Jules Lemaître, he has no verses *faits d'avance*. He may not always have been successful, but at least he never tries to *deceive* his reader. His prosody is based upon what Mr Bridges has called 'the natural speech-stress', rather than on that which is ordered by the 'numeration of syllables', and a strict regularity of accent. Only, indeed, in this way could he get that admirable variety into his metres which makes their music so wonderful. As a rule, of course, the metre has syllabic regularity, but the accents, the pauses, are exquisitely varied, and in a poem like *The Host of the Air*, the metrical effect depends primarily upon this variation. If you have the right ear, his verse is the easiest verse in the world to read, because the tune coincides so exactly with the sense. Read it *for* the sense, indeed, and you cannot fail to read it rightly, the accent naturally falling on those syllables that must be stressed to give the tune its value. In other words, the rhythm is governed by 'true speech-stresses', never, or very rarely, imposing, for the sake of metre, a false accent, which is not in the 'natural speech-intonation'. There are lyrics which have fine qualities, but which it is impossible to read aloud without sacrifice either of the sense or of the music. That this defeats the principal end for which a lyric exists, ought to be obvious. Every misplaced accent, every rhyme that is but a rhyme for the printed page, and which the speaking voice cannot rest upon, is a blot, a fault in technique. You will find few such faults in Mr Yeats' poems. . . .

In *Responsibilities* (1914) obscurity has to a large extent disappeared. A certain bewilderment may be experienced by the reader of *The Grey Rock*, but only if he is careless enough not to keep the threads of the poem separate, which the typography will help him to do. For myself, I admit that the method of weaving together two distinct poems, one very personal, and the other a narrative poem – a method Mr Yeats had already employed in *Baile and Aillinn* – does not seem a happy one. It really weakens the grip of both, and I cannot see what compensating advantage is gained. *Responsibilities*, nevertheless, is particularly interesting, because it shows such a remarkable recovery from the rather feeble and arid *Green Helmet*. The poems exhibit a great variety of form. We have narrative poems; short gnomic pieces like *The Witch*; fables like the charming *Dolls*; verses suggested by passing events, such as the Lane controversy; songs like *The Mountain Tomb*; and ballads like *September, 1913*. It is intensely interesting to watch how through the hard ruggedness of the new style the individuality of the poet shows unaltered. There are lines, too, and particularly in that fine narrative poem, *The Two Kings*, which have much of the old satisfying beauty. What more perfect image of love was ever given than this?

She builds her nest upon a narrow ledge
Above a windy precipice.

All the old beauty, yet with a subtle difference, is reborn in lines like these:

Where certain beeches mixed a pale green light
With the ground-ivy's blue, he saw a stag
Whiter than curds, its eyes the tint of the sea.

And again, when the King has fought with, and is about to kill, this stag, which of course is no ordinary stag, but an immortal lover of his Queen:

On the instant
It vanished like a shadow, and a cry
So mournful that it seemed the cry of one
Who had lost some unimaginable treasure
Wandered between the blue and the green leaf
And climbed into the air, crumbling away,
Till all had seemed a shadow or a vision
But for the trodden mire, the pool of blood,
The disembowelled horse.

This poem proves once again Mr Yeats' genius for narrative verse. Straightforward, lucid, compelling, it is marred only by an occasional line of rhetoric, as when Eochaid says, fearing for his sick brother:

If he be living still the whole world's mine
But if not living, half the world is lost.

Such lines come like an echo from the stage, and the whole style indeed, with its much freer employment of enjambment, has obviously been influenced by dramatic writing.

At times, as in *Beggar to Beggar Cried*, the directness of speech is a little startling. Mr Yeats is no longer afraid to bring fleas and lice into his verse, and in this particular lyric there is a line as bewilderingly, and I think unnecessarily, frank as anything in Whitman. Some of the rhythms are swifter than any he has yet created, and there is one song at least, *The Player Queen*, which comes with all the authority of an old masterpiece that has sung its way triumphantly down the ages. Something of the naïve magic of *The Happy Townland* lives again in *Running to Paradise*; and *September, 1913*, with its lilting refrain,

Romantic Ireland's dead and gone,
It's with O'Leary in the grave:

is a ballad whose stirring patriotism, made poetic, lifts it among the
finest national songs. Even a few of the poems that might be classed
as occasional poems have a quality of permanence about them which
such things very rarely have. There is this quality, surely, in the
splendid concluding lines of *To a Shade*, particularly in the last line
of all, with its harsh masculine restraint:

> Unquiet wanderer
> Draw the Glasnevin coverlet anew
> About your head till the dust stops your ear,
> The time for you to taste of that salt breath
> And listen at the corners has not come;
> You had enough of sorrow before death –
> Away, away! You are safer in the tomb.

I fancy that Mr Yeats' poetry in the future will not differ much
from the poetry in *Responsibilities*. It will be principally dramatic and
narrative, with now and then a song, and an epigram called forth by
some passing event. It will not have the beauty of the earlier verse.
It will be less rapturous, less inspired, less filled with the 'vision and
the faculty divine'. Its beauty will have what we find in most of these
lyrics, a hard intellectual quality. It will be a little mannered, a little
cold; and its colour will have something of the greyness of granite.
For that declination from the highest beauty to a lower beauty, in
which skill and theory occupy a larger place and inspiration and
emotion a smaller, seems to be the inevitable fate of every artist,
once he has reached his own particular perfection; and to the poet,
one knows not why, it seems to come sooner than to others. . . .

He is not a universal poet: his art does not come out of the whole
of life, as Shakespeare's art comes, or even as Whitman's comes: and
if we judge poetry by the breadth of the poet's vision of life it is
possible that compared with Whitman he will seem a secondary poet.
If we judge it, however, as I believe we must, by its intensity, its
ecstasy, its sheer beauty and music, then, of course, the position will
be exactly reversed. If Shelley is a great poet, if Keats and Coleridge
and Rossetti are great poets, then Mr Yeats is a great poet also,

greater, I think, than any of these. Even in quantity, if we compare his first-rate work with the first-rate work of the writers I have mentioned, has any of them more to show? has any of them as much? That scrupulous care for perfection which characterizes certain writers who are also artists – Rossetti, or Flaubert, and today Mr Yeats – is often misleading; so that what we sometimes take for a sign of greater wealth in others is often really only a sign either of a lack of a critical faculty, or of an unwillingness to make sacrifices. . . .

In his whole conception of the art of poetry Mr Yeats, to my mind, approaches more nearly to Milton than to any other poet. With both, poetry is sacred, something more than life, a faith, an enthusiasm, a passionate religion, that kind of enthusiasm for which men long ago went to the stake, and in the devouring heart of the flame saw the glory of God. Up to the year 1900 he was far more in touch with the seventeenth century than with any other. No one had come closer to Milton in his poetry, or to Jeremy Taylor in his prose. The likeness lies below the surface, for he shared few of their ideas. But it is there – he is of their kin, he is closer to them than to any of his contemporaries. One breathes in this world, which was his true world, the same exalted, perhaps, for most people, over-rarefied atmosphere. Very likely he prefers the Elizabethans, but he is not of them, and when a touch of their earthiness comes into his later work it is because he has put it there deliberately. He would have been an uneasy guest at the Mermaid Tavern. The very fact that all his finest work could have been done, like Milton's or Taylor's, in the seclusion of a Horton, or a Golden Grove, is significant. And that work has a beauty, a strange bright glory, that seem to me imperishable.

John Butler Yeats

from a letter to W. B. Yeats   27 February 1916

Have you noticed that poets use ideas in a way quite different from prose writers – the latter treat ideas as matters in which they believe, as scientists believe in the law of gravitation. With poets ideas are consciously or unconsciously part of their technique and of the machinery of poetry. We do not know and we do not care whether

Wordsworth actually believed in Plato's doctrine of prenatal existence, the idea is not really an integral part of the poetry. Did Shelley believe in what Keats called his 'magnanimity', fine ideas, which came to him second hand from the cold brains of Godwin. At any rate, his verse when he writes about these things is very different from when he writes concrete things. The callow American poet is all for ideas, if these are true and fine, then the poetry is true and fine etc. To ideas outside those of science and mathematics, we extend only a half belief. When I proclaim that the soul is immortal, what am I really thinking of? This and that person who is dear to me, and of the sad reality of death and also of the reality of my own longing – and when I write of immortality, apart from these, the verse will grow languid as my beliefs, for in my terrible sincerity in presence of any sufferings, perforce, I will avoid the emphasis of a real belief. We know that it was the practice of Socrates and his school to affirm nothing and to know the boundaries dividing the regions of belief and half belief – 'Men of Athens, we now separate you to your various vocations, and I to die, which is what I know not.' Those are the last words of his Apology.

Let poets, by all means, touch on ideas, but let it be only a 'touching' and a tentative groping with the sensitive poetical fingers. It is bad poetry which proclaims a definite belief – because it is a sin against sincerity. Wordsworth was full of 'beliefs' and ideas – yet always is it evident that he knew them to be only longings – and so it is with every poet that writes of ideas. It is a fault with Browning that he is too confident – he was at heart a practical man, and after the manner of his sort must have even in matters of the spirit definite grounds upon which to work. People talk with complacent superficiality of vagueness and a mere suggestiveness as necessary in poetry. But this is only true when they enter the regions where we all spend so much time – the blissful regions of longing and half belief – here not the certainties of joyous conviction are audible but the plaintive longing of half belief. Nay, there is not even this – only a faint hope – and for this there is as far as I can make out no foundation except the consciousness of mortal ignorance.

W. B. Yeats

from *Per Amica Silentia Lunae* 1917 (reprinted in *Mythologies*, 1959)

We make out of the quarrel with others, rhetoric, but of the quarrel with ourselves, poetry. Unlike the rhetoricians, who get a confident voice from remembering the crowd they have won or may win, we sing amid our uncertainty; and, smitten even in the presence of the most high beauty by the knowledge of our solitude, our rhythm shudders. I think, too, that no fine poet, no matter how disordered his life, has ever, even in his mere life, had pleasure for his end. Johnson and Dowson, friends of my youth, were dissipated men, the one a drunkard, the other a drunkard and mad about women, and yet they had the gravity of men who had found life out and were awakening from the dream; and both, one in life and art and one in art and less in life, had a continual preoccupation with religion. Nor has any poet I have read of or heard of or met with been a sentimentalist. The other self, the anti-self or the antithetical self, as one may choose to name it, comes but to those who are no longer deceived, whose passion is reality. The sentimentalists are practical men who believe in money, in position, in a marriage bell, and whose understanding of happiness is to be so busy whether at work or at play, that all is forgotten but the momentary aim. They find their pleasure in a cup that is filled from Lethe's wharf, and for the awakening, for the vision, for the revelation of reality, tradition offers us a different word – ecstasy.

A poet, when he is growing old, will ask himself if he cannot keep his mask and his vision without new bitterness, new disappointment. Could he if he would, knowing how frail his vigour from youth up, copy Landor who lived loving and hating, ridiculous and unconquered, into extreme old age, all lost but the favour of his muses?

The mother of the muses we are taught
Is memory; she has left me; they remain
And shake my shoulder urging me to sing.[1]

Surely, he may think, now that I have found vision and mask I need not suffer any longer. He will buy perhaps some small old house

1 The opening lines of *Memory* by Walter Savage Landor. [Ed.]

where like Ariosto he can dig his garden, and think that in the return of birds and leaves, or moon and sun, and in the evening flight of the rooks he may discover rhythm and pattern like those in sleep and so never awake out of vision. Then he will remember Wordsworth withering into eighty years, honoured and empty-witted, and climb to some waste room and find, forgotten there by youth, some bitter crust.

John Middleton Murry

from 'Mr Yeats' Swan Song', *Aspects of Literature*   1919

... Although it has little mysterious and haunting beauty, *The Wild Swans at Coole* is indeed a swan song. It is eloquent of final defeat; the following of a lonely path has ended in the poet's sinking exhausted in a wilderness of gray. Not even the regret is passionate; it is pitiful.

I am worn out with dreams,
A weather-worn, marble triton
Among the streams;
And all day long I look
Upon this lady's beauty
As though I had found in book
A pictured beauty,
Pleased to have filled the eyes
Or the discerning ears,
Delighted to be but wise,
For men improve with the years;
And yet, and yet
Is this my dream, or the truth?
O would that we had met
When I had my burning youth;
But I grow old among dreams,
A weather-worn, marble triton
Among the streams.
    (Men Improve with the Years)

It is pitiful because, even now in spite of all his honesty, the poet mistakes the cause of his sorrow. He is worn out not with dreams, but with the vain effort to master them and submit them to his own creative energy. He has not subdued them nor built a new world from them; he has merely followed them like will-o'-the-wisps away from the world he knew. Now, possessing neither world, he sits by the edge of a barren road that vanishes into a no-man's land, where is no future, and whence there is no way back to the past.

My country is Kiltartan Cross,
My countrymen Kiltartan's poor;
No likely end could bring them loss
Or leave them happier than before.
    (An Irish Airman Foresees his Death)

It may be that Mr Yeats has succumbed to the malady of a nation. We do not know whether such things are possible; we must consider him only in and for himself. From this angle we can regard him only as a poet whose creative vigour has failed him when he had to make the highest demands upon it. His sojourn in the world of the imagination, far from enriching his vision, has made it infinitely tenuous. Of this impoverishment, as of all else that has overtaken him, he is agonisedly aware.

I would find by the edge of that water
The collar-bone of a hare,
Worn thin by the lapping of the water,
And pierce it through with a gimlet, and stare
At the old bitter world where they marry in churches,
And laugh over the untroubled water
At all who marry in churches,
Through the white thin bone of a hare.
    (The Collar-Bone of a Hare)

Nothing there remains of the old bitter world, which for all its bitterness is a full world also; but nothing remains of the sweet world of imagination. Mr Yeats has made the tragic mistake of thinking that to contemplate it was sufficient. Had he been a great poet he would have made it his own, by forcing it into the fetters of speech. By re-creating it, he would have made it permanent; he would have built landmarks to guide him always back to where the effort of his last discovery had ended. But now there remains nothing but a handful of the symbols with which he was content:

A Sphinx with woman breast and lion paw,
A Buddha, hand at rest,
Hand lifted up that blest;

And right between these two a girl at play....
    (*The Double Vision of Michael Robartes*)

These are no more than the dry bones in the valley of Ezekiel, and, alas! there is no prophetic fervour to make them live.

Whether Mr Yeats, by some grim fatality, mistook his phantasmagoria for the product of the creative imagination, or whether (as we prefer to believe) he made an effort to discipline them to his poetic purpose and failed, we cannot certainly say. Of this, however, we are certain, that somehow, somewhere, there has been disaster. He is empty, now. He has the apparatus of enchantment, but no potency in his soul. He is forced to fall back upon the artistic honesty which has never forsaken him. That it is an insufficient reserve let this passage show: –

For those that love the world serve it in action,
Grow rich, popular, and full of influence,
And should they paint or write still it is action:
The struggle of the fly in marmalade.
The rhetorician would deceive his neighbours,
The sentimentalist himself; while art
Is but a vision of reality....
    (*Ego Dominus Tuus*)

Mr Yeats is neither rhetorician nor sentimentalist. He is by structure and impulse an artist. But structure and impulse are not enough. Passionate apprehension must be added to them. Because this is lacking in Mr Yeats those lines, concerned though they are with things he holds most dear, are prose and not poetry.

John Butler Yeats

Letter to W. B. Yeats   30 June 1921

When is your poetry at its best? I challenge all the critics if it is not when the wild spirit of your imagination is wedded to concrete fact. Had you stayed with me and not left me for Lady Gregory, and her friends and associations, you would have loved and adored concrete life for which as I know you have a real affection. What would have resulted? Realistic and poetical plays – poetry in closest and most intimate union with the positive realities and complexities of life. And that is the world that waits, so far in vain, its poet. I have always hoped and do still hope that your wife may do for you what I would have done. Not ideas but the game of life should have been your preoccupation, as it was Shakespeare's and the old English writers', notably the kinglike Fielding. The moment you touch however lightly on concrete fact, how alert you are! and how attentive we your readers become! Whistler was a fine artist, but as a portrait painter a failure. His Carlyle is ridiculous, a mere conventional coat of a prophet, the picture merely a good decorative arrangement. Every artist, poet and painter, should have many visions – first the poem itself or the picture – and with Whistler this included the frame – and then as part and parcel of that the vision of the man or woman or landscape. Da Vinci had his immortal vision of that great lady with the smile. But Whistler was too arrogant or rather too insolent – and insolence I do not love, it makes me think of the nobleman's footman. So he had not the patience to become the student and lover of life itself. Carlyle the man was to him nothing except an occasion for an artistic picture. In Shakespeare's time that kind of insolence was not known among the poets. France had not ennobled and decorated them, they were little better than noblemen's servants or servants to the public – so that there was nothing to prevent their making a close study of life itself – and they had not despised their fellow creatures as did the Puritan and does the modern English gentleman. For this kind of study you have by nature every natural qualification – your conversation shows it. Never are you happier and never more felicitous in words than when in your conversation you describe life and comment on it. But when you write poetry you as it were put on your dress coat and shut yourself in and forget what is vulgar to a man in a dress coat.

Probably you will have a long life, in which will be many revolutions and epochs. It is my belief that some day you will write a play of real life in which poetry will be the inspiration as propaganda is of G. B. Shaw's plays.

Am I talking wildly? Am I senile? I don't think so, for I would have said the same any time these 20 or 30 years. The best thing in life is the game of life, and some day a poet will find this out. I hope you will be that poet. It is easier to write poetry that is far away from life, but it is *infinitely more exciting* to write the poetry of life – and it is what the whole world is crying out for as pants the hart for the water brook. I bet it is what your wife wants – ask her. She will know what I mean and drive it home. I have great confidence in her. Does she lack the courage to say it?

Had you stayed with me, we would have collaborated and York Powell would have helped. We should have loved the opportunity of a poet among us to handle the concrete which is now left in the hands of the humorists and the politicians.

My play which you did have and probably did not read, is a poetical play dealing with the concrete – though of course not very profound, and very demoded, but it is the right sort.

W. B. Yeats

from *The Trembling of the Veil* 1922 (reprinted in *Autobiographies*, 1955)

I generalized a great deal and was ashamed of it. I thought it was my business in life to be an artist and a poet, and that there could be no business comparable to that. I refused to read books and even to meet people who excited me to generalization, all to no purpose. I said my prayers much as in childhood, though without the old regularity of hour and place, and I began to pray that my imagination might somehow be rescued from abstraction and became as preoccupied with life as had been the imagination of Chaucer. For ten or twelve years more I suffered continual remorse, and only became content when my abstractions had composed themselves into picture and dramatization. My very remorse helped to spoil my early poetry, giving it an element of sentimentality through my refusal to permit it any share of an intellect which I considered impure. Even in practical life I only very gradually began to use generalizations, that have since become the foundation of all I have done, or shall do, in Ireland. For all I know all men may have been so timid, for I am persuaded that our intellects at twenty contain all the truths we shall ever find, but as yet we do not know truths that belong to us from opinions caught up in casual irritation or momentary fantasy. As life goes on we discover that certain thoughts sustain us in defeat, or give us victory, whether over ourselves or others, and it is these thoughts, tested by passion, that we call convictions. Among subjective men (in all those, that is, who must spin a web out of their own bowels) the victory is an intellectual daily recreation of all that exterior fate snatches away, and so that fate's antithesis; while what I have called 'the Mask' is an emotional antithesis to all that comes out of their internal nature. We begin to live when we have conceived life as tragedy.

A conviction that the world was now but a bundle of fragments possessed me without ceasing. I had tried this conviction on the Rhymers, thereby plunging into greater silence an already too-silent evening. 'Johnson,' I was accustomed to say, 'you are the only man I know whose silence has beak and claw.' I had lectured on it to some London Irish society, and I was to lecture upon it later on in Dublin, but I never found but one interested man, an official of the Primrose League, who was also an active member of the Fenian Brotherhood. 'I am an extreme conservative apart from Ireland,' I have heard him explain; and I have no doubt that personal experience made him share the sight of any eye that saw the world in fragments. I had been put into a rage by the followers of Huxley, Tyndall, Carolus Duran, and Bastien-Lepage, who not only asserted the unimportance of subject whether in art or literature, but the independence of the arts from one another. Upon the other hand, I delighted in every age where poet and artist confined themselves gladly to some inherited subject-matter known to the whole people, for I thought that in man and race alike there is something called 'Unity of Being', using that term as Dante used it when he compared beauty in the *Convito* to a perfectly proportioned human body. My father, from whom I had learned the term, preferred a comparison to a musical instrument so strung that if we touch a string all the strings murmur faintly. There is not more desire, he had said, in lust than in true love, but in true love desire awakens pity, hope, affection, admiration and, given appropriate circumstance, every emotion possible to man. When I began, however, to apply this thought to the state and to argue for a law-made balance among trades and occupations my father displayed at once the violent free trader and propagandist of liberty. I thought that the enemy of this unity was abstraction, meaning by abstraction not the distinction but the isolation of occupation, or class or faculty –

Call down the hawk from the air
Let him be hooded, or caged,
Till the yellow eye has grown mild,
For larder and spit are bare,
The old cook enraged,
The scullion gone wild.
      (*The Hawk*)

   I knew no mediaeval cathedral, and Westminster, being a part of abhorred London, did not interest me, but I thought constantly of Homer and Dante, and the tombs of Mausolus and Artemisia, the great figures of King and Queen and the lesser figures of Greek and Amazon, Centaur and Greek. I thought that all art should be a Centaur finding in the popular lore its back and its strong legs. I got great pleasure too from remembering that Homer was sung, and from that tale of Dante hearing a common man sing some stanza from *The Divine Comedy*, and from Don Quixote's meeting with some common man that sang Ariosto. Morris had never seemed to care greatly for any poet later than Chaucer and though I preferred Shakespeare to Chaucer I begrudged my own preference. Had not Europe shared one mind and heart, until both mind and heart began to break into fragments a little before Shakespeare's birth? Music and verse began to fall apart when Chaucer robbed verse of its speed that he might give it greater meditation, though for another generation or so minstrels were to sing his lengthy elaborated *Troilus and Criseyde*; painting parted from religion in the later Renaissance that it might study effects of tangibility undisturbed; while, that it might characterize, where it had once personified, it renounced, in our own age, all that inherited subject-matter which we have named poetry. Presently I was indeed to number character itself among the abstractions, encouraged by Congreve's saying that 'passions are too powerful in the fair sex to let humour' or as we say character, 'have its course'. Nor have we fared better under the common daylight, for pure reason has notoriously made but light of practical reason, and has been made light of in its turn from that morning when Descartes discovered that he could think better in his bed than out of it; nor needed I original thought to discover, being so late of the school of Morris, that machinery had not separated from handicraft wholly for the world's good, nor to notice that the distinction of classes had become their isolation. If the London merchants of our day competed together in writing lyrics they would not, like the Tudor merchants, dance in the open street before the house of the victor; nor do the great ladies of London finish their balls on the pavement before their doors as did the great Venetian ladies, even in the eighteenth century, conscious of an all-enfolding sympathy. Doubtless because fragments broke into even smaller fragments we saw one another in a light of bitter comedy, and in the arts, where now one technical element reigned and now another, generation hated generation, and accomplished beauty was snatched away when it had most engaged our affections. One thing I did not foresee, not having the courage of my own thought: the growing murderousness of the world.

Turning and turning in the widening gyre
The falcon cannot hear the falconer;
Things fall apart; the centre cannot hold;
Mere anarchy is loosed upon the world,
The blood-dimmed tide is loosed and everywhere
The ceremony of innocence is drowned;
The best lack all conviction while the worst
Are full of passionate intensity.
    (The Second Coming)

I know now that revelation is from the self, but from that age-long memoried self, that shapes the elaborate shell of the mollusc and the child in the womb, that teaches the birds to make their nest; and that genius is a crisis that joins that buried self for certain moments to our trivial daily mind. There are, indeed, personifying spirits that we had best call but Gates and Gate-keepers, because through their dramatic power they bring our souls to crisis, to Mask and Image, caring not a straw whether we be Juliet going to her wedding, or Cleopatra to her death; for in their eyes nothing has weight but passion. We have dreamed a foolish dream these many centuries in thinking that they value a life of contemplation, for they scorn that more than any possible life, unless it be but a name for the worst crisis of all. They have but one purpose, to bring their chosen man to the greatest obstacle he may confront without despair. They contrived Dante's banishment, and snatched away his Beatrice, and thrust Villon into the arms of harlots, and sent him to gather cronies at the foot of the gallows, that Dante and Villon might through passion become conjoint to their buried selves, turn all to Mask and Image, and so be phantoms in their own eyes. In great lesser writers like Landor and like Keats we are shown that Image and that Mask as something set apart; Andromeda and her Perseus – though not the sea-dragon – but in a few in whom we recognize supreme masters of tragedy, the whole contest is brought into the circle of their beauty. Such masters – Villon and Dante, let us say – would not, when they speak through their art, change their luck; yet they are mirrored in all the suffering of desire. The two halves of their nature are so completely joined that they seem to labour for their objects, and yet to desire whatever happens, being at the same instant predestinate and free, creation's very self. We gaze at such men in awe, because we gaze not at a work of art, but at the re-creation of the man through that art, the birth of a new species of man, and, it may even seem that the hairs of our heads stand up, because that birth, that re-creation, is from terror. Had not Dante and Villon understood that their fate wrecked what life could not rebuild, had they lacked their Vision of Evil, had they cherished any species of optimism, they could but have found a false beauty, or some momentary instinctive beauty, and suffered no change at all, or but changed as do the wild creatures, or from devil well to devil sick, and so round the clock.

They and their sort alone earn contemplation, for it is only when the intellect has wrought the whole of life to drama, to crisis, that we may live for contemplation, and yet keep our intensity.

And these things are true also of nations, but the Gate-keepers who drive the nation to war or anarchy that it may find its Image are different from those who drive individual men, though I think at times they work together. And as I look backward upon my own writing, I take pleasure alone in those verses where it seems to me I have found something hard and cold, some articulation of the Image, which is the opposite of all that I am in my daily life, and all that my country is; yet man or nation can no more make this Mask or Image[1] than the seed can be made by the soil into which it is cast [. . .]

Somewhere about 1450, though later in some parts of Europe by a hundred years or so, and in some earlier, men attained to personality in great numbers, 'Unity of Being', and became like a 'perfectly proportioned human body', and as men so fashioned held places of power, their nations had it too, prince and ploughman sharing that thought and feeling. What afterwards showed for rifts and cracks were there already, but imperious impulse held all together. Then the scattering came, the seeding of the poppy, bursting of pea-pod, and for a time personality seemed but the stronger for it. Shakespeare's people make all things serve their passion, and that passion is for the moment the whole energy of their being – birds, beasts, men, women, landscape, society, are but symbols, and metaphors, nothing is studied in itself, the mind is a dark well, no surface, depth only. The men that Titian painted, the men that Jongsen painted, even the men of Van Dyck, seemed at moments like great hawks at rest. In the Dublin National Gallery there hung, perhaps there still hang, upon the same wall, a portrait of some Venetian gentleman by Strozzi and Mr Sargent's painting of President Wilson. Whatever thought broods in the dark eyes of that Venetian gentleman, has drawn its life from his whole body; it feeds upon it as the flame feeds upon the candle –and should that thought be changed, his prose would change, his very cloak would rustle for his whole body thinks. President Wilson lives only in the eyes, which are steady and intent; the flesh about the

[1] There is a form of Mask or Image that comes from life and is fated, but there is a form that is chosen.

mouth is dead, and the hands are dead, and the clothes suggest no movement of his body, nor any movement but that of the valet, who has brushed and folded in mechanical routine. There, all was an energy flowing outward from the nature itself; here, all is the anxious study and slight deflection of external force; there man's mind and body were predominantly subjective; here all is objective, using those words not as philosophy uses them, but as we use them in conversation [. . .]

When Edmund Spenser described the islands of Phaedria and of Acrasia he aroused the indignation of Lord Burleigh, 'that rugged forehead' and Lord Burleigh was in the right if morality were our only object.

In those islands certain qualities of beauty, certain forms of sensuous loveliness were separated from all the general purposes of life, as they had not been hitherto in European literature – and would not be again, for even the historical process has its ebb and flow, till Keats wrote his *Endymion*. I think that the movement of our thought has more and more so separated certain images and regions of the mind, and that these images grow in beauty as they grow in sterility. Shakespeare leaned, as it were, even as craftsman, upon the general fate of men and nations, had about him the excitement of the play-house; and all poets, including Spenser in all but a few pages, until our age came, and when it came almost all, have had some propaganda or traditional doctrine to give companionship with their fellows. Had not Matthew Arnold his faith in what he described as the best thought of his generation? Browning his psychological curiosity, Tennyson, as before him Shelley and Wordsworth, moral values that were not aesthetic values? But Coleridge of the *Ancient Mariner*, and *Kubla Khan*, and Rossetti in all his writing made what Arnold has called that 'morbid effort', that search for 'perfection of thought and feeling, and to unite this to perfection of form', sought this new, pure beauty, and suffered in their lives because of it. The typical men of the classical age (I think of Commodus, with his half-animal beauty, his cruelty and his caprice), lived public lives, pursuing curiosities of appetite, and so found in Christianity, with its Thebaid and its Mareotic Sea the needed curb. But what can the Christian confessor say to those who more and more must make all out of the privacy of their thought, calling up perpetual images of desire, for he cannot say 'Cease to be artist, cease to be poet', where the whole life is art and poetry, nor can he bid men leave the world, who suffer from the terrors that pass before shut-eyes. Coleridge, and Rossetti though his dull brother did once persuade him that he was an agnostic, were devout Christians, and Steinbock and Beardsley were so towards their lives' end, and Dowson and Johnson always, and yet I think it but deepened despair and multiplied temptation.

Dark Angel, with thine aching lust,
To rid the world of penitence:
Malicious angel, who still dost
My soul such subtil violence!

When music sounds, then changest thou
A silvery to a sultry fire:
Nor will thine envious heart allow
Delight untortured by desire.

Through thee, the gracious Muses turn
To Furies, O mine Enemy!
And all the things of beauty burn
With flames of evil ecstasy.

Because of thee, the land of dreams
Becomes a gathering place of fears:
Until tormented slumber seems
One vehemence of useless tears.[1]

Why are these strange souls born everywhere today? with hearts that Christianity, as shaped by history, cannot satisfy. Our love letters wear out our love; no school of painting outlasts its founders, every stroke of the brush exhausts the impulse, Pre-Raphaelitism had some twenty years; Impressionism thirty perhaps. Why should we believe that religion can never bring round its antithesis? Is it true that our air is disturbed, as Mallarmé said, by 'the trembling of the veil of the temple', or 'that our whole age is seeking to bring forth a sacred book'? Some of us thought that book near towards the end of last century, but the tide sank again.

1 From *The Dark Angel* by Lionel Johnson, 1893. [Ed.]

I. A. Richards

from 'Some Contemporary Poets', *Science and Poetry*   1927

Mr Yeats and Mr Lawrence present two further ways of dodging those difficulties which come from being born into this generation rather than into some earlier age. Mr De la Mare takes shelter in the dream-world of the child, Mr Yeats retires into black velvet curtains and the visions of the Hermetist, and Mr Lawrence makes a magnificent attempt to reconstruct in himself the mentality of the Bushman. There are other modes of escape open to the poet. Mr Blunden, to name one other poet only, goes into the country, but few people follow him there in his spirit, whereas Mr Yeats and Mr Lawrence, whether they are widely read or not, do represent tendencies among the defeated which are only too easily observable.

Mr Yeats' work from the beginning was a repudiation of the most active contemporary interests. But at first the poet of *The Wanderings of Usheen*, *The Stolen Child* and *Innisfree* turned away from contemporary civilization in favour of a world which he knew perfectly, the world of folklore as it is accepted, neither with belief nor disbelief, by the peasant. Folklore and the Irish landscape, its winds, woods, waters, islets and seagulls, and for a while an unusually simple and direct kind of love poetry in which he became something more than a minor poet, these were his refuge. Later, after a drawn battle with the drama, he made a more violent repudiation, not merely of current civilization but of life itself, in favour of a supernatural world. But the world of the 'eternal moods', of supernal essences and immortal beings is not, like the Irish peasant stories and the Irish landscape, part of his natural and familiar experience. Now he turns to a world of symbolic phantasmagoria about which he is desperately uncertain. He is uncertain because he has adopted as a technique of inspiration the use of trance, of dissociated phases of consciousness, and the revelations given in these dissociated states are insufficiently connected with normal experience. This, in part, explains the weakness of Mr Yeats' transcendental poetry. A deliberate reversal of the natural relations of thought and feeling is the rest of the explanation. Mr Yeats takes certain feelings – feelings of conviction attaching to certain visions – as evidence for the thoughts which he supposes his visions to symbolize. To Mr Yeats the value of *The Phases of the Moon* lies not in any attitudes which it arouses or embodies but in the doctrine which for an initiate it promulgates.

The resort to trance, and the effort to discover a new world-picture to replace that given by science, are the two most significant points for our purpose in Mr Yeats' work. A third might be the singularly bitter contempt for the generality of mankind which occasionally appears.

Theodore Spencer

'*The Tower*', New Republic, vol. 56   10 October 1928

In no age except our own have all serious poets been so consistently occupied with one problem; in no other age has a single problem been so steadily forced upon them. The cause is fairly obvious. Science, and particularly anthropological science, has taken away from man the sense of order, of external arrangement in the world, which for centuries had been his defense against a Nature otherwise heartlessly impartial. She has stripped him of his armor, and, as a result, though he may feel that

> there's more enterprise
> In walking naked,

the thoughtful individual realizes that such a condition, since it leaves him without an authority to substantiate his reactions to the world, comes dangerously near to ending in despair. To the poet this situation is particularly acute. For the poet expresses his emotions best when he can feel them, not only as his own, but a part of a generally accepted system: the way the Elizabethans felt about death is an example. He must be aware, that is, not only that other people feel the same way he does, but that they regard their feelings in the same light; according to the same hierarchy of values. The advantage of an external order, such as that embodied in *The Divine Comedy*, is that it gives the poet this necessary sense of emotional values. The chief difficulty facing the modern poet it not so much that he has lost what Mr I. A. Richards calls 'the magical view of the universe', but that he no longer shares a common background which can give him an ordered emotional symbolism. He has to make his system for himself, as Blake did, or he has to get along with no system at all. And since the latter is the obvious path for him to take, practically the only sense which modern poetry as a whole communicates is a sense of futility.

No one has been more aware of the contemporary problem than Mr Yeats; the question of an external order, and the individual's relation to it, has been his constant preoccupation. In his earliest poems he sought 'some symbolic language reaching far back into the past and associated with familiar names and conspicuous hills that I might not be alone amid the obscure impressions of the senses'; and in the poems of his second period he strove to express 'those simple emotions which resemble the more, the more powerful they are, everybody's emotion. . . . I was soon to write many poems where an always personal emotion was woven into a general pattern of myth and symbol.'

But a reference to Irish legend or the mere expression of emotion, no matter how universal it may be, was, to Mr Yeats, not enough. Description and analysis must be followed by synthesis, and for the past ten or fifteen years, the construction of such a synthesis, in a form outside of poetry, has been Mr Yeats' chief concern. He has worked out an elaborate scheme, which explains, on the authority of medieval magic, spiritism, and personal revelation, the relationship between the elements of the individual life, between different lives, and between the individual and his age. An account of this system was privately printed in 1925 under the title, A Vision.

This is not the place to discuss the validity of Mr Yeats' philosophy; what we are concerned with is its effect on his poetry. And for a time it seemed unfortunate. Such poems as The Phases of the Moon, and Ego Dominus Tuus, written some eight years ago, though they are by no means without fine lines, are jerky and uneven; they are too didactic to be musical; they do not represent the proper marriage between thought and emotion.

One awaited, therefore, Mr Yeats' next volume of verse with considerable interest, and one was prepared to attack it with several questions. Would the philosophy be sufficiently absorbed not to override the emotion? Would the escapist element, now that a philosophic symbolism had been substituted for a nationalistic one, still be too predominant? Would the personal feeling be so related to the external order that they would be fused into a single whole?

And now that *The Tower* has appeared, one may answer all these questions to Mr Yeats' advantage. It is true that there are some reservations, and these will appear in a moment, but, on the whole, the poems in this book are among the finest Mr Yeats has written. They are, in a sense, less dependent on *A Vision* than their immediate predecessors; they are not, that is, expository. The philosophy is used as a mine for symbols, instead of itself being the subject-matter of the poems; this is, of course, the way in which poetry should always make use of philosophy. And it is symbolism employed in this fashion which gives to Mr Yeats' poems a quality peculiar to them alone. They have, in the first place, an air of authority obtained by their reference to a system outside themselves, and, in the second place, they have a richness of tone which makes them echo and reëcho in the mind.

But the use of a symbolism drawn from personal philosophy implies a considerable danger. The symbols may be too private, they may fail to communicate the emotion they represent. And if this is the case, then the construction of the philosophy will have, for poetry, little immediate significance, and the poet will have to wait, like Blake, a century or so before he is understood. Such, however, it is safe to remark, will not be the fate of Mr Yeats. His symbols are, as a rule, sufficiently related to the common cultured memory so that they awaken a response in the intelligent reader. Where the danger comes is in the assignation to certain symbols of a greater emotional value than they would have for anyone unacquainted with Mr Yeats' own system. The subject of the poem called *Sailing to Byzantium*, for instance, is the determination of the poet, now he has become old, to leave sensuous things, and turn to the things of the spirit.

And therefore I have sailed the seas and come
To the holy city of Byzantium.

This is perfectly satisfactory, for one is willing to accept the use of Byzantium as a symbol for age and wisdom, especially when it is qualified by what follows:

O sages standing in God's holy fire
As in the gold mosaic of a wall,
Come from the holy fire, perne in a gyre
And be the singing masters of my soul.
Consume my heart away: sick with desire
And fastened to a dying animal
It knows not what it is; and gather me
Into the artifice of eternity.

This is admirable writing, and the only snag is the reference to Mr
Yeats' system in the words, 'perne in a gyre'. But when, as the climax
of the poem, the poet tells us that once 'out of nature', he will only
take his bodily form from

Such a form as Grecian goldsmiths make
Of hammered gold and gold enamelling
To keep a drowsy emperor awake,

one feels, without a knowledge of Mr Yeats' sense of values, that
this is a trivial ambition, unworthy of the strong feeling that has
preceded it, and it is only when one turns to page 191 of *A Vision* and
finds that the craftsmanship of sixth-century Byzantium has for Mr
Yeats a special significance, that one can feel the poem as it was
meant to be felt.

Privacies like this are the chief fault of this book. They are largely
responsible for a sensation of trailing off, of inconclusiveness, that
the reader is not infrequently aware of. Just as, in Mr Yeats' prose,
one feels that thought and emotion are not clearly enough distinguished, so here one sometimes gets an impression of mistiness, of a
mind clad too obviously in flesh, that prevents successful communication.

But such blemishes are outweighed by the positive achievement
which this book represents. There is no one living to whom poetry
is more important than to Mr Yeats, there is hardly anyone more
important to poetry. He has made of poetry a method of life, and he
has kept his art steadily alive by adapting it to the changing circumstances of his thought. This book is different from its predecessors,
not only because it is concerned with different emotions, and because
its style is in many ways different from Mr Yeats' previous style, but

also because it gets closer to reality; it is more centripetal. Even if the symbolism is on occasion remote, the emotions, particularly those connected with old age, are more convincing than they ever have been, and many of these poems – *The Tower*, *Nineteen Nineteen*, *Among School Children* – will remain a permanent part of English poetry.

William Empson

from *Seven Types of Ambiguity*   1930 Reprinted by permission of New Directions Publishing Corporation and Chatto & Windus Ltd. All rights reserved.

The strength of vagueness, in fact, is that it allows of secret ambiguity; it seems to have forced itself on nineteenth-century poets when they felt they needed ambiguity, but would have considered its more discoverable forms improper. If I may once more attempt to give reasons for this fact, it may spring from their respect for logical punctuation, from their admiration for simple ecstasies (it was no longer courtiers and administrators who wrote poetry), from their resulting admiration for smoothness of lyrical flow, and from the fact that the language had become less fluid, a less subtle mirror of the mind (though a more precise mirror of the scientific world), since the clarifying labours of the eighteenth century. This cult of vagueness produced the nonsense writers like Lear and Lewis Carroll (the Carpenter was a castle; the Walrus, who could eat so many more oysters because he was crying into his handkerchief, was a *bishop*, in the chessboard scheme. It was the cult of vagueness which saved their extraordinary author from thinking himself a satirist); and the dowagers of Oscar Wilde's plays, who by the gentle indifference of their vagueness could give insults beside which violence must pale. My next example shows the extreme beauty which such a technique can sustain.

One of the finest poems of W. B. Yeats is an example of an ambiguity of the sixth type, under the sub-heading 'irrelevant statements'.

Who will go drive with Fergus now,
And pierce the deep wood's woven shade,
And dance upon the level shore?
Young man, lift up your russet brow,
And lift your tender eyelids, maid,
And brood on hopes and fears no more.[1]

And no more turn aside and brood
Upon Love's bitter mystery;
For Fergus rules the brazen cars,
And rules the shadows of the wood,
And the white breast of the dim sea
And all dishevelled wandering stars.
  (*Who Goes with Fergus?*)

There is another poem in the volume explaining about Fergus.[2] He appears as a king, who has left the judgement-hall, and the pleasures of the court, and the chariot races by the seashore, who has grown weary of active life, and has sought out a Druid to be given the bag of dreams. The Druid warns him that

No woman loves me, no man seeks my help,
Because I be not of the things I dream.

Fergus, insisting, is given the dreams and awakes to what they imply, the intellectual or contemplative life, so that

    now I am grown nothing, being all,
And the whole world weighs down upon my heart,

and so that he cries out

Ah! Druid, Druid, how great webs of sorrow
Lay hidden in the small slate-coloured bag!

One may notice the way a foreign idiom is implied by the two uses of *how*: 'how great were the webs' and 'how the webs of sorrow lay hidden'.

The first poem, of course, assumes this story, but *now* may mean before or after the transformation. If after, the first line means:

1 The line now properly reads 'And brood on hopes and fear no more.' [Ed.]
2 *Fergus and the Druid.* [Ed.]

'Now that the awful example of Fergus is in front of you, surely you will not be so unwise as to brood?'; to *drive* with him would be to wander through the woods like a ghost, as he does; the *dancing* would be that of the fairy child who danced upon the mountains like a flame and stole away the children. Or 'Now who will be so loyal as to follow him?' or 'Can you be so cruel as to abandon him now?'; or with a different feeling: 'Now that Fergus knows everything, who will come and join in his meditations; who will share his melancholy and his knowledge; which of you will pierce the mystery of the forest and rejoice in sympathy with the whole of nature?' If before, so that the force of *now* is: 'There is still time to drive with Fergus, as he is still a king in the world,' or 'There is still time to give a warning, as the fatal thing has not yet happened'; then the first line gives: 'Who will come out with the great figures of the court, and join in their sensible out-of-door pleasures?'

If before, the second verse means: 'You need not brood, because Fergus is guardian of common-sense; he is a strong man to drive war-chariots, as you should be; he owns all the territory on which magic takes place; he will keep it under decent control; there is no need for you to worry about it.' If after: 'Do not brood; be warned by Fergus, who though still king, still technically in command of war-chariots, is true ruler only of the dim appurtenances of magic dreams,' or, since there is no mistaking the triumph of the line about *cars* into whatever melancholy the verse trails away, 'Remember that though Fergus is a great poet or philosopher or what not, though he drives some mythological chariot of the Muses,' of whose details I am afraid I am ignorant, 'yet even he, because these victories involved brooding, is reduced to the dim and ghostly condition of the last three lines.'

I said that an example of the sixth type must say nothing, and this poem says: 'Do not brood.' But the words have little of the quality of an order; they convey rather: 'How strange and sad that you should still be brooding!'; and one may interpret variously the transition from advice to personal statement, from such of an imperative as was intended to the mere pain of loss, in the repetition of *no more*. 'I, in that I am Fergus, can no more turn aside from brooding,' is a sort of false grammar by juxtaposition, which may be felt in the line, and there is a suggestion that they must now lose their dreams, as they have already lost the real world, without getting anything in exchange for either. 'All has grown bitter, and who can join in either activity of Fergus any longer?' One might finally distinguish the erotic brooding of the young persons from the philosophical brooding of Fergus, which as hoping for nothing is at once grander and more empty; no doubt this distinction is only intended faintly, since it is part of the wisdom of the language of the poet that it treats these two as of the same kind. But, in so far as it is intended, it allows of an opposite meaning for 'Do not brood' – 'Do not brood in this comparatively trivial fashion but go and drive with Fergus, who will teach you to brood about everything, who will teach you to wander, untouchable, and all-embracing, in an isolation like that of the stars.'

The wavering and suggestive indefiniteness of nineteenth-century poetry is often merely weak. When, as here, it has a great deal of energy and sticks in your head, it is usually because the opposites left open are tied round a single strong idea; thus here, on the one hand, the condition of brooding is at once to be sought out and to be avoided; on the other, the poet, 'nothing, being all', contemporaneously living all lives, may fitly be holding before him both the lives of Fergus, and drawing the same moral from either of them.

Edmund Wilson

from 'W. B. Yeats', *Axel's Castle* 1932

Yeats has shown himself, in his prose writings, a man of both exceptionally wide information and exceptional intellectual curiosity; but, for all the variety of his interests and the versatility of his intelligence, he has, in rejecting the methods of modern science, cut himself off in a curious way from the general enlightened thought of his time. Yet his mind is so comprehensive and so active that he has felt the need of constructing a system: and, finding it impossible to admit the assumptions upon which most modern systems are based, he has had recourse to the only science which his position has allowed him to accept, the obsolete science of astrology. As a young man, Yeats frequented clairvoyants and students of astrology and magic; Madame Blavatsky, the necromantic Theosophist, seems to have made upon him a considerable impression. And in 1901 he was led to formulate, in an essay on magic, the following set of beliefs, to which he still apparently adheres:

1. That the borders of our mind are ever shifting, and that many minds can flow into one another, as it were, and create or reveal a single mind, a single energy.

2. That the borders of our memories are as shifting, and that our memories are a part of one great memory, the memory of Nature herself.

3. That this great mind and great memory can be evoked by symbols.

What Yeats was really approaching here was some such systematic study of the symbolism of myths, trances, dreams and other human visions as psychoanalysis and anthropology were attempting from a different direction. And despite the obvious charlatanism or naïveté of most of his instructors and fellow investigators, Yeats' account of his researches is interesting. For it is not merely that Yeats loves the marvellous: he is also intent upon discovering symbols which may stand for the elements of his own nature or which shall seem to possess some universal significance. The results of this research are very curious. When we read Yeats' account of his adventures among the mediums, it becomes plain that, in spite of his repudiation of science, he has always managed to leave himself a margin of scientific doubt. Like Huysmans, he betrays an instinct to scrutinize and check up on the supernatural which is disastrous to genuine mysticism. Just as in Huysmans' case, we always feel that the wistful student of Satanism has too much solid Dutch common-sense really to deceive himself about his devils, so in Yeats – he himself has confessed it – the romantic amateur of magic is always accompanied and restrained by the rationalistic modern man. 'He and I often quarrelled,' Yeats writes of himself and A. E., 'because I wanted him to examine and question his visions, and write them out as they occurred; and still more because I thought symbolic what he thought real like the men and women that had passed him on the road.' Yet Huysmans went so far as to claim – or at least to make one of his characters claim – as genuine examples of demoniacal possession those very hysteria cases of Charcot's which at that moment were leading Charcot's young pupil Freud to his first great discovery of the principle of emotional repression; and Yeats attributes to a sort of supernatural being designated as *Anima Mundi* precisely such universal symbols as are studied by such psychologists as Jung. What is most curious is that Yeats should at last have constructed out of these symbols an elaborate mystical-metaphysical system.

This system was set forth in *A Vision*, a work which occupied Yeats for many years and which he published privately in 1926. *A Vision* presented an elaborate theory of the variation of human personality, of the vicissitudes of human history and of the transformations of the soul in this world and the next. This theory was worked out with geometrical diagrams and set forth in terms of such unfamiliar conceptions as *daimons*, *tinctures*, *cones*, *gyres*, *husks* and *Passionate Bodies*.

Yeats asserts that human personality follows the pattern of a 'Great Wheel'. That is, the types of personality possible constitute a kind of closed circle – they are regular stages in a circular journey to and fro between complete objectivity at one pole and complete subjectivity at the other; and this journey may be represented by the orbit of the moon, to which it corresponds. Let the moon represent subjectivity and the sun, objectivity: then the dark of the moon, when it is closest to the sun, is the phase of complete objectivity; and the full moon, which is farthest from the sun, is the phase of complete subjectivity. At these two opposite poles of the circle, human life is impossible: there exist only antipodal types of supernatural beings. But along the circumference of the circle, between these two ultra-human poles, there occur twenty-six phases which cover all possible types of human personality.

Yeats' theory of the variation of these types is extremely complicated. He begins by assigning to 'incarnate man' four 'faculties': the Will, 'by which is understood feeling that has not become desire ... and energy as yet uninfluenced by thought, action or emotion'; the Mask, which means 'the image of what we wish to become, or of that to which we give our reverence'; the Creative Mind, 'the intellect ... all the mind that is consciously constructive'; and the Body of Fate, 'the physical and mental environment, the changing human body, the stream of Phenomena as this affects a particular individual, all that is forced upon us from without.' The

Will is always opposite the Mask: 'it looks into a painted picture.' The Creative Mind is opposite the Body of Fate: 'it looks into a photograph; but both look into something which is the opposite of themselves.' We follow the Will around the clock, and by combining it with the other elements according to geometrical laws we calculate the characters of the different phases. Starting at the right of the objective pole, the soul passes first through varieties of almost purely physical life – Yeats takes his examples here from the Bacchuses and shepherds of the poets. It is moving toward subjectivity, however – Walt Whitman, Alexandre Dumas: it is seeking itself, and as it progresses, it becomes more beautiful. The ultra-human subjective phase, which apparently includes Christ, is described as 'a phase of complete beauty', where 'Thought and Will are indistinguishable, effort and attainment are indistinguishable – nothing is apparent but dreaming Will and the Image that it dreams'. This is preceded and followed by phases which include Baudelaire and Beardsley; Keats and Giorgione; Blake and Rabelais; Dante and Shelley; and presumably Yeats himself: men who have withdrawn from the life of the world in order to live in their dream. But once the all-subjective phase is past, the soul

... would be the world's servant, and as it serves,
Choosing whatever task's most difficult
Among tasks not impossible, it takes
Upon the body and upon the soul
The coarseness of the drudge.
                                        Before the full
It sought itself and afterwards the world.

And it is now leaving beauty behind and headed toward deformity:

Reformer, merchant, statesman, learned man,
Dutiful husband, honest wife by turn,
Cradle upon cradle, and all in flight and all
Deformed because there is no deformity
But saves us from a dream.
    (The Phases of the Moon)

The soul has now come full circle: the three final human phases before the phase of complete objectivity are the Hunchback, the Saint and the Fool.

Yeats has worked all this out with great care and with considerable ingenuity. He has described each of the twenty-eight phases and supplied us with typical examples. What we find in this part of the book is Yeats' familiar preoccupation with the conflict between action and philosophy, reality and imagination. (It is amusing and characteristic that, according to his system, the side of humanity closest to the sun – that is, closest the objective nature – should be the side that is bathed in darkness, whereas the side which is furthest from the sun – that is, nearest the subjective nature – should be the side that is bright!) Now this is a subject which has hitherto, in Yeats' prose as well as in his verse, usually inspired him well; the symbols of the Mask, the Sun and Moon, etc., if they have sometimes been a little disconcerting when we encountered them in his critical writings, have created just the right impression of significance in mystery for Symbolistic poetry. And there are, to be sure, certain passages of *A Vision* as brilliant as Yeats at his best. He writes, for example, of the phase of 'the Receptive Man', to which he assigns Rembrandt and Synge: 'The man wipes his breath from the window pane, and laughs in his delight at all the varied scene.' And of the phase of 'the Obsessed Man', to which he assigns Giorgione and Keats:

When we compare these images with those of any
subsequent phase, each seems studied for its own sake; they
float as in serene air, or lie hidden in some valley, and if
they move it is to music that returns always to the same
note, or in a dance that so returns upon itself that they
seem immortal.

And, in what is perhaps the most eloquent passage in the book, he returns to a certain type of beautiful uncontemplative woman who has already haunted his poetry:

Here are born those women who are most touching in
their beauty. Helen was of this phase; and she comes before
the mind's eye elaborating a delicate personal discipline as
though she would make her whole life an image of a
unified antithetical (that is, subjective) energy. While
seeming an image of softness, and of quiet, she draws
perpetually upon glass with a diamond. Yet she will not

number among her sins anything that does not break that personal discipline, no matter what it may seem according to others' discipline; but if she fail in her own discipline she will not deceive herself, and for all the languor of her movements, and her indifference to the acts of others, her mind is never at peace. She will wander much alone as though she consciously meditated her masterpiece that shall be at the full moon, yet unseen by human eye, and when she returns to her house she will look upon her household with timid eyes, as though she knew that all power of self-protection had been taken away, and that of her once Primary Tincture (that is, objective element) nothing remained but a strange irresponsible innocence. . . . Already perhaps, through weakness of desire, she understands nothing, while alone seeming of service. Is it not because she desires so little and gives so little that men will die and murder in her service?

And there is a strange imaginative power in the conception behind the final sequence of the Hunchback, the Saint and the Fool.

Yet *A Vision*, when we try to read it, makes us impatient with Yeats. As a rule, he expounds his revelations as if he took them seriously – that is, as if he believed that masks and husks and daimons and Passionate Bodies were things which actually existed, as if they were as real as those visions of A. E.'s which had been as real to A. E. as the people in the street, but which Yeats had tried to induce him to question; and indeed one would think that to elaborate a mystical system so complicated and so tedious, it would be necessary to believe in it pretty strongly. Yet now and then the skeptical Yeats reasserts himself and we are startled by an unexpected suggestion that, after all, the whole thing may be merely 'a background for my thought, a painted scene'. If the whole thing, we ask ourselves, has been merely an invented mythology, in which Yeats himself does not believe, what right has he to bore us with it – what right has he to expect us to explore page after page of such stuff as the following description of the habits of the soul after death:

The Spirit first floats horizontally within the man's dead body, but then rises until it stands at his head. The Celestial

Body is also horizontal at first but lies in the opposite position, its feet where the Spirit's head is, and then rising, as does the Spirit, stands up at last at the feet of the man's body. The Passionate Body rises straight up from the genitals and stands in the centre. The Husk remains in the body until the time for it to be separated and lost in *Anima Mundi*.

In 'A Packet for Ezra Pound' (1929) a new light is thrown on *A Vision*.[1] We learn that Yeats' wife is a medium, and that the theories set forth in this book were communicated through her by supernatural beings. Yeats tells us how, four days after their marriage in 1917, Mrs Yeats surprised him by attempting automatic writing.

What came in disjointed sentences, in almost illegible writing was so exciting, sometimes so profound, that I persuaded her to give an hour or two day after day to the unknown writer, and after some half-dozen such hours offered to spend what remained of life explaining and piecing together those scattered sentences. 'No,' was the answer, 'we have come to give you metaphors for poetry.' The unknown writer took his theme at first from my just published *Per Amica Silentia Lunae*. I had made a distinction between the perfection that is from a man's combat with himself and that which is from a combat with circumstances, and upon this simple distinction he built up an elaborate classification of men according to their more or less complete expression of one type or the other. He supported his classification by a series of geometrical symbols and put these symbols in an order that answered the question in my essay as to whether some prophet could not prick upon the calendar the birth of a Napoleon or a Christ.

Yeats describes the manifestations which accompanied these revelations: the perfumes, whistlings, smells of burnt feathers, bursts of music, apparitions of great black birds and of 'persons in clothes of the late sixteenth century and of the seventeenth'. On one occasion, when an owl was hooting in the garden, the dictating spirit asked

1 The revised 1937 edition of *A Vision* incorporates *A Packet for Ezra Pound* as its first section. [Ed.]

for a recess: 'Sounds like that,' the spirit explained, 'give us great pleasure.' And here were also mischievous obstructive spirits who attempted to mislead the Yeatses and who were designated as 'Frustrators';

> the automatic script would deteriorate, grow sentimental or confused, and when I pointed this out the communicator would say 'from such and such an hour, on such and such a day, all is frustration.' I would spread out the script and he would cross all out back to the answer that began it, but had I not divined frustration he would have said nothing.

We learn also, by the way, a fact which might, for a psychologist, throw a good deal of light on the development of Yeats' personality. It appears that not only has Yeats always succeeded in steering clear of science: he has never till recently read philosophy.

> Apart from two or three of the principal Platonic Dialogues I knew no philosophy. Arguments with my father, whose convictions had been formed by John Stuart Mill's attack upon Sir William Hamilton, had destroyed my confidence and driven me from speculation to the direct experience of the Mystics. I had once known Blake as thoroughly as his unfinished confused Prophetic Books permitted, and I had read Swedenborg and Boehme, and my initiation into the 'Hermetic Students' had filled my head with Cabalistic imagery.

Now, however, he wants to study philosophy as an aid to understanding the 'system'. The spirits ask him to wait till they have finished. At the end of three years when the supernatural revelations have ceased, and A Vision is actually in proof, Yeats takes down from Mrs Yeats, who, it appears, did not share her husband's ignorance, a list of the philosophers she had read. For four years, Yeats applies himself to these, and what he finds makes him uneasy about A Vision: he feels that he must partly have misinterpreted what the spirits have told him. But the spirits themselves intervene to put an end to this disquieting situation: they make him stop his philosophical studies.

As we read all this, we say to ourselves that Yeats, growing older, has grown more credulous. But we come, at the end, to the following passage:

Some will ask if I believe all that this book contains, and I will not know how to answer. Does the word belief, used as they will use it, belong to our age, can I think of the world as there and I here judging it?

And he intimates that, after all, his system may be only a set of symbols like another – a set of symbols, we recognize, like the Irish myths with which he began.

Into the personal situation suggested by Yeats' account of his revelations, it is inappropriate and unnecessary to go: the psychological situation seems plain. When Yeats, at the crucial period of his life, attempted to leave fairyland behind, when he became aware of the unsatisfying character of the life of iridescent reverie, when he completely recreated his style so as to make it solid, homely and exact where it had formerly been shimmering or florid – the need for dwelling with part of his mind – or with his mind for part of the time – in a world of pure imagination, where the necessities of the real world do not hold, had, none the less, not been conjured away by the new artistic and intellectual habits he was cultivating. Where the early Yeats had studied Irish folk-lore, collected and sorted Irish fairy tales, invented fairy tales for himself, the later Yeats worked out from the mediumistic communications of his wife the twenty-eight phases of the human personality and the transformations of the soul after death. Yeats' sense of reality today is inferior to that of no man alive – indeed, his greatness is partly due precisely to the vividness of that sense. In his poetry, in his criticism and in his memoirs, it is the world we all live in with which we are confronted – the world we know, with all its frustrations, its defeats, its antagonisms and its errors – the mind that sees is not naïve, as the heart that feels is not insensitive. They meet reality with comprehension and with passion – but they have phases, we are astonished to discover, when they do not seem to meet it at all. Yet the scientific criticism of supernatural phenomena is actually as much a part of the reality of Yeats' world as it is of that of most of the rest of us. And when Yeats writes of his supernatural experiences, this criticism, though it may be kept in the background, is nevertheless always present – his realistic sense is too strong, his intellectual integrity too high, to leave it out of the picture. Though he is much addicted to these fantastic imaginings, though he no doubt needs their support to enable him to sustain his rôle of great poet – yet when he comes to write about his spirits and their messages, he cannot help letting us in on the imposture. He believes, but – he does not believe: the impossibility of believing is the impossibility which he accepts most reluctantly, but still it is there with the other impossibilities of this world which is too full of weeping for a child to understand.

It is interesting to compare *A Vision* with that other compendious treatise on human nature and destiny by that other great writer from Dublin: Bernard Shaw's *Guide to Socialism and Capitalism.* Here we can see unmistakably the differences between the kind of literature which was fashionable before the War and the kind which has been fashionable since. Shaw and Yeats, both coming as young men to London from eighteenth-century Dublin, followed diametrically opposite courses. Shaw shouldered the whole unwieldy load of contemporary sociology, politics, economics, biology, medicine and journalism, while Yeats, convinced that the world of science and politics was somehow fatal to the poet's vision, as resolutely turned away. Shaw accepted the scientific technique and set himself to master the problems of an industrial democratic society, while Yeats rejected the methods of Naturalism and applied himself to the introspective plumbing of the mysteries of the individual mind. While Yeats was editing Blake, Shaw was grappling with Marx; and Yeats was appalled by Shaw's hardness and efficiency. 'I hated it,' he says of *Arms and the Man*; 'it seemed to me inorganic, logical straightness and not the crooked road of life and I stood aghast before its energy.' And he tells us that Shaw appeared to him in a dream in the form of a sewing machine, 'that clicked and shone, but the incredible thing was that the machine smiled, smiled perpetually.'

In his Great Wheel of the twenty-eight phases, Yeats has situated Shaw at a phase considerably removed from his own, and where the individual is headed straight for the deformity of seeking, not the soul, but the world. And their respective literary testaments – *A Vision* and the *Guide* – published almost at the same time, mark the extreme points of their divergence: Shaw bases all human hope and happiness on an equal distribution of income, which he believes will finally make impossible even the pessimism of a Swift or a Voltaire; while Yeats, like Shaw a Protestant for whom the Catholic's mysticism was impossible, has in *A Vision* made the life of humanity contingent on the movements of the stars. 'The day is far off,' he concludes, 'when the two halves of man can divine each its own unity in the other as in a mirror, Sun in Moon, Moon in Sun, and so escape out of the Wheel.'

Yet, in the meantime, the poet Yeats has passed into a sort of third phase, in which he is closer to the common world than at any previous period. He is no longer quite so haughty, so imperturbably astride his high horse, as during his middle Dantesque period. With the Dantesque mask, he has lost something of intensity and something of sharpness of outline. In *The Tower* (1928), certain words such as 'bitter', 'wild', and 'fierce', which he was able, a few years ago, to use with such thrilling effect, have no longer quite the same force. He writes more loosely, and seems to write more easily. He has become more plain-spoken, more humorous – his mind seems to run more frankly on his ordinary human satisfactions and chagrins: he is sometimes harsh, sometimes sensual, sometimes careless, sometimes coarse.

Though he now inhabits, like Michael Robartes, a lonely tower on the outermost Irish coast, he has spent six years in the Irish senate, presiding at official receptions in a silk hat, inspecting the plumbing of the government schools and conscientiously sitting through the movies which it is one of his official duties to censor. He is much occupied with politics and society, with general reflections on human life – but with the wisdom of the experience of a lifetime, he is passionate even in age. And he writes poems which charge now with the emotion of a great lyric poet that profound and subtle criticism of life of which I have spoken in connection with his prose.

We may take, as an example of Yeats' later vein, the fine poem in *The Tower* called *Among School Children*. The poet, now 'a sixty year old smiling public man', has paid an official visit to a girls' school kept by nuns; and as he gazes at the children there, he remembers how the woman he had loved had told him once of some 'harsh reproof or trivial event' of her girlhood which had changed 'some childish day to tragedy'. And for a moment the thought that she may once have looked like one of the children before him has revived the excitement of his old love. He remembers the woman in all her young beauty – and thinks of himself with his present sixty years – 'a comfortable kind of old scarecrow'. What use is philosophy now? – is not all beauty bound up with the body and doomed to decay with it? – is not even the divine beauty itself which is worshipped there by the nuns inseparable from the images of it they adore?

Labour is blossoming or dancing where
The body is not bruised to pleasure soul,
Nor beauty born out of its own despair,
Nor blear-eyed wisdom out of midnight oil.
O chestnut tree, great rooted blossomer,
Are you the leaf, the blossom or the bole?
O body swayed to music, O brightening glance,
How can we know the dancer from the dance?

Here the actual scene in the convent, the personal emotions it awakens and the general speculations which these emotions suggest, have been interwoven and made to play upon each other at the same time that they are kept separate and distinct. A complex subject has been treated in the most concentrated form, and yet without confusion. Perceptions, fancies, feelings and thoughts have all their place in the poet's record. It is a moment of human life, masterfully seized and made permanent, in all its nobility and lameness, its mystery and actuality, its direct personal contact and abstraction.

Yvor Winters

from 'T. Sturge Moore', *Hound and Horn*, vol. 6   April–June 1933

In my opinion Mr Moore is a greater poet than Mr Yeats. He has lived obscurely, and has not displayed Mr Yeats' talent for self-dramatization; for these reasons and others he has never become a public figure or a popular writer. Mr Yeats began as a rather bad poet of a kind exactly suited to the popular taste of his decade, and through some miracle of destiny retained his following when he became serious, whereas Mr Moore has been a master, of a kind, from the outset. Mr Yeats, as a dramatist of his own personality, writes with

an histrionic tone seldom entirely justified by his ideas and perceptions but which beguiles many readers: it is a similar tone (but super-
imposed on extremely bad poetry) which accounts for the popularity
for Mr Jeffers. Mr Moore, on the other hand, is never his own dupe,
and has received the neglect that is commonly the lot of a perfectly
lucid mind.

Most interesting of all the reasons for this difference in reputation,
however, are the relationships in which the two poets stand to the
generation of poets which succeeded them, the generation of Pound,
Eliot, Stevens, Williams, Miss Moore, and Miss Loy, and of which
Hart Crane, a much younger writer, was probably the last important
disciple and, so far as the crucial defects of the generation are concerned, perhaps the most illuminating example. The generation bore
the same relationship to the Romantic poets which the French
Symbolists bore: that is, they endeavored to correct the stylistic
defects of looseness and turgidity tolerated by the Romantics, without
understanding the conceptual confusion which had debauched
Romantic style and Romantic character alike. The result has been a
poetry superior to most Romantic poetry, but, by virtue of its
superiority, rendering the Romantic deficiencies even more plain
than they appeared in the Romantics. That is, the looseness of
Whitman's form is more clearly demonstrated in Pound's *Cantos* than
in Whitman; the confusion of Whitman's ideas is more clearly
demonstrated in *The Bridge*, by Hart Crane, than in Whitman;
because Pound and Crane write precisely enough in detail to point
directly to those issues with which they cannot deal precisely. All
cats are gray in the dark, and everything is gray in Whitman.

The fundamental post-Romantic defect is the abandonment of
logic, either in favor of an undisguised form of what Mr Kenneth
Burke calls 'qualitative progression' (that is, progression governed
wholly by mood), as in the *Cantos*, or as in *Anna Livia Plurabelle*, or in
favor of a pseudo-logic, such as one finds discreetly distributed (amid
much real logic) throughout Mr Eliot's *Gerontion*, in most of Crane,
and frequently at crucial moments in poems by Mr Yeats. The
abandonment of logic is a defect for two reasons: it eliminates a half
of human experience, and so limits the poet's range and often falsifies
his feeling; and it is an uneconomical use of words, half only of the

power of the words being brought into play. These types of non-logical writing represent the ultimate boundary of the uncritical emotionalism of the Romantics: they represent the stylistic *definition* of that emotionalism, its ultimate formal equivalent, to which the Romantics seldom attained, an emotionalism which is frequently merely sensationalism, and which is largely unmotivated (that is, un-formulable).

The defect which gives rise to Romantic irony, the intellectual confusion which causes a greater or less measure of meaningless feeling, Mr Yeats shares with the entire generation subsequent to him. His irreducible obscurities, his moments of inexplicable excitement, have appeared to be kinds of profundity. . . .

Theodore Spencer

from 'The Later Poetry of W. B. Yeats', *Hound and Horn*, vol. 7 October 1933 (reprinted in Morton Dauwen Zabel (ed.), *Literary Opinion in America*, 1938)

A distinguished critic, Mr Yvor Winters, has recently compared the poetry of W. B. Yeats with the poetry of T. Sturge Moore. His remarks are challenging and need to be discussed. In his opinion, Moore is a greater poet than Yeats; he says that Yeats, at crucial moments, suffers from the 'fundamental post-Romantic defect, the abandonment of logic', that Yeats achieves a 'factitious coherence', is guilty of intellectual confusion, and is an 'unregenerate Romantic'. These adverse criticisms sum up very well the case against Yeats as an important poet, and the reason they need to be discussed by anyone concerned with Yeats's poetry is that they have a plausibility which may make them a serious obstacle to a satisfactory judgement of Yeats's position.

There is not much to be said about the first of them. To say that Moore is a better poet than Yeats seems to me meaningless, and I cannot imagine any standards of criticism by which such a statement can be defended. In subtlety of rhythm, in intensity, in richness of verbal association, in force, in everything which implies an original and individual style, the later poems of Yeats are superior to anything by Moore. Compare, for example, the opening lines of Moore's sonnet, *Apuleius Meditates*, which Mr Winters praises very highly, with the opening of Yeats's sonnet on *Leda and the Swan*. This is Moore:

An old tale tells how Gorgo's gaze distilled
Horror to petrify men's mobile limbs:
Endymion's moonlit beauty never dims,
Hard-frozen as the fond chaste goddess willed.

And Yeats:

A sudden blow: the great wings beating still
Above the staggering girl, her thighs caressed
By the dark webs, her nape caught in his bill,
He holds her helpless breast upon his breast.

There is an important distinction illustrated here, a distinction which applies to other poetry than that of Moore and Yeats. It is the distinction between the poetry of revery and the poetry of immediacy. I do not, of course, mean by the poetry of revery poetry which is written necessarily about past events; what I am describing, to put it loosely, is the associative climate into which we feel the poet has moved when he got himself ready for writing, and in which he has remained during the composition of the poem. Even without the revealing phrase 'An old tale tells', which begins Moore's sonnet, we know from the rhythm, the fairly obvious and hence unregenerated adjectives, that the subject is being viewed from a distance, that it is not apprehended immediately. The poet and his material have not passed through a period of 'intimate welding'; they have been contiguous, not fused. But, 'A sudden blow: the great wings beating still': here the poet has put the reader in the midst of the action; the subject is not considered and contemplated from outside; we are convinced that the matter has been so vividly an essential part of the poet's experience, that it becomes, if we are reading with the proper attention, an equally vivid part of the reader's experience too.

The distinction between these two ways of regarding the subject matter of a poem becomes obvious if we think of Wordsworth's famous definition of the origin of poetry. 'It takes its origin,' he says, 'from emotion recollected in tranquillity; the action is contemplated till, by a species of reaction, the tranquillity gradually disappears, and an emotion, kindred to that which was before the subject of contemplation, is gradually produced, and does itself actually exist in the mind.' It is the last part of this sentence, the part usually left unquoted, which is important. Without the disappearance of tranquillity no good poem can be written, and the trouble with the kind of poetry I have called the poetry of revery is that when we are reading it we feel the tranquillity is still there; the 'emotion which was before the subject of contemplation' has not turned up. It is because we never feel like this about Shakespeare that we consider Shakespeare so great a poet, and it is because we often feel like this about Tennyson, that Tennyson's reputation is dubious.

The difference between immediate poetry and the poetry of revery is a reflection of a difference in poetic temperament, and like all differences in temperament it shows itself in a number of ways. One does not expect that a temperament addicted to revery will seek for startling words or for arrangements of images and thoughts that will surprise the mind. Revery in any form not being a function of the human personality as a whole, its aim, when expressed in poetry, will be to lull rather than excite, to describe, or even lament, as beautifully as possible, rather than to assert or protest. Not that poetry of this kind is without intensity; one has only to think of sections 54 to 56 of *In Memoriam*; but it is not the intensity of immediacy, of anger, or of satire, because it is not an intensity which fully includes the intellect.

Of course the contrast between these two kinds of poetic temperament may be carried too far, and one can waste one's time in putting various poets into the various categories they imply, which is foolish because in many cases it is impossible to draw a satisfactory line between them. The reason I mention the matter at all is that it throws an interesting light on the poetry of Yeats. He is a striking example of a man whose poetic development has been from the one way of writing to the other, of a man who has tried to move from a partial to a complete way of looking at the experience he is putting into words. This change, and the success with which he has brought it about, is one of the reasons why his later poetry is so interesting, and it is one of the facts which justify the assertion that Yeats is the greatest of living English poets.

R. P. Blackmur

'The Later Poetry of W. B. Yeats', *Southern Review*, vol. 2, no. 2
1936 (reprinted in *Form and Value in Modern Poetry*, 1957)

The later poetry of William Butler Yeats is certainly great enough in
its kind, and varied enough within its kind, to warrant a special
approach, deliberately not the only approach, and deliberately not a
complete approach. A body of great poetry will awaken and exem-
plify different interests on different occasions, or even on the same
occasions, as we may see in the contrasting and often contesting
literatures about Dante and Shakespeare: even a relation to the poetry
is not common to them all. I propose here to examine Yeats's later
poetry with a special regard to his own approach to the making of it;
and to explore a little what I conceive to be the dominant mode of his
insight, the relations between it and the printed poems, and – a
different thing – the relations between it and the readers of his poems.

The major facts I hope to illustrate are these: that Yeats has, if you
accept his mode, a consistent extraordinary grasp of the reality of
emotion, character, and aspiration; and that his chief resort and
weapon for the grasping of that reality is magic; and that if we would
make use of that reality for ourselves we must also make some use of
the magic that inspirits it. What is important is that the nexus of
reality and magic is not by paradox or sleight of hand, but is logical
and represents, for Yeats in his poetry, a full use of intelligence.
Magic performs for Yeats the same fructifying function that Christianity does for Eliot, or that ironic fatalism did for Thomas Hardy;
it makes a connection between the poem and its subject matter and
provides an adequate mechanics of meaning and value. If it happens
that we discard more of Hardy than we do of Yeats and more of Yeats
than we do of Eliot, it is not because Christianity provides better
machinery for the movement of poetry than fatalism or magic, but
simply because Eliot is a more cautious craftsman. Besides, Eliot's
poetry has not even comparatively worn long enough to show what
parts are permanent and what merely temporary. The point here is
that fatalism, Christianity, and magic are none of them disciplines to
which many minds can consciously appeal today, as Hardy, Eliot, and
Yeats do, for emotional strength and moral authority. The super-

natural is simply not part of our mental furniture, and when we meet it in our reading we say: Here is debris to be swept away. But if we sweep it away without first making sure what it is, we are likely to lose the poetry as well as the debris. It is the very purpose of a supernaturally derived discipline, as used in poetry, to set the substance of natural life apart, to give it a form, a meaning, and a value which cannot be evaded. What is excessive and unwarranted in the discipline we indeed ought to dismiss; but that can be determined only when what is integrating and illuminating is known first. The discipline will in the end turn out to have had only a secondary importance for the reader; but its effect will remain active even when he no longer considers it. That is because for the poet the discipline, far from seeming secondary, had an extraordinary structural, seminal, and substantial importance to the degree that without it he could hardly have written at all.

Poetry does not flow from thin air but requires always either a literal faith, an imaginative faith, or, as in Shakespeare, a mind full of many provisional faiths. The life we all live is not alone enough of a subject for the serious artist; it must be life with a leaning, life with a tendency to shape itself only in certain forms, to afford its most lucid revelations only in certain lights. If our final interest, either as poets or as readers, is in the reality declared when the forms have been removed and the lights taken away, yet we can never come to the reality at all without the first advantage of the form and lights. Without them we should *see* nothing but only glimpse something unstable. We glimpse the fleeting but do not see what it is that fleets.

So it was with Yeats; his early poems are fleeting, some of them beautiful and some that sicken, as you read them, to their own extinction. But as he acquired for himself a discipline, however unacceptable to the bulk of his readers, his poetry obtained an access to reality. So it is with most of our serious poets. It is almost the mark of the poet of genuine merit in our time – the poet who writes serious works with an intellectual aspect which are nonetheless poetry – that he performs his work in the light of an insight, a group of ideas, and a faith, with the discipline that flows from them, which taken together form a view of life most readers cannot share, and which, furthermore, most readers feel as repugnant, or sterile, or simply inconsequential.

All this is to say generally – and we shall say it particularly for Yeats later – that our culture is incomplete with regard to poetry; and the poet has to provide for himself in that quarter where authority and value are derived. It may be that no poet ever found a culture complete for his purpose; it was a welcome and arduous part of his business to make it so. Dante, we may say, completed for poetry the Christian culture of his time, which was itself the completion of centuries. But there was at hand for Dante, and as a rule in the great ages of poetry, a fundamental agreement or convention between the poet and his audience about the validity of the view of life of which the poet deepened the reality and spread the scope. There is no such agreement today. We find poets either using the small conventions of the individual life as if they were great conventions, or attempting to resurrect some great convention of the past, or, finally, attempting to discover the great convention that must lie, willy-nilly, hidden in the life about them. This is a labor, whichever form it takes, which leads as often to subterfuge, substitution, confusion, and failure, as to success; and it puts the abnormal burden upon the reader of determining what the beliefs of the poet are and how much to credit them before he can satisfy himself of the reality which those beliefs envisage. The alternative is to put poetry at a discount – which is what has happened.

This the poet cannot do who is aware of the possibilities of his trade: the possibilities of arresting, enacting, and committing to the language through his poems the expressed value of the life otherwise only lived or evaded. The poet so aware knows, in the phrasing of that prose-addict Henry James, both the sacred rage of writing and the muffled majesty of authorship; and knows, as Eliot knows, that once to have been visited by the muses is ever afterwards to be haunted. These are qualities that once apprehended may not be discounted without complete surrender, when the poet is no more than a haunt haunted. Yeats has never put his poetry at a discount. But he has made it easy for his readers to do so – as Eliot has in his way – because the price he has paid for it, the expense he has himself been to in getting it on paper, have been a price most readers simply do not know how to pay and an expense, in time and labor and willingness to understand, beyond any initial notion of adequate reward.

The price is the price of a fundamental and deliberate surrender to magic as the ultimate mode for the apprehension of reality. The expense is the double expense of, on the one hand, implementing magic with a consistent symbolism, and on the other hand, the greatly multiplied expense of restoring, through the *craft* of poetry, both the reality and its symbols to that plane of the quickened senses and the concrete emotions. That is to say, the poet (and, as always, the reader) has to combine, to fuse inextricably into something like an organic unity the constructed or derived symbolism of his special insight with the symbolism animating the language itself. It is, on the poet's plane, the labor of bringing the representative forms of knowledge home to the experience which stirred them: the labor of keeping in mind *what* our knowledge is of: the labor of craft. With the poetry of Yeats this labor is, as I say, doubly hard, because the forms of knowledge, being magical, do not fit naturally with the forms of knowledge that ordinarily preoccupy us. But it is possible, and I hope to show it, that the difficulty is, in a sense, superficial and may be overcome with familiarity, and that the mode of magic itself, once familiar, will even seem rational for the purposes of poetry – although it will not thereby seem inevitable. Judged by its works in the representation of emotional reality – and that is all that can be asked in our context – magic and its burden of symbols may be a major tool of the imagination. A tool has often a double function; it performs feats for which it was designed, and it is heuristic, it discovers and performs new feats which could not have been anticipated without it, which it indeed seems to instigate for itself and in the most unlikely quarters. It is with magic as a tool in its heuristic aspect – as an agent for discovery – that I wish here directly to be concerned.

One of the finest, because one of the most appropriate to our time and place, of all Yeats's poems, is his *The Second Coming*.

Turning and turning in the widening gyre
The falcon cannot hear the falconer;
Things fall apart; the centre cannot hold;
Mere anarchy is loosed upon the world,
The blood-dimmed tide is loosed, and everywhere
The ceremony of innocence is drowned;
The best lack all conviction, while the worst
Are full of passionate intensity.

Surely some revelation is at hand;
Surely the Second Coming is at hand.
The Second Coming! Hardly are those words out
When a vast image out of *Spiritus Mundi*
Troubles my sight: somewhere in sands of the desert
A shape with lion body and the head of a man,
A gaze blank and pitiless as the sun,
Is moving its slow thighs, while all about it
Reel shadows of the indignant desert birds.
The darkness drops again; but now I know
That twenty centuries of stony sleep
Were vexed to nightmare by a rocking cradle,
And what rough beast, its hour come round at last,
Slouches towards Bethlehem to be born?

There is about it, to any slowed reading, the immediate conviction of
pertinent emotion; the lines are stirring, separately and in their
smaller groups, and there is a sensible life in them that makes them
seem to combine in the form of an emotion. We may say at once
then, for what it is worth, that in writing his poem Yeats was able to
choose words which to an appreciable extent were the right ones to
reveal or represent the emotion which was its purpose. The words
deliver the meaning which was put into them by the craft with which
they were arranged, and that meaning is their own, not to be segre-
gated or given another arrangement without diminution. Ultimately,
something of this sort is all that can be said of this or any poem, and
when it is said, the poem is known to be good in its own terms or bad
because not in its own terms. But the reader seldom reaches an
ultimate position about a poem; most poems fail, through craft or
conception, to reach an ultimate or absolute position: parts of the
craft remain machinery and parts of the conception remain in limbo.
Or, as in this poem, close inspection will show something questionable
about it. It is true that it can be read as it is, isolated from the rest of
Yeats's work and isolated from the intellectual material which it
expresses, and a good deal gotten out of it, too, merely by submitting
to it. That is because the words are mainly common, both in their
emotional and intellectual senses; and if we do not know precisely
what the familiar words drag after them into the poem, still we know

vaguely what the weight of it feels like; and that seems enough to make a poem at one level of response. Yet if an attempt is made at a more complete response, if we wish to discover the precise emotion which the words mount up to, we come into trouble and uncertainty at once. There is an air of explicitness to each of the separate fragments of the poem. Is it, in this line or that, serious? Has it a reference? – or is it a rhetorical effect, a result only of the persuasive overtones of words? – or is it a combination, a mixture of reference and rhetoric?

Possibly the troubled attention will fasten first upon the italicized phrase in the twelfth line: *Spiritus Mundi*; and the question is whether the general, the readily available senses of the words are adequate to supply the specific sense wanted by the poem. Put another way, can the poet's own arbitrary meaning be made, merely by discovering it, to participate in and enrich what the 'normal' meanings of the words in their limiting context provide? The critic can only supply the facts; the poem will in the end provide its own answer. Here there are certain facts that may be extracted from Yeats' prose writings which suggest something of what the words symbolize for him. In one of the notes to the limited edition of *Michael Robartes and the Dancer*, Yeats observes that his mind, like another's, has been from time to time obsessed by images which had no discoverable origin in his waking experience. Speculating as to their origin, he came to deny both the conscious and the unconscious memory as their probable seat, and finally invented a doctrine which traced the images to sources of supernatural character. I quote only that sentence which is relevant to the phrase in question 'Those [images] that come in sleep are firstly from the state immediately preceding our birth; secondly from the *Spiritus Mundi* – that is to say, from a general storehouse of images which have ceased to be a property of any personality or spirit.' It apparently follows, for Yeats, that images so derived have both an absolute meaning of their own and an operative force in determining meaning and predicting events in this world. In another place (the Introduction to 'The Resurrection' in *Wheels and Butterflies*) he describes the image used in this poem, which he had seen many times, 'always at my left side just out of the range of sight, a brazen winged beast that I associated with laughing, ecstatic destruction'. Ecstasy, it should be added, comes for Yeats just before death, and at death comes the moment of revelation, when the soul is shown its kindred dead and it is possible to see the future.

Here we come directly upon that central part of Yeats' magical beliefs which it is one purpose of this poem emotionally to represent: the belief in what is called variously *Magnus Annus*, the Great Year, the Platonic Year, and sometimes in a slightly different symbolism, the Great Wheel. This belief, with respect to the history of epochs, is associated with the procession of the equinoxes, which bring, roughly every two thousand years, a Great Year of death and rebirth, and this belief, with respect to individuals, seems to be associated with the phases of the moon; although individuals may be influenced by the equinoxes and there may be a lunar interpretation of history. These beliefs have a scaffold of geometrical figures, gyres, cones, circles, etc., by the application of which exact interpretation is secured. Thus it is possible to predict, both in biography and history, and in time both forwards and backwards the character, climax, collapse, and rebirth in antithetical form of human types and cultures. There is a subordinate but helpful belief that signs, warnings, even direct messages, are always given, from *Spiritus Mundi* or elsewhere, which the poet and the philosopher have only to see and hear. As it happens, the Christian era, being nearly two thousand years old, is due for extinction and replacement, in short for the Second Coming, which this poem heralds. In his note to its first publication (in *Michael Robartes and the Dancer*) Yeats expresses his belief as follows:

At the present moment the life gyre is sweeping outward,
unlike that before the birth of Christ which was
narrowing, and has almost reached its greatest expansion.
The revelation which approaches will however take its
character from the contrary movement of the interior gyre.
All our scientific, democratic, fact-accumulating,
heterogeneous civilization belongs to the outward gyre and
prepares not the continuance of itself but the revelation as in
a lightning flash, though in a flash that will not strike only in
one place, and will for a time be constantly repeated, of the
civilization that must slowly take its place.

So much for a major gloss upon the poem. Yeats combined, in the best verse he could manage, the beliefs which obsessed him with the image which he took to be a specific illustration of the beliefs. Minor and buttressing glosses are possible for many of the single words and phrases in the poem, some flowing from private doctrine and some from Yeats's direct sense of the world about him, and some from both at once. For example: The 'ceremony of innocence' represents for Yeats one of the qualities that made life valuable under the dying aristocratic social tradition; and the meaning of the phrase in the poem requires no magic for completion but only a reading of other poems. The 'falcon and the falconer' in the second line has, besides its obvious symbolism, a doctrinal reference. A falcon is a hawk, and a hawk is symbolic of the active or intellectual mind; the falconer is perhaps the soul itself or its uniting principle. There is also the apposition which Yeats has made several times that 'Wisdom is a butterfly/And not a gloomy bird of prey.' Whether the special symbolism has actually been incorporated in the poem, and in which form, or whether it is private debris merely, will take a generation of readers to decide. In the meantime it must be taken provisionally for whatever its ambiguity may seem to be worth. Literature is full of falcons, some that fly and some that lack immediacy and sit, archaic, on the poet's wrist; and it is not always illuminating to determine which is which. But when we come on such lines as

The best lack all conviction, while the worst
Are full of passionate intensity,

we stop short, first to realize the aptness of the statement to every plane of life in the world about us, and then to connect them with the remote body of the poem they illuminate. There is a dilemma of which the branches grow from one trunk but which cannot be solved; for these lines have, not two meanings, but two sources for the same meaning. There is the meaning that comes from the summary observation that this is how men are – and especially men of power – in the world we live in; it is knowledge that comes from knowledge of the 'fury and mire in human veins'; a meaning the contemplation of which has lately (April 1934) led Yeats to offer himself to any government or party that, using force and marching men, will 'promise not this or that measure but a discipline, a way of life'. And there is in effect the same meaning, at least at the time the poem was written, which comes from a different source and should have, one would think, very different consequences in prospective party loyalties. Here the meaning has its source in the doctrines of the Great Year and the Phases of the Moon; whereby, to cut exegesis short, it is predicted as necessary that, at the time we have reached, the best minds, being subjective, should have lost all faith though desiring it, and the worst minds, being so nearly objective, have no need of faith and may be full of 'passionate intensity' without the control of any faith or wisdom. Thus we have on the one side the mirror of observation and on the other side an imperative, magically derived, which come to the conclusion of form in identical words.

The question is, to repeat, whether the fact of this double control and source of meaning at a critical point defeats or strengthens the unity of the poem; and it is a question which forms itself again and again in the later poems, sometimes obviously but more often only by suggestion. If we take another poem on the same theme, written some years earlier, and before his wife's mediumship gave him the detail of his philosophy, we will find the question no easier to answer in its suggested than in its conspicuous form. There is an element in the poem called *The Magi* which we can feel the weight of but cannot altogether name, and of which we can only guess at the efficacy.

Now as at all times I can see in the mind's eye,
In their stiff, painted clothes, the pale unsatisfied ones
Appear and disappear in the blue depths of the sky
With all their ancient faces like rain-beaten stones,
And all their helms of silver hovering side by side,
And all their eyes still fixed, hoping to find once more,
Being by Calvary's turbulence unsatisfied,
The uncontrollable mystery on the bestial floor.

I mean the element which, were Yeats a Christian, we could accept as a species of Christian blasphemy or advanced heresy, but which since he is not a Christian we find it hard to accept at all: the element of emotional conviction springing from intellectual matters without rational source or structure. We ought to be able, for the poem's sake, to accept the conviction as an emotional possibility, much as we accept *Lear* or Dostoyevsky's *Idiot* as valid, because projected from represented experience. But Yeats's experience is not represented consistently on any one plane. He constantly indicates a supernatural validity for his images of which the authority cannot be reached. If we come nearer to accepting *The Magi* than *The Second Coming* it is partly because the familiar Christian paradigm is more clearly used, and, in the last two lines what Yeats constructs upon it is given a more immediate emotional form, and partly because, *per contra*, there is less demand made upon arbitrary intellectual belief. There is, too, the matter of scope; if we reduce the scope of *The Second Coming* to that of *The Magi* we shall find it much easier to accept; but we shall have lost much of the poem.

We ought now to have enough material to name the two radical defects of magic as a tool for poetry. One defect, which we have just been illustrating, is that it has no available edifice of reason reared upon it conventionally independent of its inspiration. There is little that the uninspired reader can naturally refer to for authority outside the poem, and if he does make a natural reference he is likely to turn out to be at least partly wrong. The poet is thus in the opposite predicament; he is under the constant necessity of erecting his beliefs into doctrines at the same time that he represents their emotional or dramatic equivalents. He is, in fact, in much the same position that Dante would have been had he had to construct his Christian doctrine while he was composing *The Divine Comedy*: an impossible labour. The Christian supernaturalism, the Christian magic (no less magical than that of Yeats), had the great advantage for Dante, and imaginatively for ourselves, of centuries of reason and criticism and elaboration: It was within reason a consistent whole; and its supernatural element had grown so consistent with experience as to seem supremely *natural* – as indeed it may again. Christianity has an objective form, whatever the mysteries at its heart and its termini, in which all the phenomena of human life may find place and meaning. Magic is none of these things for any large fraction of contemporary society. Magic has a tradition, but it is secret, not public. It has not only central and terminal mysteries but has also peripheral mysteries, which require not only the priest to celebrate but also the adept to manipulate. Magic has never been made 'natural'. The practical knowledge and power which its beliefs lead to can neither be generally shared nor overtly rationalized. It is in fact held to be dangerous to reveal openly the details of magical experience: they may be revealed, if at all, only in arbitrary symbols and equivocal statements.

Thus we find Yeats, in his early and innocuous essay on magic, believing his life to have been imperiled for revealing too much. Again, the spirits or voices through whom magical knowledge is gained are often themselves equivocal and are sometimes deliberately confusing. Yeats was told to remember, 'We will deceive you if we can,' and on another occasion was forbidden to record anything that was said, only to be scolded later because he had failed to record every word. In short, it is of the essence of magical faith that the supernatural cannot be brought into the natural world except through symbol. The distinction between natural and supernatural is held to be substantial instead of verbal. Hence magic may neither be criticized nor institutionalized; nor can it ever reach a full expression of its own intention. This is perhaps the justification of Stephen Spender's remark that there is more magic in Eliot's *The Hollow Men* than in any poem of Yeats; because of Eliot's Christianity, his magic has a rational base as well as a supernatural source: it is the magic of an orthodox, authoritative faith. The dogmas of magic, we may say, are all heresies which cannot be expounded except each on its own authority as a fragmentary insight; and its unity can be only the momentary unity of association. Put another way, magic is in one respect in the state of Byzantine Christianity, when miracles were quotidian and the universal frame of experience, when life itself was held to be supernatural and reason was mainly a kind of willful sophistication.

Neither Yeats nor ourselves dwell in Byzantium. At a certain level, though not at all levels, we conceive life, and even its nonrational features, in rational terms. Certainly there is a rational bias and a rational structure in the poetry we mainly agree to hold great – though the content may be what it will; and it is the irrational bias and the confused structure that we are mainly concerned to disavow, to apologize or allow for. It was just to provide himself with the equivalent of a rational religious insight and a predictable rational structure for the rational imagination that in his book, *A Vision* (published, in 1925, in a limited edition only, and then withdrawn),[1] he attempted to convert his magical experience into a systematic philosophy. 'I wished,' he writes in the Dedication to that work, 'for a system of thought that would leave my imagination free to create

1 It was revised and republished in 1937. [Ed.]

as it chose and yet make all that it created, or could create, part of the one history, and that the soul's.' That is, Yeats hoped by systematizing it to escape from the burden of confusion and abstraction which his magical experience had imposed upon him. 'I can now,' he declares in this same dedication, 'if I have the energy, find the simplicity I have sought in vain. I need no longer write poems like *The Phases of the Moon* nor *Ego Dominus Tuus*, nor spend barren years, as I have done three or four times, striving with abstractions that substitute themselves for the play that I had planned.'

'Having inherited', as he says in one of his poems, 'a vigorous mind', he could not help seeing, once he had got it all down, that his system was something to disgorge if he could. Its truth as experience would be all the stronger if its abstractions could be expunged. But it could not be disgorged; its thirty-five years of growth was an intimate part of his own growth, and its abstractions were all of a piece with his most objective experience. And perhaps we, as readers, can see that better from outside than Yeats could from within. I suspect that no amount of will could have rid him of his magical conception of the soul; it was by magic that he knew the soul; and the conception had been too closely associated with his profound sense of his race and personal ancestry. He has never been able to retract his system, only to take up different attitudes towards it. He has alternated between granting his speculations only the validity of poetic myth and planning to announce a new deity. In his vacillation – there is a poem by that title – the rational defect remains, and the reader must deal with it sometimes as an intrusion upon the poetry of indeterminate value and sometimes as itself the subject of dramatic reverie or lyric statement. At least once he tried to force the issue home; and in a section of *A Packet for Ezra Pound* called 'Introduction to the Great Wheel' he meets the issue by transforming it, for the moment, into wholly poetic terms. Because it reveals a fundamental honesty and clarity of purpose in the midst of confusion and uncertainty the section is quoted entire.

Some will ask if I believe all that this book contains, and I will not know how to answer. Does the word belief, as they will use it, belong to our age, can I think of the world as there and I here judging it? I will never think any thoughts

but these, or some modification or extension of these;
when I write prose or verse they must be somewhere
present though it may not be in the words; they must
affect my judgement of friends and events; but then there
are many symbolisms and none exactly resembles mine.
What Leopardi in Ezra Pound's translation calls that
'concord' wherein 'the arcane spirit of the whole mankind
turns hardy pilot' – how much better it would be without
that word 'hardy' which slackens speed and adds nothing –
persuades me that he has best imagined reality who has best
imagined justice.

The rational defect, then, remains; the thought is not always in the
words; and we must do with it as we can. There is another defect of
Yeats's magical system which is especially apparent to the reader but
which may not be apparent at all to Yeats. Magic promises precisely
matters which it cannot perform – at least in poetry. It promises, as
in *The Second Coming*, exact prediction of events in the natural
world; and it promises again and again, in different poems, exact
revelations of the supernatural, and of this we have an example in
what has to many seemed a great poem, *All Souls' Night*, which had
its first publication as an epilogue to *A Vision*. Near the beginning of
the poem we have the explicit declaration : 'I have a marvellous thing
to say'; and near the end another: 'I have mummy truths to tell'.
'Mummy truths' is an admirable phrase, suggestive as it is of the
truths in which the dead are wrapped, ancient truths as old as Egypt
perhaps, whence mummies commonly come, and truths, too, that
may be unwound. But there, with the suggestion, the truths stop
short; there is, for the reader, no unwinding, no revelation of the
dead. What Yeats actually does is to summon into the poem various
of his dead friends as 'characters' – and this is the greatness, and only
this, of the poem: the summary, excited, even exalted presentation
of character. Perhaps the rhetoric is the marvel and the evasion the
truth. We get an impact as from behind, from the speed and weight
of the words, and are left with an ominous or terrified frame of mind,
the revelation still to come. The revelation, the magic, was in Yeats's
mind; hence the exaltation in his language; but it was not and could
not be given in the words of the poem.

It may be that for Yeats there was a similar exaltation and a similar self-deceit in certain other poems, but as the promise of revelation was not made, the reader feels no failure of fulfillment. Such poems as *Easter 1916*, *In Memory of Major Robert Gregory*, and *Upon a Dying Lady* may have buried in them a conviction of invocation and revelation; but if so it is no concern of ours: we are concerned only, as the case may be, with the dramatic presentations of the Irish patriots and poets, Yeats's personal friends, and Aubrey Beardsley's dying sister, and with, in addition, for minor pleasure, the technical means – the spare and delicate language, the lucid images, and quickening rhymes – whereby the characters are presented as intensely felt. There is no problem in such poems but the problem of reaching, through a gradual access of intimacy, full appreciation; here the magic and everything else are in the words. It is the same, for bare emotion apart from character, in such poems as *A Deep-Sworn Vow*, where the words accumulate by the simplest means an intolerable excitement, where the words are, called as they may be from whatever source, in an ultimate sense their own meaning.

Others because you did not keep
That deep-sworn vow have been friends of mine;
Yet always when I look death in the face,
When I clamber to the heights of sleep,
Or when I grow excited with wine,
Suddenly I meet your face.

Possibly all poetry should be read as this poem is read, and no poetry greatly valued that cannot be so read. Such is one ideal towards which reading tends; but to apply it as a standard of judgement we should first have to assume for the poetic intelligence absolute autonomy and self-perfection for all its works. Actually, autonomy and self-perfection are relative and depend upon a series of agreements or conventions between the poet and his readers, which alter continually, as to what must be represented by the fundamental power of language (itself a relatively stable convention) and what, on the other hand, may be adequately represented by mere reference, sign, symbol, or blue-print indication. Poetry is so little autonomous from the technical point of view that the greater part of a given work must be conceived as the manipulation of conventions that the reader will, or will not, take for granted; these being crowned, or animated, emotionally transformed, by what the poet actually represents, original or not, through his mastery of poetic language. Success is provisional, seldom complete, and never permanently complete. The vitality or letter of a convention may perish although the form persists. *Romeo and Juliet* is less successful today than when produced because the conventions of honour, family authority, and blood-feud no longer animate and justify the action; and if the play survives it is partly because certain other conventions of human character do remain vital, but more because Shakespeare is the supreme master of representation through the reality of language alone. Similarly with Dante; with the cumulative disintegration, even for Catholics, of medieval Christianity as the ultimate convention of human life, the success of *The Divine Comedy* comes more and more to depend on the exhibition of character and the virtue of language alone – which may make it a greater, not a lesser poem. On the other hand, it often happens that a poet's ambition is such that, in order to get his work done at all, he must needs set up new conventions or radically modify old ones which fatally lack that benefit of form which can be conferred only by public recognition. The form which made his poems available was only gradually conferred upon the convention of evil in Baudelaire and, as we may see in translations with contrasting emphases, its limits are still subject to debate; in his case the more so because the life of his language depended more than usual on the viability of the convention.

Let us apply those notions, which ought so far to be commonplace, to the later work of Yeats, relating them especially to the predominant magical convention therein. When Yeats came of poetic age he found himself, as Blake had before him, and even Wordsworth, but to a worse extent, in a society whose conventions extended neither intellectual nor moral authority to poetry; he found himself in a rational but deliberately incomplete, because progressive, society. The *emotion* of thought, for poetry, was gone, along with the emotion of religion and the emotion of race – the three sources and the three aims of the great poetry of the past. Tyndall and Huxley are the villains, Yeats records in his *Autobiographies*, as Blake recorded Newton; there were other causes, but no matter, these names may serve as symbols. And the dominant aesthetics of the time were as rootless in the realm of poetic import and authority as the dominant conventions. Art for Art's sake was the cry, the Ivory Tower the retreat, and Walter Pater's luminous languor and weak Platonism the exposition. One could say anything but it would mean nothing. The poets and society both, for opposite reasons, expected the poet to produce either exotic and ornamental mysteries or lyrics of mood; the real world and its significance were reserved mainly to the newer sciences, though the novelists and the playwrights might poach if they could. For a time Yeats succumbed, as may be seen in his early work, even while he attempted to escape; and of his poetic generation he was the only one to survive and grow in stature. He came under the influence of the French Symbolists, who gave him the clue and the hint of an external structure but nothing much to put in it. He read, with a dictionary, Villiers de L'Isle-Adam's *Axel's Castle*, and so came to be included in Edmund Wilson's book of that name – although not, as Wilson himself shows, altogether correctly. For he began in the late nineties, as it were upon his own account, to quench his thirst for reality by creating authority and significance and reference in the three fields where they were lacking. He worked into his poetry the substance of Irish mythology and Irish politics and gave them a symbolism, and he developed his experiences with Theosophy and Rosicrucianism into a body of conventions adequate, for him, to animate the concrete poetry of the soul that he wished to write. He did not do these things separately; the mythology, the politics, and the magic are conceived, through the personalities that reflected them, with an increasing unity of apprehension. Thus more than any poet of our time he has restored to poetry the actual emotions of race and religion and what we call abstract thought. Whether we follow him in any particular or not, the general poetic energy which he liberated is ours to use if we can. If the edifice that he constructed seems personal, it is because he had largely to build it for himself, and that makes it difficult to understand in detail except in reference to the peculiar unity which comes from their mere association in his life and work. Some of the mythology and much of the politics, being dramatized and turned into emotion, are part of our common possessions. But where the emphasis has been magical, whether successfully or not, the poems have been misunderstood, ignored, and the actual emotion in them which is relevant to us all decried and underestimated, merely because the magical mode of thinking is foreign to our own and when known at all is largely associated with quackery and fraud.

We do not make that mistake – which is the mistake of unwillingness -- with Dante or the later Eliot, because, although the substance of their modes of thinking is equally foreign and magical, it has the advantage of a rational superstructure that persists and which we can convert to our own modes if we will. Yeats lacks, as we have said, the historical advantage and with it much else; and the conclusion cannot be avoided that this lack prevents his poetry from reaching the first magnitude. But there are two remedies we may apply, which will make up, not for the defect of magnitude, but the defect of structure. We can read the magical philosophy in his verse *as if* it were converted into the contemporary psychology with which its doctrines have so much in common. We find little difficulty in seeing Freud's preconscious as a fertile myth and none at all in the general myth of extroverted and introverted personality; and these may be compared with, respectively, Yeats's myth of *Spiritus Mundi* and the Phases of the Moon: the intention and the scope of the meaning are identical. So much for a secular conversion. The other readily available remedy is this: to accept Yeats's magic literally as a machinery of meaning, to search out the prose parallels and reconstruct the symbols he uses on their own terms in order to come on the emotional reality, if it is there, actually in the poems – when the machinery may be dispensed with. This method has the prime advantage over secular conversion of keeping judgement in poetic terms, with the corresponding disadvantage that it requires more time and patience, more 'willing suspension of disbelief', and a stiffer intellectual exercise all around. But exegesis is to be preferred to conversion on still another ground, which may seem repellent: that magic, in the sense that we all experience it, is nearer the represented emotions that concern us in poetry than psychology, as a generalized science, can ever be. We are all, without conscience, magicians in the dark.

But even the poems of darkness are read in the light. I cannot, of course, make a sure prognosis; because in applying either remedy the reader is, really, doctoring himself as much as Yeats. Only this much is sure: that the reader will come to see the substantial unity of Yeats's work, that it is the same mind stirring behind the poems on Crazy Jane and the Bishop, on Cuchulain, on Swift, the political poems, the biographical and the doctrinal – a mind that sees the fury and the mire and passion of the dawn as contrary aspects of the real world. It is to be expected that many poems will fail in part and some entirely, and if the chief, magic will not be the only cause of failure. The source of a vision puts limits upon its expression which the poet cannot well help overpassing. 'The limitation of his view,' Yeats wrote of Blake, 'was from the very intensity of his vision; he was a too-literal realist of imagination, as others are of nature'; and the remark applies to himself. But there will be enough left to make the labor of culling worth all its patience and time. Before concluding, I propose to spur the reader, or inadvertently dismay him, by presenting briefly a few examples of the sort of reconstructive labor he will have to do and the sort of imaginative assent he may have to attempt in order to enter or dismiss the body of the poems.

As this is a mere essay in emphasis, let us bear the emphasis in, by repeating, on different poems, the sort of commentary laid out above on *The Second Coming* and *The Magi*, using this time *Byzantium* and *Sailing to Byzantium*. Byzantium is for Yeats, so to speak, the heaven of the man's mind; there the mind or soul dwells in eternal or miraculous form; there all things are possible because all things are known to the soul. Byzantium has both a historical and an ideal form, and the historical is the exemplar, the dramatic witness, of the ideal. Byzantium represents both a dated epoch and a recurrent state of insight, when nature is magical, that is, at the beck of mind, and magic is natural – a practical rather than a theoretic art. If with these notions in mind we compare the two poems named we see that the first, called simply *Byzantium*, is like certain cantos in the *Paradiso* the poetry of an intense and condensed declaration of doctrine; not emotion put into doctrine from outside, but doctrine presented as emotion. I quote the second stanza.

Before me floats an image, man or shade,
Shade more than man, more image than a shade:
For Hades' bobbin bound in mummy-cloth
May unwind the winding path;
A mouth that has no moisture and no breath
Breathless mouths may summon;
I hail the superhuman;
I call it death-in-life and life-in-death.

The second poem, *Sailing to Byzantium*, rests upon the doctrine but is not a declaration of it. It is, rather, the doctrine in action, the doctrine actualized in a personal emotion resembling that of specific prayer. This is the emotion of the flesh where the other was the emotion of the bones. The distinction should not be too sharply drawn. It is not the bones of doctrine but the emotion of it that we should be aware of in reading the more dramatic poem: and the nearer they come to seeming two reflections of the same thing the better both poems will be. What must be avoided is a return to the poem of doctrine with a wrong estimation of its value gained by confusion of the two poems. Both poems are serious in their own kind, and the reality of each must be finally in its own words whatever clues the one supplies to the other. I quote the third stanza.

O sages standing in God's holy fire
As in the gold mosaic of a wall,
Come from the holy fire, perne in a gyre,
And be the singing-masters of my soul.
Consume my heart away; sick with desire
And fastened to a dying animal
It knows not what it is; and gather me
Into the artifice of eternity.

We must not, for example, accept 'perne in a gyre' in this poem merely because it is part of the doctrine upon which the poem rests. Its magical reference may be too explicit for the poem to digest. It may be merely part of the poem's intellectual machinery, something that will *become* a dead commonplace once its peculiarity has worn out. Its meaning, that is, may turn out not to participate in the emotion of the poem: which is an emotion of aspiration. Similarly a note of aspiration would have been injurious to the stanza quoted from *Byzantium* above.

Looking at other poems as examples, the whole problem of exegesis may be put another way; which consists in joining two facts and observing their product. There is the fact that again and again in Yeats's prose, both in that which accompanies the poems and that which is independent of them, poems and fragments of poems are introduced at strategic points, now to finish off or clinch an argument by giving it as proved, and again merely to balance argument with witness from another plane. *A Vision* is punctuated by five poems.

And there is the complementary fact that, when one has read the various autobiographies, introductions, and doctrinal notes and essays, one continually finds echoes, phrases and developments from the prose in the poems. We have, as Wallace Stevens says, the prose that wears the poem's guise at last; and we have, too, the poems turning backwards, reilluminating or justifying the prose from the material of which they sprang. We have, to import the dichotomy which T. S. Eliot made for his own work, the prose writings discovering and buttressing the ideal, and we have the poems which express as much as can be actualized – given as concrete emotion – of what the prose discovered or envisaged. The dichotomy is not so sharp in Yeats as in Eliot. Yeats cannot, such is the unity of his apprehension, divide his interests. There is one mind employing two approaches in the labor of representation. The prose approach lets in much that the poetic approach excludes; it lets in the questionable, the uncertain, the hypothetic, and sometimes the incredible. The poetic approach, using the same material, retains, when it is successful, only what is manifest, the emotion that can be made actual in a form of words that need only to be understood, not argued. If props of argument and vestiges of idealization remain, they must be felt as qualifying, not arguing, the emotion. It should only be remembered and repeated that the poet invariably requires more machinery to secure *his* effects – the machinery of his whole life and thought – than the reader requires to secure what he takes as the *poem's* effects; and that, as readers differ, the poet cannot calculate what is necessary to the poem and what is not. There is always the debris to be cut away.

In such a fine poem as *A Prayer for My Son*, for example, Yeats cut away most of the debris himself, and it is perhaps an injury to judgement provisionally to restore it. Yet to this reader at least the poem seems to richen when it is known from what special circumstances the poem was freed. As it stands we can accept the symbols which it conspicuously contains – the strong ghost, the devilish things, and the holy writings – as drawn from the general stock of literary conventions available to express the evil predicament in which children and all innocent beings obviously find themselves. Taken so, it is a poem of natural piety. But for Yeats the conventions were not merely literary but were practical expressions of the actual terms of the predicament, and his poem is a prayer of dread and supernatural piety. The experience which led to the poem is recounted in *A Packet for Ezra Pound*. When his son was still an infant Yeats was told through the mediumship of his wife that the Frustrators or evil spirits would henceforth 'attack my health and that of my children, and one afternoon, knowing from the smell of burnt feathers that one of my children would be ill within three hours, I felt before I could recover self-control the mediaeval helpless horror of witchcraft.' The child *was* ill. It is from this experience that the poem seems to have sprung, and the poem preserves all that was actual behind the private magical conventions Yeats used for himself. The point is that the reader has a richer poem if he can substitute the manipulative force of Yeats's specific conventions for the general literary conventions. Belief or imaginative assent is no more difficult for either set. It is the emotion that counts.

That is one extreme to which the poems run – the extreme convention of personal thought. Another extreme is that exemplified in *A Prayer for My Daughter*, where the animating conventions *are* literary and piety *is* natural, and in the consideration of which it would be misleading to introduce the magical convention as more than a foil. As a foil it is nevertheless present; his magical philosophy, all the struggle and warfare of the intellect, is precisely what Yeats in this poem *puts out of mind*, in order to imagine his daughter living in innocence and beauty, custom and ceremony.

A third extreme is that found in the sonnet *Leda and the Swan*, where there is an extraordinary sensual immediacy – the words meet and move like speaking lips – and a profound combination of the generally available or literary symbol and the hidden, magical symbol of the intellectual, philosophical, impersonal order. Certain longer poems and groups of poems, especially the series called *A Woman Young and Old*, exhibit the extreme of combination as well or better; but I want the text on the page.

A sudden blow: the great wings beating still
Above the staggering girl, her thighs caressed
By the dark webs, her nape caught in his bill,
He holds her helpless breast upon his breast.

How can those terrified vague fingers push
The feathered glory from her loosening thighs?
And how can body, laid in that white rush,
But feel the strange heart beating where it lies?

A shudder in the loins engenders there
The broken wall, the burning roof and tower
And Agamemnon dead.
                         Being so caught up,
So mastered by the brute blood of the air,
Did she put on his knowledge with his power
Before the indifferent beak could let her drop?

It should be observed that in recent years new images, some from
the life of Swift, and some from the Greek mythology, have been
spreading through Yeats's poems; and of Greek images he has used
especially those of Oedipus and Leda, of Homer and Sophocles. But
they are not used as we think the Greeks used them, nor as mere
drama, but deliberately, after the magical tradition, both to represent
and hide the myths Yeats has come on in his own mind. Thus *Leda
and the Swan* can be read on at least three distinct levels of significance,
none of which interferes with the others: the levels of dramatic
fiction, of condensed insight into Greek mythology, and a third level
of fiction and insight combined, as we said, to represent and hide a
magical insight. This third level is our present concern. At this level
the poem presents in interfusion among the normal terms of the poem
two of Yeats' fundamental magical doctrines in emotional form.
The doctrines are put by Yeats in the following form in his essay on
magic: 'That the borders of our mind are ever shifting, and that many
minds can flow into one another, as it were, and create or reveal a
single mind, a single energy. . . . That this great mind can be evoked
by symbols.' Copulation is the obvious nexus for spiritual as well as
physical seed. There is also present I think some sense of Yeats's
doctrine of Annunciation and the Great Year, the Annunciation, in
this case, that produced Greek culture. It is a neat question for the
reader, so far as this poem is concerned, whether the poetic emotion
springs from the doctrine and seizes the myth for a safe home and
hiding, or whether the doctrine is correlative to the emotion of the
myth. In neither case does the magic matter as such; it has become

poetry, and of extreme excellence in its order. To repeat the interrogatory formula with which we began the commentary on *The Second Coming*, is the magical material in these poems incorporated in them by something like organic reference or is its presence merely rhetorical? The reader will answer one way or the other, as, to his rational imagination, to all the imaginative understanding he can bring to bear, it either seems to clutter the emotion and deaden the reality, or seems rather, as I believe, to heighten the emotional reality and thereby extend its reference to what we call the real world. Once the decision is made, the magic no longer exists; we have the poetry.

Other approaches to Yeats's poetry would have produced different emphases, and this approach, which has emphasized little but the magical structure of Yeats's poetic emotions, has made that emphasis with an ulterior purpose: to show that magic may be a feature of a rational imagination. This approach should be combined with others, or should have others combined with it, for perspective and reduction. No feature of a body of poetry can be as important as it seems in discussion. Above all, then, this approach through the magical emphasis should be combined with the approach of plain reading – which is long reading and hard reading – plain reading of the words, that they may sink in and do as much of their own work as they can. One more thing: When we call man a rational animal we mean that reason is his great myth. Reason is plastic and takes to any form provided. The rational imagination in poetry, as elsewhere, can absorb magic as a provisional method of evocative and heuristic thinking, but it cannot be based upon it. In poetry, and largely elsewhere, imagination is based upon the reality of words and the emotion of their joining. Yeats's magic, then, like every other feature of his experience, is rational as it reaches words; otherwise it is his privation, and ours, because it was the rational defect of our society that drove him to it.

W. B. Yeats

Fragment of a letter to Lady Elizabeth Pelham 4 January 1939

I know for certain that my time will not be long. I have put away everything that can be put away that I may speak what I have to speak, and I find 'expression' is a part of 'study'. In two or three weeks – I am now idle that I may rest after writing much verse – I will begin to write my most fundamental thoughts and the arrangements of thought which I am convinced will complete my studies. I am happy, and I think full of an energy, of an energy I had despaired of. It seems to me that I have found what I wanted. When I try to put all into a phrase I say, 'Man can embody truth but he cannot know it.' I must embody it in the completion of my life. The abstract is not life and everywhere draws out its contradictions. You can refute Hegel but not the Saint or the *Song of Sixpence*.

W. H. Auden

'The Public *v.* the Late Mr William Butler Yeats',
Partisan Review vol. 6, no. 3 Spring 1939

The Public Prosecutor:

Gentlemen of the jury. Let us be quite clear in our minds as to the nature of this case. We are here to judge, not a man, but his work. Upon the character of the deceased, therefore, his affectations of dress and manner, his inordinate personal vanity, traits which caused a fellow countryman and former friend to refer to him as the greatest literary fop in history, I do not intend to dwell. I must only remind you that there is usually a close connection between the personal character of a poet and his work, and that the deceased was no exception.

Again I must draw your attention to the exact nature of the charge. That the deceased had talent is not for a moment in dispute; so much is freely admitted by the prosecution. What the defence are asking you to believe, however, is that he was a great poet, the greatest of this century writing in English. That is their case, and it is that which the prosecution feels bound most emphatically to deny.

A great poet. To deserve such an epithet, a poet is commonly required to convince us of these things: firstly a gift of a very high order for memorable language, secondly a profound understanding of the age in which he lived, and thirdly a working knowledge of and sympathetic attitude toward the most progressive thought of his time.

Did the deceased possess these? I am afraid, gentlemen, that the answer is, no.

On the first point I shall be brief. My learned friend, the counsel for the defence, will, I have no doubt, do his best to convince you that I am wrong. And he has a case, gentlemen. O yes, a very fine case. I shall only ask you to apply to the work of the deceased a very simple test. How many of his lines can you remember?

Further, it is not unreasonable to suppose that a poet who has a gift for language will recognize that gift in others. I have here a copy of an anthology edited by the deceased entitled *The Oxford Book of Modern Verse*. I challenge anyone in this court to deny that it is the most deplorable volume ever issued under the imprint of that highly respected firm which has done so much for the cause of poetry in this country, the Clarendon Press.

But in any case you and I are educated modern men. Our fathers imagined that poetry existed in some private garden of its own, totally unrelated to the workaday world, and to be judged by pure aesthetic standards alone. We know that now to be an illusion. Let me pass, then, to my second point. Did the deceased understand his age?

What did he admire? What did he condemn? Well, he extolled the virtues of the peasant. Excellent. But should that peasant learn to read and write, should he save enough money to buy a shop, attempt by honest trading to raise himself above the level of the beasts, and O, what a sorry change is there. Now he is the enemy, the hateful huxter whose blood, according to the unseemly boast of the deceased, never flowed through *his* loins. Had the poet chosen to live in a mud cabin in Galway among swine and superstition, we might think him mistaken, but we should admire his integrity. But did he do this? O dear no. For there was another world which seemed to him not only equally admirable, but a deal more agreeable to live in, the world of noble houses, of large drawing rooms inhabited by the rich and the decorative, most of them of the female sex. We do not have to think very hard or very long, before we shall see a connection between these facts. The deceased had the feudal mentality. He was prepared to admire the poor just as long as they remained poor and deferential, accepting without protest the burden of maintaining a little Athenian band of literary landowners, who without their toil could not have existed for five minutes.

For the great struggle of our time to create a juster social order, he felt nothing but the hatred which is born of fear. It is true that he played a certain part in the movement for Irish Independence, but I hardly think my learned friend will draw your attention to that. Of all the modes of self-evasion open to the well-to-do, nationalism is the easiest and most dishonest. It allows to the unjust all the luxury of righteous indignation against injustice. Still, it has often inspired men and women to acts of heroism and self-sacrifice. For the sake of a free Ireland the poet Pearse and the Countess Markovitz gave their all. But if the deceased did give himself to this movement, he did so with singular moderation. After the rebellion of Easter Sunday 1916, he wrote a poem on the subject which has been called a masterpiece. It is. To succeed at such a time in writing a poem which could offend neither the Irish Republicans nor the British Army was indeed a masterly achievement.

And so we come to our third and last point. The most superficial glance at the last fifty years is enough to tell us that the social struggle toward a greater equality has been accompanied by a growing intellectual acceptance of the scientific method and the steady conquest of irrational superstition. What was the attitude of the deceased toward this? Gentlemen, words fail me. What are we to say of a man whose earliest writings attempted to revive a belief in fairies and whose favourite themes were legends of barbaric heroes with unpronounceable names, work which has been aptly and wittily described as Chaff about Bran!

But you may say, he was young: youth is always romantic; its silliness is part of its charm. Perhaps it is. Let us forgive the youth, then, and consider the mature man, from whom we have a right to expect wisdom and common sense. Gentlemen, it is hard to be charitable when we find that the deceased, far from outgrowing his folly, has plunged even deeper. In 1900 he believed in fairies; that was bad enough; but in 1930 we are confronted with the pitiful, the deplorable spectacle of a grown man occupied with the mumbo-jumbo of magic and the nonsense of India. Whether he seriously believed such stuff to be true, or merely thought it petty, or imagined it would impress the public, is immaterial. The plain fact remains that he made it the centre of his work. Gentlemen, I need say no more. In the last poem he wrote, the deceased rejected social justice and reason, and prayed for war. Am I mistaken in imagining that somewhat similar sentiments are expressed by a certain foreign political movement which every lover of literature and liberty acknowledges to be the enemy of mankind?

The Counsel for the Defence:

Gentlemen of the jury. I am sure you have listened with as much enjoyment as I to the eloquence of the prosecution. I say enjoyment because the spectacle of anything well done, whether it be a feat of engineering, a poem, or even an outburst of impassioned oratory, must always give pleasure.

We have been treated to an analysis of the character of the deceased which for all I know, may be as true as it is destructive. Whether it proves anything about the value of his poetry is another matter. If I may be allowed to quote my learned friend, 'We are here to judge, not a man but his work.' We have been told that the deceased was conceited, that he was a snob, that he was a physical coward, that his taste in contemporary poetry was uncertain, that he could not understand physics and chemistry. If this is not an invitation to judge the man I do not know what is. Does it not bear an extraordinary resemblance to the belief of an earlier age that a great artist must be chaste? Take away the frills, and the argument of the prosecution is reduced to this: 'A great poet must give the right answers to the problems which perplex his generation. The deceased gave the wrong answers. Therefore the deceased was not a great poet.' Poetry in such a view is the filling up of a social quiz; to pass with honours the poet must score not less than 75 per cent. With all due respect to my learned friend, this is nonsense. We are tempted so to judge contemporary poets because we really do have problems which we really do want solved, so that we are inclined to expect everyone, politicians, scientists, poets, clergymen, to give us the answer, and to blame them indiscriminately when they do not. But who reads the poetry of the past in this way? In an age of rising nationalism, Dante looked back with envy to the Roman Empire. Was this socially progressive? Will only a Catholic admit that Dryden's *The Hind and the Panther* is a good poem? Do we condemn Blake because he rejected Newton's theory of light, or rank Wordsworth lower than Baker, because the latter had a deeper appreciation of the steam engine?

Can such a view explain why

Mock Emmet, Mock Parnell
All the renown that fell. . . .

is good; and bad, such a line as

Somehow I think that you are rather like a tree. . . .

In pointing out that this is absurd, I am not trying to suggest that art exists independently of society. The relation between the two is just as intimate and important as the prosecution asserts.

Every individual is from time to time excited emotionally and intellectually by his social and material environment. In certain individuals this excitement produces verbal structures which we call poems; if such a verbal structure creates an excitement in the reader, we call it a good poem. Poetic talent, in fact, is the power to make personal excitement socially available. Poets, i.e. persons with poetic talent, stop writing good poetry when they stop reacting to the world they live in. The nature of that reaction, whether it be positive or negative, morally admirable or morally disgraceful, matters very little, what is essential is that the reaction should genuinely exist. The later Wordsworth is not inferior to the earlier because the poet had altered his political opinions, but because he had ceased to feel and think so strongly, a change which happens, alas, to most of us as we grow older. Now, when we turn to the deceased, we are confronted by the amazing spectacle of a man of great poetic talent, whose capacity for excitement not only remained with him to the end, but actually increased. In two hundred years when our children have made a different and, I hope, better social order, and when our science has developed out of all recognition, who but a historian will care a button whether the deceased was right about the Irish Question or wrong about the transmigration of souls? But because the excitement out of which his poems arose was genuine, they will still, unless I am very much mistaken, be capable of exciting others, different though their circumstances and beliefs may be from his.

However since we are not living two hundred years hence, let us play the schoolteacher a moment, and examine the poetry of the deceased with reference to the history of our time.

The most obvious social fact of the last forty years is the failure of liberal capitalist democracy, based on the premises that every individual is born free and equal, each an absolute entity independent of all others. And that a formal political equality, the right to vote, the right to a fair trial, the right of free speech, is enough to guarantee his freedom of action in his relations with his fellow men. The results are only too familiar to us all. By denying the social nature of personality, and by ignoring the social power of money, it has created the most impersonal, the most mechanical, and the most unequal civilization the world has ever seen, a civilization in which the only emotion common to all classes is a feeling of individual isolation from everyone else, a civilization torn apart by the opposing emotions born of economic injustice, the just envy of the poor and the selfish terror of the rich.

If these latter emotions meant little to the deceased, it was partly because Ireland compared with the rest of western Europe was economically backward, and the class struggle was less conscious there. My learned friend has sneered at Irish nationalism, but he knows as well as I that nationalism is a necessary stage towards socialism. He has sneered at the deceased for not taking arms, as if shooting were the only honourable and useful form of social action. Has the Abbey Theatre done nothing for Ireland?

But to return to the poems. From first to last they express a sustained protest against the social atomization caused by industrialism, and both in their ideas and their language a constant struggle to overcome it. The fairies and heroes of the early work were an attempt to find through folk tradition a binding force of society; and the doctrine of Anima Mundi found in the later poems is the same thing, in a more developed form, which has left purely local peculiarities behind, in favour of something that the deceased hoped was universal; in other words, he was working for a world religion. A purely religious solution may be unworkable, but the search for it is, at least, the result of a true perception of a social evil. Again, the virtues that the deceased praised in the peasantry and aristocracy, and the vices he blamed in the commercial classes were real virtues and vices. To create a united and just society where the former are fostered and the latter cured is the task of the politician, not the poet.

For art is a product of history, not a cause. Unlike some other products, technical inventions for example, it does not re-enter history as an effective agent, so that the question whether art should or should not be propaganda is unreal. The case for the prosecution rests on the fallacious belief that art ever makes anything happen, whereas the honest truth, gentlemen, is that, if not a poem had been written, not a picture painted, not a bar of music composed, the history of man would be materially unchanged.

But there is one field in which the poet is a man of action, the field of language, and it is precisely in this that the greatness of the deceased is most obviously shown. However false or undemocratic his ideas, his diction shows a continuous evolution toward what one might call the true democratic style. The social virtues of a real democracy are brotherhood and intelligence, and the parallel linguistic virtues are strength and clarity, virtues which appear even more clearly through successive volumes by the deceased.

The diction of *The Winding Stair* is the diction of a just man, and it is for this reason that just men will always recognize the author as a master.

W. H. Auden

'In Memory of W. B. Yeats',
from *Collected Poetry of W. H. Auden*   1945[1]

I

He disappeared in the dead of winter:
The brooks were frozen, the airports almost deserted,
And snow disfigured the public statues;
The mercury sank in the mouth of the dying day.
O all the instruments agree
The day of his death was a dark cold day.

Far from his illness
The wolves ran on through the evergreen forests,
The peasant river was untempted by the fashionable quays;
By mourning tongues
The death of the poet was kept from his poems.

But for him it was his last afternoon as himself,
An afternoon of nurses and rumours;
The provinces of his body revolted,
The squares of his mind were empty,
Silence invaded the suburbs,
The current of his feeling failed: he became his admirers.

Now he is scattered among a hundred cities
And wholly given over to unfamiliar affections;
To find his happiness in another kind of wood
And be punished under a foreign code of conscience.
The words of a dead man
Are modified in the guts of the living.

But in the importance and noise of tomorrow
When the brokers are roaring like beasts on the floor of the
    Bourse,

1 The poem was originally published in *New Republic*, 8 March 1939, without part 2. In recent editions Auden has eliminated stanzas 2-4 from part 3.
[Ed.]

And the poor have the sufferings to which they are fairly
    accustomed,
And each in the cell of himself is almost convinced of his
    freedom;
A few thousand will think of this day
As one thinks of a day when one did something slightly unusual.

O all the instruments agree[1]
The day of his death was a dark cold day.

2

You were silly like us: your gift survived it all;
The parish of rich women, physical decay,
Yourself; mad Ireland hurt you into poetry.
Now Ireland has her madness and her weather still,
For poetry makes nothing happen: it survives
In the valley of its saying where executives
Would never want to tamper; it flows south[2]
From ranches of isolation and the busy griefs,
Raw towns that we believe and die in; it survives,
A way of happening, a mouth.

3

Earth, receive an honoured guest;
William Yeats is laid to rest:
Let the Irish vessel lie
Emptied of its poetry.

Time that is intolerant
Of the brave and innocent,
And indifferent in a week
To a beautiful physique,

1 The line now reads: 'What instruments we have agree'. [Ed.]
2 The line now reads: 'Would never want to tamper,/Flows on South'. [Ed.]

Worships language and forgives
Everyone by whom it lives;
Pardons cowardice, conceit,
Lays its honours at their feet.

Time that with this strange excuse
Pardoned Kipling and his views,
And will pardon Paul Claudel,
Pardons him for writing well.

In the nightmare of the dark
All the dogs of Europe bark,
And the living nations wait,
Each sequestered in its hate;

Intellectual disgrace
Stares from every human face,
And the seas of pity lie
Locked and frozen in each eye.

Follow, poet, follow right
To the bottom of the night,
With your unconstraining voice
Still persuade us to rejoice;

With the farming of a verse
Make a vineyard of the curse,
Sing of human unsuccess
In a rapture of distress;

In the deserts of the heart
Let the healing fountain start,
In the prison of his days
Teach the free man how to praise.

Part Two Later Criticism (after 1939)

The 1940s and 1950s witness Yeats' canonization, as anyone who read literature in the universities at that time will attest. The volume of essays which most demonstrates this enshrinement was published in 1950, appropriately titled *The Permanence of Yeats*, and contained substantial contributions by the American New Critics, bolstered by Eliot, Auden, Leavis, and Edmund Wilson. Though not without exception, the prevailing tones were reverence and admiration; the poems most dwelt on were those from *The Tower* and much attention was paid to the relation between Yeats' 'magical' beliefs and the poems into which, to some extent at least, they found their way. The present selection from criticism of Yeats over the thirty years since his death naturally begins with Eliot's Dublin lecture, delivered in 1940 and amounting to, at long last, the seal of approval. Eliot assured his audience, and in so doing assured critics to come, that Yeats' influence on younger poets was wholly good, since he was too strange to be imitated. But he also located the major area of argument and definition in future criticism of Yeats by pointing to the 'power of development' revealed in his work as a whole; further, Eliot insisted that this development was not merely personal in its reach, since Yeats 'was one of those few whose history is the history of their own time, who are a part of the consciousness of an age which cannot be understood without them'.

The word 'development' turns up regularly in those who followed Eliot and attempted some assessment of the true shape of Yeats' career. In the Yeats issue of the *Southern Review* (1942), Randall Jarrell makes up a list of the most-encountered words in the early poems, then a similar list for the post-*Responsibilities* ones: the dramatic difference between the lists is to be understood by, in the language of his essay-title, 'The Development of Yeats' Sense of Reality' – reality thus being seen as essentially harsh, spare and bitter, rather than misty or curd-pale. But in the same issue Arthur Mizener puts the stress elsewhere, on the continuity of 'romantic' attitudes in a poetry that was always committed to the heart's desire. Eliot had thought it marvellous that Yeats, like Dickens, could have perfected a style early on, then started over from scratch and written 'later' poetry as dramatically different from the early work as was *Bleak House* from *Pickwick Papers*. Mizener demurs, arguing that the greatness of Yeats' later poetry was a kind 'inherent' in the early nineties work; that the later symbolic poems were as exotic in their splendour as anything written earlier, and that though it might be thought Yeats developed a true language for representing reality – the way things are – the later poetry never truly represents the surfaces of things as they are, is as selective and brilliantly arbitrary in what it calls up as was ever *The Lake Isle of Innisfree*. So the emphasis is placed on inherent continuity rather than dramatic change.

Mizener described Yeats' romanticism as a fact to be accepted. From another angle one might insist that such self-dramatization was self-indulgence, and find deplorable the violence of tone which particularly marked Yeats' later work. In writing to Olivia Shakespear he himself professed astonishment in discovering how bitter a book was *The Tower*; as for *Last Poems*, F. R. Leavis characterized its effect in sharply adverse terms, calling it a 'saddening volume' and speaking of the wastage of Yeats' powers, his unpleasant arrogance and bitterness of manner. The accusation made in particular by *Scrutiny* critics, that Yeats' poetry was insufficiently human, received further expression as L. C. Knights found that his career of romantic idealization, looked at as a whole, had to be considered a 'heroic failure'. One could of course emphasize the heroism of the failure, but Knights' essay seemed to come down harder on the latter term. And two years later D. S. Savage provided a summary and culmination of the adversely critical tradition by defining and severely commenting on what he termed Yeats' 'aestheticism' and the ways in which this attitude was anti-life, inadequately sympathetic to human and religious aspirations. There is a particularly striking moment toward the end of his essay where Savage quotes the 'Irish poets learn your trade' section from the end of 'Under Ben Bulben' that concludes 'Cast your minds on other days/That we in coming days may be/Still the indomitable Irishry', at which point Savage casts up his eyes and exclaims:

The indomitable Irishry! It is one of the enigmas of Yeats as a poet that he should be capable of mixing real tragic grandeur with such fatal vulgarity and commonplaceness. Whatever may be the conventional verdict on his work, it is certain that at its centre is a hollowness which time is bound increasingly to reveal.

And he provided a new twist to the notion of Yeats' 'development' by picking up the word, then calling it a 'development in a vacuum'.

George Orwell's little-known essay (actually a review of a book on Yeats by V. K. Menon) is included in this selection for the blunt way in which it raises the question of Yeats' political tendencies. Orwell is unimpressed by claims for 'development' in Yeats' work, since he believes that what remains significantly constant in that work is a hatred of modern Western civilization. But Orwell isn't content (as a recent book like John Harrison's *The Reactionaries* was) simply to extract reactionary opinions from the poems so that Yeats can be charged with some form of fascism. Beginning with the language, which he finds often characterized by artificiality and 'quaintness' ('Till I am Timon and Lear/Or that William Blake' – where it is the 'that' which bothers Orwell), he goes on to ask what relationship this quaintness bears to the kinds of extreme opinions assembled in *A Vision* as well as to more explicitly political ones. Politics and one's use of the English language, Orwell assumes (and elsewhere argues) would be most intimately involved.

It should be emphasized that Mizener, Knights, Savage, and Orwell are not typical of Yeats' critics during the 1940s. Their selectively weighted attention can afford, must afford, something more than head-nodding affirmation at everything the poet wrote or every move he made. But in a good many classes or lectures and in published or unpublished essays, the attitude taken toward Yeats was rather more respectfully admiring, as the teacher directed his pupils into an appreciation of the symbolic richness of the Byzantium poems or the ironic splendours of 'Among School Children'. In other words much consolidation, much agreement on what the best poems were, a generally patronizing attitude toward pre-1900 Yeats, much respect directed at how he reformed his style and came to terms with Reality, a good deal of identification with his self-dramatizing voice at a time when very un-Yeatsian attitudes were being practised and prudently adjusted to in society and politics. In my own case at least, I paid little attention in 1952 to the exploits of Senator Joseph McCarthy or to the Korean War, since I was busy memorizing and learning to declaim *Lapis Lazuli* and *Two Songs from a Play*. Yet explication of individual poems sometimes ran into snags: how much should one rely on *A Vision*, or on Yeats' other prose, or on the facts of his biography (as they were being set down by Joseph Hone and Richard Ellmann) to clear up what was murky, puzzling, or simply not quite *there* in the individual poem? New Critics held that Yeats had bequeathed us many marvellous lyrics which were coherent unto themselves. Couldn't these be approached in the pages of any anthology and there appreciated just as fully as if they had been encountered in the text of the *Complete Poems*?

Hugh Kenner's answer was that they couldn't, since Yeats had written not poems but 'A Sacred Book of the Arts' which demanded to be studied and appreciated not in relation to biography or occultism, but for its architecture, particularly for the relations between a poem and its immediate predecessors and successors – not chronologically considered, but as Yeats arranged them in the volumes at least from *Responsibilities* through *A Full Moon in March*. Kenner argued that this act of arrangement was an act of deliberate personality, a brilliant expression of Yeats' quarrel with nineteenth-century popular Romanticism. Whether or not that is so (one thinks of Wordsworth's 'personal' but hardly comprehensible arranging of his poems into the maddening categories of his collected edition) Kenner's readings of one poem in the light of its neighbours provided an alternative to dragging in some prose gloss aimed at rescuing the stranded reader. (In this connection John Wain's wrestling with the problem of how seriously to take Yeats' note on 'Honey of generation' in the fifth stanza of *Among School Children* is an example of a reading that refuses to subordinate itself to any gloss handed down from on high, even if by the artist himself.) In relation to earlier attempts to see Yeats' 'development' as an enlargement of his sense of reality, or to deny that such an enlargement ever took place ('development in a vacuum'), Kenner suggests in his review of Yeats' *Letters* that what developed was 'the art of putting things more and more arrestingly, and setting the matters that interested him in closer, more electrifying relationships with one another'.

Kenner's procedure opened up the *oeuvre* to more playful and interesting kinds of critical speculation than were usually to be found in analytical treatments of Yeats' poems in terms of what their symbols really meant – a tendency most doggedly pursued in two long books from the 1950s by F. A. C. Wilson. Over the last fifteen years there has been a variety of useful approaches to Yeats that suggests how very alive, perhaps more alive than they were in 1908 or 1939, are the words of this dead man. Frank Kermode's *Romantic Image* was centrally concerned with Yeats as the pre-eminent modern poet who committed himself to 'the

Image' and all that Kermode argues this commitment implies about one's consequent attitude toward life. However much Kermode admires the poetry Yeats wrote under or out of this theory, he has reservations about the theory itself, especially insofar as writers are still unwitting prisoners to it. So that there is a sense in which *Romantic Image* provided a demythologizing of the Yeats who preoccupied himself with composing The Sacred Book of the Arts, the Yeats who is not just a heroic figure but also on occasions a bore and a windbag. Such demythologizing could of course only occur after a sufficient body of critical writings had been built up in description of Yeats' poetry as terribly complex. It needed, in other words, an F. A. C. Wilson rather loftily explicating the symbolism of the Byzantium poems in order for a playful critic like William Empson to come along and say, see here, you are ignoring the story in this poem which is told with much humour and good sense. Or it needed the whole weight of adulatory commentary on all the poems of Yeats for an equally though more sternly playful critic like Yvor Winters to attempt to blow the whole thing sky-high by confessing that he could make no sense of an assertion, or by remarking offhandedly that of course this line or that poem is rhythmically coarse or undistinguished.

Both Empson and Winters (one in praise, the other in blame) insist on being, in Marianne Moore's fine phrase, 'literalists of the imagination' intent on considering whatever real toads do or do not exist in the imaginary gardens of a Yeats poem. During the last decade there have been many book-length studies of Yeats' aesthetic, his idea of the heroic, his relationship to eighteenth-century Ireland, or of relations (notably in Helen Vendler's book) between *A Vision* and the plays. And with the many centenary tributes in 1965 every nook of the artist's work and many aspects of his life seem to have been well explored. But in my judgement the most valuable work of opening up the poems for further inspection has been done by certain 'literalist' writers on Yeats who have asked questions about the kinds and qualities of experience, the human reality found in the poems. In particular, C. K. Stead and Donald Davie have paid intelligent attention to the ones written around 1916–20 in those 'middle' years when Yeats was perhaps most richly involved in many kinds of life. Here, in *The Wild Swans at Coole* and *Michael Robartes and the Dancer*, Davie finds Yeats a good influence on succeeding poets, and not because (as in T. S. Eliot's argument) he is inimitable. For poems like *Prayer for my Daughter* and *Easter 1916* are models of poetic diction, also models of the sanely human response to life which both the earlier and later Yeats found difficult to sustain.

The two concluding essays in this section, by Helen Vendler and myself, attempt to look at Yeats' career as a whole and to make some judgements about the relationship of 'heart-mysteries' to the images and symbols that were chosen by Yeats – or chose Yeats – to express them. If Yeats' reputation, like that of any artist's, exists on discussion, argument, comparison of poems, flashes of annoyance along with momentary thrills and chills, it should profit by a criticism that, since most of the symbols have now been explicated, keeps asking about the human sense a particular poem does or doesn't make. And in seeking that human sense, our most lively and problematic moments of response will occur when we speak back to the dazzle and brilliance of this poet's most irrepressible voice.

T. S. Eliot

'Yeats', a lecture delivered at the Abbey Theatre, Dublin 1940
(reprinted in *On Poetry and Poets*, 1957)

The generations of poetry in our age seem to cover a span of about
twenty years. I do not mean that the best work of any poet is limited
to twenty years: I mean that it is about that length of time before a
new school or style of poetry appears. By the time, that is to say,
that a man is fifty, he has behind him a kind of poetry written by
men of seventy, and before him another kind written by men of
thirty. That is my position at present, and if I live another twenty
years I shall expect to see still another younger school of poetry.
One's relation to Yeats, however, does not fit into this scheme.
When I was a young man at the university, in America, just beginning to write verse, Yeats was already a considerable figure in the
world of poetry, and his early period was well defined. I cannot
remember that his poetry at that stage made any deep impression
upon me. A very young man, who is himself stirred to write, is not
primarily critical or even widely appreciative. He is looking for masters
who will elicit his consciousness of what he wants to say himself, of
the kind of poetry that is in him to write. The taste of an adolescent
writer is intense, but narrow: it is determined by personal needs. The
kind of poetry that I needed, to teach me the use of my own voice,
did not exist in English at all; it was only to be found in French.
For this reason the poetry of the young Yeats hardly existed for me
until after my enthusiasm had been won by the poetry of the older
Yeats; and by that time – I mean, from 1919 on – my own course of
evolution was already determined. Hence, I find myself regarding
him, from one point of view, as a contemporary and not a predeces-
sor; and from another point of view, I can share the feelings of younger men, who came to know and admire him by that work from
1919 on, which was produced while they were adolescent.

Certainly, for the younger poets of England and America, I am
sure that their admiration for Yeats' poetry has been wholly good.
His idiom was too different for there to be any danger of imitation,
his opinions too different to flatter and confirm their prejudices. It
was good for them to have the spectacle of an unquestionably great

living poet, whose style they were not tempted to echo and whose ideas opposed those in vogue among them. You will not see, in their writing, more than passing evidences of the impression he made, but the work, and the man himself as poet, have been of the greatest significance to them for all that. This may seem to contradict what I have been saying about the kind of poetry that a young poet chooses to admire. But I am really talking about something different. Yeats would not have this influence had he not become a great poet; but the influence of which I speak is due to the figure of the poet himself, to the integrity of his passion for his art and his craft which provided such an impulse for his extraordinary development. When he visited London he liked to meet and talk to younger poets. People have sometimes spoken of him as arrogant and overbearing. I never found him so; in his conversations with a younger writer I always felt that he offered terms of equality, as to a fellow worker, a practitioner of the same mistery. It was, I think, that, unlike many writers, he cared more for poetry than for his own reputation as a poet or his picture of himself as a poet. Art was greater than the artist: and this feeling he communicated to others; which was why younger men were never ill at ease in his company.

This, I am sure, was part of the secret of his ability, after becoming unquestionably the master, to remain always a contemporary. Another is the continual development of which I have spoken. This has become almost a commonplace of criticism of his work. But while it is often mentioned, its causes and its nature have not been often analysed. One reason, of course, was simply concentration and hard work. And behind that is character: I mean the special character of the artist as artist – that is, the force of character by which Dickens, having exhausted his first inspiration, was able in middle age to proceed to such a masterpiece, so different from his early work, as *Bleak House*. It is difficult and unwise to generalize about ways of composition – so many men, so many ways – but it is my experience that towards middle age a man has three choices: to stop writing altogether, to repeat himself with perhaps an increasing skill of virtuosity, or by taking thought to adapt himself to middle age and find a different way of working. Why are the later long poems of Browning and Swinburne mostly unread? It is, I think, because one gets the essential Browning or Swinburne entire in earlier poems; and in the later, one is reminded of the early freshness which they lack, without being made aware of any compensating new qualities. When a man is engaged in work of abstract thought – if there is such a thing as wholly abstract thought outside of the mathematical sciences – his mind can mature, while his emotions either remain the same or only atrophy, and it will not matter. But maturing as a poet means maturing as the whole man, experiencing new emotions appropriate to one's age, and with the same intensity as the emotions of youth.

One form, a perfect form, of development is that of Shakespeare, one of the few poets whose work of maturity is just as exciting as that of their early manhood. There is, I think, a difference between the development of Shakespeare and Yeats, which makes the latter case still more curious. With Shakespeare, one sees a slow, continuous development of mastery of his craft of verse, and the poetry of middle age seems implicit in that of early maturity. After the first few verbal exercises you say of each piece of work: 'This is the perfect expression of the sensibility of that stage of his development.' That a poet should develop at all, that he should find something new to say, and say it equally well, in middle age, has always something miraculous about it. But in the case of Yeats the kind of development seems to me different. I do not want to give the impression that I regard his earlier and his later work almost as if they had been written by two different men. Returning to his earlier poems after making a close acquaintance with the later, one sees, to begin with, that in technique there was a slow and continuous development of what is always the same medium and idiom. And when I say development, I do not mean that many of the early poems, for what they are, are not as beautifully written as they could be. There are some, such as Who Goes with Fergus?, which are as perfect of their kind as anything in the language. But the best, and the best known of them, have this limitation: that they are as satisfactory in isolation, as 'anthology pieces', as they are in the context of his other poems of the same period.

I am obviously using the term 'anthology piece' in a rather special sense. In any anthology, you find some poems which give you complete satisfaction and delight in themselves, such that you are hardly curious who wrote them, hardly want to look further into the work of that poet. There are others, not necessarily so perfect or complete, which make you irresistibly curious to know more of that poet through his other work. Naturally, this distinction applies only to short poems, those in which a man has been able to put only a part of his mind, if it is a mind of any size. With some such you feel at once that the man who wrote them must have had a great deal more to say, in different contexts, of equal interest. Now among all the poems in Yeats' earlier volumes I find only in a line here or there, that sense of a unique personality which makes one sit up in excitement and eagerness to learn more about the author's mind and feelings. The intensity of Yeats' own emotional experience hardly appears. We have sufficient evidence of the intensity of experience of his youth, but it is from the retrospections in some of his later work that we have our evidence.

I have, in early essays, extolled what I called impersonality in art, and it may seem that, in giving as a reason for the superiority of Yeats' later work the greater expression of personality in it, I am contradicting myself. It may be that I expressed myself badly, or that I had only an adolescent grasp of that idea – as I can never bear to re-read my own prose writings, I am willing to leave the point unsettled – but I think now, at least, that the truth of the matter is as follows. There are two forms of impersonality: that which is natural to the mere skilful craftsman, and that which is more and more achieved by the maturing artist. The first is that of what I have called the 'anthology piece', of a lyric by Lovelace or Suckling, or of Campion, finer poet than either. The second impersonality is that of the poet who, out of intense and personal experience, is able to express a general truth; retaining all the particularity of his experience, to make of it a general symbol. And the strange thing is that Yeats, having been a great craftsman in the first kind, became a great poet in the second. It is not that he became a different man, for, as I have hinted, one feels sure that the intense experience of youth had been lived through – and indeed, without this early experience he could never have attained anything of the wisdom which appears in his later writing. But he had to wait for a later maturity to find expression of early experience; and this makes him, I think, a unique and especially interesting poet.

Consider the early poem which is in every anthology, *When you are old and grey and full of sleep*, or *A Dream of Death* in the same volume of 1893. They are beautiful poems, but only craftsman's work, because one does not feel present in them the particularity which must provide the material for the general truth. By the time of the volume of 1904 there is a development visible in a very lovely poem, *The Folly of Being Comforted*, and in *Adam's Curse*; something is coming through and in beginning to speak as a particular man he is beginning to speak for man. This is clearer still in the poem *Peace*, in the 1910 volume. But it is not fully evinced until the volume of 1914, in the violent and terrible epistle dedicatory of *Responsibilities*, with the great lines

Pardon that for a barren passion's sake,
Although I have come close on forty-nine. . . .

And the naming of his age in the poem is significant. More than half a lifetime to arrive at this freedom of speech. It is a triumph.

There was much also for Yeats to work out of himself, even in technique. To be a younger member of a group of poets, none of them certainly of anything like his stature, but further developed in their limited path, may arrest for a time a man's development of idiom. Then again, the weight of the pre-Raphaelite prestige must have been tremendous. The Yeats of the Celtic twilight – who seems to me to have been more the Yeats of the Pre-Raphaelite twilight – uses Celtic folklore almost as William Morris uses Scandinavian folklore. His longer narrative poems bear the mark of Morris. Indeed, in the Pre-Raphaelite phase, Yeats is by no means the least of the Pre-Raphaelites. I may be mistaken, but the play, *The Shadowy Waters*, seems to me one of the most perfect expressions of the vague enchanted beauty of that school: yet it strikes me – this may be an impertinence on my part – as the western seas descried through the back window of a house in Kensington, an Irish myth for the Kelmscott Press, and when I try to visualize the speakers in the play, they have the great dim, dreamy eyes of the knights and ladies of Burne-Jones. I think the phase in which he treated Irish legend in the manner of Rossetti or Morris is a phase of confusion. He did not master this legend until he made it a vehicle for his own creation of character – not, really, until he began to write the *Plays for Dancers*. The point is, that in becoming more Irish, not in subject-matter but in expression, he became at the same time universal.

The points that I particularly wish to make about Yeats' development are two. The first, on which I have already touched, is that to have accomplished what Yeats did in the middle and later years is a great and permanent example – which poets-to-come should study with reverence – of what I have called 'character of the artist': a kind of moral, as well as intellectual, excellence. The second point, which follows naturally after what I have said in criticism of the lack of complete emotional expression in his early work, is that Yeats is pre-eminently the poet of middle age. By this I am far from meaning that he is a poet only for middle-aged readers: the attitude towards him of younger poets who write in English, the world over, is enough evidence to the contrary. Now, in theory, there is no reason why a poet's inspiration or material should fail, in middle age or at any time before senility. For a man who is capable of experience finds himself in a different world in every decade of his life; as he sees it with different eyes, the material of his art is continually renewed. But in fact, very few poets have shown this capacity of adaptation to the years. It requires, indeed, an exceptional honesty and courage to face the change. Most men either cling to the experiences of youth, so that their writing becomes an insincere mimicry of their earlier work, or they leave their passion behind, and write only from the head, with a hollow and wasted virtuosity. There is another and even worse temptation: that of becoming dignified, of becoming public figures with only a public existence – coat-racks hung with decorations and distinctions, doing, saying, and even thinking and feeling only what they believe the public expects of them. Yeats was not that kind of poet: and it is, perhaps, a reason why young men should find his later poetry more acceptable than older men easily can. For the young can see him as a poet who in his work remained in the best sense always young, who even in one sense became young as he aged. But the old, unless they are stirred to something of the honesty with oneself expressed in the poetry, will be shocked by such a revelation of what a man really is and remains. They will refuse to believe that *they* are like that.

You think it horrible that lust and rage
Should dance attendance upon my old age;

They were not such a plague when I was young:
What else have I to spur me into song?

    (*The Spur*)

These lines are very impressive and not very pleasant, and the sentiment has recently been criticized by an English critic whom I generally
respect. But I think he misread them. I do not read them as a personal
confession of a man who differed from other men, but of a man who
was essentially the same as most other men; the only difference is in
the greater clarity, honesty and vigour. To what honest man, old
enough, can these sentiments be entirely alien? They can be subdued
and disciplined by religion, but who can say that they are dead?
Only those to whom the maxim of La Rochefoucauld applies: '*Quand
les vices nous quittent, nous nous flattons de la créance que c'est nous qui
les quittons.*' The tragedy of Yeats' epigram is all in the last line.

    Similarly, the play *Purgatory* is not very pleasant, either. There
are aspects of it which I do not like myself. I wish he had not given it
this title, because I cannot accept a purgatory in which there is no
hint, or at least no emphasis upon Purgation. But, apart from the
extraordinary theatrical skill with which he has put so much action
within the compass of a very short scene of but little movement, the
play gives a masterly exposition of the emotions of an old man. I
think that the epigram I have just quoted seems to me just as much to
be taken in a dramatic sense as the play *Purgatory*. The lyric poet – and
Yeats was always lyric, even when dramatic – can speak for every
man, or for men very different from himself; but to do this he must
for the moment be able to identify himself with every man or other
men; and it is only his imaginative power of becoming this that
deceives some readers into thinking that he is speaking for and of
himself alone – especially when they prefer not to be implicated.

    I do not wish to emphasize this aspect only of Yeats' poetry of
age. I would call attention to the beautiful poem in *The Winding
Stair*: *In Memory of Eva Gore-Booth and Con Markiewicz*, in which
the picture at the beginning, of:

Two girls in silk kimonos, both
Beautiful, one a gazelle,

gets great intensity from the shock of the later line:

When withered old and skeleton-gaunt,

and also to *Coole Park*, beginning

I meditate upon a swallow's flight,
Upon an aged woman and her house.

In such poems one feels that the most lively and desirable emotions of youth have been preserved to receive their full and due expression in retrospect. For the interesting feelings of age are not just different feelings; they are feelings into which the feelings of youth are integrated.

Yeats' development in his dramatic poetry is as interesting as that in his lyrical poetry. I have spoken of him as having been a lyric poet – in a sense in which I should not think of myself, for instance, as lyric; and by this I mean rather a certain kind of selection of emotion rather than particular metrical forms. But there is no reason why a lyric poet should not also be a dramatic poet; and to me Yeats is the type of lyrical dramatist. It took him many years to evolve the dramatic form suited to his genius. When he first began to write plays, poetic drama meant plays written in blank verse. Now, blank verse has been a dead metre for a long time. It would be outside of my frame to go into all the reasons for that now: but it is obvious that a form which was handled so supremely well by Shakespeare has its disadvantages. If you are writing a play of the same type as Shakespeare's, the reminiscence is oppressive; if you are writing a play of a different type, it is distracting. Furthermore, as Shakespeare is so much greater than any dramatist who has followed him, blank verse can hardly be dissociated from the life of the sixteenth and seventeenth centuries: it can hardly catch the rhythms with which English is spoken nowadays. I think that if anything like regular blank verse is ever to be re-established, it can be after a long departure from it, during the course of which it will have liberated itself from period associations. At the time of Yeats' early plays it was not possible to use anything else for a poetry play: that is not a criticism of Yeats himself, but an assertion that changes in verse forms come at one moment and not at another. His early verse-plays, including the *Green Helmet*, which is written in a kind of irregular rhymed fourteener, have a good deal of beauty in them, and, at least, they are the best verse-plays written in their time. And even in these, one notices some development of irregularity in the metric. Yeats did not quite invent a new metre, but the blank verse of his later plays shows a great advance towards one; and what is most astonishing is the virtual abandonment of blank verse metre in *Purgatory*. One device used with great success in some of the later plays is the lyrical choral interlude. But another, and important, cause of improvement is the gradual purging out of poetical ornament. This, perhaps, is the most painful part of the labour, so far as the versification goes, of the modern poet who tries to write a play in verse. The course of improvement is towards a greater and greater starkness. The beautiful line for its own sake is a luxury dangerous even for the poet who has made himself a virtuoso of the technique of the theatre. What is necessary is a beauty which shall not be in the line or the isolable passage, but woven into the dramatic texture itself; so that you can hardly say whether the lines give grandeur to the drama, or whether it is the drama which turns the words into poetry. (One of the most thrilling lines in *King Lear* is the simple:

Never, never, never, never, never

but, apart from a knowledge of the context, how can you say that it is poetry, or even competent verse?) Yeats' purification of his verse becomes much more evident in the four *Plays for Dancers* and in the two in the posthumous volume: those, in fact, in which he had found his right and final dramatic form.

It is in the first three of the *Plays for Dancers*, also, that he shows the internal, as contrasted with the external, way of handling Irish myth of which I have spoken earlier. In the earlier plays, as in the earlier poems, about legendary heroes and heroines, I feel that the characters are treated, with the respect that we pay to legend, as creatures of a different world from ours. In the later plays they are universal men and women. I should, perhaps, not include *The Dreaming of the Bones* quite in this category, because Dermot and Devorgilla are characters from modern history, not figures of pre-history; but I would remark in support of what I have been saying that in this play these two lovers have something of the universality of Dante's Paolo and Francesca, and this the younger Yeats could not have given them. So with the Cuchulain of *The Hawk's Well*, the Cuchulain, Emer and Eithne of *The Only Jealousy of Emer;* the myth is not presented for its own sake, but as a vehicle for a situation of universal meaning.

I see at this point that I may have given the impression, contrary to my desire and my belief, that the poetry and the plays of Yeats' earlier period can be ignored in favour of his later work. You cannot divide the work of a great poet so sharply as that. Where there is the continuity of such a positive personality and such a single purpose, the later work cannot be understood, or properly enjoyed, without a study and appreciation of the earlier; and the later work again reflects light upon the earlier, and shows us beauty and significance not before perceived. We have also to take account of the historical conditions. As I have said above, Yeats was born into the end of a literary movement, and an English movement at that: only those who have toiled with language know the labour and constancy required to free oneself from such influences – yet, on the other hand, once we are familiar with the older voice, we can hear its individual tones even in his earliest published verse. In my own time of youth there seemed to be no immediate great powers of poetry either to help or to hinder, either to learn from or to rebel against, yet I can understand the difficulty of the other situation, and the magnitude of the task. With the verse-play, on the other hand, the situation is reversed, because Yeats had nothing, and we have had Yeats. He started writing plays at a time when the prose-play of contemporary life seemed triumphant, with an indefinite future stretching before it, when the comedy of light farce dealt only with certain privileged strata of metropolitan life; and when the serious play tended to be an ephemeral tract on some transient social problem. We can begin to see now that even the imperfect early attempts he made are probably more permanent literature than the plays of Shaw; and that his dramatic work as a whole may prove a stronger defence against the successful urban Shaftesbury Avenue vulgarity which he opposed as stoutly as they. Just as, from the beginning, he made and thought his poetry in terms of speech and not in terms of print, so in the drama he always meant to write plays to be played and not merely to be read. He cared, I think, more for the theatre as an organ for the expression of the consciousness of a people than as a means to his own fame or achievement; and I am convinced that it is only if you serve it in this spirit that you can hope to accomplish anything worth doing with it. Of course, he had some great advantages, the recital of which does not rob him of any of his glory: his colleagues, a people with a natural and unspoilt gift for speech and for acting. It is impossible to disentangle what he did for the Irish theatre from what the Irish theatre did for him. From this point of advantage, the idea of the poetic drama was kept alive when everywhere else it had been driven underground. I do not know where our debt to him as a dramatist ends – and in time, it will not end until that drama itself ends. In his occasional writings on dramatic topics he has asserted certain principles to which we must hold fast: such as the primacy of the poet over the actor, and of the actor over the scene-painter; and the principle that the theatre, while it need not be concerned only with 'the people' in the narrow Russian sense, must be for the people; that to be permanent it must concern itself with fundamental situations. Born into a world in which the doctrine of 'Art for Art's sake' was generally accepted, and living on into one in which art has been asked to be instrumental to social purposes, he held firmly to the right view which is between these, though not in any way a compromise between them, and showed that an artist, by serving his art with entire integrity, is at the same time rendering the greatest service he can to his own nation and to the whole world.

To be able to praise, it is not necessary to feel complete agreement; and I do not dissimulate the fact that there are aspects of Yeats' thought and feeling which to myself are unsympathetic. I say this only to indicate the limits which I have set to my criticism. The questions of difference, objection and protest arise in the field of doctrine, and these are vital questions. I have been concerned only with the poet and dramatist, so far as these can be isolated. In the long run they cannot be wholly isolated. A full and elaborate examination of the total work of Yeats must some day be undertaken; perhaps it will need a longer perspective. There are some poets whose poetry can be considered more or less in isolation, for experience and delight. There are others whose poetry, though giving equally experience and delight, has a larger historical importance. Yeats was one of the latter: he was one of those few whose history is the history of their own time, who are a part of the consciousness of an age which cannot be understood without them. This is a very high position to assign to him: but I believe that it is one which is secure.

W. H. Auden

'Yeats: Master of Diction', *Saturday Review*, vol. 22,   8 June 1940
(review of *Last Poems and Plays*)

'Everything he wrote was read', Yeats said in one of his last poems,
and, indeed, he was unusually fortunate, for few poets have so
managed to complete their career without suffering any reverses of
reputation, at least with the young, and still fewer have written their
most widely-acclaimed work in the second half of their life. The
universal admiration which his later poems have commanded is all
the more surprising when one remembers how antagonistic were both
his general opinions and his conception of his art to those current in
recent literary movements.

> Sing the peasantry, and then
> Hard-riding country gentlemen,
> The holiness of monks, and after
> Porter-drinkers' randy laughter;
> Sing the lords and ladies gay
> That were beaten into the clay
> Through seven heroic centuries;
> Cast your mind on other days. . . .
>   *(Under Ben Bulben)*

This shows scant sympathy with the 'social consciousness' of the
thirties, and

> Processions that lack high stilts have nothing that catches the
>   eye. . . .
> Because piebald ponies, led bears, caged lions, make but poor
>   shows,
> Because children demand Daddy-long-legs upon his timber toes,
> Because women in the upper storeys demand a face at the pane.
>   *(High Talk)*

is far removed from those who, reacting during the twenties against
inflated Victorian rhetoric, made understatement their God, and
sacrificed grammar to terseness. I find it encouraging that, despite
this, Yeats was recognized as a great poet, for it indicates that readers

are less bigoted, less insistent upon the identity of the poet's beliefs with their own, and, when they can find some that is not completely trivial in subject, more appreciative of poetry that sounds well, that *sings*, than they sometimes appear.

The first thing that strikes one about Yeats is that he really enjoyed writing poetry. Some moderns make one feel that they regard it merely as a necessary means to some other end, the communication of ideas, mystical experience, self-analysis, castigation of abuses or what-have-you, and that the medium in which they work, the sounds and patterns of words, irrespective of the subject, give them little or no pleasure. Yeats, on the other hand, was always more concerned with whether or not a phrase sounded effective, than with the truth of its idea or the honesty of its emotion.

Both attitudes, the Puritanical and the Aesthetic, have their dangers. The first, in forgetting that poetry is an *art*, i.e., artificial, a *factibile* not an *agibile*, may defeat its own purpose by producing drab stuff which is so harsh to the ear and lacking in pattern, that no one can take any pleasure in reading it; the second, by ignoring the fact that the artist is a human being with a moral responsibility to be honest, humble, and self-critical, may leave the poet too easily content with ideas which he finds poetically useful and effective. Not bothering to re-examine them, to throw out the false elements and develop the rest further, he is prevented from reaching his full potential poetic stature, and remains playing variations on the old tune which has served him so well in the past.

It cannot be said that Yeats completely escaped this second temptation. There are, particularly in this volume, more frequent echoes from his own previous work, both in phrasing and rhythm, than there ought to be, and, though every short poem, no doubt, expresses an attitude which in so far as it is one out of many possible moods may be called a pose, its singularity should not obtrude, and on occasion Yeats indulges in an embarrassing insistence upon an old man's virility, which some one who was more self-critical, not as a poet, but as a man, would have avoided.

Further, his utter lack of effort to relate his aesthetic *Weltanschauung* with that of science, a hostile neglect which was due, in part at least, to the age in which he was born when science was avidly mechanistic, was perhaps the reason why he never succeeded in writing a long poem. For, as he himself says so beautifully in *The Circus Animals' Desertion*:

Character isolated by a deed
To engross the present and dominate memory.
Players and painted stage took all my love,
And not those things that they were emblems of.

Those masterful images because complete
Grew in pure mind, but out of what began?
A mound of refuse or the sweepings of a street,
Old kettles, old bottles, and a broken can,
Old iron, old bones, old rags, that raving slut
Who keeps the till. Now that my ladder's gone,
I must lie down where all the ladders start,
In the foul rag-and-bone shop of the heart.

But it was just this that he never did.

Much of his best work, such as the poem just quoted or *Ego Dominus Tuus*, is concerned with the relation of Life and Art. In this relation he had, like Thomas Mann and Valéry, a profound sense of what Kierkegaard called the 'dialectic', but his vision of other kinds of relations was two-dimensional. Hence his onesided determinist and 'musical' view of history, and the lack of drama which not all his theatre can conceal. I cannot but feel, for instance, that the two plays in this volume are worthless.

Yet how little we care. For it is the lyrics we read. In lyric writing what matters more than anything else, more than subject-matter or wisdom, is diction, and of diction, 'simple, sensuous and passionate', Yeats is a consummate master.

Louis MacNeice

'Yeats's Epitaph', *New Republic*, vol. 102   24 June 1940
(review of *Last Poems and Plays*)

During the last ten years, Yeats has had more bouquets from the critics than any other poet of our time. It was refreshing to see these

critics and also many of the younger poets committing themselves
to enthusiasm for an older contemporary; their praise, however, was
sometimes uncritical and sometimes, on a long-term view, injurious
to its subject. There were reviewers who felt Yeats was a safe bet –
safe because he was an exotic; anyone can praise a bird of paradise
but you have to have some knowledge before you go buying
Rhode Island Reds. There is a double point that needs making – first
that Yeats was not so exotic as is popularly assumed, second that on
the whole his exoticism was not an asset but a liability. He was
partly aware of this himself; in his middle period he fought clear of
the dead hand of Walter Pater and deliberately set out to make his
poetry less 'poetic' and in his later years (the years when he was a
devotee of Balzac) he paid at least lip-homage to the principle of
Homo sum. . . . His failure fully to practise this principle was due to a
constitutional inhumanity.

I say this in honour to his memory. If you believe a man was a
genius, it is an insult to him to ignore his deficiencies and peculiarities.
One of the most peculiar poets in our history, Yeats was also extraordinarily lacking in certain qualities which the greater poets usually
possess; in so far as he achieved greatness it proves, not the power of
inspiration or any other such woolly miracle – all that it proves is the
miracle of artistic integrity. For this was a quality he possessed even
though as a man he may sometimes have been a fraud. His more
naïve enemies regard him as knave or fool all through – at best as a
'silly old thing'; his more naïve admirers regard him as God-intoxi-
cated and therefore impeccable. It is high time for us to abandon this
sloppy method of assessment; if poetry is important it deserves more
from us than irresponsible gibes on the one hand or zany gush on the
other.

Take Yeats's two passions – Ireland and Art. We have to remember
that, in regard to both, his attitude was conditioned by a comparatively narrow set of circumstances and that, in judging his services
to Ireland and Art, we shall be very shortsighted if we reapply his
own heavily blinkered concepts of either; it is a lucky thing for the
artist that his work usually outruns his ideology. Yeats talked a good
deal about magic and beauty and mysticism, but his readers have no
right to gabble these words like parrots and call what they are doing
appreciation. Beauty is *not* the mainspring of poetry and, although a

few poets have been genuine mystics, Yeats, unlike his friend A. E., was certainly not one of them; he had what might be called a mystical sense of value, but that is a different thing and a thing which perhaps for *all* artists is a *sine qua non*.

Yeats's poetry reached its peak in *The Winding Stair* (1933). The 'Last Poems' now published represent the Indian summer of his virile, gossipy, contumacious, arrogant, magnificently eccentric old age. Although the book as a whole certainly lacks the depth and range of *The Tower* or *The Winding Stair*, although the septua-genarian virility is sometimes too exhibitionist, although he overdoes certain old tricks and falls into needless obscurities, and although the two plays here included are flat failures, there is still enough vitality and elegance to compensate for certain disappointments. Few poets in English literature have been able to write lyrics after thirty-five; the astonishing thing about Yeats is that he remained essentially a lyric poet till the last. Even the enormous cranky pseudo-philosophy of *A Vision* only served as an occasion for further lyrics. Yeats's ingred-ients became odder and odder, but because they were at least dry and hard, they helped him to assert a joy of life which was comparatively lacking in his early Celtic or Pre-Raphaelite twilights. The great discovery of the later Yeats was that joy need not imply softness and that boredom is something more than one gets in dreams. Axel has been refuted; 'Hamlet and Lear are gay'.

Ireland is very prominent in these last poems. Yeats had for a long time regarded the essential Ireland as incarnate in the country gentry and the peasantry, his ideal society being static and indeed based upon caste. The Irish 'Troubles', however, evoked in him an admiration, even an envy, for the dynamic revolutionary. His thought, in assimilating this element, became to some extent dialectical; he began to conceive of life as a developing whole, a whole which depends upon the conflict of the parts. He even began to write in praise of war, a false inference from a premise which is essentially valid –

... when all words are said
And a man is fighting mad,
Something drops from eyes long blind,
He completes his partial mind. ...
    (Under Ben Bulben)

Physical violence being a simple thing, the Yeats who honoured it took to writing in ballad forms, while the contemplative Yeats continued to use a grand rhetorical manner and a complex inlay of esoteric ideas and images; there are good examples of both in this book. There are also, as in the preceding volumes, a number of poems about himself and his friends; once again he goes around with a highly coloured spotlight; it is amusing to turn from one of these poems, *Beautiful Lofty Things*, which contains a reference to a public banquet in Dublin, to George Moore's account of the same banquet in *Ave*. The most revealing poem in this book is *The Circus Animals' Desertion*, where Yeats with admirable ruthlessness looks back on his various elaborate efforts to project himself on to the world – Celtic legend, Maud Gonne, symbolic drama. In this excellent and moving poem a self-centred old man rises above his personality by pinning it down for what it is.

Randall Jarrell

from 'The Development of Yeats's Sense of Reality',
Southern Review, vol. 7   Winter 1942

If you look at the poems Yeats was writing in the first year or two of this century, you are surprised at how much they resemble the poems he was writing fifteen years before, at how little he had managed to improve; even the improvement had been, largely, technical improvement, growth inside the narrow limits his poetry had originally confined itself to. The lyrics are thin, pale tapestries of a sentimental and romantic past – at first Indian, later Irish, but always completely unreal. The poetry is intolerably pure; the qualities that make Yeats's later poems notable are exactly what these lack. The most common subject of the poems is a passive, Platonic and hopelessly unrequited love. They are an odd combination of Pre-Raphaelite and *fin de siècle* poetry – the Pre-Raphaelite corpse possessed by the decadent spirit: they represent a culminating point of one kind of Romanticism, so much so that the worst of them are their own most effective parodies. A list of the words Yeats used most frequently will show exactly what kind of poetry he was writing. His early poetry is full of the following words (and of words derived from them or related to them): 'dream', 'rose', 'heart', 'lonely', 'wandering', 'gentle', 'sorrow', 'sweet', 'mournful', 'holy', 'tender', 'quiet', 'faery', 'Druid', 'beauty', 'peace', 'lofty', 'high', 'pitiful', 'wan', 'murmur', 'worn', 'grief', 'tears', 'weary', 'sigh', 'old', 'desolate', 'piteous', 'faint', 'dreaming', 'foam', 'flame', 'fade', 'woven', 'tremble', 'shadowy', 'grey', 'dim', 'white', 'pale' ('curd-pale', 'cloud-pale', 'honey-pale', 'pearl-pale', 'death-pale'). The metre and construction match the words; the limp wan rhythms, the enormous quantities of adjectives and intransitive verbs, are exactly what one would expect. (I always think with affection of the poem in which a woman expresses her hatred of a rival by saying: 'And may some dreadful ill befall her quick!')

The reader may want to compare with these the words that occur most frequently in Yeats's late poetry: 'foul', 'passionate', 'ignorant', 'ignorance', 'malicious', 'abstract', 'crazy', 'lunatic', 'mad', 'bitter', 'famous', 'frenzy', 'frenzied', 'violent', 'violence', 'fantasy', 'rage', 'daemonic', 'horrible', 'furious', 'bloody', 'triumphant', 'insolent', 'arrogant', 'arrogance', 'mock', 'mockery', 'murderous', 'bone', 'blood', 'stone', 'malice', 'sensual', 'fanatic', 'intellect', 'shriek', 'rascal', 'knave', 'rogue', 'fool', 'gyres', 'miraculous', 'cold', 'indifferent', 'raddled', 'blind', 'wild', 'naked', 'dumb', 'rag', 'ragged', 'tumult', 'joy', 'death', 'hate', 'night', 'wine', 'ditch', 'mummy', 'barren', 'murderous', 'torn', 'terrible', 'great', 'brilliant', 'fabulous', 'drunken', 'mire'. The words are full of violence, of toughness and strength; some have a rhetorical magnificence, others a sensual colloquial sharpness. This list is the antithesis of the other; one needs only to read the two to realize how completely Yeats's poetry changed.

Just then there were several reasons for a change. He had carried these particular romantic tendencies to a limit and exhausted them; he began constantly writing for the theatre, and soon saw the necessity for a language that would be balder and more dramatic, more like speech; and, most important of all, the dreams that made up his life were going to pieces, and his poetry changed with their ruin. He had loved and worked for several things, and only one of them (mysticism, supernaturalism) remained whole. Another one was Irish independence, which he had worked hardest at during the last years of the century, travelling all over England and Scotland, taking pride in evenings spent with 'some small organizer into whose spittoon I secretly poured my third glass of whiskey', enduring 'some of the worst months of my life', always hoping to become what he was not and could never be. All this was mixed with, partly caused by, the 'miserable love affair' that was for a great many years the most important thing in his life; he was in love with a revolutionary agitator who cared for nothing but Irish independence – he once said ruefully that his devotion 'might as well have been offered to an image in a milliner's window, or a statue in a museum'. Both his private life and his political life, from year to year, grew more and more hopeless; and Yeats began slowly to realize that his other great desire – bringing himself, his country, and its literature back to the 'unity of culture' of the Middle Ages – was hopeless too. For years the chief subject of his lyrics was his despair at seeing what was happening to himself and his love, his disillusionment with the politics he had wasted himself on. He became full of bitter resentment at the revolutionary politics that made it impossible for his love to be anything but miserable and hopeless; that seemed to him to be transforming the woman he loved into a fanatic; that separated him both from his natural work and his natural surroundings. Years later he could write angrily that he had always forsaken poetry for anything: 'One time it was a woman's face, or worse – the seeming needs of my fool-driven land'. Still later he wrote that he had seen 'the loveliest woman born' ruin herself 'for an old bellows full of angry wind'; the woman ruined by fanaticism became one of his obsessions.

It was all this, and what happened because of it, that began to put reality into Yeats's poetry. Yeats had identified Irish politics with his own interests and desires: his own love affair, his own hope for the restoration of an aristocratic, legendary, theological, folkish state like those he calls the 'pure' Asiatic cultures. All his life his one overwhelming desire was for the defeat of science and industrialism, the return of the world to the old order of things – and everything he ever cared about, from politics to spiritualism, he managed to join to this desire. Until the time we have come to – when Yeats was almost forty – he believed that he and people like him could *make* the world change, 'reverse the cinematograph' of history. (But he made his poetry represent, not the struggle to get the world he wanted, but a vague, wistful, and sentimental propaganda-picture of an unreal universe; he made a romantic Utopia out of a legendary past.) Now Yeats began to realize that it was impossible to make all this happen – that it was impossible, really, to make any of it happen: he saw the Ireland he wanted, the world he wanted, the woman he wanted, moving farther and farther away – and he saw, too, that his work and misery had been useless, that all these things had from the beginning been beyond his reach. Reality had crushed Yeats's picture of it, his plans for it; the real world – and the real Yeats who lived in that world – began to force their way into the poetry that had for so long been innocent of either.

Arthur Mizener

from 'The Romanticism of W. B. Yeats', *Southern Review*, vol. 7 Winter 1942

> Never had I more
> Excited, passionate, fantastical
> Imagination, nor an ear and eye
> That more expected the impossible. . . .
>   *(The Tower)*

There seems to be pretty general agreement among critics that the later poetry of Yeats is superior to the kind he was writing at the turn of the century. But the tendency has been to analyse the difference between the two either in terms of the change in Yeats's style, of the development of what Mr MacNeice thinks 'we might call the neo-classic beauty' of the later poetry, or in terms of the part played in this change by Yeats's commitment to magic and the system set forth in *A Vision*. It seems to me possible that the points aimed at by these analyses can be made clearer if we are willing to recognize that Yeats was, to the end of his career, a poet of the Romantic nineties and that the greatness of the later poetry is a kind of greatness inherent in the nineties' attitude.

No one, I suppose, will wish to argue that the style of the later poems is not different from the style of the earlier ones, but it is a curious fact that Yeats remained all his life devoted to the idea of 'style' in the 1890s' sense, scoring, as he must have supposed, some of his most telling points off George Moore, for instance, with anecdotes which demonstrated Moore's inability to write like Pater. And late in *Dramatis Personae* he is still talking, with all the lack of historical perspective which characterized the 1890s on this point, of 'style, as it has been understood from the translators of the Bible to Walter Pater' as distinguished from 'a journalistic effectiveness' (*Autobiographies*). Yeats's own conception of his later style was that he had cunningly used 'occasional prosaic words' because 'if we dramatize some possible singer or speaker we remember that he is moved by one thing at a time, certain words must be dull and numb' (*Autobiographies*.) The achievement of the end suggested by these quotations was, I think, very near the heart of Yeats's astonishing success in the later poems. But that success did not consist in making 'something memorable and even sensuous out of ordinary words, austere rhythms and statements bleakly direct' (*The Poetry of W. B. Yeats*), or at least this is a distorted account of both the means and their result.

If we are to talk of style in the abstract, as both Yeats and Mr MacNeice are inclined to, it would be better to say that Yeats, retaining to the end an 1890s conception of style, learned to use for the purpose of style a much larger vocabulary and a number of colloquial – though never either loose or simple – rhythms; that above all he learned to give an impression of the 'active man' speaking, to dramatize the speaker of the poem, by a cunning mixture of the 'dull and numb' words and the colloquial rhythms with the romantic diction and rhythms of his earlier poetry. But he never sought to write verse that was 'journalistically effective', and the result of supposing so is the notion that in Yeats's later poetry there is 'an almost Wordsworthian simplicity' – a somewhat curious gloss on 'neo-classic beauty'. This is a description patently inappropriate to Yeats' great symbolic poems, for these poems are as exotic in their splendour as anything well could be. And it is a description equally if perhaps less obviously inappropriate to the great poems of meditation. I think Yeats would not forgive us for so describing these achievements of what he believed the 'calm ... of ordered passion'. Wordsworth was certainly capable of that combination of great dignity and passion which Yeats is aiming at in these poems, but not when he was being 'simple'. The difference between a poem by the early Yeats and the late Yeats is not the difference between a rhetorical poem and a poem of Wordsworthian simplicity. It is the difference between a poem where rhythm and vocabulary are obvious and conventional, because the poet has deliberately eliminated from it the dramatic and the concrete, and a poem where neither is obvious or conventional – in either the bad or the good sense – because the poet is bent on including both.

What happened to make Yeats's later poetry different from his early poetry was that he came to feel the early poetry unsatisfactory, not because its theme was unsatisfactory, but because its manner of realizing its theme was. He wanted not only to present his theme but to present it in terms of the 'real' world; he wanted his poems to be true not only to the dreams where his responsibility began but also to the facts; he wanted, when he wrote, to hold not only justice but reality in a single thought. This is a development rather than a conversion, a technical change rather than a substantial one. And it is the development of something present in Yeats from the start, for he was a very young man on that occasion when he walked down the street eyeing himself in the shop windows and wondering why his tie did not blow out in the wind as Byron's did in the picture.

The obvious moral of this incident is that Yeats was not satisfied simply to dream the pictures in which his desires were realized; he wanted to realize them in fact. It is, if less obviously, also its moral that the picture he dreamed was always a romantic one and that it never occurred to Yeats to modify it at any point in order that it might conform with the demonstrable habits of the wind. Yeats could not change the habits of the wind, nor could he ever quite bring himself to leave the miraculous intervention to which he was committed in other hands than his own. What he could do was his best always to stand on corners where the wind was most likely to blow to his satisfaction; and he tried hard to believe that the ensuing flutter of tie-ends was the result of the wind's ordinary habits, not the result of his careful selection of corners. As a consequence his poetry and, I suspect, his life were, when the wind came up to snuff, intensely dramatic, if they were also sometimes merely theatrical.

Yeats was, as he knew, a man with a 'faint perception of things in their weight and mass' as such, who nevertheless had a desire for the world of these things, the world where men were 'almost always partisans, propagandists and gregarious'. He therefore sought, as he says in *A Vision* men of his phase must, 'simplification by intensity'. For he knew himself also one of those who define themselves 'mainly through an image of the mind', and he was too much of a romantic ever to believe the task of defining the world of weight and mass could be anything like of equal importance with the definition of self:

I turn away and shut the door, and on the stair
Wonder how many times I could have proved my worth
In something that all others understand or share;
But O! ambitious heart, had such a proof drawn forth
A company of friends, a conscience set at ease,
It had but made us pine the more. The abstract joy,
The half-read wisdom of daemonic images,
Suffice the ageing man as once the growing boy.
  (*Meditations in Time of Civil War*)

Speaking in the *Autobiographies* of the early career here referred to Yeats said that he 'overrated the quality of anything that could be connected with my general beliefs about the world'; and, he might have added, was willing to use almost any ingenuity of interpretation in order to connect what he found moving with these general beliefs. He was, as Rothenstein remarked (*Scattering Branches*), 'too easily impressed by work which showed a superficial appearance of romance or mysticism'. He never wholly conquered this habit; it sufficed the ageing man as once the growing boy. It is a result of this fact that Yeats's later poetry never has a consistently representational surface, never represents the shows of things. What it does have is a marvellous concreteness and immediacy which is the result of Yeats's presenting with the maximum specification of sensuous detail a startling variety of objects which were attached, by some more or less obscure implication which Yeats found in them, to his general beliefs; it is here, and here only, that they find their unity and value for Yeats.

The later Yeats, then, desired what he called 'reality', that is simplicity, order and concreteness; and in this sense it is true, as Mr Reed

Whittemore has said, that Yeats was a romantic who did not want to be one; not, however, because he wanted to be something different, but because he wanted to be something more. He wanted reality, but only on his own terms, and the main requirement of these terms was that particular version of the romantic objective on which the nineties concentrated: intensity of feeling. In desiring reality only on his own terms, Yeats was of course desiring something he could not get, since this pragmatical, preposterous pig of a world, its farrow that so solid seem, have a certain stubborn independence of the mind's theme, in spite of God-appointed Berkeley, whom Yeats seems to have thought God appointed to prove He does not exist rather than that He does. Imagination, by which he meant emotion, he thought 'is always justified by time, thought hardly ever. It can only bring us back to emotion' (*Autobiographies*). This devotion to imagination in the sense of emotion, to what the heart says, was for Yeats, as for all romantics, the defining characteristic of the artist. 'Since Phase 12,' he wrote in *A Vision*, 'the *Creative Mind* has been so interfused by the *antithetical tincture* that it has more and more confined its contemplation of actual things to those that resemble images of the mind desired by the *Will*. The being has . . . been more and more the artist.'

The 1890s, in their *reductio ad absurdum* way, were prepared to sacrifice 'reality' altogether ('as for living. . .') to the aesthetic expression of the passionate self, for 'to maintain this ecstasy is success in life'. But Yeats, knowing the lives of Johnson and Wilde, knew that one could not live wholly in the imagination. It was plain from the experience of the nineties that to refine ecstasy to perfection, to a purely aesthetic and contemplative thing, was self-defeating. It was self-defeating because life will have its revenge; it was self-defeating because, since passion and energy were physical things, to have them only in contemplation, or in the ritual of manners and the ancestral houses out of which the 'bitter and violent' living had passed, was not to have them.

O what if gardens where the peacock strays
With delicate feet upon old terraces,
Or else all Juno from an urn displays
Before the indifferent garden deities;
O what if levelled lawns and gravelled ways

Where slippered Contemplation finds his ease
And Childhood a delight for every sense,
But take our greatness with our violence?
    (*Meditations in Time of Civil War*)

It was, then, in life, with its bitterness and violence, its fury and
mire, and not in the contemplative peace of the imagination, that
ecstasy could be realized. In one sense it was an intolerable insult that
this should be so, an insult to the doll-gods, the Magi in their stiff
painted clothes, the lifeless but beautiful gods of the poet's imagination. For it was in the Great Memory, that conglomeration of all that
men with high imaginations like Yeats's had dreamed, that ecstasy
was perfectly conceived, and to such, mere human love was 'A noisy
and filthy thing'. Always Yeats found it 'a poor and crazy thing that
we who have imagined so many noble persons cannot bring our flesh
to heel' (*Autobiographies*). On the other hand, it was precisely in what
was temporal and evanescent, in the unaesthetic mess of physical life,
that ecstasy had its realized being.

It was thus that Yeats came to think of life as at once a horror and
a glory:

Why must those holy, haughty feet descend
From emblematic niches and what hand
Ran that delicate raddle through their white?
My heart is broken, yet must understand.
What do they seek for? Why must they descend?
For the desecration and the lover's night.

It was thus that he came to dream of a paradise where ecstasy could
disdain ('distain', as Yeats first wrote it, free itself from the stain of
and so be free to scorn)

All that man is,
All mere complexities,
The fury and the mire of human veins. . . .
    (*Byzantium*)

Here ecstasy would achieve perfection and permanence of simplicity
and intensity, though at the terrible cost of not being able really to
burn at all:

Where blood-begotten spirits come
And all complexities of fury leave,
Dying into a dance,
An agony of trance,
An agony of flame that cannot singe a sleeve.
    (Byzantium)

In such a paradise one could burn with this hard gem-like flame,
could maintain this ecstasy, eternally; here 'religious, aesthetic and
practical life were one' and 'the strain one upon another of opposites',
the conflict of desires for the subjective and objective lives, was resolved. Yet Yeats so loved the flame that can singe a sleeve, that all
his poems which describe this paradise are prayers that he may be
relieved of that love:

O sages standing in God's holy fire . . .
Consume my heart away; sick with desire
And fastened to a dying animal
It knows not what it is. . . .
    (Sailing to Byzantium)

For all his conviction that

He who can read the signs nor sink unmanned . . .
Has but one comfort left: all triumph would
But break upon his ghostly solitude;

for all this conviction, he could not forget the ecstasy of the heart:

But is there any comfort to be found?
Man is in love and loves what vanishes,
What more is there to say?
    (Nineteen Hundred and Nineteen)

Sometimes, for a moment, Yeats was able to visualize a romanti-
cized version of some actual life which approached what he wanted.
This privately mythologized version of actuality he could give his
heart to because it seemed actually to realize his heart's desire, a life
of that 'calm which is . . . an ordered passion'. 'Yet is not ecstasy,'
he wrote, speaking of the proper end of tragedy, 'some fulfilment
of the soul in itself, some slow or sudden expansion of it like an overflowing well? Is not this what is meant by beauty?' (Autobiographies).

And precisely this same metaphor he applied, conditionally, to the life of the Irish gentry:

Surely among a rich man's flowering lawns,
Amid the rustle of his planted hills,
Life overflows without ambitious pains;
And rains down life until the basin spills,
And mounts more dizzy high the more it rains
As though to choose whatever shape it wills
And never stoop to a mechanical
Or servile shape, at others' beck and call.
   (*Meditations in Time of Civil War*)

But the mood of romantic irony follows quickly upon this always. . . .

   The later poetry of Yeats is far finer than the poetry he wrote for the nineties and it is finer because in it he sought to shape life to his heart's desire not merely in fancy but in fact. But it remains the poetry of a man committed to the heart's desire, a romantic poetry. As such it is at once colloquial and orotund, straightforward and full of astounding, 'irrelevant' implications. As such it is full of enthusiastic and crotchety extremes which are forever on the verge of destroying its coherence or statement or its unity of style. It knows neither decorum of idea ('For love has pitched its mansion in/The place of excrement') nor decorum of vocabulary ('perne in a gyre'). This is not the logical, decorous, 'neo-classical' poetry so many of Yeats's critics appear to be trying to make it out, and it is not because it rests on that conviction which Hulme the neo-classicist was at such pains to deny: that the divine is life at its intensest. Mr Winters's low opinion of it is a perfectly logical judgement from his point of view, and I do not see how we are to dissent from his account of Yeats's procedure, however much we may disagree with his evaluation of its results. The poetry of *The Tower* is not harder and drier and more logical than the poetry of *The Rose*; it is only more concrete, more skillful in rhetoric, and more crowded with what Yeats found solid in life. For he might have been speaking of himself when he wrote of the Irish story-teller:

His art, too, is often at its greatest when it is most
extravagant, for he only feels himself among solid things,

among things with fixed laws and satisfying purposes, when he has reshaped the world according to his heart's desire. He understands as well as Blake that the ruins of time build mansions in eternity (*Cuchulain in Muirthemne*, p. 13).

L. C. Knights

from 'W. B. Yeats: The Assertion of Values', *Southern Review*, vol. 7 Winter 1942 (reprinted as 'Poetry and Social Criticism: The Work of W. B. Yeats', *Explorations*, 1946)

Romanticism in literature, we may say, is the expression of a sensibility deliberately limited, both as regards its objects of interest and the modes of consciousness that it employs. In Yeats's early verse, for example, a narrow range of uncomplicated emotional attitudes is expressed in a technique incapable of variety, force or subtlety. What is less obvious is that even when in the interest of a fuller and more abounding life he had developed a technique of flexible and forceful speech, persistent habits of Romantic simplification remained. An example of what I mean can be found in his use of figures from heroic legend. Instead of impossible heroes and languishing queens with cloud-pale eyelids and dream-dimmed eyes, we now have 'Helen and her boy', Soloman with Sheba 'planted on his knees', and Leda, 'that sprightly girl was trodden by a bird'. At first reading it seems that the purpose served by these and similar phrases is the re-creation of the heroic world in modern idiom, the ironic application – in Elizabethan fashion – of old fable to contemporary needs. That perhaps was the intention, but the references also serve a deeper need, a nostalgia for an imagined past in which painful complexities are evaporated. Mr MacNeice says rightly that Yeats 'was orientated ... towards a simplified past'; and it is significant that in the poem *Ancestral Houses* the irony relies on an absolute acceptance of the past – 'a haughtier age' – and is directed solely against the present: there is no suggestion of the two-way irony which in *The Waste Land* sets present *and* past in a clearer light. To romanticize *any* element in a given situation is to admit an inability to deal with it completely and with a full awareness of all that is involved; and

Yeats, even in his middle and later periods, continued to use Romantic glamour as an escape from difficult or painful problems. The poem *No Second Troy* opens in the tones of straightforward speech:

Why should I blame her that she filled my days
With misery, or that she would of late
Have taught to ignorant men most violent ways,
Or hurled the little streets upon the great,
Had they but courage equal to desire?

But from the sixth line the poem draws largely on Romantic idealization:

What could have made her peaceful with a mind
That nobleness made simple as a fire,
With beauty like a tightened bow, a kind
That is not natural in an age like this,
Being high and solitary and most stern?

And in the end a woman with whom only difficult relations were possible is transformed into that Helen who exists only for the imagination:

Why, what could she have done being what she is?
Was there another Troy for her to burn?

In *Easter 1916* the refrain,

All changed, changed utterly:
A terrible beauty is born.

represents an escape from full realization. Sometimes, as in the instances just quoted, the nature of the transformation is indicated by a change in diction, a lapse into something like Yeats's earlier manner. At other times it is half concealed by the assured use of an idiom professedly non-Romantic. Yeats in fact uses his later colloquial technique with such self-confident swagger that often one gives him credit for doing all that he merely claims to do. The speech of 'My Self' which ends *A Dialogue of Self and Soul* (*The Winding Stair*) has a sinewy vigour:

I am content to live it all again
And yet again, if it be life to pitch
Into the frog-spawn of a blind man's ditch,
A blind man battering blind men.

But when the poem ends,

I am content to follow to its source
Every event in action or in thought;
Measure the lot; forgive myself the lot!

we have no warrant that 'follow to its source', 'measure' and 'forgive
myself' stand for explorations actually undertaken. And if the poems
dealing explicitly with contemporary chaos are, in the long run,
disappointing, it is for a similar reason. In *Meditations in Time of
Civil War* and *Nineteen Hundred and Nineteen* (*The Tower*) there are
memorable lines and striking images:

Nothing but grip of claw, and the eye's complacency,
The innumerable clanging wings that have put out the moon.

Violence upon the roads: violences of horses. ....
Herodias' daughters have returned again
A sudden blast of dusty wind and after
Thunder of feet, tumult of images,
Their purpose in the labyrinth of the wind;

but if the success of the poems seems partial and fragmentary it is
because 'the half read wisdom of daemonic images' (which, we are
told, 'suffice the ageing man as once the growing boy') is made to
take the place of a deeper understanding.

Perhaps the best way of defining the disappointment that one feels
on returning to so many of Yeats's poems that had previously seemed
deeply moving is to say that they fail to 'gather strength of life, with
being', to grow, that is, with one's own developing experience –
unlike so much of Eliot's poetry where each fresh reading brings fresh
discovery. For not only does Yeats tend to simplify his problems,
there is in much of his poetry a static quality which can be traced to
the adoption of certain fixed attitudes in the face of experience.
'There is a relation,' he said, 'between discipline and the theatrical
sense. .... Active virtue as distinguished from the passive acceptance

of a current code is therefore theatrical, consciously dramatic, the wearing of a Mask' (*Dramatis Personae*).[1] But his preoccupation with the Mask was not merely a search for a discipline: sometimes it seems like the rationalization of a self-dramatizing egotism which made him feel happier if he could see himself ('Milton's Platonist') in an appropriate light. Consider, for example, his attitude of pride. One can relish his criticism of those who 'long for popularity that they may believe in themselves' and of poets who 'want marching feet', and at the same time recognize a danger to sincerity in a too persistent assertion of 'something steel-like and cold within the will, something passionate and cold'.[2] There is a smack of the nineties here; and one remembers his fondness for Dowson's lines,

> Unto us they belong,
>   Us the bitter and gay.
> Wine and women and song.
>   (*Villanelle of The Poet's Road*)

' "Bitter and gay", that is the heroic mood,' he wrote in 1935. Like the aristocratic order that he imagined, pride is valued as an assertion of the living spirit confronted with democratic commonness; but there is something unliving in the use he makes of 'cold' and 'bitter' and 'proud' – adjectives that tend to appear with the same regularity as the 'emblems' which, in his later poetry, too often take the place of living metaphor. There is no doubt that the sap flows most freely when the conscious pride is forgotten, remaining only as a temper of mind that is sufficiently assured not to insist on its own firmness. The pose that results from over-insistence is most obvious in admittedly minor poems, like the short sequence *Upon a Dying Lady* and those verses that celebrate 'the discipline of the looking-glass', which he seems to have continued to regard as the appropriate discipline for beautiful women; but it also betrays itself in work of greater power. In the third section of the title poem of *The Tower* he writes of 'upstanding men',

1 Compare *Dramatis Personae*, p. 79 ('Style, personality – deliberately adopted and therefore a mask – is the only escape from the hot-faced bargainers and the money-changers') and many passages in the *Autobiographies*.
2 The references are to *Dramatis Personae* and *Letters on Poetry*.

> I declare
> They shall inherit my pride,
> The pride of people that were
> Bound neither to Cause nor to State,
> Neither to slaves that were spat on,
> Nor to the tyrants that spat,
> The people of Burke and of Grattan
> That gave, though free to refuse –

The rhythm of these lines suggests Tom Moore rather than the man who wrote the vigorous protest against old age with which the same poem opens. The pride, in short, sometimes seems like another form of the escape from complexity. Referring, once more, to the Mask, he wrote: 'I think all happiness depends on the energy to assume the Mask of some other self; that all joyous or creative life is a re-birth as something not oneself. . . . We put on a grotesque or solemn painted face to hide us from the terrors of judgement, invent an imaginative Saturnalia where one forgets reality, a game like that of a child, where one loses the infinite pain of self-realization' (*Dramatis Personae*). Yeats knew as well as anyone that 'the infinite pain of self-realization' is the price paid for 'life'; and in the lines that he wrote for his epitaph there is a deep and unintended pathos:

> Cast a cold eye
> On life, on death.
> Horseman, pass by.

Measured by potentiality, by aspiration, and by the achievement of a few poems, it is as an heroic failure that one is forced to consider Yeats's poetic career as a whole. The causes were complex. Something, no doubt, must be attributed to defects of 'character'; and a very great deal must be attributed to the literary tradition of the nineteenth century which, as he came to see so clearly, offered the very opposite of an incitement to maturity. But, since 'the death of language . . . is but a part of the tyranny of impersonal things' (*Essays*), that tradition itself appears as the symptom of a deeper disease. Yeats wrote of W. E. Henley: 'He never understood how small a fragment of our nature can be brought to expression, nor that but with great toil, in a much divided civilization'; and of himself as a young man, already half-conscious that 'nothing so much matters as Unity of Being': 'Nor did I understand as yet how little that Unity, however wisely sought, is possible without a Unity of Culture in class or people that is no longer possible at all' (*Autobiographies*). These passages, representative of many others, are part of a diagnosis that is valuable not merely for the light that it throws on Yeats's poetry. For those who would understand our divided and distracted civilization, in which the 'passionate intensity' of partial men offers itself as a substitute for the vitality that springs from the whole consciousness, few things are more profitable than a study of Yeats's poetry and prose together. 'The mischief,' he said, 'began at the end of the seventeenth century when man became passive before a mechanized nature' (Introduction to *The Oxford Book of Modern Verse*).

George Orwell

'W. B. Yeats', *Horizon* January 1943 (reprinted in *Collected Essays, Journalism and Letters*, vol. 2, 1968)

One thing that Marxist criticism has not succeeded in doing is to trace the connection between 'tendency' and literary style. The subject-matter and imagery of a book can be explained in sociological terms, but its texture seemingly cannot. Yet some such connection there must be. One knows, for instance, that a Socialist would not write like Chesterton or a Tory imperialist like Bernard Shaw, though *how* one knows it is not easy to say. In the case of Yeats, there must be some kind of connection between his wayward, even tortured style of writing and his rather sinister vision of life. Mr Menon[1] is chiefly concerned with the esoteric philosophy underlying Yeats' work, but the quotations which are scattered all through his interesting book serve to remind one how artificial Yeats' manner of writing was. As a rule, this artificiality is accepted as Irishism, or Yeats is even credited with simplicity because he uses short words, but in fact one seldom comes on six consecutive lines of his verse in which there is

1 V. K. Narayana Menon, *The Development of William Butler Yeats*, Oliver & Boyd.

not an archaism or an affected turn of speech. To take the nearest example:

Grant me an old man's Frenzy,
My self must I remake
Till I am Timon and Lear
Or that William Blake
Who beat upon the wall
Till truth obeyed his call.
 (An Acre of Grass)

The unnecessary 'that' imports a feeling of affectation, and the same tendency is present in all but Yeats' best passages. One is seldom long away from a suspicion of 'quaintness', something that links up not only with the nineties, the Ivory Tower and the 'calf covers of pissed-on green', but also with Rackham's drawings, Liberty art-fabrics and the *Peter Pan* never-never land, of which, after all, *The Happy Townland* is merely a more appetizing example. This does not matter, because, on the whole, Yeats gets away with it, and if his straining after effect is often irritating, it can also produce phrases ('the chill, footless years', 'the mackerel-crowded seas') which suddenly overwhelm one like a girl's face seen across a room. He is an exception to the rule that poets do not use poetical language:

How many centuries spent
The sedentary soul
In toils of measurement
Beyond eagle or mole,
Beyond hearing or seeing,
Or Archimedes' guess,
To raise into being
That loveliness?
 (The Only Jealousy of Emer)

Here he does not flinch from a squashy vulgar word like 'loveliness', and after all it does not seriously spoil this wonderful passage. But the same tendencies, together with a sort of raggedness which is no doubt intentional, weaken his epigrams and polemical poems. For instance (I am quoting from memory) the epigram against the critics who damned *The Playboy of the Western World*:

Once when midnight smote the air
Eunuchs ran through Hell and met
On every crowded street to stare
Upon great Juan riding by;
Even like these to rail and sweat,
Staring upon his sinewy thigh.
(On Those that Hated The Playboy of the Western World, 1907)

The power which Yeats has within himself gives him the analogy
ready made and produces the tremendous scorn of the last line, but
even in this short poem there are six or seven unnecessary words. It
would probably have been deadlier if it had been neater.

Mr Menon's book is incidentally a short biography of Yeats, but
he is above all interested in Yeats' philosophical 'system', which in
his opinion supplies the subject-matter of more of Yeats' poems than
is generally recognized. This system is set forth fragmentarily in
various places, and at full length in A Vision, a privately printed book
which I have never read but which Mr Menon quotes from exten-
sively. Yeats gave conflicting accounts of its origin, and Mr Menon
hints pretty broadly that the 'documents' on which it was ostensibly
founded were imaginary. Yeats' philosophical system, says Mr
Menon, 'was at the back of his intellectual life almost from the
beginning. His poetry is full of it. Without it his later poetry becomes
almost completely unintelligible'. As soon as we begin to read about
the so-called system we are in the middle of a hocus-pocus of Great
Wheels, gyres, cycles of the moon, reincarnation, disembodied
spirits, astrology and what-not. Yeats hedges as to the literalness with
which he believed in all this, but he certainly dabbled in spiritualism
and astrology, and in earlier life had made experiments in alchemy.
Although almost buried under explanations, very difficult to understand, about the phases of the moon, the central idea of his philosophical system seems to be our old friend, the cyclical universe, in
which everything happens over and over again. One has not, perhaps,
the right to laugh at Yeats for his mystical beliefs – for I believe it
could be shown that some degree of belief in magic is almost universal
– but neither ought one to write such things off as mere unimportant
eccentricities. It is Mr Menon's perception of this that gives his book
its deepest interest. 'In the first flush of admiration and enthusiasm,'

he says, 'most people dismissed the fantastical philosophy as the price we have to pay for a great and curious intellect. One did not quite realize where he was heading. And those who did, like Pound and perhaps Eliot, approved the stand that he finally took. The first reaction to this did not come, as one might have expected, from the politically minded young English poets. They were puzzled because a less rigid or artifical system than that of *A Vision* might not have produced the great poetry of Yeats' last days.' It might not, and yet Yeats' philosophy has some very sinister implications, as Mr Menon points out.

Translated into political terms, Yeats' tendency is Fascist. Throughout most of his life, and long before Fascism was ever heard of, he had had the outlook of those who reach Fascism by the aristocratic route. He is a great hater of democracy, of the modern world, science, machinery, the concept of progress – above all, of the idea of human equality. Much of the imagery of his work is feudal, and it is clear that he was not altogether free from ordinary snobbishness. Later these tendencies took clearer shape and led him to 'the exultant acceptance of authoritarianism as the only solution. Even violence and tyranny are not necessarily evil because the people, knowing not evil and good, would become perfectly acquiescent to tyranny. . . . Everything must come from the top. Nothing can come from the masses.' Not much interested in politics, and no doubt disgusted by his brief incursions into public life, Yeats nevertheless makes political pronouncements. He is too big a man to share the illusions of Liberalism, and as early as 1920 he foretells in a justly famous passage (*The Second Coming*) the kind of world that we have actually moved into. But he appears to welcome the coming age, which is to be 'hierarchical, masculine, harsh, surgical', and is influenced both by Ezra Pound and by various Italian Fascist writers. He describes the new civilization which he hopes and believes will arrive: 'an aristocratic civilization in its most completed form, every detail of life hierarchical, every great man's door crowded at dawn by petitioners, great wealth everywhere in a few men's hands, all dependent upon a few, up to the Emperor himself, who is a God dependent on a greater God, and everywhere, in Court, in the family, an inequality made law'. The innocence of this statement is as interesting as its snobbishness. To begin with, in a single phrase, 'great wealth in a few men's hands',

Yeats lays bare the central reality of Fascism, which the whole of its propaganda is designed to cover up. The merely political Fascist claims always to be fighting for justice: Yeats, the poet, sees at a glance that Fascism means injustice, and acclaims it for that very reason. But at the same time he fails to see that the new authoritarian civilization, if it arrives, will not be aristocratic, or what he means by aristocratic. It will not be ruled by noblemen with Van Dyck faces, but by anonymous millionaires, shiny-bottomed bureaucrats and murdering gangsters. Others who have made the same mistake have afterwards changed their views, and one ought not to assume that Yeats, if he had lived longer, would necessarily have followed his friend Pound, even in sympathy. But the tendency of the passage I have quoted above is obvious, and its complete throwing overboard of whatever good the past two thousand years have achieved is a disquieting symptom.

How do Yeats' political ideas link up with his leaning towards occultism? It is not clear at first glance why hatred of democracy and a tendency to believe in crystal-gazing should go together. Mr Menon only discusses this rather shortly, but it is possible to make two guesses. To begin with, the theory that civilization moves in recurring cycles is one way out for people who hate the concept of human equality. If it is true that 'all this', or something like it, 'has happened before', then science and the modern world are debunked at one stroke and progress becomes for ever impossible. It does not matter if the lower orders are getting above themselves, for, after all, we shall soon be returning to an age of tyranny. Yeats is by no means alone in this outlook. If the universe is moving round on a wheel, the future must be foreseeable, perhaps even in some detail. It is merely a question of discovering the laws of its motion, as the early astronomers discovered the solar year. Believe that, and it becomes difficult not to believe in astrology or some similar system. A year before the war, examining a copy of *Gringoire*, the French Fascist weekly, much read by my officers, I found in it no less than thirty-eight advertisements of clairvoyants. Secondly, the very concept of occultism carries with it the idea that knowledge must be a secret thing, limited to a small circle of initiates. But the same idea is integral to Fascism. Those who dread the prospect of universal suffrage, popular education, freedom of thought, emancipation of women, will start off with a predilection towards secret cults. There is another link between Fascism and magic in the profound hostility of both to the Christian ethical code.

No doubt Yeats wavered in his beliefs and held at different times many different opinions, some enlightened, some not. Mr Menon repeats for him Eliot's claim that he had the longest period of development of any poet who has ever lived. But there is one thing that seems constant, at least in all of his work that I can remember, and that is his hatred of modern Western civilization and desire to return to the Bronze Age, or perhaps to the Middle Ages. Like all such thinkers, he tends to write in praise of ignorance. The Fool in his remarkable play, *The Hour-Glass*, is a Chestertonian figure, 'God's fool' the 'natural born innocent', who is always wiser than the wise man. The philosopher in the play dies in the knowledge that all his lifetime of thought has been wasted (I am quoting from memory again)—

The stream of the world has changed its course,
And with the stream my thoughts have run
Into some cloudy, thunderous spring
That is its mountain-source;
Ay, to a frenzy of the mind,
That all that we have done's undone
Our speculation but as the wind.[1]

Beautiful words, but by implication profoundly obscurantist and reactionary; for if it is really true that a village idiot, as such, is wiser than a philosopher, then it would be better if the alphabet had never been invented. Of course, all praise of the past is partly sentimental, because we do not live in the past. The poor do not praise poverty. Before you can despise the machine, the machine must set you free from brute labour. But that is not to say that Yeats' yearning for a more primitive and more hierarchical age was not sincere. How much of all this is traceable to mere snobbishness, product of Yeats' own position as an impoverished offshoot of the aristocracy, is a different question. And the connection between his obscurantist opinions and

1 The last three lines actually read:
'Aye, to some frenzy of the mind
For all that we have done's undone
Our speculation but as the wind.'
[Ed.]

his tendency towards 'quaintness' of language remains to be worked out; Mr Menon hardly touches upon it.

This is a very short book, and I would greatly like to see Mr Menon go ahead and write another book on Yeats, starting where this one leaves off. 'If the greatest poet of our times is exultantly ringing in an era of Fascism, it seems a somewhat disturbing symptom,' he says on the last page, and leaves it at that. It *is* a disturbing symptom, because it is not an isolated one. By and large the best writers of our time have been reactionary in tendency, and though Fascism does not offer any real return to the past, those who yearn for the past will accept Fascism sooner than its probable alternatives. But there are other lines of approach, as we have seen during the past two or three years. The relationship between Fascism and the literary intelligentsia badly needs investigating, and Yeats might well be the starting-point. He is best studied by someone like Mr Menon, who can approach a poet primarily as a poet, but who knows that a writer's political and religious beliefs are not excrescences to be laughed away, but something that will leave their mark even on the smallest detail of his work.

D. S. Savage

'The Aestheticism of W. B. Yeats', *The Personal Principle* 1944
(also published in *Kenyon Review*, Winter 1945)

The intellect of man is forced to choose
Perfection of the life, or of the work,
And if it take the second must refuse
A heavenly mansion, raging in the dark.
    (The Choice)

No question is of greater moment for the understanding of modern poetry than that of the relationship of art to life. The various schools and movements of the last hundred years have all been conditioned in one way or another by the disparity existing between the poet's private world and the public world in which he is situated as a social being and which, with the expansion of mechanical civilization, has increasingly separated itself from the private and personal values. In this way all later movements may be seen as offshoots of the Romantic Revival, which was the initial movement of the creative mind in its attempt deliberately to dissociate itself from the realm of collective values and to centre itself upon the personal life of the individual. After the Romantics the movement known in France as Symbolism took the personalistic revolution a stage further, purifying poetry of the social and moralistic elements within romanticism, and in doing this it helped to clarify the essential nature of poetry. But Symbolism in turn led to the weakened, inverted Romanticism of Aestheticism. And it is from the point of view of Aestheticism that we must consider the career of W. B. Yeats.

The Symbolists attempted to purge poetry of all that was foreign to it, to concentrate upon essentials, and this meant the exclusion from art of those elements which in life had receded into the realm of the general, the commonplace. Thus the Symbolists tended to repudiate outer actuality, which they identified with bourgeois civilization, and, retiring into themselves, to concentrate upon their own experience, which became more and more private and personal. The Symbolists, if by that word we mean principally the poets Baudelaire, Verlaine and Mallarmé, were not led by their ideas to a repudiation of life, i.e. of experience. But in their search for an ideal Beauty lying behind the world of appearances their grip on actual life was weakened, and this made it easier for successors to turn away from actuality altogether and to preoccupy themselves with dreams. All art is rooted in experience. The flaw in Symbolism, which helped to make possible its utilization by the exponents of Aestheticism, was its imperfect realization of this truth and its too intense endeavour to break outside the limits of life, its over-specialization and the reactionary tendency which made it concentrate too exclusively upon the exotic, the bizarre. Symbolism and Aestheticism must not, however, be confused. The first is a doctrine of art, springing from artistic practice; the second derives from theory and tends to become an attitude to life – a very different thing. Yet it is not hard to see how this doctrine of art lent itself to the less austere and integral gospel of Aestheticism which, as a way of apprehending life rather than a way of writing poetry, involved a turning away from actuality and a concentration upon certain elements in life which were considered to be superior to the rest.

As is well enough known, Yeats began his career in a literary environment heavily saturated with the Aestheticism of Pater, of Wilde, and of the lesser figures of the 1890s, the dominant influences upon his mind being those of Pater and Villiers de L'Isle Adam, *Axel* being one of his 'sacred books'. Of the three main threads which ran together through his life and thought, each deriving from a common source: that is, Aestheticism, nationalism and occultism, it is the first which may most profitably be taken as the key to his development. Yeats absorbed certain of the doctrines of Symbolism (as preached by Mallarmé) through the medium of Arthur Symons, who called him 'the chief representative of that movement in our country'. Nevertheless, Symbolism meant something quite different to the English followers than to their French masters. Baudelaire, Verlaine and Mallarmé were not aesthetes; they were poets, seekers after reality, visionaries, and the practice of their art was rooted in, although it was an attempt to transcend, experience. It had a religious quality about it, and was in a sense the culmination of a mystical way of life, of apprehension. The aesthetes, however, who took over and adapted for their own uses the doctrines of Symbolism, lacked this intense seriousness. They were dilettantes, and interested less in the ardours of artistic creation than in the use to which artistic precepts could be put in the alleviation of living. The elements in life which aestheticism took to be superior to the others were its poetic elements, and therefore when they took to creative work their art was a reflection of a reflection. Dream and decoration were characteristics of their work because dream and decoration were what they sought for in life. Where the practice of poetry for Mallarmé implied a mystical vision of life, for Yeats it meant a turning away from life and the making of poetry out of moods and dreams, while his 'mysticism', so far from being inherent in his artistic practice, was imported from outside in the form of the alien paraphernalia of theosophy, magic and the rest.

Art can never be divorced entirely from life, from experience, although it can concentrate on certain limited aspects of life and disregard others. The serious artist cannot afford not to take life seriously. For, although art is the creation of a superior world – superior to that of commonplace existence – it must take its elements from life. It is not so much the creation of an ideal world remote from life as the record of the perception of an organic and meaningful order within the disparate universe of day-to-day experience. The life of the poet is thus in the nature of a religious discipline, in which the whole personality engages, to find forms within which experience can be held in organic wholeness, where it becomes illuminated with meaning. Life and art thus become united and yet separate, each dwelling within the other. Art grows from life, and in return illuminates it. Yet they remain distinct, and for their continued existence the boundaries between each must be clearly preserved.

The aesthetes obliterated this distinction. They wanted life to be art – in other words, they wanted a life purged of all its coarse, vulgar, trivial elements. Accordingly they turned away in life from all its inartistic elements. Where the poet's primary impulse may be said to be a 'religious' one, the attempt to grapple with experience and to find order and significance in it, and his artistic impulse only secondary, a continuation of the same impulse – the desire to embody and transmit his vision – the aesthetes made a religion out of art. They inverted the order of the creative mind and replaced the dynamic 'religious' principle at the centre by the static 'artistic' principle and relegated the 'religious' principle to the periphery, where it became immobilized and nullified.

It was such a doctrine of Aestheticism, to which the Symbolists were already pointing the way, that Yeats came to accept. His difference from his fellow-aesthetes of the nineties is shown by his combination of Aestheticism with apparently alien factors – with Irish nationalism and occult supernaturalism. Where the Aestheticism of many of the minor poets of that time, with its colourful bohemian diabolism, shows a reaction from bourgeois social and moral standards, Yeats's attitude appears as remarkably pure of such taints. Yeats did not become an aesthete only through circumstances, his Aestheticism derived straight from a central detachment. And he remained an aesthete throughout his life.

Poets are commonly of two kinds, or of intermixtures of those kinds. There are those creative spirits whose work is a process of self-revelation and self-realization, who proceed from an inner impulse working through their personal experience, through which experience is formulated and compelled into organic patterns. Their work is a personal, dynamic activity deriving from personal necessity, their impulse is essentially spiritual. And there are those men of talent whose work, deriving from a much weaker inner impulse, is much more impersonal, miscellaneous, exterior in character. These latter writers are they who, less vehemently original, are able to share to a much greater extent than the former the values of the society in which they are brought up. In a culturally homogeneous society they will be quite at home, and busy writing the long narratives or pastorals or didactic poems which their society demands. Their main preoccupation will be with the mechanics of their craft, their subject-matter will be readily available, dictated to them by the conventions of their age. And their religious life will be adequately cared for by the current orthodoxy. Yet what happens to writers of this kind in a culturally *disrupted* society – those, in particular, who, through the nature of their gift and mental inclination, remain writers of verse? Deprived on the one hand of that cultural give-and-take between poet and public which sustains the classical poet, and on the other hand lacking that fiery inner dynamism which distinguishes the original poet, the creative mind, will they not easily drift towards the acceptance of such doctrines as the Aestheticism of the *fin-de-siècle*, the doctrines of art for art's sake? This, it seems to me, was the position of Yeats. Essentially a non-dynamic mind, he was saved from dissipation or vulgarization of his gifts by the narrowness of his interests and the strictness of his devotion to his craft. Inwardly he lacked the visionary intensity of the creative spirit, and his art developed peripherally, unaccompanied by any very interesting inward, personal development.

Yeats's view of art as a religious surrogate is expressed in an essay, 'William Blake and the Imagination', written in 1897, in which he says of Blake that

He announced the religion of art, of which no man dreamed in the world he knew. . . . In his time educated people believed that they amused themselves with books of imagination, but that they 'made their souls' by listening to sermons and by doing or by not doing certain things. When they had to explain why serious people like themselves honoured the great poets greatly, they were hard put to it for lack of good reasons. In our time we are agreed that we

'make our souls' out of some one of the great poets of
ancient times, or out of Shelley or Wordsworth, or
Goethe or Balzac, or Flaubert, or Count Tolstoy, in the books
he wrote before he became a prophet and fell into a lesser
order, or out of Mr Whistler's pictures, while we amuse
ourselves, or, at best, make a poorer sort of soul, by
listening to sermons or by doing or by not doing certain
things.

This is hardly an adequate representation of Blake, who, whatever he
might have been, was certainly not cut to the shape of a nineties
aesthete. Yet the passage is enlightening for its revelation of Yeats's
completely impervious Aestheticism, to which he seems to have felt
a special impulse to attach the writings of mystics like Böhme,
Blake and Swedenborg, using them as elements in a purely aesthetic
scheme of his own.[1]

Lacking inner dynamism, the religious impulse to grasp hold of
life and make it surrender its meaning, and lacking, by the exigencies
of his situation, the classical artist's interest in a variety of outward
expressions of life and his participation in an orthodox form of religious worship, Yeats, looking inwards, could see only a static universe
of moods and dreams, and this he translated into his work. The re-
pugnance to the world of actuality which Aestheticism typifies
severely limits the material and scope of art, and in the early Yeats this
is restricted to a small range of dream-imagery used to convey a predominant, static emotion of world-weariness and ineffectual and
objectless longing. 'Dream' is itself a recurrent key-word. There is
no need to give examples of this sort of writing, although *The Song
of the Happy Shepherd* might be given as a good expression of Yeats's
central theme:

The woods of Arcady are dead,
And over is their antique joy;
Of old the world on dreaming fed;

[1] There is a revealing account in the *Autobiographies* of how Yeats, wandering
in a remote part of Ireland and discovering an old castle in a romantic spot, falls
to thinking what an excellent retreat this would make for some esoteric religious
order, and then begins to attempt the formulation of the rule and mysteries of
some such order which could suitably make use of the castle. The inversion is
characteristic.

Grey Truth is now her painted toy;
Yet still she turns her restless head:
But O, sick children of the world,
Of all the many changing things
In dreary dancing past us whirled,
To the cracked tune that Chronos sings,
Words alone are certain good. . . .

Here we note – a significant inversion – that the world *feeds* on dreams, but merely *toys* with Truth.

Practice apart, Yeats's idea of the nature and function of poetry is formulated in certain essays written in the 1890s, from which it is apparent that he regards it as having no commerce with the world of experience, its task being to conjure up certain enchanted states of mind in which the mind is made aware of some bodiless, timeless reality. As he writes in *The Symbolism of Poetry*:

The purpose of rhythm, it has always seemed to me, is to prolong the moment of contemplation, the moment when we are both asleep and awake, which is the one moment of creation, by hushing us with an alluring monotony, while it holds us waking by variety, to keep us in that state of perhaps real trance, in which the mind liberated from the pressure of the will is unfolded in symbols.

And he continues:

If people were to accept the theory that poetry moves us because of its symbolism, what change should one look for in the manner of our poetry? A return to the way of our fathers, a casting out of descriptions of nature for the sake of nature, of the moral law for the sake of the moral law, a casting out of all anecdotes and of that brooding over scientific opinion that so often extinguished the central flame in Tennyson, and of that vehemence that would make us do or not do certain things; or, in other words, we should come to understand that the beryl stone was enchanted by our fathers that it might unfold the pictures in its heart, and not to mirror our own excited faces, or the boughs waving outside the window. With this change of

substance, this return to imagination, this understanding
that the laws of art, which are the hidden laws of the
world, can alone bind the imagination, would come a
change of style, and we would cast out of serious poetry
those energetic rhythms, as of a man running, which are the
invention of the will with its eyes always on something to
be done or undone; and we would seek out those
wavering, meditative, organic rhythms, which are the
embodiment of the imagination, that neither desires nor
hates, because it has done with time, and only wishes to
gaze upon some reality, some beauty. . . .

An Aestheticism of this kind has a similar effect upon both art and
life. As an essentially static attitude to life, an attitude which 'has
done with time', it fails to see meaning or purpose in everyday
living, and therefore turns from this to preoccupy itself with that
which lies outside the borders of normal human life. Thus Yeats'
interest in dreams, in magic, in spiritualism, in astrology, in theosophy,
in anything of a religiose or mystical flavour which did not, like true
religion, invade and claim the right to transform the actual texture of
existence. The texture of existence for Yeats remained, for this
reason, commonplace.

In art, the same applies. To avoid a monotonous reiteration of the
same mood and imagery, this attitude necessitates a continual search
for subject-matter, and this it likewise tends to seek in that which is
exotic and remote. Together with his early vein of dreamy sorrow
and Romantic longing to have 'done with time', Yeats learned to
exploit Irish legend, as later he was to exploit his own personal
legend and Irish nationalist politics. But always his first interest in
these things was as material for poetry.

The static nature of Yeats' life-attitude is revealed in his doctrine
of the Mask, the need for the poet to cultivate a style, both in art and
in life. He wrote in 1909 that 'Style, personality – deliberately adopted
and therefore a Mask – is the only escape from the hot-faced bargainers and the money-changers.' And: 'There is a relation between
discipline and the theatrical sense. If we cannot imagine ourselves as
different from what we are and assume that second self, we cannot
impose a discipline upon ourselves, though we may accept one from

others. Active virtue as distinguished from the passive acceptance of a current code is therefore theatrical, consciously dramatic, the wearing of a Mask. It is the condition of arduous, full life.' And again, late in life, he writes in his diary: '. . . my character is so little myself that all my life it has thwarted me. It has affected my poems, my true self, no more than the character of a dancer affects the movements of a dance.' Throughout his work the negative and static quality of Yeats' personality is revealed. The famous undulating prose style derives directly from it. In his *Essays* we find, not an active, dynamic intellect driving towards some object, not a style, which subordinated to the power of thought, becomes tense, supple and directioned, a vehicle for meaning; but a meandering intermixture of speculation and reminiscence in which the style turns upon itself, becomes ornamental and florid. Everything is shadowy and vague, the ideas are powerless and do not grip, rhetoric and incantation flood the meaning. A similar vagueness and paucity is discovered in the *Autobiographies*. Where we might expect a delineation of the organic growth of an original personality, shaping itself through its manifold contacts with life, we are given a series of blurred impressions, an aesthetic drifting in which scene follows scene but statically and without development. Throughout the *Autobiographies*, Yeats, despite the information he gives about himself, remains a flat and shadowy figure.

Yeats, as we have seen, made a 'religion' of art, which means in effect that he neutralized religion. Religious activity is the dynamism of the soul in its efforts to comprehend ultimate or absolute truth, meaning and purpose, and to bring actual life into a relationship with them. This did not concern Yeats. The effort to bring actual life into the radius of the ultimate implies the possibility of correspondence between the supernatural and the natural worlds, through which the life of man is given meaning and purpose. It is therefore interesting to find, in Yeats, the predication of a supernatural realm, the world of Faery, of the 'Ever Living', which, however, exists in an *antithetical* relationship to the world of humanity. This means that for him human life is lived in a closed circle, a purposeless efflorescence denied the significance which can be given it only by an integral relationship with the absolute, while the supernatural world is such another closed circle. This is a perfect theological justification for

Aestheticism! There are certain inevitable consequences of such a view of the independence of the natural and supernatural spheres. Not only will the supernatural sphere be seen as the realm of the *inhuman*, but the natural will be de-spiritualized. In Yeats' poems and plays, mortals who have felt the attraction of the land of Faery wander about in a hopeless daze, fall into trances, or feel themselves to be under some accursed enchantment which turns life to ashes in their mouth.

Yeats's development from the poet of a monotonous dreamy twilight to the poet of the harsh and acrid light of day is to some extent involved with his changing attitude towards the supernatural. But basically his view remained the same, the alteration being one of emphasis. As a young man he dreamed and wrote about the inhuman world of Faery, and this naturally limited the scope of his art. In middle life he approached nearer humanity, but because of his view of the separation of the two worlds he wrote poetry of disenchantment, was not able to take human life seriously, and in his old age fell back on the de-spiritualized natural world and celebrated the brutal, sensual life of the blood. There is something inhuman, or soulless, about Yeats all the way through.

His concern with fairies was apparent from the start. A juvenile poem began:

A man has the hope of heaven
But soulless a fairy dies . . .
    (*Song of the Faeries*)

and an early poem, *The Stolen Child*, has for refrain:

Come away, O human child!
To the waters and the wild
With a faery, hand in hand,
For the world's more full of weeping than you can understand.

In the early play, *The Land of Heart's Desire*, the theme is of a young woman who is wrapt away to the deathless but inhuman world of the fairies. And in the *Wanderings of Oisin* (1889) this legendary Irish hero who has lived three hundred years with Niamh his bride in the land of the immortals returns only by a mishap to find his years fall suddenly on him and himself condemned to drag out the rest of his existence in a Christianized Ireland which has no place for the ancient heroes. *The Shadowy Waters*, the final version of which appeared in 1910, has a similar theme in that it represents the voyage of the life-rejecting poet and lover Forgael over the 'waste seas' in search of an ideal happiness in that ' "country at the end of the world/Where no child's born but to outlive the moon"'. While he was writing in this vein, Yeats's language was decorative and languorous. But it was not an inexhaustible vein, and a poet of Yeats's artistic conscientiousness could not be content with endless repetition of himself. After *The Shadowy Waters* his verse began to show a more personal bitterness than that contained in the musical melancholy of the early poems. The rather fluent world-weariness gives place to a more acrid dissatisfaction with life. The poem *Adam's Curse* reveals a movement towards realism and away from a lofty, other-world Romanticism, and this trend is continued in *Responsibilities* (1914). The bitterness of disillusionment and waste of life runs through the prefatory verses to the latter collection, in which the poet, addressing his ancestors, requests:

Pardon that for a barren passion's sake,
Although I have come close on forty-nine
I have no child, I have nothing but a book,
Nothing but that to prove your blood and mine.
(*Prologue to Responsibilities*)

It is notable that in these volumes begins utterance occasioned by public events. And here too is the poem in which the poet speaks of the lying days of his youth when he swayed his leaves and flowers in the sun and now prays that he may 'wither into the truth'. In these poems generally the language is barer, more sinewy, the metaphors more exact:

      . . . There's something ails our colt
That must, as if it had not holy blood,
Nor on Olympus leaped from cloud to cloud,
Shiver under the lash, strain, sweat and jolt
As though it dragged road metal. My curse on plays
That have to be set up in fifty ways,

On the day's war with every knave and dolt,
Theatre business, management of men. . . .
    (*The Fascination of What's Difficult*)

and from this time on, it is to be observed, occurs the more frequent
and ironical use of broken rhythm and false rhyme.

The cause of this change of mood, subject-matter and style lay in
Yeats's dissatisfaction with a poetry of dreams which reflected his
dissatisfaction with dreams themselves. Yeats was growing older, the
woman about whom he had woven his Romantic fantasies appeared
with time in a different perspective, he could now admit his to be 'a
barren passion'. 'Theatre business, management of men' had brought
his idealistic visions of a national cultural renascence to the hard test
of practical realization, and in writing for the stage he had had to
adapt his style to the understanding of the theatre audience. And
with all this he had come to be convinced of the wrongness of his
own poetic method of the exclusion of what seemed non-essential
from his search for Beauty. But that his attitude to life had indeed
changed, or more truly that the perspective of his vision of the relationship of the ideal to the actual world had shifted, is made apparent
in the fabular poem entitled *The Two Kings*, in which the old theme
of the human and the supernatural lover is taken up for the last time,
but is given a new and significant twist. In this poem Edain, the
wife of King Eochaid, is tricked to a meeting-place where she is
confronted by a supernatural being who claims her love on the
grounds of pre-natal priority. In spite of all the spirit's arguments of
the transitoriness of mortal love and the superiority of life among the
immortals, Edain rejects him and returns to her husband, to whom
she recounts her adventure. Here, though the variance in emphasis
which differentiates it from previous allegories is apparent, it should
be noted that the alteration is merely one of emphasis: the situation
remains basically the same. Edain rejects the supernatural and
chooses the human, but there is no suggestion that human life is anything more than merely mortal, that there is any mitigation of the
absolute cleavage between natural and supernatural. The inference
clearly is that Yeats has turned away from an impossible ideal for the
sake of a reality known to be and accepted as unspiritual, and which
is still, therefore, something less than human.

In *The Hour Before Dawn* the altered emphasis is brought out even more unmistakably. The beggar, 'a cursing rogue with a merry face' who stumbles on a deep hollow where he finds a drinker with a tub of enchanted beer which will keep him asleep till the day of judgement when all phenomena will pass away, represents the acceptance of life; the drinker, whom he curses and pummels and flees from with prayers and curses on his lips, is an obvious symbol of rejection. The reversal here in Yeats's implied attitude to 'dreams' is complete. But here again human life, whose values the poem implicitly decides for, is represented by a beggar, sensual humanity at its commonest level. To the same period belongs to the poem *Beggar to Beggar Cried* which, foreshadowing Yeats's later 'frenzied' manner, is also a fairly frank piece of self-revelation.

The volume in which Yeats approaches most nearly to the condition of humanity, in which there is some indication of an awareness of the pathos, irony and suffering within human existence, *The Wild Swans at Coole*, is also that which marks Yeats's weakest level of creation. There is little dramatizing here, and less adventitious supernaturalism. The book conveys, as a whole, an impression of a cold, ashy sadness, the sadness of the unachieved and the unrealized; but this sadness is not fully faced and poetically overcome, and it lingers miasmally around the verge of the poems, where its effect is desolate and depressing. The total effect is only to show how far from a deep and rich human sympathy Yeats really is. His lack of grasp is reflected in a technical laxity, and some of the poems, *The People*, *The Dawn*, *The Sad Shepherd*, *Presences*, *Broken Dreams* and others, are garrulous and prosy, while such didactic pieces as *The Phases of the Moon* and *Ego Dominus Tuus* suffer from a flatness where all is on the surface, mere dissertation. The movement towards a deeper sympathy with and a greater honesty of approach to human life is partial only, and is not a success, nor is it surprising to find in such a poem as *The Collar-Bone of a Hare*, to me a strangely unpleasing and distasteful poem, what amounts to a confession of inhumanity. The slightly 'touched' irresponsibility of this, the half-idiotic cackle at the 'old bitter world where they marry in churches', is not pretty, particularly in the reminiscential, old-mannish context of the book.

Yeats was not happy with humanity: he refused to suffer. Nor did any miracle occur to alter his approach and cause him to accept

human life in a far deeper sense than he had ever done hitherto·
Instead, after the hesitations of *The Wild Swans at Coole*, he made a
sudden and decisive movement towards entrenching himself in his old
supernatural-natural dualism. *Ego Dominus Tuus* and *The Phases of
the Moon*, besides the prose essay *Per Amica Silentia Lunae*, has shown
his gropings towards some kind of private esoteric system, and now
in the years after the Great War, in the early days of his marriage,
there came the ideas and inspirations which were to result in the
work eventually published under the title, *A Vision*.

Yeats himself described the system expounded in this book as a
construction which enabled him to purge his poetry of explanation
and abstraction and to find a simplicity he had previously sought in
vain. The system itself is entirely peculiar to Yeats, it is doubtful
whether it would be of use to any other person. The theses upon which
it is built are all put forward as *a priori* arguments; the entire construction is arbitrary and seems to have no nexus in real existence.
The material upon which it is based purports to have been supplied
by 'spirits', and it is entirely in keeping that when Yeats, as he says,
offered to spend the rest of his life explaining and piecing together
the material they gave him, they should have replied. 'No, we have
come to give you metaphors for poetry.' It seems clear that the purpose of this peculiar and ingenious system in relation to Yeats was
purely functional. Yeats's static aestheticism precluded him from the
living pursuit of truth within experience. Truth was of no interest to
him, he wanted either material for poetry or material for that which
would provide the pre-conditions for poetry, in this case an idiosyncratic, self-sufficient system which, cutting arbitrarily across all living
currents of thought, would enshrine his own feelings about life and
justify his concentration upon his deep and narrow vein of poetry.
'Some will ask,' he wrote in *A Vision*,

whether I believe in the actual existence of my circuits of
sun and moon. . . . To such a question I can but answer that
if sometimes, overwhelmed by miracle as all men must be
when in the midst of it, I have taken such periods literally,
my reason has soon recovered; and now that the system
stands out clearly in my imagination I regard them as
stylistic arrangements of experience comparable to the cubes

in the drawing of Wyndham Lewis and to the ovoids in the sculpture of Brancusi. They have helped me to hold in a single thought reality and justice.

The system here expounded confirms Yeats's fast division between natural and supernatural, with the difference that here the 'supernatural' as spiritual reality is virtually eliminated, existing only as a blind power driving the wheel of birth and rebirth in which man and the cosmos are involved. The system is rigidly deterministic. Man, according to it, is an inert substance caught up in a cyclic mechanism of successive incarnations in which he passes from pure subjectivity to pure objectivity, the tension between which poles of being determines fate, life and character. Human life exists for no purpose beyond its own mere being, nor is there seemingly any escape from the wheel. The static, deterministic nature of the cosmic process precludes progress of any kind, even individual striving. Thus, by implication, moral effort is redundant, both as operating within the personal life and as directed towards the maintenance of the equilibrium of society. The individual is freed from all responsibility, since everything is regulated automatically by the cosmic mechanism, and there is no possibility of really changing or improving things. While war, famine, destruction of civilizations, are all inevitable and preordained, this is cancelled out by the inevitability of renewal and reconstruction, so that catastrophes are not to be taken very seriously and may, indeed, be accepted with rejoicing as providing a little interest and excitement in the tedium of a prearranged existence. There is obviously no place for the humane emotions, love, pity and the rest. All the individual can do is to accept the life thus thrust upon him and, since there is really no alternative, exult in it. Vitality becomes a value in its own right.

It will be seen how such a system fitted in with Yeats's predilections, and how it helped to make possible the attitude to life of hard, scornful acceptance out of which the poems in *The Tower* and *The Winding Stair* drew their origin. Freed from all uncertainties he could go on to that celebration of blind, passionate, aimless life out of which some of his most magnificent verse arose:

I am content to live it all again
And yet again, if it be life to pitch

Into the frog-spawn of a blind man's ditch,
A blind man battering blind men;
Or into that most fecund ditch of all,
The folly that man does
Or must suffer, if he woos
A proud woman not kindred of his soul.

I am content to follow to its source
Every event in action or in thought;
Measure the lot; forgive myself the lot!
When such as I cast out remorse
So great a sweetness flows into the breast
We must laugh and we must sing,
We are blest by everything,
Everything we look upon is blest.
   (Dialogue of Self and Soul)

Yeats's poetry has received a greater degree of recognition than that of any other modern British poet. Therefore no harm will be done if for a moment we refuse to be hypnotized by his reputation and probe more critically into the nature of his achievement than current valuations might seem to encourage. And that there are unsatisfactory features about his poetry seems to me apparent.

The sense of dissatisfaction with the poetry of Yeats – to speak from my own experience – is faint at the first but increases after familiarity, when the mind has recovered from its first bedazzlement and begins to grope after a permanent relationship, to find a place for it in its life. And Yeats's poetry, it seems to me, is one which, though it compels our admiration, contains an element (or the absence of such) which prevents us from finding a place for it close to our heart. It is too remote, both too characteristic and too impersonal; it is, again for want of a better word, too inhuman. We can live with a speaking or a singing voice, but not with a bellow or shriek pitched violently or ecstatically beyond the range of the human ear. This inhumanness is not a feature of the later verse only. It runs throughout Yeats's work. I have never been able to think of Yeats's work in the abstract or to read a number of poems concretely without receiving the impression of a sort of ghostly shining phosphorescence, and this impression puzzled me for a long time until I began to see its origin and meaning.

It is this peculiar quality which imparts an atmosphere of unreality to his work. This unrealness is very noticeable in the early poetry:

You need but lift a pearl-pale hand,
And bind up your long hair and sigh;
And all men's hearts must burn and beat;
And candle-like foam on the dim sand,
And stars climbing the dew-dropping sky,
Live but to light your passing feet.
    (*He Gives His Beloved Certain Rhymes*)

This is very delightful; but nothing could be falser, more exaggerated, more out of touch with life. We are able to accept the poem only if we accept the poet's premises and permit ourselves to enter into his dream. Now although as Yeats developed he left behind this dim world of dreams and began to incorporate more of concrete imagery into his verse, and although a dreamy vagueness of mood gave place to the sharpness of disenchantment and bitterness or a kind of ironical joy, nevertheless he retained his ineradicable tendency to exaggerated statement the effect of which was necessarily to place his poetry at a remove from human life and sympathy. Even in his middle period his love-poetry is born out of a dramatic attitude rather than out of an honest relationship to experience. This exaggeration and over-heightening, this indulgence in dramatics, is exemplified by the repeated use of hyperbolic phrases and of resounding words whose effect is to inflate the meaning. Some of Yeats's favourite words of his later period: passionate, rage, turbulent, frenzy, murderous, agony, miraculous, bitter, blind, wild, he overworked no less than, during his early period, he overworked words like: dim, dreams, pale, desolate, sorrow and the rest. Yeats carries off his use of these words, and the over-dramatic attitude implied in that use, in his later verse no less successfully than in his earlier work; but they do not ring any truer to the perceptive ear. As with the early poems, one must grant the poet his own ground, which means here entering the remote world of reminiscence and reverie which he has built up around his lonely ego, before one is able to accept his work. Yeats's art persuades us to do so. But his is a world which we cannot endure, or interest ourselves in, for long. Yeats's pattern of experience is provincial not only thematically but spiritually, and while we can force it into temporary relationship with our own we cannot truly make it ours.

This hyperbolism of Yeats which on familiarity becomes wearisome and hollow, and which sometimes leads him into tremendous, nonsensical asseverations, finds a counterpart in his lack of contemporaneity, itself a grave fault in any poet when, as nearly always, it signifies a poverty of observation which in turn reflects an incapability before the fullness of experience. On Yeats's part it is certain that it does reflect an inability to overcome and bring into the scope of his art more than a strictly limited range of experience, namely, that which lends itself to a stylized 'dramatic' treatment. It is not necessary to suppose that no modern poem can be regarded as valid unless it contains repeated references to pylons, gas-works or grain-elevators to realize the truth that we live in a world which is full of these and similar things, that these therefore constitute much of the background of our experience, and that in mastering experience and translating it into the terms of poetry we are bound to use the images with which experience presents us. Yeats ignores the contemporary scene, which means that he ignores much of his own experience, and when he attempts at times to incorporate a contemporary reference into his verse requiring the exploitation of modern imagery the result is not fortunate. Modern war, for instance, is hardly presented adequately to the imagination in his otherwise admirable poem *Lapis Lazuli*, when he writes:

For everybody knows or else should know
That if nothing drastic is done
Aeroplane and Zeppelin will come out,
Pitch like King Billy bomb-balls in
Until the town lie beaten flat.

Yeats is much happier in the same poem when he is describing an antique work of art:

Two Chinamen, behind them a third,
Are carved in lapis lazuli,
Over them flies a long-legged bird,
A symbol of longevity;
The third, doubtless a serving man,
Carries a musical instrument.

Every discoloration of the stone,
Every accidental crack or dent,
Seems a water-course or an avalanche,
Or lofty slope where it still snows
Though doubtless plum or cherry-branch
Sweetens the little half-way house
Those Chinamen climb towards, and I
Delight to imagine them seated there. . . .

And might it not also be possible to view Yeats's attachment to an
idiosyncratic use of mechanical verse-metres in the light of his insen-
sibility to those rhythmical currents in the life of our time which
have been influential in determining the subtler verse-forms of more
sensitively contemporary poets? Yeats's complete absence of discrim-
ination in his response to contemporary work – *vide* the unfortunate
Oxford Book of Modern Verse – seems to bear this out.

The substance of the poems in *The Tower* and *The Winding Stair*,
superficially so impressively full, dwindles on acquaintance and in-
vestigation to a very small residue. Yeats's exploitation of his personality and of his personal history is consciously dramatic. The resounding dramatic *effect* achieved, there is very little to hold on to. The
poem sequence which gives its title to *The Tower* opens effectively
enough, and the second section promises to unfold the poem well,
with:

I pace upon the battlements and stare
On the foundations of a house, or where
Tree, like a sooty finger, starts from the earth;
And send imagination forth
Under the day's declining beam, and call
Images and memories
From ruin or from ancient trees,
For I would ask a question of them all.

But thereafter, instead of a fulfilment of the expectancy aroused in
these opening lines, we have – a descent to anecdote:

Beyond that ridge lived Mrs French, and once
When every silver candlestick or sconce

Lit up the dark mahogany and the wine,
A serving man that could divine
That most respected lady's every wish,
Ran and with the garden shears
Clipped an insolent farmer's ears
And brought them in a little covered dish.

And the poem continues in such a reminiscential, rambling, inconsequent manner, only held together by the poet's rhythmical and rhetorical skill.

The poems in these two volumes, indeed, bear out the implications of attitude made in such a poem as *The Hour Before Dawn*. Here sensual human life is celebrated: but a life which, when detached from all intercourse with spiritual meaning, is regarded as an aimless and meaningless proliferation. Yeats's creed consists in the not very interesting or subtle exaltation of brute vitality:

Whatever stands in field or flood,
Bird, beast, fish or man,
Mare or stallion, cock or hen,
Stands in God's unchanging eye
In all the vigour of its blood;
In that faith I live or die.

In choosing 'perfection of the work' in false opposition to perfection of the life', Yeats, through his artistic devotedness, was able to develop his poetry without developing at the same time a wider and deeper insight into life, and his early other-worldliness, springing from a defect of deep and warm humanity, being too rarefied and phantasmal, found its level in the blood, lust and mud of the last poems. For Yeats there is no human mean between the supernatural and the bestial, the inhuman purity of the moon and the animal ragings of the blood. The culmination of this tendency is to be seen in Yeats's last works, *A Full Moon in March* and the *Last Poems and Plays*. In the play which gives its title to the former volume, the virginal Queen, 'whose emblem is the moon', promises to give herself to whatever man can move her by his song. A swineherd, dressed in 'foul rags' and with hair 'more foul and ragged than' his rags, and with 'scratched foul flesh', comes to sing before her:

I tended swine, when I first heard your name.
I rolled among the dung of swine and laughed.
What do I know of beauty?

And when the Queen asks what she gains if, proclaiming his song the best, she leaves her throne for his sake, he answers:

A song – the night of love,
An ignorant forest and the dung of swine,

adding to himself:

She shall bring forth her farrow in the dung.

Insulted, the Queen has the swineherd beheaded. The severed head being brought to her, she takes it in her hands and dances, pressing her lips to the lips of the head. In the *Last Poems and Plays* we have the glorification of violence and war, the celebration of sexuality, the same inner emptiness revealed either in an expression of a sense of personal futility or in the insistence upon a hysterical and nihilistic exultation. In certain of the poems, *Why Should Not Old Men Be Mad?*, *Are You Content?*, *What Then?*, Yeats questions himself, but then drowns any conceivable reply with a randy ballad or a ballad of violence, a political lampoon or a marching song. 'Come swish around, my pretty punk' and 'What shall I do for pretty girls/Now my old bawd is dead' alternate with 'The Ghost of Roger Casement/ Is beating on the door' and 'The Roaring Tinker if you like,/But Mannion is my name,/And I beat up the common sort/And think it is no shame'. In *The Circus Animals' Desertion* the poet speaks of his search for a theme, enumerates half regretfully, half ironically, his earlier use of legendary subjects, and concludes:

Now that my ladder's gone,
I must lie down where all the ladders start,
In the foul rag-and-bone shop of the heart. . . .

while in *The Spur* he confesses:

You think it horrible that lust and rage
Should dance attention on my old age;
They were not such a plague when I was young;
What else have I to spur me into song?

Certain of these last poems have a barbaric beauty and splendour, although it is a splendour of desolation and emptiness, and an inhuman beauty. But what are we to think of a poet who, with all his occasional impressiveness, is in one moment capable of such a descent into banality as the following:

Irish poets, learn your trade
Sing whatever is well made,
Scorn the sort now growing up
All out of shape from toe to top,
Their unremembering hearts and heads
Base-born products of base beds.
Sing the peasantry, and then
Hard-riding country gentlemen,
The holiness of monks, and after
Porter-drinkers' randy laughter;
Sing the lords and ladies gay
That were beaten into the clay
Through seven heroic centuries;
Cast your mind on other days
That we in coming days may be
Still the indomitable Irishry.
  (Under Ben Bulben)

The indomitable Irishry! It is one of the enigmas of Yeats as a poet that he should be capable of mixing real tragic grandeur with such fatal vulgarity and commonplaceness. Whatever may be the conventional verdict on his work, it is certain that at its centre is a hollowness which time is bound increasingly to reveal.

Other things apart, Yeats is a demonstration of the superficiality of the 'Romantic-classical' antithesis as commonly applied to poetry. On the surface, there has never been a more 'Romantic' poet than Yeats, with his self-dramatization, his dandyism, his exaggerated emotionalism (springing from an inner coldness: one thinks of his impossible love and his marriage in middle age) and the rest. Yet, probing beneath the surface, we find a contradictory conservatism and reliance upon outward conditions. The qualities and conditions of a stable, hierarchical social order in which poetry and the poet would have their recognized official places. As Mr MacNeice says in his study of Yeats:

His desire for a creed and for poetry whose imagery, as well as ideas, is based on that creed, is in tune with his desire for schools of poetry. In spite of his Romantic genealogy he had a Roman liking for the poet in a formal niche; poets were to be members of a priesthood, handing down their mysteries to their successors, and conferring with one another when they wished to develop or modify their ritual.

This is nothing if not retrogressive. The fact that he regarded the poet's function as ideally a public (i.e. impersonal) one is shown in several of his remarks about his own poetry during his later life, and by his reversion to the 'bard' in his ballad-writing on Irish political themes.

We cannot understand Yeats until we realize that his inner attitude was quite static; his philosophy, his politics, his life and his work were all shaped by this fact. Custom and ceremony are the conditions he exalts when he writes, in *A Prayer for My Daughter*, of the perquisites of the good life. His 'Romantic' peculiarities were developed only as a substitute for that acceptable external framework of convention and custom which, given him by a different society, a different age, would have proved him indubitably a 'classical' artist. Yeats flaunts his 'personality', but in reality is an extremely impersonal artist; his personality is a 'mask', a dramatic convenience for the writing of verse; true personality is not idiosyncratic but anonymous, and does not flaunt itself. Yeats did not place any high value upon the personal qualities and upon human personality itself. He evaded Christianity, which exalts and enshrines the values of human personality(and which brings the supernatural down into the natural), and it is not therefore surprising to find that he took great pride in his ancestry, his family, the nation of his birth. The fact that he toyed with fascism in his later years and took a keen interest in eugenics (racial purity) is but another revelation of his anti-personalism. In default of a principle of personal dynamism within himself, and of such a stable classical order and accepted orthodoxy, Yeats assembled a homemade, gimcrack order and 'religious' system out of the exotic fragments he found here and there beyond the borders of commonplace life; thus his apparent Romanticism. An artificer or bard, without a context, without standards he could accept from outside and without an inner spiritual pressure directed upon life, he turned inwards to centre his attention upon art, he became an aesthete, and there resulted the development which is revealed in his work: a development in a vacuum.

John Crowe Ransom

from 'The Severity of Mr Savage', *Kenyon Review*, vol. 7
Winter 1945

If Yeats had been merely an unreflective lyric poet without torturing religious preoccupations, I suppose Mr Savage would not have brought charges against him. Otherwise it must have occurred to us that Aestheticism was probably a vain thing, but that one thing surely malignant was religionism. I am glad I do not have to say that at Mr Savage's expense. But actually Yeats tried one religion after another, and what is left of Mr Savage's complaint is that he never arrived at the true one. This is not a language that I should care to use, and here I must be careful once again, this time to say that it is Mr Savage's complaint only in effect, and that he does not commit himself actually to a locution of such specific complacency.

There must be many kinds of aspiration and conviction that express the truly religious spirit. It need not matter much if the vanities of the dandiacal body irrupt into one's poems, nor even if one accepts the ravage of old age with the poorest grace. The noble poems of Yeats's maturity are too many and too unmistakable to deny, the reality is too compelling, and the quality of the metaphysic is too religious.

In this sense I will quote a very little, in order not to finish this note upon an argument but in the immediate presence of the poetic fact. I could use some splendid passages out of *The Tower*, the rich poem whose anecdote about Mrs French is objectionable to Mr Savage. But I will take a more typical passage from *Meditations in Time of Civil War*, another poem in which the poet forgets to temper his natural arrogance, and specifically the section called 'My Descendants'. Like an Israelitish patriarch the poet regards himself as the worthy descendant of his ancestors, and like a man acutely sensitive to fact allows for the event of the degeneration of his line after him:

And what if my descendants lose the flower
Through natural declension of the soul,
Through too much business with the passing hour,
Through too much play, or marriage with a fool?
May this laborious stair and this stark tower
Become a roofless ruin that the owl
May build in the cracked masonry and cry
Her desolation to the desolate sky.

The *Primum Mobile* that fashioned us
Has made the very owls in circles move;
And I, that count myself most prosperous,
Seeing that love and friendship are enough,
For an old neighbour's friendship chose the house
And decked and altered it for a girl's love,
And know whatever flourish and decline
These stones remain their monument and mine.

Though I could cite many passages from Yeats that are religious in a more conventional style, I cannot but regard this as a genuine religious utterance. For it is magnificent, being both large and intense; it is uncompromising in its sense of values; and it is austere and humble enough in its expectations.

Hugh Kenner

'The Sacred Book of the Arts', *Gnomon* 1958
(first published 1955)

The way out is via the door, how is it no one will use this method? (Confucius)

Catechism

Q In *Among School Children* we read of a 'Ledaean body'. Where are we to seek information about that?

A Not from the mythological dictionary, but as everybody knows, from the poem *Leda and the Swan*.

Q And where is this poem to be discovered?

A On the previous page.

Q Very good. You are on the way to noticing something. Now consider the last stanza of *Among School Children*. After an apostrophe to 'self born mockers of man's enterprise' we read:

> Labour is blossoming or dancing where
> The body is not bruised to pleasure soul,
> Nor beauty born out of its own despair,
> Nor blear-eyed wisdom out of midnight oil.
> O chestnut-tree, great-rooted blossomer,
> Are you the leaf, the blossom or the bole?
> O body swayed to music, O brightening glance,
> How can we know the dancer from the dance?

That 'where' is by its placing in the line made very emphatic. Its gesture implies a place or a state intensely real to Yeats. Does he print lines elsewhere that might be taken as descriptive of that place or state?

A He does; in *Colonus' Praise*, after invoking 'immortal ladies' who 'tread the ground/Dizzy with harmonious sound' (which invocation of course we are meant to connect with 'O body swayed to music'), he goes on,

> And yonder in the gymnasts' garden thrives
> The self-sown, self-begotten shape that gives
> Athenian intellect its mastery. . . .

the self-born no longer a mocker, body and intellect thriving in unison, neither bruised to pleasure the other; and the miraculous olive-tree that, as he goes on to tell us, symbolizes that perfection, is to be connected with the domestic 'chestnut-tree, great-rooted blossomer' of the famous peroration.

Q Excellent, excellent. And now tell me where, in relation to *Among School Children*, this song in praise of Colonus is to be found?

A On the following page.

Q You are answering today with admirable point and economy.

Now tell me: were the three poems you have mentioned as bearing upon one another written, as it were, simultaneously?

A I find by the chronology at the back of Mr Ellmann's *Identity of Yeats* that the first was written nearly four years before the last. I notice furthermore that the arrangement of the poems in the volume we are discussing, *The Tower*, is far from chronological. *Sailing to Byzantium* (26 September 1926), with which it begins, was written *after* *Among School Children* (14 June 1926), which is located two-thirds of the way through the book. In between there are poems dating as far back as 1919, and the volume ends with *All Souls' Night*, 1920.

Q We should be lost without these American scholars. You would say, then, that the arrangement of poems within the volume was deliberate rather than casual or merely chronological?

A I would indeed. But wait, I have just noticed something else. In *Sailing to Byzantium*, at the beginning of the book, the speaker has abandoned the sensual land of 'dying generations' and is asking the 'sages standing in God's holy fire' to emerge from it and be his singing-masters. At the end, in *All Souls' Night*, he announces that he has 'mummy truths to tell' and would tell them to some mind that despite cannon-fire from every quarter of the world, can stay

Wound in mind's pondering
As mummies in the mummy-cloth are wound.

In the former poem he was calling forth sages to teach him; throughout *All Souls' Night* he is calling up ghosts to hear him. Pupil has become master.

Q How often must I enjoin precision on you? It is the land of sensual *music* he has left: bird-song, love-songs. *All Souls' Night* opens, by contrast, with the formal tolling of 'the great Christ Church Bell', like the 'great cathedral gong' that dissipates 'night walkers' song' in *Byzantium*. Furthermore, there is a calling up of ghosts near the beginning of the book too, in the poem called *The Tower*, where he summons them not (as later) to instruct them but to ask a question. What else have you noticed?

A Why, it gets more and more deliberate as one examines it. He began the volume by renouncing his body; he ends it in the possession of disembodied thought:

Such thought – such thought have I that hold it tight
Till meditation master all its parts . . .
Such thought, that in it bound
I need no other thing,
Wound in mind's wandering
As mummies in the mummy-cloth are wound.

Earlier he had expected to need the body of a jeweled bird.
Through that volume, *The Tower*, runs a dramatic progression if
I ever saw one. And the presence of such a progression, once it is
discerned, modifies all the parts. Now I have a theory. . . .

Q Stop, you grow prolix. Write it out, write it out as an explanation
that I may read at my leisure. And please refrain from putting in
many footnotes that tire the eyes.

Explanation

Among School Children, to begin with that again, is as centrifugal a
major poem as exists in the language. Whoever encounters it out of
the context Yeats carefully provided for it, for instance in an Anthology Appointed to be Taught in Colleges, will find himself after
twenty minutes seeking out who Leda was and what Yeats made of
her, and identifying the daughter of the swan with Maud Gonne
(excursus on her biography, with anecdotes) and determining in what
official capacity, through what accidents of a destiny sought and
ironically accepted, the poet found himself doubling as school
inspector. So true is this of the majority of his major poems, that the
anthologists generally restrict themselves to his minor ones, his critics
practise mostly a bastard mode of biography, and his exegetists a
Pécuchet's industry of copying parallel passages from *A Vision* (first
and second versions), from letters and diaries, from unpublished
drafts, and occasionally from other poems. Even Dr Leavis calls his
poetry 'little more than a marginal comment on the main activities
of his life'. Occasionally someone feels that Yeats's poems need to be
reclaimed for the modern critic's gallery of self-sufficient objects,
and rolling up his sleeves offers to explain *Two Songs from a Play*
without benefit of *A Vision*. This requires several thousand words of
quasi-paraphrase. The least gesture of unannounced originality on a
poet's part suffices to baffle critical presupposition completely, and the

two regnant presuppositions of the mid-twentieth century – the old one, that poems reflect lives and announce doctrines, the new one, that poems are self-contained or else imperfect – are rendered helpless by Yeats's most radical, most casual, and most characteristic maneuver: he was an architect, not a decorator; he didn't accumulate poems, he wrote books.

It would have been surprising if he had not, preoccupied as he was with sacred writings. When he functioned as a critic, as in his essay on Shelley or his useful generalizations on Shakespeare, it was the oeuvre, not the fragment, that held his attention.

The place to look for light on any poem is in the adjacent poems, which Yeats placed adjacent to it because they belonged there. And the unit in which to inspect and discuss his development is not the poem or sequence of poems but the volume, at least from *Responsibilities* (1914) to *A Full Moon in March* (1935).[1] This principle is sometimes obvious enough; anyone can see that the six songs following *The Three Bushes* belong in its entourage, or that *The Phases of the Moon* incorporates the half-dozen poems appended to it. Such obvious instances are, however, slightly misleading; one is apt to think of the main poem as not quite completed, raveling out into lyrical loose ends, or not quite definitive in scope, making shift to appropriate, like a handful of minnows, lesser foci of energy that ought to have been brought within its sphere at the time of composition. In the age of Eliot, the poet is supposed to gather his interests and impulses and discharge them utterly in a supreme opus every so often, and evades this responsibility at the price of being not quite a major poet. Those weren't the terms in which Yeats was thinking; we misread him if we suppose either that the majority of the poems are casual or that in each he was trying for a definitive statement of all that, at the time of composition, he was.

Men Improve with the Years looks like an attempt of this kind; it cuts off, of course, too neatly. The poet was once young, and a lover; now he is a monument, and no lady will love him. The quality of the rhetoric is impeccable, but the poem, on some acquaintance, appears to reduce itself to its mere theme, and that theme so simple-minded as to invite biographical eking out. The unspoken

1 It isn't clear how much, if any, of *Last Poems* was arranged by Yeats himself. [But see Curtis Bradford, *Yeats at Work*, 1965, for clarification. Ed.]

premise of Yeats criticism is that we have to supply from elsewhere
– from his life or his doctrines – a great deal that didn't properly get
into the poems: not so much to explain the poems as to make them
rich enough to sustain the reputation. It happens, however, that
Men Improve with the Years has for context not Yeats's biography
but two poems about a man who did not undergo that dubious improvement: at the climax of *In Memory of Major Robert Gregory* we
read,

Some burn damp faggots, others may consume
The entire combustible world in one small room
As though dried straw, and if we turn about
The bare chimney is gone black out
Because the work had finished in that flare.
Soldier, scholar, horseman, he,
As 'twere all life's epitome,
What made us dream that he could comb grey hair?

Dried straw, damp faggots; in *Men Improve with the Years* we discover a 'burning youth' succeeded by water:

A weather-worn, marble triton
Among the streams.

Major Robert Gregory, 'all life's epitome', concentrated all in an
instantaneous conflagration; the speaker of 'Men Improve with the
Years' has advanced serially through phases one can enumerate to the
condition of a statue. Statues, of course, have their immortality,
their nobility of arrested gesture. Yeats isn't being picturesque in
specifying the kind of statue; tritons blow their wreathèd horns,
and a marble one would be puffing soundlessly at a marble trumpet,
like an official Poet; not even in the open sea, but amid the fountains
of Major Gregory's mother's garden. The poem isn't a small clearing
in which Yeats sinks decoratively to rest, it is a counter-rhetoric to
the rhetorical memorial poem. It doesn't come quite on the heels of
that poem, however; between the two we hear the dry tones of the
Irish Airman ('soldier, scholar, horseman') himself:

Those that I fight I do not hate,
Those that I guard I do not love.

Midway between Yeats's contrasting rhetorics, Gregory (*An Irish Airman Foresees His Death*) hasn't a rhetoric but a style. He wasn't exhilarated by the prospect of consuming 'the entire combustible world'; 'a lonely impulse of delight' redeems from calculation the decision born of an explicit disenchantment:

I balanced all, brought all to mind,
The years to come seemed waste of breath,
A waste of breath the years behind
In balance with this life, this death.

Those are the words from which we pass to these:

I am worn out with dreams:
A weather-worn, marble triton
Among the streams.
    (*Men Improve with the Years*)

– the traditional sonorities, the diction ('my burning youth!'), the conventional elegances of cadence evoking (while just evading) a 'literary' tradition against which is poised the next poem in the volume: *The Collarbone of a Hare*.

Would I could cast a sail on the water
Where many a king has gone
And many a king's daughter,
And alight at the comely trees and the lawn,
The playing upon pipes and the dancing,
And learn that the best thing is
To change my loves while dancing
And pay but a kiss for a kiss.

This live rhythm quickens a remote, folkish idiom, unsonorous and wry. *Men Improve with the Years* seems in retrospect heavier than ever. In this pastoral kingdom not only are there no marble tritons (its tone has nothing in common with that of the *Land of Heart's Desire* where the Princess Edain was 'busied with a dance'), but the newcomer's characteristic gesture is to look back through 'the collarbone of a hare' and laugh at 'the old bitter world where they marry in churches' with a lunatic peasant slyness. The symbol of trivial death proffers a peephole or spyglass; it doesn't, as death is reputed to do, open vistas. You can squint with its aid at the old world, from fairyland. Yeats is trying out different arrangements of a poetic universe with the blunt fact of death in it. In the next poem he reverses the situation and rearranges the perspective. Stretched for nonchalant slumber 'On great grandfather's battered tomb', Beggar Billy sees the dancing-world: not

> the comely trees and the lawn,
The playing upon pipes and the dancing,

but

> a dream
Of sun and moon that a good hour
Bellowed and pranced in the round tower,

That golden king and that wild lady
Sang till stars began to fade,
Hands gripped in hands, toes close together,
Hair spread on the wind they made;
That lady and that golden king
Could like a brace of blackbirds sing.
  (*Under the Round Tower*)

This is the celebrated music of the spheres; and Beggar Billy decides that 'great grandfather's battered tomb' that educes such noisy and energetic visions is no place for him. So the book, having degraded its initial persona to beggardom (there are curious analogies with *Lear*) and preoccupied itself with themes and images of death until it has set the celestial boiler shop going, takes leave of this theme for a time and turns to quieter matters like the dead lovers Solomon and Sheba.

That initial persona now wants looking at. The volume we are examining, *The Wild Swans at Coole*, began not with the Gregory elegy – that is its second poem – but with the poem *The Wild Swans at Coole* itself: an image of personal dejection ('And now my heart is sore') that uses the permanent glory of the swans to silhouette the transience attending human beings who must keep their feet on the ground and try to assimilate the 'brilliant creatures' by counting them.

All's changed since I, hearing at twilight
The first time on this shore,
The bell-beat of their wings above my head
Trod with a lighter tread.

Unwearied still, lover by lover,
They clamber in the cold
Companionable streams or climb the air;
Their hearts have not grown old; ...

'All's changed' is a mood, not a summary of presented facts; this initial poem confines itself to a wholly familiar *Angst*, a setting documented in a spare but traditional manner –

The trees are in their autumn beauty,
The woodland paths are dry –

a specified month and time of day, a poet who does and thinks and feels nothing unusual, verbs no more than inert copulas, and swans that are scarcely more than swans. We are in the presence of a mind reflecting nature and then reflecting Locke-wise upon what it reflects: tantalized – not teased, but undergoing the pangs of Tantalus – because it must undergo change while nature – the swans – remains other, 'unwearied still'. Though none of the great Romantics could have written it with such economy and directness, the poem remains within, say, the Coleridgean orbit of experience.

It is upon experience resignedly ordered in this plane that the brilliant death of Major Robert, the Irish Airman, impinges; he took wing like the swans; his heart has not grown old; he demonstrated that it lay within human capacity to

consume
The entire combustible world in one small room
As though dried straw.

This death and the contemplation of the poet's impotent middle age ferment and interact throughout the volume, entoiling other materials, discovering unexpected resonances in the pastoral mode (*Shepherd and Goatherd*) and in the lingering end of Mabel Beardsley (*Upon a Dying Lady*), never for long oblivious of the piercing hypothesis that maximum human intensity coincides with human extinction. What

is arrived at is an extinction not of the person but of his natural context.
At the end of the volume October water no more mirrors a natural
sky:

On the grey rock of Cashel the mind's eye
Has called up the cold spirits that are born
When the old moon has vanished from the sky
And the new still hides her horn.
  (The Double Vision of Michael Robartes)

The mind's eye, no longer the Newtonian optic; and that moon
isn't nature's moon. Nor does the mind's eye see swans that fly away,
but calls up three arresting figures – one a sphinx – observed not in
placidity but in active intensity:

Mind moved but seemed to stop
As 'twere a spinning-top.

In contemplation had those three so wrought
Upon a moment, and so stretched it out
That they, time overthrown,
Were dead yet flesh and bone.
    (ibid.)

The poem – and the volume – closes on a note of triumph; Yeats
tells us he 'arranged' – deliberate word – his vision in a song –

Seeing that I, ignorant for so long
Had been rewarded thus
In Cormac's ruined house.
    (ibid.)

The poles of this volume are its first and last poems, *The Wild
Swans at Coole* and *The Double Vision of Michael Robartes*, as the poles
of *The Tower* are *Sailing to Byzantium* and *All Souls' Night*. Between
the observation of the swans and the vision of the sphinx passes the
action of the book. The crisis occurs when, in *Ego Dominus Tuus*
(which immediately follows the account of the Dying Lady's heroic
arrogance) *Ille*[1] determines to 'set his chisel to the hardest stone' and
forget about the kind of self-fulfillment envisaged by people who

1 'Willy', commented Ezra Pound.

tell us that men improve with the years. Immediately a long poem devotes itself to the moon, the faded cliché of a thousand mewling nature poets; and examining it not as they do in the Irish sky but by way of the sort of diagram one discovers in a penny astrology book, sets the stage for the double vision of Michael Robartes.

The Wild Swans at Coole is a book about death and the will. A component poem like *Men Improve with the Years* will no more pull loose from it than the 'foolish fond old man' speech will pull loose from *King Lear*. It is a radical mistake to think of Yeats as a casual or fragmentary poet whose writings float on a current discoverable only in his biographable life. How much time does he not spend telling us that he has carefully rendered the mere events of his life irrelevant!

Anti-Nature

Yeats's quarrel with nineteenth-century popular Romanticism encompassed more than its empty moons. He turned with increasing vehemence against a tradition that either laid streams of little poems like cod's eggs or secreted inchoate epics. Against the poet as force of nature he placed of course the poet as deliberate personality, and correspondingly against the usual *Collected Poems* (arranged in the order of composition) he placed the oeuvre, the deliberated artistic Testament, a division of that new Sacred Book of the Arts of which, Mr Pound has recalled, he used to talk. It was as a process of fragmentation, into little people and little poems, that he viewed the history of European poetry, from the *Canterbury Tales* to the Collected Poems of, say, Lord Byron.

If Chaucer's personages had disengaged themselves from Chaucer's crowd, forgot their common goal and shrine, and after sundry magnifications become each in turn the centre of some Elizabethan play, and had after split into their elements and so given birth to romantic poetry, must I reverse the cinematograph?

The *Canterbury Tales*, it should be recalled, isn't a bloated descant on some epic idea but, like *The Divine Comedy* or *The Wild Swans at Coole* – or *The Cantos* – a unity made by architecture out of separate and ascertainable components. And the cinematograph seemed indeed reversible:

> ... a nation or an individual with great emotional
> intensity might follow the pilgrims as it were to some
> unknown shrine, and give to all those separated elements
> and to all that abstract love and melancholy, a symbolical, a
> mythological coherence.

This unity isn't substituted for the existing traditions of poetry, it unites them. Ireland, furthermore, might well be the chosen nation:

> I had begun to hope, or to half hope, that we might be the
> first in Europe to seek unity as deliberately as it had been
> sought by theologian, poet, sculptor, architect, from the
> eleventh to the thirteenth century.

For Ireland had her autochthonous mythology, and 'have not all races had their first unity from a mythology, that marries them to rock and hill?'[1]

It was natural that he should inspect the practice of any discoverable forerunners, and inevitable that he should see himself as standing in the same relation to Irish folklore as Wordsworth to the English folk ballads. One of his own false starts (seduced by this parallel) had been to write ballads; Wordsworth's unconsidered false start, it must finally have seemed to Yeats, had been to marry only himself and not his race to 'rock and hill'. Wordsworth had undertaken his work with an insufficient sense of hieratic dedication; for him a poet was only 'a man speaking to men' (though a more than usually conscious man), not the amanuensis of revelation. That is why old age overtook not only his body but his speech. *The Prelude* is a narrative of self-discovery, in which the lesson of life, muffled by the automatic grand style, is that knowledge and experience will not synchronize.

Hic   And I would find myself and not an image.
Ille   That is our modern hope, and by its light
           We have lit upon the gentle, sensitive mind
           And lost the old nonchalance of the hand;

[1] Above quotations from *The Trembling of the Veil*, Book I, Ch. 23–24.

> Whether we have chosen chisel, pen or brush,
> We are but critics, or but half create,
> Timid, entangled, empty and abashed. . . .
> (*Ego Dominus Tuus*)

That is the formula of Wordsworth's decline. As Yeats moved into middle age, the sole survivor of the Rhymers' Club's 'Tragic Generation', the parallel between his destiny and Wordsworth's grew more insistent; had Wordsworth not in the same way survived for a quarter of a century Keats, Shelley, and Byron, the other members of the last great wave of creative force? And had he not, assuming the laureateship, turned into a 'sixty year old smiling public man', moving further and further from the only time in his life when he had been alive, and lamenting over the dead imaginative vigour of his boyhood? That is the context of the defiant opening of *The Tower*:

> Never had I more
> Excited, passionate, fantastical
> Imagination, nor an ear and eye
> That more expected the impossible –
> No, not in boyhood when with rod and fly,
> Or the humbler worm, I climbed Ben Bulben's back
> And had the livelong summer day to spend.

'Or the humbler worm' is a tip to the reader; it isn't Yeatsian diction but a parody of Wordsworth's. Unlike Wordsworth, Yeats the poet has passed sixty undiminished and needs no man's indulgence.

Wordsworth had developed 'naturally', moving on the stream of nature; and streams run downhill. For the natural man the moment of lowest vitality is the moment of death; in the mid-eighteenth century the image of an untroubled decline into the grave fastened itself upon the imagination of England, and *Siste viator* was carved on a thousand tombstones. 'Pause, traveller, whoever thou art, and consider thy mortality; as I am, so wilt thou one day be.' The traveller came on foot, examined the inscription, and went on his way pondering, his vitality still lower than before. This was one of the odd versions of pastoral sentiment that prepared the way for Wordsworth's career of brilliance and decline; Yeats turns powerfully against it in the Goatherd's song on Major Gregory (see *Shepherd and Goatherd*), more powerfully still in the epitaph he designed for himself. The last division of his Sacred Book closes with an apocalypse, superhuman forms riding the wintry dawn, Michelangelo electrifying travellers with his Creation of Adam, painters revealing heavens that opened. The directions for his own burial are introduced with a pulsation of drums:

Ún dér báre Bén Búl bén's héad
In DRUMcliff churchyard. ...
    (*Under Ben Bulben*)

The *mise en scène* is rural and eighteenth century – the churchyard, the ancestral rector, the local stonecutters; but the epitaph flies in the face of traditional invocations to passers-by:

Cast a cold eye
On life, on death.
Horseman, pass by.
    (ibid.)

Much critical ingenuity has been expended on that horseman. He is simply the designated reader of the inscription, the heroic counter-image of the footweary wanderer who was invited to ponder a '*siste viator*';[1] the only reader Yeats can be bothered to address. And he is not to be weighed down by the realization of his own mortality; he is to defy it.

The life a counterlife, the book not a compendium of reflections but a dramatic revelation, the sentiments scrupulous inversions of received romantic sentiment; what more logical than that Yeats should have modelled the successive phases of his testament on the traditional collections of miscellaneous poems, and (as he always did when he touched a tradition) subverted the usual implications? He dreamed as a young man of creating some new *Prometheus Unbound*. One applauds his wisdom in not attempting that sort of *magnum opus*, but it was not likely that he should forget the idea of a work operating on a large scale. Each volume of his verse, in fact, *is* a large-scale work, like a book of the Bible. And as the Bible was once treated by exegetists as the self-sufficient divine book mirroring the

1 Though Swift wrote '*Abi, Viator, et imitare si poteris* ...' which Yeats paraphrased as 'Imitate him if you dare/World-besotted traveller.'

other divine book, Nature, but possessing vitality independent of natural experience, so Yeats considered his Sacred Book as similar to 'life' but radically separated from it, 'mirror on mirror mirroring all the show'. In *The Phases of the Moon*, Aherne and Robartes stand on the bridge below the poet's tower, where the candle burns late, and in mockery of his hopeless toil expound, out of his earshot, the doctrine of the lunar wheel. It is clear that they know what he can never discover; they toy with the idea of ringing his bell and speaking

> Just truth enough to show that his whole life
> Will scarcely find for him a broken crust
> Of all those truths that are your daily bread.

It is an entrancing idea:

> He'd crack his wits
> Day after day, yet never find the meaning.

But it is late; Aherne determines to pass up this satisfaction.

> And then he laughed to think that what seemed hard
> Should be so simple – a bat rose from the hazels
> And circled round him with its squeaky cry,
> The light in the tower window was put out.

Why is it put out? Because Yeats has finished writing the poem! Aherne, Robartes, the doctrine of the phases, the baffled student, all of them, we are meant suddenly to realize, are components in a book, and so is the man who is supposed to be writing the book. What we see in this mirror, the page, is reflected from that one, 'life'; but the parallel mirrors face each other, and in an infinite series of interreflections life has been acquiring its images from the book only that the book may reflect them again. The book, then, is (by a Yeatsian irony) self-contained, like the Great Smaragdine Tablet that said, 'Things below are copies', and was itself one of the things below; a sacred book like the Apocalypse of St John, not like most poetry a marginal commentary on the world to be read with one eye on the pragmatical pig of a text.

'Day after day,' Yeats wrote at the end of *A Vision*, 'I have sat in my chair turning a symbol over in my mind, exploring all its details, defining and again defining its elements, testing my convictions and those of others by its unity. . . . It seems as if I should know all if I could but banish such memories and find everything in the symbol.' On that occasion nothing came; the symbol was perhaps too limited. But the conviction remains with Yeats that a book, if not a symbol, can supplant the world; if not supplant it, perpetually interchange life with it. Nothing, finally, is more characteristic than his dryly wistful account of the perfected sage for whom the radiance attending the supernatural copulation of dead lovers serves but as a reading light:

> Though somewhat broken by the leaves, that light
> Lies in a circle on the grass; therein
> I turn the pages of my holy book.

Hugh Kenner

from 'At the Hawk's Well', *Gnomon* 1958

Unpurged Images

There is nothing essentially new here.[1] The reader will already be familiar with the outlines of this development from diffident youth to outrageous passionate sage. It has been for some years the theme of the standard books about Yeats, which, bending to the temptations of the subject, have gotten themselves written out of a division of interest in which poetry – the part of himself Yeats designedly gave to the public – is treated chiefly as a body of evidence throwing light on the personal integration of an old man now many years dead. He wanted the integration so as to be more wholly a poet – 'Man can embody truth but he cannot know it' – but one is led to suppose that it had some independent importance. Dr Jeffares' book is called *W. B. Yeats, Man and Poet*; it ends, 'He had made himself a great poet.' Mr Ellmann's first book is called *Yeats: the Man and the Masks*; in its summary chapter we read how 'with great courage and will, he tried to become the hero of whom he had dreamed. . . . His amazing achievement was to succeed partially. . . . He looked the poet, and he lived the poet.' Even Miss Koch, who pretends (*W. B. Yeats: The Tragic Phase*) to guide us through the last poems by the unaided light

1 Kenner is referring to Allan Wade's edition of Yeats's letters. [Ed.]

of the poems themselves, in fact does nothing of the kind. Her initial premise is but the orthodox one inverted: 'In old age, Yeats became a great poet but he was more than conscious that he had not become a great man.' She dilates on the Steinach operation, fusses with interim drafts, and boxes the bibliographic compass in – of all places – her discussion of that cryptic but admirably direct poem *The Statues*.

It is arguable that Yeats would be better read if less were accessible that he didn't mean the reader of his poetry to see. One advantage of having the *Letters* to plow through is that one can learn in an evening how the principle of obfuscation operates. We find him thanking Sarah Purser for her 'charming embroidered book cover' (235), or anxiously writing Lady Gregory about his forgotten trouser stretcher (543), or requesting Olivia Shakespear to send him from a bird shop a bundle of nesting material 'to help my canaries who are nest-making but with sheep's wool and green moss which they dislike' (680), and observe, in the contexts, a progressive tightening. It is an effort for him (1894) to seem at ease about the book cover, but it is part of the serene bardic role (1922) to be occupied in the Tower with his canaries. The random social gestures, we note with satisfaction, are becoming the very repertoire of the self-dramatizing style. But there are hundreds of paragraphs that won't fit into this comfortable progression, and these contain the very things that Yeats is intent on *telling* his correspondents, in a constant obsession with stating with exactness something of importance:

It is not inspiration that exhausts one, but art (87).

The best argumentative and learned book is like a mechanical invention and when it ceases to contain the newest improvements becomes, like most things, not worth an old song (246).

I hold as Blake would have held also, that the intellect must do its utmost 'before inspiration is possible'. It clears the rubbish from the mouth of the sybil's cave but it is not the sybil (262).

I do not understand what you mean when you distinguish between the word that gives your idea and the more beautiful word (343).

The subjects which people think suitable for drama get fewer every day (361).

Drama for them consists in a tension of wills excited by commonplace impulses, especially by those impulses that are the driving force of rather common natures . . . The commonplace will, that is, the will of the successful business man, the business will, is the root of the whole thing. Indeed when I see the realistic play of our time, even Ibsen and Sudermann, much more when I see the plays of their imitators, I find that blessed business will keeping the stage most of the time. What would such writers or their stage managers do with the mockery king of snow? Or with Lear upon his heath? (441)

One thing I am now quite sure of is that all the finest poetry comes logically out of the fundamental action, and that the error of late periods like this is to believe that some things are inherently poetical, and to try to pull them on to the scene at every moment (460).

These are all early; the date of the latest of them is 1904. Their range and point need no comment. They exhibit none of the dreaminess we have been trained to expect from the Yeats of that period. Nor, really, does the context from which they are excerpted, much of it a tissue of shrewd maneuvers for earning necessary money or arranging sympathetic reviews. What developed wasn't the grip of his mind, though it came to grip more and more things; what developed was the art: specifically, the art of putting things more and more arrestingly, and setting the matters that interested him in closer, more electrifying relationship with one another. This is a technical development; what makes it look like a development of personality is our proneness to forget that we are not after all in touch with a *person*, but with written words.

The reader of the early letters, then, confronted by so many things pointing in so many directions, soon grows inured to their penetrative force and starts listening to the Yeatsian voice, which grows, plainly, more assured. In the same way, it is natural to assume that that is the outline of Yeats's poetic development too – the personality ramifying, consolidating itself, assuming control; hence that what his published books are 'about' is the effort to fabricate a durable self. This is an especially natural assumption for the reader of the *Letters* because of the color it acquires from whatever he remembers of whatever books about Yeats he may have read: Mr Henn's, Mr Jeffares', Mr Ellmann's. Each of these writers, one may surmise, has fallen victim to the experience of reading through a great deal of material which Yeats did not intend for the public eye; this is exactly the position of a reader of the *Letters*. His ostensible subjects, when he writes for himself alone or for friends, are so miscellaneous that one ignores them and attends to the constant element, the style; and what the developing style does – so runs the account – is to parallel, as one mushroom does another, the fostered growth of the famous personality. QED.

Hence the Yeatsian critical tradition: an industry erected on the premise that the coherence of the poetic oeuvre not only reflects supinely some coherence lying outside the volumes of poetry themselves, but cannot even be said with confidence to exist until that external center has been located, delimited, and surveyed. The usual procedure is to play down his activities as too miscellaneous to keep track of, and offer, as fulcrum, *A Vision*, of which Yeats wrote in a letter of 1931,

The young men I write for may not read my *Vision* – they may care too much for poetry – but they will be pleased that it exists. Even my simplest poems will be the better for it. . . . I have constructed a myth, but then one can believe in a myth – one only assents to philosophy (781).

He was sanguine if he thought that the books about him would be one day written by these young men who cared much for poetry. Instead of addressing themselves to the poems, a brief generation of critics assaulted the doors of that Gothic fortress, *A Vision*, or scrutinizing its interior by periscope reported that it was full of bats. Worse followed: an immense limbo, consisting of the poet's diaries, notebooks, drafts, and unpublished mss., was opened to certified explorers after his death, and the heady possibility that the clues to what Yeats had been making lay in his lumber room, or in the chips from his workbench, overwhelmed everyone who has so far reported. It is doubtful if what a major writer actually published has ever been so little trusted.

What you can reconstruct from such materials is the poet's biography, or one level of it; the current postulate of Yeats criticism is that the poems depend from the life, not so much the public life as the inner life, the diary life, and are explicated one by one in the light of their author's private obsessions and self-communings:

Caught in that sensual music, all neglect
Monuments of unaging intellect.
    (Sailing to Byzantium)

One hears at great length what Yeats's notebooks contained on the subject of Byzantium ('Idea for a poem ...' etc.), and receives assurance, from a letter to Lady Gregory on the death of Mabel Beardsley, that Yeats didn't invent the rouged cheeks or the trousered dolls. It grows harder and harder for the tradition to preserve him as a major poet, except by an act of assertion, or by transposing to the verse the impressiveness of the persona of the last decade. Gradually, in the texture of critical emphasis, the poems whose strings lead back to some inner crisis are allowed to supplant all the rest (which, when clues turn up, get explicated as puzzles), and no poem is allowed, as Yeats intended, to explicate its neighbour in the cunningly arranged volumes.

John Wain

'Among School Children', Interpretations 1957

The main subject of the poem is the relationship or interpenetration of matter and spirit. Broadly speaking, it is a meditation on the riddle that has puzzled us all when we have thought of it, and to which various answers, theological, philosophical, and psychological, have been proposed. We say that Jones dies and goes to Heaven; but *which* Jones goes there? The squalling infant Jones, the undergraduate Jones, the full-blooded middle-aged Jones as *père de famille*, or the old shrunken Jones who actually dies? Obviously they are all the same, in a sense; but in *what* sense are they all the same? This question is the major preoccupation of the poem, and there is also the secondary theme, present as a strong undertow, which is expressed by the word 'labour'. Our identities – our souls, if you like – manifest themselves in our activities, in our *work*; the heads of the schoolchildren bowed over their reading-books and histories, the hard speculations of the philosophers, the straining of the youthful mother in labour, and finally the blossoming and dancing, the work of beings in a state of perfection and rightness. To show how these themes are interwoven, it is necessary first to cross the *pons asinorum*, to give, as bluntly as possible, the paraphrasable content of the poem (one does not speak, in this connection, of its 'meaning').

The poet, at sixty, is performing part of his public duty by being shown over a school. To the children, he is just one more of the genial fogies who represent age and authority. But inwardly, he is visited by thoughts of the woman he loves, and how, late one night, she spoke of some incident of her own childhood. (There was a 'sinking fire', over which she was 'bent'; it was the hour of confidences. Leda was the mother of Helen, the father being Jove in the form of a swan; as the next stanza makes clear, the woman is Ledaean in the sense that she is like Helen rather than like Leda. The conclusion that the poet is in love with her is, to my mind, inescapable, though it can be contested.[1]) This confidence gave the poet a precious sense of kinship with the woman, which he expresses by an indirect use of Plato's image, from the *Symposium*, of the twin halves of a single sphere.

This train of thought sends his mind back to the school-children, and brings with it the realization that she, too, the daughter of the swan, must have looked something like this. Inevitably, the pendulum swings back at once to 'her present image', which is something like a Quattrocento painting. (She is hollow-cheeked, but I cannot take this as necessarily conveying that she is old; she is just one of those very beautiful women, one sees them everywhere, who look as if they did not get quite enough to eat.) He himself has to repress the dangerous and painful thought that in younger days, before he became an old scarecrow, he was handsome enough. He pulls himself up with the thought that the best thing to do is to put a good face on it, and seem at least to be 'comfortable'.

1 And was contested, with tremendous cogency, by Mr Richard Hughes in a conversation with me in November 1954. I bring in his name as a means of offering him an oblique apology for not accepting his argument.

This cluster of contrasts between youth and age leads on to the next step, which is the first generalized thought in the poem, the first one to have no immediate bearing on the poet's personal situation. A man of sixty would hardly seem worth the trouble of bearing and bringing up, if he appeared before his mother at the moment of parturition. That is the broad sense of stanza 5; the detail is complicated. The young mother is in the midst of childbirth; she is being given an anaesthetic, but, since birth has to be at least intermittently conscious or it could not be performed, she is divided between consciousness and recollection (a marvellously exact use of the word). This is for her, unmistakably, an ordeal; she would escape if she could; it was the 'honey of generation', the pleasant activity of conceiving the child, which let her in for this: it 'betrayed' her. The grammar of 'had', in the second line, is ambiguous; it could equally well be 'has', but the pluperfect is more final; none of the other verbs in the stanza is a straight present tense, for 'would' and 'did' are conditional, and 'must' is a verb that does not change in the preterite.

It is necessary to pause here to consider Yeats' note on this stanza, which reads as follows:

I have taken the 'honey of generation' from Porphyry's essay on 'The Cave of the Nymphs', but find no warrant in it for considering it the 'drug' that destroys the 'recollection' of prenatal freedom. He blamed a cup of oblivion given in the zodiacal sign of Cancer.

Here we come head-on against the huge recurrent problem that faces the reader of Yeats. It is, briefly, the problem of how much notice to take of Yeats' personal fandango of mysticism and superstition. To many readers it will seem intolerably arrogant if I say that I propose simply to brush aside his reading of his own words. Obviously, they will say, if the poet himself tells us that it is the 'shape' who is 'betrayed' – it is the child who loses the remembrance of his ideal prenatal existence by having the practical joke of birth played on him – then that is all; away with this obstinate insistence that it is the 'mother' who was betrayed by the pleasure of generation.

I can only answer, in absolute seriousness, that I must respect the poem more than the poet, and try to serve it rather than to serve him. Substitute Yeats' own rendering, and what becomes of the argument of the poem? The stanza is absolutely clear; it relates logically to the rest of the poem; it develops the argument; it is intelligible, compassionate, and human. By contrast, the interpretation which is proffered as Yeats' 'intention' is an affair of solemn childishness, a product of the side of his nature which found it necessary to construct a system of beliefs in order to write poetry at all. I am not contemptuous of this system; it was valuable for Yeats in that it overcame his despair in the face of a world which appeared to have no beliefs that he could share; it was responsible for his change from a minor 'aesthetic' poet into a major human one. But what, in all humility, I would insist on is this: these beliefs were necessary for him, *but that does not make them necessary for us*. He had to have them in order to write his poetry; we do not have to have them in order to read it.

This is not an attempt to set the critic above the poet; it is merely an attempt to avoid setting the poet above the poem. If we admit the interpretation that is imported by Yeats' note, we give that note an authority which, in the last resort, can only be claimed *by the poem*. A poem must dictate its own meaning, and define for itself the area within which it chooses to operate. In this instance, we have a clear case of attempted interference with the poem; the argument requires the juxtaposed images of the young mother, in painful labour, and the scarred, compromised man of sixty; it requires the painful contrast between the cost of producing him and sending him out into life, and his performance considered as the return for that cost.

Having got so far, I must pause to admit that I do not *like* having to be so peremptory; it is never pleasant to feel that one's interpretation of a poem can be carried through only by pushing against the author's. And indeed, if anyone were to claim that, without going outside the poem at all, the grammar and grouping of the words on the page demand the interpretation that it *must* be the shape that is betrayed, it must be the child who is divided between sleeping, shrieking and struggling to escape – I should not know how to answer him. My own feeling is the other way; but the lines could take that interpretation: Jones does not want to be born; he is happier where he is. In the process of being born, he has flashes of 'recollection', in which his prenatal consciousness comes back; then he 'struggles to escape' – from the womb. If his mother saw him at sixty, she might regret, not only her labour, but the fact of her having called him from his previous and happier existence to enter upon this unsatisfactory soul-and-body relationship. If any reader insisted on this interpretation, I should have to grant it, though I personally do not find it helpful with regard to the poem as a whole. As for Porphyry and the zodiacal sign of Cancer, of course, I cannot away with them. To invoke them is a mere flourish: the kind of flourish that is sometimes necessary to the writer, never to the reader. If this reading is valid, it is valid simply as a piece of Yeats's familiar pessimism, to document which we need not go outside his verse. We do not need magical explanations for what he found already developed in Sophocles:

Never to have lived is best, ancient writers say:
Never to have drawn the breath of life, never to have looked
  into the eye of day;
The second best's a gay goodnight and quickly turn away.
    (*Oedipus at Colonus*)

To return to the argument of the poem: the question has now been posed, in one at least of its possible forms; and we turn, naturally, to the philosophers. All these philosophers, as we realize when he names them, had theories about the soul and the body, though these theories are not conspicuously set in the poem. Pythagoras suggests to us the transmigration of souls. Aristotle is the scientist of the trio, the man who invented logic; what doctrines of his about the soul Yeats may have had in mind, I do not know, but that is just my ignorance. As regards Plato, his doctrine of the existence of archetypal forms, of which the physical world affords only imitations, has never been so adroitly captured by a single metaphor. What precise associations the word 'paradigm' had for Yeats, I do not know; in my experience I have very seldom met it except in the pages of a Greek grammar, where it meant a *schema* of the principle parts of a verb: an excellent parallel for the intellectually conceived framework which gives shape and body to the 'spume' that plays on it. These two lines alone would prove that Yeats was a great poet, if nothing else of his had survived. Aristotle, by contrast, leathered Alexander's bottom; the language becomes earthy and solid, pointing the contrast be-

tween the two. Pythagoras was 'world-famous', which as Mr G. S.
Fraser remarked,[1] is an odd way to talk of a philosopher; it is more
the sort of description one would expect to hear of an athlete or
film-star; perhaps, Mr Fraser goes on, it signifies something about
the character of Pythagoras – that he enjoyed being world-famous,
even to the extent of tolerating absurd rumours about himself, such
as that he had golden thighs. Since the tendency of this stanza, taken
as a whole, is to make fun of the philosophers, to reduce them to
figures of helplessness, such an interpretation is very easily admissible,
though in fact we learn from Diogenes Laertius that Pythagoras did
have a great personal standing and was not unaware of it:

Indeed, his bearing is said to have been most dignified, and
his disciples held the opinion about him that he was Apollo
come down from the far north. There is a story that once,
when he was disrobed, his thigh was seen to be of gold; and
when he crossed the river Nessus, quite a number of people
said they heard it welcome him.[2]

The two lines describing what Pythagoras did to earn his place in
this *galère* (vol. 6, 6, 7) can be put into non-metaphorical language
quite easily; we need not do it for ourselves; what is the *Encyclopaedia
Britannica* for?

Pythagoras's greatest discovery was, perhaps, that of the
dependence of the musical intervals on certain arithmetical
ratios of lengths of string at the same tension, 2 : 1 giving the
octave, 3 : 2 the fifth and 4 : 3 the fourth. This discovery
could not but have powerfully contributed to the idea that
'all things are numbers'. According to Aristotle, the theory
in its original form regarded numbers, not as relations
predicable of things, but as actually constituting their
essence or substance. Numbers, he says, seemed to the
Pythagoreans to be the first things in the whole of nature,
and they supposed the elements of numbers to be the
elements of all things, and the whole heaven to be a
musical scale and a number (*Metaph* A 986a).

1 'Yeats and the New Criticism', *Colonnade*, no. 1–2.
2 From *Lives of Eminent Philosophers*, vol. 2, trans. Hicks, Loeb.

To say, therefore, that Pythagoras 'fingered upon a fiddlestick or strings/What a star sang and careless Muses heard' is a brilliant piece of metaphor-spinning, almost on a level with the superb one about Plato; what it has to do with the immediate question is not clear, but the point is that Pythagoras was a very brilliant and deep-thoughted man, and yet it made no difference; the Muses, who work by being careless, did not allow it to matter to them. All three philosophers are, in fact, given up with a sad shrug; they are nothing but a lot of scarecrows like the poet himself. This is profoundly Yeatsian: he enjoyed reading about people's experiments with ideas, but was at the same time profoundly anti-philosophic. Of course the philosophers could have nothing relevant to say; they were in the same trap themselves; it had taken them so long to work out their ideas that they had become scarecrows in the process. 'Bodily decrepitude is wisdom; young/We loved each other and were ignorant.' It is no use asking the old what they think about these matters, any more than the young. Time has taken away their physical vitality, and added, after all, nothing very valuable in exchange. It is, of course, a familiar Yeatsian theme:

Come let us mock at the great
That had such burdens on the mind
And toiled so hard and late
To leave some monument behind,
Nor thought of the levelling wind.
    (Nineteen Hundred and Nineteen)

And again, one is perfectly well aware that the familiar gesture towards occultism can be seen, by those curious enough to want to see it, behind this stanza as it could behind the 'youthful mother' stanza. The reason why philosophers are never allowed a look in (the philosopher in The Hour Glass comes off worst in a speculating match with the village idiot, for instance) is because they represent something incompatible with the virtues typified by the three key figures of the Yeatsian world, 'Hunchback and Saint and Fool'. The poem in which this hocus-pocus is 'explained', The Phases of the Moon, is followed by a group of others on related themes, and in one of them the Saint is made to say:

I shall not cease to bless because
I lay about me with the taws
That night and morning I may thrash
Greek Alexander from my flesh.
    (The Saint and the Hunchback)

As far as we are concerned here, the important fact is that the philosophers are declared out of the running.

In short, this question of the inter-relation of body and spirit must be referred at last to those who love. The three kinds of human love, 'passion, piety and affection', are all present in the poem; we have already seen the poet with his heart driven wild as the image of his beloved comes before him; now we see the two other emblematic figures, the nun and the mother, worshipping their own kind of images. What ties the three kinds together, for the purposes of the poem, is the fact that they are all *composite* images, depending partly on the memory and partly on the imagination; a mother thinks of her son simultaneously as he was in his cradle, in early childhood, in boyhood proper, and fuses these images with his 'present image' in manhood. The piety of a nun sees eternity and holiness in the stillness of marble or bronze statues; indeed, the actualization of religious truth is for her principally an affair of images. She cannot be disappointed in these images in the way a mother might be disappointed in her son, could she but see him with sixty or more winters on his head, but she can suffer the harshness of a dedicated life; her images can break her heart too, in their own way.

When memory and imagination work in this way on an image, they transform it into a composite thing, with its own order of existence, which Yeats here calls a Presence. The Presences are the composite images of love which are known to the three kinds of lover. But they are not merely called forth by the emotions of the lovers; they are 'self-born'; they existed before the love to which they correspond, or at any rate they are independent of it. They are the symbols of heavenly glory; paraphrase cannot get any closer than that, because if one asks the paraphraser's prime question – 'What is the literal truth of which this is the metaphorical expression?' – one is left with the circular answer that heaven, for living men, is itself a metaphor, that its glory is metaphorical, and that a symbol is something that cannot be reduced. The Presences correspond, simply, to 'heavenly glory' – and what *that* may be, we shall find out one day; it lies outside the poem, because it lies outside human life and language. No wonder that the Presences are 'mockers of man's enterprise', especially (one suspects) the sort of enterprise the philosophers have.

At all events, the poet now addresses these Presences directly; not for their information, not to ask them anything, but simply because they are, rhetorically, the only possible audience for his words. And he tells them something about Labour. Labour, here, is the condition of being; it is performing one's function. It is the only continuity that runs through the bewildering series of changes that are the life of Jones. Trees grow leaves and blossoms; men grow hair and nails, but with them it cannot stop there; activity is the expression of identity, and identity is the one link that binds bank-manager Jones with schoolboy Jones. But – and this is part of the problem – something has gone wrong; just as we can never grasp and arrest the Protean identity, so we can never achieve a perfect relationship between activity and nature; between 'labour' and 'blossoming or dancing'. It is unfortunately true that the body has to be 'bruised to pleasure soul'; witness the patient toil of the nun as she teaches the children a few simple lessons, which for them are as arduous as the speculations of the philosophers; witness the asceticism of the nun; witness the 'pang' of the mother in setting the whole process going and making passion, piety and affection attainable in the first place. 'Beauty' also is 'born out of its own despair', in the sense that beautiful poems are written by old scarecrows who had better not even think of the fact that they used to be good-looking. Similarly the philosophers get bleary eyes as they ponder their problems instead of going to sleep, which turns them into scarecrows all the faster. But in a perfect state, such as we are now imagining, all these things would be attainable without paying such a crushing price for them. 'Labour' would be 'blossoming' – simply unconscious growth – or 'dancing' – a natural if stylized activity – in such a state. 'Where' at the end of the first line means either 'in the place where' or 'when such conditions are present' – cf. 'where you've got a good referee, the game is played fairly'; it is a familiar concentration of meanings in the word. 'Labour' means, of course, the act of birth as well as the various activities of work; the two are not, at this level, distinguishable. The Presences are 'self-born' – they do not owe their existence to labour; they are, I suppose, identical with the 'self-begotten' who are elsewhere the subject of a short, but complete, poem (see stanza 24 of *Words For Music Perhaps*).

This would indeed be the perfect state; but even then there is no guarantee that we should escape from the confused relationship of matter and spirit. Even blossoming and dancing are accompanied by this confusion; a chestnut-tree has a massive trunk, cool green leaves, and delicate blossoms; at which point is one most in touch with its essential identity? Again, a dancer is the embodiment of the dance; without the tangible, moving human body, the dance would not exist; nevertheless, it is a perceptible thing in itself. This question is brought up, but it is not the function of the poem to propound a solution; the last two sentences are interrogative, reminding us that a poet differs from other kinds of sage by the fact that he makes his poems out of his ignorances as much as his certainties. So we are left with the question, which it was the purpose of the poem to bring before us: not in order to set us to work finding a solution, but merely to force upon us the realization that the question exists.

Exists, that is, as a reality, something to be humanly reckoned with; and what we are concerned with as literary critics is the success of this actualization and the concrete means employed to bring it about.

It is, of course, far easier to indicate in general terms what these means are, than to instance in detail their manner of action. Anyone can see that the success of the poem is due to the suppleness and force of its language, and the dramatic coherence of its construction. But to illustrate these things in the concrete is to approach the vanishing centre of literary criticism, which, not being an exact science, is bound sooner or later to reach a point at which demonstration breaks down and is replaced by a shared sensibility; though, of course, this point is very much more distant than the anti-critical writers on literature would have us think. It remains true, however, that anyone who does not see, without prompting, the peculiarly Yeatsian excellence of language attained in this poem, will not see it with any amount of prompting. It is an affair of variation within a well-defined area, which the reader must be capable of inhabiting. The area is the area of dignity and passion; the language can become familiar, with its 't'other', 'paddler', 'bottom'; it can name common-place objects, with its 'reading-books',' yolk', 'scarecrow'; it can rise to the heights of what is conventionally thought of as 'poetic' language, as in the first four lines of stanza IV; but it remains always within the area. Every word used is consonant with dignity and passion. This Yeatsian style, peculiar to this poet but common in his poems, is a high plateau; it has its valleys and hills, but the traveller can never for an instant forget that he is close to the clouds. One recalls how Edmund Wilson, in *Axel's Castle*, tried to pin down the bare nobility of Yeats' 'middle period' style by using an image of the common-place transmuted into the priceless: 'His words, no matter how prosaic, are always somehow luminous and noble, as if pale pebbles smoothed by the sea were to take on some mysterious value and become more precious than jewels or gold.' It is 'the proud full sail of his great verse', of course, that does it; that opulence of movement which is the justification both of Yeats' arrogance and of the silly mystery-worship of his disposition. Too much humility, too much common-sense, would have left him incapable of sustaining this loftiness; the parallel case is Milton's. The harmony is so rich – I need not bore the reader by pointing out instances of assonance, verbal music, etc. – that the style can afford its familiarities, can interrupt itself with 'enough of that', can, alternatively, rise to its peaks without losing concreteness. It is the writing of a man who has schooled himself to see everything in concrete terms; a handful of abstractions sown here and there would ruin the poem. This was the fruit of Yeats' fierce simple-mindedness; all the abstractions were concrete in his eyes – poverty was a ragged man with a wooden leg, riches the contemplation of great art in a palace. He had undergone, that is, the essential training of the poet, which is to unlearn the discipline of abstract thought insisted on by modern education, and thus to make himself, by the standards of that education, a simpleton.

You must become an ignorant man again,
And see the sun again with an ignorant eye,
    (*Notes Toward a Supreme Fiction*)

as Wallace Stevens has it; and in Yeatsian terms, and a context only slightly different,

John Synge, I and Augusta Gregory, thought
All that we did, all that we said or sang
Must come from contact with the soil, from that
Contact everything Antaeus-like grew strong.
We three alone in modern times had brought
Everything down to that sole test again,
Dream of the noble and the beggar-man.
    (*The Municipal Gallery Revisited*)

Yeats was, in fact, a specialized intelligence; his mind was perfectly adapted to the writing of poetry, and able to invest poetry with a pantherine play of intelligence that animated its ceremony and mystery. Outside poetry, he tended to be an albatross; most subjects of inquiry do call for a certain power of abstract thought, and abstract thought was next door to impossible for Yeats. Owing to the irregular nature of his education, he never learnt it in the first place, and would in any case have had to unlearn it. To conclude this digression, I am not of course saying that Yeats was, or that any poet can afford to be, anything but supremely intelligent; merely that the order of intelligence required in poetry does not usually enable its possessor to shine in other fields.

This use of language, then, was the product of a temperament. It is a compound of the robust and the fastidious, wedded together by the balance of the verse. This balance, like the poem's structure, is essentially dramatic; it assumes complete control of the speaking voice, dictating its pace and pitch. Anyone who would trouble to read an essay like this would not be interested in having examples heaped up; the kind of thing I am thinking of is the free-ranging and varied run of stanza 7: after the easy flow of the first line, the initial statement, we have the difference between the stillness of the nun's adoration and the rapid vicissitudes of a mother's emotions, brought out by the fact that the line

But those the candles light are not as those

consists mainly of single syllables, and therefore must be spoken slowly, while

That animate a mother's reveries

is spoken flowingly, and turns mainly on the softer, tenderer consonants, m, n, r, v. Then immediately we are back in the world of bronze and marble with the heavy impact of the single syllables

And yet they too break hearts.

I have not much stomach for this kind of work; it easily becomes absurd, and can best be done by the reader; and here I leave the diction of the poem.

With regard to its structure, the first thing one notices is that the poem breaks into two halves. Of its eight stanzas, the last four contain all the essential argumentation of the piece; they could be printed alone, and the result would be a concentrated intellectual poem of the greatest difficulty, but perfectly coherent, perfectly ready to yield to analysis. What, then (to begin with the elementary question), do the first four stanzas contribute to the poem?

Elementary as the question is, the answer to it can be made to open out much of the poem's essential secret. These four stanzas serve, in the first place, to make the poem easier to understand. By presenting the personal situation of the poet, and the concrete setting in which he is thinking of it, they enable us to enter on the independent speculation of the second half with a good head of steam to drive us along. Further, since the essence of poetry is the actualization of the concepts it deals with (what it *feels like* to be two and two making four, or alternatively what it feels like to *understand* that two and two make four), they help us towards participation in the poem. This is a well-understood convention of poetry; *Among School Children* is best put in perspective by seeing it as one of the great romantic odes; it is the culminating achievement in the tradition which begins with the odes of Wordsworth and Coleridge. And it is of course a common feature of this kind of poem that it begins with the personal, concrete statement:

Well, if the bard was weather-wise, who made
The grand old ballad of Sir Patrick Spens,
We shall have rain to-night. . . .
    (Dejection: An Ode)

The man is looking through the window of his lonely room, talking to himself between set teeth. The prosaic opening helps to moor down the soaring speculation which this kind of poem deals in. There is, by the way, an adroit use of the device in William Empson's poem *Camping Out*, which begins

And now she cleans her teeth into the lake,

an opening so prosaic that the poem seems to be challenging itself to get off the ground at all. Yet within a dozen lines we have climbed to

Who moves so among stars, their frame unties;
See where they blur, and die, and are out-soared.

Yeats' poem uses this convention in a way that reveals complete mastery of the formal technique of the Romantic ode. 'I walk through the long schoolroom questioning' is an exact counterpart to the Coleridgean beginning, just as the vivid realism of his description of the schoolroom is a counterpart to the elaborate scene-setting in *Resolution and Independence*. But whereas it was the tendency of the other Romantics to bring the thing round in a circle, so that

My heart aches, and a drowsy numbness pains
My sense
    (Ode to A Nightingale)

would circle round to its ending in:

Fled is that music; do I wake or sleep?

Yeats abandons the circular technique; after the half-way mark, there is no recurrence of the schoolroom, the children, the nun, the personal situation; the 'I' is banished, having done its work, as if to emphasize that the vagaries of a man's own fate only serve to lead him, by his particular route, to the frontier of that realm of speculation whose problems are universal ones. The first half of the poem has given us the three types of love and of labour, either directly or by implication; children imply the existence of mothers and motherhood; the nun implies the existence of a religion and the emotions appropriate to it; the sexual love felt by the poet involves the existence of a beloved woman. The children learn and grow, the nun teaches and worships, the poet loves, smiles and is a public man, performing his duty to the State. These are the actualities of which the abstract elements in the poem's second half are the shadows.

Within the two halves, separate rhythms are discernible. The first half is circular in the traditional manner; it begins with the concrete and ends with it again, enclosing between the two a contour of impressions and memories; the children, his beloved as she is now, as she was then, Plato, the Quattrocento, his own early days. And, since the subject-matter of the first half is the external, physical manifestations of the question that is being discussed – since it is bounded by the actual situation, the children, the woman, the figure of the poet himself – we have, as a kind of rhythm within the rhythm, a progression from the pre-natal to the all-but-senile. One after another the images peel off: in line 9 he dreams of 'a Ledaean body': Leda, not Helen; the mother, not the daughter. The next image is the egg; 'the yolk and white of the one shell'. From that we go on to the 'daughter of the swan', then to the 'living child', then to 'her present image' and finally to the oldest figure in the tableau – himself. We run heavily to a standstill on the word 'scarecrow'; all that can profitably be said in personal terms has been said. Immediately, the movement of the poem is renewed, with a question; aptly, because questioning will be the keynote of the second half, as reverie was the keynote of the first.

This series of questions is arranged as a movement away from the immediate and personal, towards the universal. The 'youthful mother' is still close to the matter of the first half, though independent of it; then come the philosophers; and finally the poem launches into unaided speculation, questioning in its own voice.

This arrangement cannot be an accident. It suits the poem's central enterprise too well, it has too much dramatic propriety, to be anything but the result of careful contrivance. Instead of circling back on itself, the poem moves forward, in the form of a bridge, then suddenly stops with no opposite shore in sight. It is not a bridge after all, but a pier. It leads nowhere; its purpose is to afford us, before we turn and retrace our steps, a bleak and chastening glimpse into the deep waters.

Frank Kermode

from 'The Dancer', *Romantic Image* 1957

I come now, having commented on some of Yeats' other dancers, to the poem in which the Dancer makes her most remarkable appearance. *Among Schoolchildren* is the work of a mind which is itself a system of symbolic correspondences, self-exciting, difficult because the particularities are not shared by the reader – but his interests are not properly in the mind but in the product, which is the sort of poetry that instantly registers itself as of the best. What I have to say of the poem should not be read as an attempt to provide another explication of it, or to provide a psychological contribution to the understanding of the poet. I have, as the preceding pages show, a rather narrow interest in its images, and that is what I propose to pursue.

The 'sixty-year-old smiling public man' of the poem is caught in the act of approving, because he has ventured out of his genre, of a way of educating children which, as we have seen, is completely inimical to his profoundest convictions. The tone is of self-mockery, gentle and indeed somewhat mincing, with a hint of unambitious irony – 'in the best modern way', we can pick up this note without prior information, but it is at any rate interesting to know that the children are engaged in the wrong labour, the antithesis of the heroic labour of the looking-glass. The old man, because he is old and a *public* man, does not protest, but sees himself as amusingly humiliated, not too seriously betrayed, putting up with the shapelessness and commonness that life has visited upon him. But children of the kind he sees before him remind him of the great image of a lady who was all they could not hope to be, a daughter of imagination, not of memory; a daughter of the swan, the perfect emblem of the soul, and like Leda the sign of an annunciation of paganism and heroic poetry, for which the soul is well-lost. But she too is old; he thinks of her present image: 'Did Quattrocento finger fashion it?' For even in old age she has that quality of the speaking body, the intransigent vision, perhaps, of Mantegna. And he himself had had beauty, though he had spent it in his isolation and intellectual effort, and become shapeless and common, the old scarecrow of the later poems. The fifth stanza develops this theme, the destruction of the body by Adam's curse, which for Yeats is the curse of labour. It is a reworking of some lines from *At The Hawk's Well*, of ten years earlier.

A mother that saw her son
Doubled over with speckled shin,
Cross-grained with ninety years,
Would cry, 'How little worth
Were all my hopes and fears
And the hard pain of his birth!'

This old man has lain in wait for fifty years, but he 'is one whom the dancers cheat'; 'wisdom', conclude the singers, 'must lead a bitter life', and he who pursues it prizes the dry stones of a well and the leafless tree above a comfortable door and an old hearth, children and the indolent meadows. This is the plight of the old man in the schoolroom, to be with the scarecrow thinkers and teachers and poets, out of life; the scarecrow is the emblem of such a man, because he is an absurd, rigid diagram of living flesh that would break the heart of the woman who suffered the pang of his birth.

But there are other heartbreakers, though these do not change with time, but 'keep a marble or a bronze repose'. 'Marble and bronze' is a recurrent minor motive in Yeats. It occurs in simple form in *The Living Beauty* (1919), where there is an antithetical relationship between it and that which is truly 'alive' – alive in the normal sense, and possessing that speaking body which includes the soul.

I bade, because the wick and oil are spent,
And frozen are the channels of the blood,
My discontented heart to draw content
From beauty that is cast out of a mould
In bronze, or that in dazzling marble appears,
Appears, but when we have gone is gone again,
Being more indifferent to our solitude
Than 'twere an apparition. O heart, we are old;
The living beauty is for younger men:
We cannot pay its tribute of wild tears.

These masterly verses have the seeds of much later poetry. The purpose of art, in the life of the poet, is to mitigate isolation by providing the Image which is the daily victory. 'I suffered continual remorse, and only became content when my abstractions had composed themselves into picture and dramatisation . . .' But the relief is impermanent; the poet discovers that 'he has made, after the manner of his kind, Mere images'. There is a tormenting contrast between the images (signified by the bronze and marble statuettes) and the living beauty. And out of this contrast grows the need for a poetic image which will resemble the living beauty rather than the marble or bronze. No static image will now serve; there must be movement, the different sort of life that a dancer has by comparison with the most perfect object of art. Here we see, in strictly poetic terms, a change comparable to that wrought by Pound in the abandonment of Imagism and the development of a dynamic image-theory. The Image is to be all movement, yet with a kind of stillness. She lacks separable intellectual content, her meanings, as the intellect receives them, must constantly be changing. She has the impassive, characterless face of Salome, so that there is nothing but the dance, and she and the dance are inconceivable apart, indivisible as body and soul, meaning and form, ought to be. The Dancer in fact is, in Yeats' favourite expression, 'self-begotten' independent of labour; as such she differs totally from the artist who seeks her. She can exist only in the predestined dancing-place where, free from Adam's curse, beauty is born of itself, without the labour of childbirth or the labour of art; where art means wholly what it *is*. The tree also means what it is, and its beauty is a function of its whole being, achieved without cost, causing no ugliness in an artist. This is one of the senses of the magnificent concluding stanza:

Labour is blossoming or dancing where
The body is not bruised to pleasure soul,
Nor beauty born out of its own despair,
Nor blear-eyed wisdom out of midnight oil.
O chestnut tree, great-rooted blossomer,
Are you the leaf, the blossom or the bole?
O body swayed to music, O brightening glance,
How can we know the dancer from the dance?
　　(*Among School Children*)

A savoir que la danseuse n'est pas une femme qui danse, pour
ces motifs juxtaposés qu'elle n'est pas une femme, mais une
métaphore résumant un des aspects élémentaires de notre
forme, glaive, coupe, fleur, etc., et qu'elle ne danse pas,
suggérant, par le prodige de raccourcis ou d'élans, avec une
écriture corporelle ce qu'il faudrait des paragraphes en prose
dialoguée autant que descriptive, pour exprimer, dans la
rédaction : poème dégagé de tout appareil du scribe.[1]

This is Mallarmé's accurate prediction of Yeats's poem.

   Among School Children might well be treated as the central statement
of the whole complex position of isolation and the Image. Later there
were many fine poems that dealt with the nature of the sacrifice, and
of the fugitive victory; like *Vacillation*, which asks the question
'What is joy?' and answers it with an image, of a sort to be achieved
only by choosing the way of Homer and shunning salvation; or like
the *Dialogue of Self and Soul*, or the simple statements of *The Choice*:

The intellect of man is forced to choose
Perfection of the life or of the work,
And if it choose the second must refuse
A heavenly mansion, raging in the dark.

When all the story's finished, what's the news?
In luck or out the toil has left its mark:
That old perplexity an empty purse,
Or the day's vanity, the night's remorse.

There are poems, too, which give the problem a more specifically
religious turn. The paradise in which labour and beauty are one,
where beauty is self-begotten and costs nothing, is the artificial

1 'I mean that the ballerina *is not a girl dancing*; that, considering the juxtaposition of those group motifs, *she is not a girl*, but rather a metaphor which
symbolizes some elemental aspect of earthly form: sword, cup, flower, etc.;
and that *she does not dance* but rather, with miraculous lunges and abbreviations,
writing with her body, she *suggests* things which the written work could *express*,
only in several paragraphs of dialogue or descriptive prose. Her poem is
written without the writer's tools.' (From Mallarmé's essay, *Ballets*, trans.
Bradford Cook) [Ed.].

paradise of a poet deeply disturbed by the cost in labour. The ambiguities of hatred and love for 'marble and bronze' inform not only those poems in which Yeats praises the active aristocratic life and its courtesies, but also the Byzantium poems, which also celebrate the paradisal end of the dilemma. In this paradise life, all those delighting manifestations of growth and change in which the scarecrow has forfeited his part, give way to a new condition in which marble and bronze are the true life and inhabit a changeless world, beyond time and intellect (become, indeed, the image truly conceived, without human considerations of cost). The artist himself may be imagined, therefore, a changeless thing of beauty, purged of shapelessness and commonness induced by labour, himself a self-begotten and self-delighting marble or bronze. 'It is even possible that being is only possessed completely by the dead'; we return to the ambiguous life or death of the Image. Those who generate and die, perpetually imperfect in their world of becoming, have praise only for that world; the old man has no part in it, praising only the withered tree and the dry well, hoping only for escape into the world of complete being, the world of the self-begotten. 'The artifice of eternity', like 'the body of this death', is a reversible term.

Sailing to Byzantium could scarcely be regarded as less than a profoundly considered poem; yet Yeats was willing to accept the criticism of the acute Sturge Moore that the antithesis of the birds of the dying generations and the golden bird was imperfect; and this consideration was one of the causes of the second poem, Byzantium. 'Your Sailing to Byzantium,' wrote Moore, 'magnificent as the first three stanzas are, lets me down in the fourth, as such a goldsmith's bird is as much nature as man's body, especially if it only sings like Homer and Shakespeare of what is past or passing or to come to Lords and Ladies.' Yeats sent him a copy of Byzantium so that he should have an idea of what was needed for the symbolic cover design of his new book (at this time he was going to call it not The Winding Stair but Byzantium) and added that Moore's criticism was the origin of the new poem – it had shown the poet that 'the idea needed exposition'. Only a little earlier, by the way, Moore had provided Yeats with a copy of Flecker's A Queen's Song, which has a certain relevance to Byzantium, being a treatment of the topic of living beauty versus bronze and marble, or in this instance, gold:

Had I the power
To Midas given of old
To touch a flower
And leave its petal gold
I then might touch thy face,
Delightful boy,
And leave a metal grace
A graven joy.

Thus would I slay –
Ah! desperate device! –
The vital day
That trembles in thine eyes,
And let the red lips close
Which sang so well
And drive away the rose
To leave a shell.

We have already seen why Yeats was so interested in Byzantine art; it gave him that sense of an image totally estranged from specifically human considerations (and particularly from discursive intellect) with meaning and form identical, the vessel of the spectator's passion, which led him to develop the Dancer image. These lines of Flecker point also towards that life-in-death, death-in-life, which characterizes the perfect being of art. The absolute difference, as of different orders of reality, between the Image and what is, in the usual sense, alive, was the crucial point upon which the first Byzantium poem had, on Moore's view, failed; it was so important to the poet that he did his work again, making the distinction more absolute, seeking some more perfect image to convey the quality, out of nature and life and becoming, of the apotheosized marble and bronze. The bird must absolutely be a bird of artifice; the entire force of the poem for Yeats depended upon this – otherwise he would scarcely have bothered about Moore's characteristic, and of course intelligent, quibble. Professor N. Jeffares has shown how full are the opening lines of *Sailing to Byzantium* of peculiarly powerful suggestions of natural life, the life of generation; the salmon carries obvious suggestions of sexual vigour, and, it might be added, of that achieved physical beauty Yeats so much admired, immense power and utter singleness of purpose, in the business of generating and dying. Of course the golden bird must be the antithesis of this, as well as the heavenly counterpart of old scarecrows. It prophesies, speaks out as the foolish and passionate need not; it uses the language of courtesy in a world where all the nature-enforced discriminations of spirit and body, life and death, being and becoming, are meaningless. 'Marbles of the dancing floor/Break bitter furies of complexity'. And it is this world that Byzantium symbolizes. Mr Jeffares says the bird is different in the second poem because 'here it is explicitly contrasted with natural birds, to their disadvantage'. In fact the same contrast is intended in the earlier poem; the new degree of explicitness is what Moore's criticism forced upon the poet. The focus of attention is no longer on the poignancy of the contrast between nature and art in these special senses; nature now becomes 'mere complexities, The fury and the mire', and the strategy of the poem is, clearly, to establish the immense paradoxical vitality of the dead, more alive than the living; still, but richer in movement than the endless agitation of becoming.

And this is precisely the concept of the dead face and the dancer, the mind moving like a top, which I am calling the central icon of Yeats and of the whole tradition. Byzantium is where this is the normal condition, where all is image and there are no contrasts and no costs, inevitable concomitants of the apparition of absolute being in the sphere of becoming. We can harm the poem by too exclusive an attention to its eschatology, and it is salutary to read it simply as a marvellously contrived emblem of what Yeats took the work of art to be. There is no essential contradiction between the readings. The reconciling force is Imagination, the creator of the symbol by which men 'dream and so create Translunar paradise'. Or, to use the completely appropriate language of Blake,

This world of Imagination is the world of Eternity; it is the divine bosom into which we shall all go after the death of the Vegetated body. This World of Imagination is Infinite & Eternal, whereas the world of Generation, or Vegetation, is Finite & Temporal ... The Human Imagination ... appear'd to Me ... throwing off the Temporal that the Eternal might be Establish'd ... In Eternity one Thing

never Changes into another Thing. Each Identity is
Eternal.

There is no better gloss on Yeats' poem, a poem impossible outside
the tradition of the Romantic Image and its corollary, the doctrine
of necessary isolation and suffering in the artist.

In poems later than these, Yeats continues the search for the reconciling image; and he constantly recurs to the theme of remorse, the
lost perfection of the life. His *Dejection Ode*, at last, is *The Circus
Animals' Desertion*. The poet sought a theme, without finding one:

> Maybe at last, being but a broken man,
> I must be satisfied with my heart . . .

The 'heart' is the self, speaking out of stilled fury and lifeless mire; it is
that which has been denied for the work. He enumerates the old
themes which had served in the past to cheat the heart, and presents
them all, unfairly bitter, as the consolations merely of his own
imperfection and estrangement. Oisin was sent through the islands of
'vain gaiety, vain battle, vain repose' to satisfy an amorous need in
the poet; *The Countess Cathleen* had its origin in a private fear for a
mistress, but

>   soon enough
> This dream itself had all my thought and love.

And this was the way with all his themes.

> And when the Fool and Blind Man stole the bread
> Cuchulain fought the ungovernable sea;
> Heart-mysteries there, and yet when all is said
> It was the dream itself enchanted me:
> Character isolated by a deed
> To engross the present and dominate memory.
> Players and painted stage took all my love,
> And not those things that they were emblems of.
>   (*The Circus Animals' Desertion*)

'Players and painted stage' are here the dream, the work of imagination which relegates 'real' life to a position of minor importance.
Hence the final stanza; like the fresh images of *Byzantium*, these
images begin in fury and mire, among the dying generations, and are

changed in the dream of imagination. When this no longer works, the poet falls back into the 'formless spawning fury', left to live merely, when living is most difficult, life having been used up in another cause.

Those masterful images because complete
Grew in pure mind, but out of what began?
A mound of refuse or the sweepings of a street,
Old kettles, old bottles, and a broken can,
Old iron, old bones, old rags, that raving slut
That keeps the till. Now that my ladder's gone,
I must lie down where all the ladders start,
In the foul rag-and-bone shop of the heart.

(ibid.)

The increasingly autobiographical quality of the later poems is justified precisely by this need to examine the relation of process to product, of dying generations to bronze and marble. We are reminded of the extraordinary proportion of biographical matter in Coleridge's poem, particularly in the first version of it. If we wanted to study Yeats as hero, we could dwell upon the astonishing pertinacity with which he faced, and the integrity with which he solved, a problem which can never be far from the surface of poetry in this tradition; the Image is always likely to be withdrawn, indeed almost any normal biographical situation is likely to cause its withdrawal – this is part of its cost. Coleridge was finished as a poet in his early thirties; Arnold's situation is in this respect rather similar. Yeats often faced the crisis; the *Autobiographies* show how often, and how desperately, and many poems are made out of it. When poetry is Image, life must, as Yeats said, be tragic.

The dead face which has another kind of life, distinct from that human life associated with intellectual activity; the dancer, inseparable from her dance, devoid of expression – that human activity which interferes with the Image – turning, with a movement beyond that of life, in her narrow luminous circle and costing everything; the bronze and marble that does not provide the satisfactions of the living beauty but represent a higher order of truth, of being as against becoming, which is dead only in that it cannot change: these are the images of the Image that I have considered in this chapter. They culminate, in Yeats, in the Dancer-image of *Among School Children*;

and so does the image of the Tree. This image summarizes the traditional Romantic critical analogy of art as organism, and, while it is intimately related to the doctrine of the Image, as I have described it, one must discuss it in its own context. In a sense the next chapter will take us no further, except in so far as it clinches my reading of Yeats' *Among School Children*; but its relation to the cult of the Image is so close that it has at any rate to be mentioned, and it can be regarded as an excursus, or an attempt to consolidate.

Yvor Winters

from *Forms of Discovery* 1967 (first published as
The Poetry of W. B. Yeats, 1960)

We have been told many times that we do not have to take the ideas of W. B. Yeats seriously in order to appreciate his poetry; but if this is true, Yeats is the first poet of whom it has ever been true. We need to understand the ideas of Donne and Shakespeare in order to appreciate their works, and we have to take their ideas seriously in one sense or another, and it is possible to take their ideas seriously much of the time. A great deal of scholarly work has been done on their ideas, and some of this work has contributed to our appreciation of what they wrote. A great deal of scholarly work has been done on Yeats in recent years; unfortunately, the better one understands him, the harder it is to take him seriously.[1]

I shall refer rather often in this essay to a book by John Unterecker. The book gives a more detailed account than any other which I know of what Yeats was doing or thought he was doing. It accepts without question Yeats's ideas regarding the nature of poetry, ideas which in my opinion are unacceptable. And like almost every other publication on Yeats, it accepts without question the notion that Yeats was a very great poet and it merely substitutes exegesis for criticism. For example, Mr Unterecker explains the meaning of an

[1] In this essay I shall discuss a good many of Yeats's poems in detail. It is impractical to quote them in full. After the title of each poem discussed, therefore, I shall give the page number of *The Collected Poems of W. B. Yeats*, The Macmillan Co., New York, 1951.

early poem, *The Two Trees*, and I think correctly. Then, with no explanation whatever, he refers to it as 'so grand a poem'. The poem is obviously a bad poem: it is sentimental and stereotyped at every point. Mr Unterecker is a split personality: on the one hand he is a careful scholar and on the other hand he is a critic with neither talent nor training. In this he resembles most of the literary scholars with whose work I am acquainted. His book is very helpful notwithstanding.

Mr Unterecker says (*A Reader's Guide*), and I believe correctly so far as Yeats's theory goes:

Because all occult symbols are linked ultimately to a universal harmony, any consistent interpretation of one of them was 'right' since it in turn led to that harmony. The only danger, as Yeats frequently pointed out, is that the reader is likely to limit the symbol's meaning and so throw it into the area of allegory.

For some readers, this passage may call for brief explanation. In terms of medieval poetry, the word *symbol* refers to an object which has a one-to-one relationship to a meaning: that is, the whale is Satan, and Dante's panther, lion, and wolf, are lust, pride, and avarice. When such symbols occur in the course of a narrative, we have allegory. But Yeats here employs the word *symbol* as we employ it in speaking of French symbolist poetry, and the meaning of the term is reversed. Mallarmé was the great theorist of this kind of thing: his aim was to produce a kind of poetic absolute in which rational meaning would be as far as possible suppressed and suggestions would be isolated. He was not wholly successful in his aim, for many – perhaps most – of his later poems appear to deal, as obscurely as possible, with the theory of this kind of poetry; but he tried. In so far as this kind of effort succeeds, we have, in the very words of the master, an *aboli bibelot d'inanité sonore*. This is what Frank Kermode calls the Romantic Image, that is, the image which is meaningless, inscrutable, the image of which the dancer with the beautiful body and the expressionless face is the perfect type. Kermode disapproves of the method, and he finds it in Yeats, but he is overcome by Yeats (like most professors and literary critics, Kermode is deeply moved by trite language) and considers him a great poet notwithstanding.

What Yeats and Unterecker mean by a 'universal harmony' it would be hard to say. Mr Unterecker says elsewhere (*A Reader's Guide*):

Any analogy we can construct for the symbol, any meaning we assign to it, is legitimate so long as we recognize that that meaning is *not* its meaning. Its meaning must be more elusive than any value we can – with words – fix to it. All that the meaning we assign to a symbol can ever be is either part of its meaning or one of its possible meanings. No symbol has a meaning.

And again (*A Reader's Guide*) he tells us that the symbol does not give us meaning 'but instead the feeling of meaning. . . . an undefined sense of order, or rightness, of congruence at the heart of things'. I discussed this theory of the feeling of meaning a good many years ago, in writing of what I called pseudo-reference, and a little later in my essay on Poe. And Mr Unterecker again: 'Yeats allows us to experience. . . . the necessary if momentary illusions of order which give us courage to live.' Foolish as these ideas may seem, they are, as nearly as I can make out, very often held by Yeats as well as by Mr Unterecker, and they are commonly accepted in our time.

Yeats, of course, often deviated from this theory of the symbol and wrote forthright poems; and he often wrote in symbols more nearly akin to medieval symbols than to Mallarméan; and Mr Unterecker throughout his book writes of particular poems as if their method were medieval; and in fact, if we accept Mr Unterecker's general theory, there is no justification for his many pages of exegesis. But the theory provides a dark and convenient little corner into which the apologist may retreat rapidly backward whenever he is embarrassed by the meaning.

I will try to summarize the principal ideas which motivate Yeats's poetry. All good comes from the emotions, and even madness is good. *Wisdom* is a pejorative term; *ignorance* is the opposite. In Yeats's later work *lust* and *rage* become increasingly prominent and they represent virtues. Sexual union is equated with the mystical experience or at least participates in the mystical experience in a literal way. This is not the same thing as the analogy of sexual union which is sometimes used by the Christian mystics. The Christian mystics tell us that the mystical experience is absolutely different from any human experience and thus cannot be described in language, but that the experience can be suggested by analogy. This leads, I think, to a more or less fraudulent poetry, for the poet is pretending to deal with an ineffable experience in dealing with something irrelevant to it; but the fraud is, in a sense, an honest one, for the rules of the procedure are known. But for Yeats the two experiences are of the same kind, the only difference being that the sexual experience of living humans is less nearly pure than would be the experience of disembodied spirits: we are given the pure experience in *Ribh at the Tomb of Baile and Ailinn*, in which Ribh reads his book by the pure light given off by the orgasm of the disembodied lovers.

Yeats's concept of what would be the ideal society is also important. Such a society would be essentially agrarian, with as few politicians and tradesmen as possible. The dominant class would be the landed gentry; the peasants would also be important, but would stay in their place; a fair sprinkling of beggars (some of them mad), of drunkards, and of priests would make the countryside more picturesque. The gentlemen should be violent and bitter, patrons of the arts, and the maintainers of order; they should be good horsemen, preferably reckless horsemen (if the two kinds may exist in one); and they should be fond of fishing. The ladies should be beautiful and charming, should be gracious hostesses (although there is a place for more violent ladies – *videlicet* Mrs French of *The Tower*), should if possible be musicians, should drive men mad, love, marry, and produce children, should not be interested in ideas, and should ride horseback, preferably to hounds. So far as I can recollect, the ladies are not required to go fishing. What Yeats would have liked would have been a pseudo-eighteenth-century Ireland of his own imagining. He disliked the political and argumentative turmoil of revolutionary Ireland; he would scarcely have thought that the order which has emerged was sufficiently picturesque to produce poetry.

Yeats's cosmological and psychological system has been so fully discussed by others that I shall merely summarize it. He believed that history proceeds through cycles of two thousand years each. Every cycle begins in a state of objectivity (which is evil) and with violence; it proceeds through subjectivity (which is good), through pure subjectivity (which is too much of a good thing), and it then proceeds toward objectivity and ultimate dispersal and a new beginning. The life of every human goes through a similar cycle. Yeats had two diagrams for this process: the diagram of the phases of the moon and the diagram of the inter-penetrating cones (gyres, pernes, or spindles). The first of these is a circle with the twenty-eight phases of the moon marked upon it. At the top is the dark of the moon (pure objectivity, where no life is possible); at the bottom is the full moon (pure subjectivity, and at this point in the cycle of the individual man the spirit may leave the body and encounter other spirits); on the opposite sides of the circle are the two half-moons, which complete the division of the circle into quarters. Between the dark and the first half-moon we have a primitive condition of violence and elementary learning, the struggle between the spirit and brutality. Between the first half and the full moon, we approach creativity; and between the full and the second half we depart from creativity. The period of the greatest creativity is on both sides of the full and close to it. Between the second half and the dark we are in the period of wisdom, in which creativity is almost at an end, and are approaching death, in the life of a man, and the end of an era, in terms of the historical cycle. The gyres are most easily represented by Richard Ellmann's diagram of the two isosceles triangles lying on their sides: the short lines of these triangles should be very short in relation to the long lines, and the tip of each triangle should reach to the middle of the short line of the other. This design gives us a cross-section of the interpenetrating cones or gyres. At the point where the long lines intersect, we have the period corresponding to the full moon on the circle. The cones rotate in opposite directions, and one of them is winding the thread of life from the other: the procedure is perning or gyring. At the end of a two-thousand-year cycle there is a sudden and violent reversal and the perning starts in the other direction.

In addition to Yeats's explicit ideas, there are certain consistent attitudes which should be mentioned. In his early work of the Celtic twilight, he relied very heavily for his subjects on the figures of Irish legend: Oisin, Cuchulain, Conchobor, Deirdre, and others, and at this time and later he created a few such characters independently, such as Red Hanrahan, Michael Robartes, and Owen Aherne. But Yeats needed heroes for his work and he came more and more to need contemporary heroes. The result was his attempt to transform himself and his friends into legendary heroes. The most important of the friends were Lady Gregory, Major Robert Gregory, John Synge, Shawe-Taylor, and Hugh Lane; but there were others, among them Douglas Hyde. None of these except Lady Gregory and John Synge would be known outside of Ireland today had Yeats not written about them, and Lady Gregory would be little known. In fact Synge's reputation in the early part of the twentieth century was due at least as much to Yeats as to Synge, and his reputation has shrunken greatly. I can remember the time when Synge was the greatest dramatist in English except Shakespeare. There is no harm in praising one's friends, but when so much hyperbole is expended on people of small importance, the discrepancy between the motive and the emotion becomes increasingly evident with time; there seems to be something ridiculous about it. Maude Gonne was a special case, for Yeats was in love with her; but his equation of Maude Gonne with Deirdre, Helen of Troy, and Cathleen ni Houlihan partakes of his dramatization of himself. His concern with his uninteresting relatives and ancestors would seem to be part of the same dramatization.

I will turn to the principal poems related to the theory of the historical cycles. *Leda and the Swan* describes the rape of Leda by Zeus in the form of a swan, a rape which led to the birth of Helen, the destruction of Troy, and the disintegration of early Greek civilization. The rape introduced the next cycle of Greek civilization, which ended with the collapse of 'Platonic tolerance', 'Doric discipline', and ultimately the Roman Empire. *Two Songs from a Play* describe the end of the second Greek cycle, and the beginning of the Christian. *The Second Coming* prophesies the imminent end of the Christian cycle. Each of these works deals with violence, for every cycle begins and ends in violence. Yeats admires violence in general and has little use for Platonic tolerance, Doric discipline, or the civilization produced by Christianity. This fact is especially important when we read *The Second Coming.*

The account of the rape in the first eight lines of *Leda and the Swan* (p. 211) is very impressively done, but an account of a rape in itself has very limited possibilities in poetry. The important thing here is this: that the rape is committed on a mortal girl by Zeus. In the significance of this fact will reside the power or weakness of the whole poem. In the first portion of the sestet, we are told that the swan has engendered the fall of Troy and the death of Agamemnon, but there is nothing about the historical cycles: this has to be read in from what we know of Yeats's theories – which are, after all, ridiculous. The greatest difficulties reside in the remainder of the sestet. 'Did she put on his knowledge with his power?' The question implies that she *did* put on his power, but in what sense? She was quite simply over-powered or raped. She did not share his power, unless we understand a mystical union in the sexual act, which I think is implied. And what about his knowledge? Was this the knowledge of the fall of Troy and the death of Agamemnon? Was it the knowledge that a new cycle was about to begin (in spite of the fact that there is no reference to the cycles in the poem)? Or was it the omniscience of the god, resulting from the sexual union, a knowledge which would include the two other forms of knowledge? I suspect the last, but I would have difficulty in proving it. Next we have to consider 'the brute blood of the air'. The swan as such is a brute and flies through the air. Zeus may be thought of as living in the air and descending from the air. But Zeus as such was not a brute in Greek myth, and his animal disguises were disguises; nevertheless he often appeared in brute forms. The brute form may be connected in the mind of Yeats with the identification of sexual union and the mystical experience. Satan, however, was referred to in the middle ages as The Prince of the Air, and he and his demons were said to live 'in darkened air'. I do not recollect that Yeats had mentioned this fact anywhere, but the fact is easily available, and it seems to me unlikely that Yeats would have overlooked it. Yeats was fascinated with the concept of demonic possession as a form of the mystical experience and with the possibility of obtaining supernatural knowledge through such possession. In *The Gift of Harun al-Rashid* (p. 439), the young wife is possessed by a Djinn, apparently as a result of sexual awakening, and in her sleep she communicates the knowledge which her husband desires. This is a pretty fantasy, I suppose, but one can scarcely take it seriously. But we return to the question: is Zeus a god or a demon, or does it make no difference? I suspect that it made no difference to Yeats, who, as Chesterton said of Blake, appears to have kept bad company in the other world; but it should make a difference if we are to adjust our feelings to the motive, for what is the motive?

Then there is the difficulty that the poem ends with a question. A question, if it is really a question, is a weak way in which to end a poem, for it leaves the subject of the poem unjudged. But this question may be, as I suspect it is, a rhetorical question: in this event the answer should be either *yes* or *no*. There is nothing in the poem to help us choose, but, from what I know of Yeats, I think that he expected us to say *yes*. This brings us to the final difficulty: the vehicle of the poem is a Greek myth, and there is no harm in this if the tenor is serious; but the tenor is a myth of Yeats's private making, and it is foolish. That is, if we are to take the high rhetoric of the poem seriously, we must really believe that sexual union is a form of the mystical experience, that history proceeds in cycles of two thousand years each, and that the rape of Leda inaugurated a new cycle; or at least we must believe that many other people have believed these things and that such ideas have seriously affected human thinking and feeling. But no one save Yeats has ever believed these things, and we are not sure that Yeats really believed them. These constitute his private fairy tale, or an important part of it, which he sometimes took seriously and sometimes did not. I see no way to make up one's mind about this poem except to decide that it is one of two things: an *aboli bibelot d'inanité sonore* or an *aboli bibelot de bêtise*. I feel sure that it is the latter, but I wish it were the former, for the former would at least be inscrutable and would call for greater skill on the part of the poet. The sonority is real, and I can appreciate it as well as the next man, but it takes more than sonority to make a great poem. Pure sonority eventually comes to seem pompous and empty.

Two Songs from a Play (p. 210) exhibit the same sonorous rhetoric and much of Yeats's private mythology: the difficulties therefore are similar to those in *Leda*. Mr Unterecker (*A Reader's Guide*) gives a page of explanation of the poem. He equates the fierce Virgin and her Star with Virgo and Spica (of the zodiac), with Astraea and the Golden Age, with the staring Virgin (Athena) and the heart of Dionysus; and he tells us that these anticipate respectively Mary and Christ, Mary and the Star of Bethlehem, Mary and the Christian Age, and Mary and Christ's heart. This set of relationships is sufficiently complicated for a poem of sixteen lines in the course of which the relationships are not explained or even suggested, but I suspect that there is one additional complication. In the poem entitled *A Nativity* (p. 332), a poem in which the symbolic method is medieval, we have the line: 'Another star has shot an ear'; and of this and other similar figures Yeats tells us: 'I had in my memory Byzantine mosaic pictures of the Annunciation, which show a line drawn from a star to the ear of the Virgin. She conceived of the Word, and therefore through the ear a star fell and was born' (*A Reader's Guide*). The fierce Virgin at the end of the first song is, of course, Mary; she must be fierce, because each new era begins in violence: we thus substitute Yeats's private myth of the Virgin for the traditional one. Similarly it was the odour of Christ's blood (in the second song) which put an end to Platonic tolerance and Doric discipline; that is, it was the violence of the new religion, the Galilean turbulence of Christ. The Babylonian starlight and the fabulous darkness indicate the same thing: we observe starlight most clearly in the dark of the moon, which is the period of pure objectivity and of the violent reversal of the gyres. The rhetorical force in the poem is close to Yeats's best – but it is purely rhetorical. What he is saying is almost as foolish as what he says in section 3 of *The Tower* (p. 195), especially the twelve lines beginning 'And I declare my faith.' These lines are uttered with a passion which is obviously meant to be convincing, but who can be convinced? The second half of the second song is an excellent elegiac stanza, but it has only a loose connection with what has preceded.

The difficulties are similar in *The Second Coming* (p. 184). In line six, the expression 'the ceremony of innocence' is misleading and awkward. By reading *A Prayer for My Daughter*, which follows, one discovers that the phrase means the ceremonious life in which innocence flourishes; but as one comes to it in the poem, it would seem to indicate some kind of ceremony, perhaps baptismal, perhaps sacrificial, perhaps some other. Otherwise the first eight lines are very impressive if one takes them phrase by phrase: the adjective *mere* in the fourth line, for example, is a stroke of genius. But what do the lines mean? One who has lived through the last thirty years or more in adulthood and who has not observed the date of the poem (the volume was published in 1921) may feel that Yeats was writing about the growth of fascism, nazism, or communism:

>   the worst
> Are full of passionate intensity.

But the first two are impossible and the third is unlikely. 'The best' are the Irish aristocrats; 'the worst' are the Irish engaged in politics, who were trying to establish a constitutional democracy and who eventually succeeded. The poem is an attack on civilized government made by a man who felt an intense dislike for democracy and the political activity without which democracy cannot survive – a dislike which was due in part to his native temperament, but largely, I fear, to the fact that Maude Gonne was more interested in politics than in Yeats; by a man who, during much of his later life, was often tempted in the direction of fascism. The first four and a half lines of the second section are an example of Yeats's rhetorical skill, but for their effect they depend upon our belief in his notion of the *Spiritus Mundi*. From there on we have his description of the beast, which is a fine description. But the account of the beast is not pure description. If we are to take it as seriously as Yeats's language indicates that we should, we must again accept his theory of the gyres as in some way valid. And if we do this, we must face the fact that Yeats's attitude toward the beast is different from ours: we may find the beast terrifying, but Yeats finds him satisfying – he is Yeats's judgement upon all that we regard as civilized. Yeats approves of this kind of brutality. When we consider all of these complications, it becomes very difficult to arrive at an acceptance of the poem, an acceptance both rational and emotional. And what would we mean if we said, in the face of these difficulties, that we accepted the poem emotionally and in no other way? The question seems to mean nothing.

I do not deny that civilization may be coming to an end – there is no way of knowing, although I think that its chances for surviving for a long time are fairly good. But if we are to have a poem dealing with the end of civilization, and one that we can suppose to be great, the poem must be based on something more convincing than a home-made mythology and a loose assortment of untenable social attitudes. We need to invoke the Mallarméan concept of the symbol to save this poem, but we cannot invoke it because the ideas are perfectly clear.

I will consider *Sailing to Byzantium* and *Byzantium*. *Sailing to Byzantium* (p. 191) opens with a very good stanza. The first four lines of the next stanza are unfortunate. In the first two lines we have Yeats's familiar figure of the scarecrow, a melodramatic characterization of his own old age, and one which becomes very tiresome. In the next two lines we have one of his melodramatic renderings of emotion through ridiculous physical action:

> unless
> Soul clap its hands and sing, etc.

The fact that this figure came from Blake does not help it. It is similar to other and earlier passages:

> Until I cried and trembled and rocked to and fro

from *The Cold Heaven* (p. 122), and:

> While up from my heart's root
> So great a sweetness flows
> I shake from head to foot

from *Friends* (p. 122). Both of these poems were published in *Responsibilities*, in 1914, when Yeats was approximately forty-nine years old. The book preceding was published in 1910. These two poems, then, were written between the ages of forty-five and forty-nine, when Yeats ought to have been too old for such immature pseudo-poetics, but actually this kind of thing went on for the rest of his life. The next four lines of the stanza are admirable, and the third stanza is one of the most impressive in Yeats except for the phrase: 'perne in a gyre'. Yeats is inviting the sages who are now in eternity to return to life (to the gyres) and become his teachers. The phrase, however, is bad in two ways: first it gives us the image of the sages stepping from the wall and then spinning like tops or dervishes; second, it does not really mean this, but is a dead metaphor for the return to life. This is one of many examples of the use of medieval symbolism, which in Yeats amounts to a kind of personal shorthand, of unrealized figures of speech. An unrealized figure of speech, as I use the term, is a figure in which the vehicle or descriptive matter is dead; in such a figure one has to deduce the tenor from the dead vehicle. It would be better to use abstract language precisely. The last stanza is well written but the view here given of the function of the poet (to say nothing of the portrait of God) is distressing; the poet, having achieved immortality, will sing to keep a drowsy emperor awake, and he will sing to lords and ladies who are, presumably, equally drowsy. This is the legendary function of the bard, a function which fascinated Yeats, a function which he seems to have tried to fulfill in the Gregory household. The stanza is no accident. We find much the same idea in an earlier piece, *On Being Asked for a War Poem* (p. 153):

I think it better that in times like these
A poet's mouth be silent, for in truth
We have no gift to set a statesman right;
He has had enough of meddling who can please
A young girl in the indolence of her youth,
Or an old man upon a winter's night.

One cannot object to Yeats's refusing to write a poem to order on war or any subject; but the reason given is feeble and characteristic – it exhibits Yeats's sentimental and anti-intellectual view of the nature of his art. The final words of *Sailing to Byzantium*, 'to come', do not in themselves indicate that the poet is in any sense a prophet (there is, of course, no reason why he should be, but this concept might appear to some readers to improve the poem), for he, like the Emperor and and the lords and ladies, is now in eternity, and they all know what is to come. What is to come, like what is past or passing, merely provides material for this kind of poetry.

Byzantium (p. 243) has often been regarded as one of the most obscure of the poems, but the meaning is fairly obvious. As most of the commentators say, the poem deals with the poet looking out from eternity on those who are coming in; it thus differs from its companion piece, which deals with the poet's voyage to eternity and his arrival there. Curiously enough, although the city of *Byzantium* is eternity, it seems to be eternity only by night; by day it is corrupted by fury, mire, and blood – but this difficulty is not really great. The starlit or moonlit dome and the bird of the third stanza have led T. R. Henn (the only commentator, so far as I can recollect, who has risked explaining them) rather far from the Yeatsian system. It seems to me unlikely that the bird is a male symbol and the moon a female. In the first stanza, a starlit dome is a dome in the dark of the moon, in the period of complete objectivity or absolute death; a moonlit dome (on this occasion one is forced to suppose that the moon is full) is a dome in the period of perfect subjectivity, when the spirit leaves the body. Either dome would thus disdain man in his essentially human periods. In the third stanza, the golden bird, like the golden bird of the other poem, is an eternal bird, a bird of absolute death; it is on a starlit golden bough and can crow like the cocks of Hades. The meaning of all this strikes me as perfectly clear, as clear as the meaning of any medieval symbol. Such a bird would be embittered by the moon because the moon marks the stages of human life; the two stanzas support this interpretation in all their details. The second stanza, which is an interruption of the argument conducted in one and three, and which would function more effectively as the third than as the second, gives us the poet's invocation of the dead, his attempt to become one with them. The fourth stanza deals with the purification of the entering spirits, and the fifth with their struggle to enter; as far as the mere logic of the discussion goes, these stanzas ought to be in reverse order. The order probably contributes as much as the esoteric symbols to the difficulty that many readers have found in the poem. The order may have been intentional – may have been an attempt to befuddle the reader into believing that medieval method was Mallarméan method – but after more than forty years of reading Yeats, I believe that the order was accidental. As we have been told, the sea is doubtless a symbol for life, and the dolphins who carry the dead to Byzantium are incidentally phallic symbols: the sea is thus tormented by the phallic symbols and by the gongs which are a call to death. We scarcely have the impenetrable image here (Mallarmé was incomparably more skilful at that); we merely have excitement and carelessness. If we study Yeats's private system, we can discover to a certainty what starlight means: its meaning is as definite as the meaning of Dante's panther. The trouble is that, like Dante's panther, it is merely a short-hand device for an idea. Starlight tells us nothing about death; the panther tells us nothing about lust. In so far as either is described well at the sensory level, it is good decoration – but it is only decoration and does nothing to clarify the subject. Yeats's poem is almost wholly decoration, and the ornaments are from his private myths. The generality of the meaning of the ornament drawn from such myths is essentially of the same kind as the generality of the cliche: it has nothing in common with the precise generalization of abstract terms. Yeats had, in fact, only a vague idea of what he was talking about. He did his talking in terms of sensory details, which everyone believes (in our time) to be essential to poetry. The fact that his sensory details do not embody definite thought (as the sensory details of Stevens and Valéry often do) and the fact that his details are often poorly realized at the sensory level do not disturb his admirers, for his language is violent. We are in search of easy emotion, and we find it in Yeats.

Among School Children (p. 212), like the poems which I have already discussed, is regarded as one of the greatest. The first stanza is quietly and effectively descriptive. The second stanza opens with one of his personal cliches, 'a Ledaean body': the body is Ledaean because it is the body of Helen, daughter of Leda – that is to say, the body of Maude Gonne. But none of us have ever seen Leda or Helen, and in a few more years there will be no one who has ever seen Maude Gonne, and the portraits of Maude Gonne which I have seen are not very convincing. This is a somewhat pretentious way of saying 'a very beautiful body', but it is not description any more than this phrase of mine would be – it is easy allusion, mechanical association. We have an overtone from the Greek myth and one from the Yeatsian myth, both very thin. Helen destroyed the civilization of her time and was thus heroic. Yeats believed that Maude Gonne was destroying the civilization of her time, and he longed to see it destroyed (although he regretted her personal part in the destruction). Therefore the two women were similar, not merely in their personal beauty but in the consequences of their behaviour. But Maude Gonne played a real, though minor, part in establishing a civilized government in Ireland, and her son Sean MacBride played a part also, as his father had done. If Maude Gonne was really heroic (I am not a specialist in Irish history nor an aficionado of the Irish temperament), it was in a way that Yeats was incompetent to understand. Maude Gonne was neither Helen nor Deirdre; she was a vigorous and practical (albeit Irish) woman. She may have had faults and virtues which are irrelevant to this discussion, but Yeats did not understand what she was doing. As Mrs Yeats is reported to have said, Yeats simply did not understand people. One can find additional testimony to the same effect in the letters of Ezra Pound – letters written when Pound was young and still a pretty shrewd observer. This may seem to be too much talk about a mere phrase: the point is that Yeats regularly employed mere phrases. Other cliches in these lines are: 'I dream' and 'bent above a sinking fire'. In the sixth line the sphere contains the idea in a general way, but not with the precision that would have been possible with abstract language or with a better figure; the egg adds nothing to the significance of the sphere and is comical in itself. The third stanza introduces fewer and less troublesome difficulties; but such phrases as 'fit of grief or rage' and 'daughters of the swan' are mechanical, and 'my heart is driven wild' is stereotyped melodrama of a sort to which I have already objected and shall object again. The fourth stanza is composed almost wholly of similar cliches and concludes with Yeats's favorite, that of the scarecrow. Stanzas five and six are of much the same kind: shoddy diction, carelessly violent diction, and further exploitation of the scarecrow. The two lines about Plato are passable but scarcely profound; the two lines about Aristotle are ridiculous without being witty; the lines about Pythagoras mean nothing and are anachronistic with regard to the history of fiddling. The seventh stanza seems to be the beginning of an important statement, but unfortunately the statement is completed in the final stanza and resolves itself into one which I can understand in terms of the pseudo-mysticism and anti-intellectualism of the past two hundred and fifty years but which I cannot grasp imaginatively – that is, in terms of human life as I know human life. The term *labour* seems to mean fruitful labor or ideal labor, and a labor which costs no effort. But where does this kind of labor exist, except, perhaps, in the life of a tree? The body is always bruised to pleasure soul; wisdom is always born out of midnight oil or out of something comparable. The diction in these lines is abominable: the first two lines are bad enough, but the third and fourth are as bad as Keats's 'Here where men sit and hear each other groan'. The question addressed to the tree is preposterous: the tree is obviously more than the leaf, the blossom or the bole, but these all exist and can be discussed, and it is because of this fact that we have words for them – the implication of the passage is that the tree is an inscrutable unit, like the Mallarméan poem. The diction of the seventh line is as bad as that of the third and fourth. The last line is similar to the fifth and sixth. When we watch the dancer we may not discriminate, although a choreographer could; but if the dancer and the dance could not be discriminated in fact, the dancer could never have learned the dance. Precisely the same ideas will be found in Emerson's *Blight*, a small affair but somewhat better written.

It may seem to the reader that I am unreasonable in objecting so strongly to trite language, when I have been willing to forgive a certain amount of it in Hardy and Bridges. But in the best of Hardy and Bridges the theme is sound and important; and in Yeats the theme is almost always foolish and ill-defined. In the best of Hardy and Bridges the amount of trite language is small; and in most of Yeats the trite language occupies most of the poem – there are a few poems of which this is not quite true, but there are only a few.

I have had something to say of Yeats's habit of excessive dramatization. I would like to be a little more explicit on this subject and then proceed to a few of his poems on his friends and on his political attitudes. I will quote two of Yeats's less ambitious poems and compare them briefly with two poems by John Synge on the same subjects. First is Yeats's poem *A Coat*: this is the last poem in *Responsibilities* and is his farewell to the style of the Celtic twilight:

I made my song a coat
Covered with embroideries
Out of old mythologies
From heel to throat;
But the fools caught it,
Wore it in the world's eyes
As though they'd wrought it,
Song, let them take it,
For there's more enterprise
In walking naked.

As I have tried to show, Yeats never learned to walk naked, although he managed to shed a few of the more obvious ribbons of the eighteen-nineties: but whether naked or bedizened, he never got over his exhibitionism. Here is Synge's poem:

After looking at one of A.E.'s pictures

Adieu, sweet Aengus, Maeve, and Fand,
Ye plumed yet skinny Shee,

That poets played with hand in hand
To learn their ecstasy.
We'll stretch in Red Dan Sally's ditch,
And drink in Tubber Fair,
Or poach with Red Dan Philly's bitch
The badger and the hare.
   (*The Passing of the Shee*)

I will now quote Yeats's poem (also from *Responsibilities*) *On Those That Hated 'The Playboy of the Western World'*:

Once when midnight smote the air,
Eunuchs ran through Hell and met
On every crowded street to stare
Upon great Juan riding by:
Even like these to rail and sweat
Staring upon his sinewy thigh.

That slow, that meditative man himself wrote as follows:

To a sister of an enemy of the author's who disapproved of 'The Playboy'

Lord, confound this surly sister,
Blight her brow with blotch and blister,
Cramp her larynx, lung, and liver,
In her guts a galling give her.

Let her live to earn her dinners
In Mountjoy with seedy sinners:
Lord, this judgment quickly bring,
And I'm your servant, J. M. Synge.
   (*The Curse*)

Yeats's poems are inflated; they are bardic in the worst sense. Synge's poems are witty and unpretentious.

   To a Friend Whose Work Has Come to Nothing (p. 107) exhibits the same inflated style and Yeats's predilection for madness. The first ten lines are plain and honest and exhibit a certain moral nobility; the last six, however, recommend madness as a cure for the problem the poem propounds. We have been told that the poem was addressed to Lady Gregory. Lady Gregory never followed the advice here given, but as she appears in this poem she is merely one in a long series of Yeatsian lunatics.

In Memory of Major Robert Gregory (p. 130) is in praise of Lady Gregory's son, who was killed in the First World War. It is commonly described as one of the greatest poems in our language; I confess that I think it is a very bad poem. The first two stanzas deal with Yeats's recent settling in his new house and with his thoughts about dead friends; the next three stanzas deal with three dead friends in particular: Lionel Johnson, John Synge, and Yeats's uncle George Pollexfen. The next six stanzas deal with Robert Gregory; the final stanza is a conclusion. The first stanza is quiet and acceptable, though undistinguished. The second stanza, undistinguished in general, contains two very awkward details: the third and fourth lines employ a conversational and verbose stereotype to embody simple matter, and the fifth line employs another. The fifth line, however, is bad in other ways: the words *up upon* make a crude combination, and the whole line, 'And quarrels are blown up upon that head', gives us, like the two lines preceding, a dead metaphor but this time a mixed metaphor as well. Unless we are imperceptive of the possibilities of language, we visualize something being blown up on top of a head. This kind of thing is common in newspaper writing and in other vulgar writing. I remember a freshman composition from many years ago, in which the student wrote: 'This line of study is basic to my field of endeavour'. The line by Yeats is the same kind of thing as my freshman's effort, and no apologetic reference to the virtues of colloquialism is an adequate defense. The third stanza, which deals with Lionel Johnson, is stereotyped throughout, but it contains two especially unfortunate details. Johnson is described as 'much falling', a sufficiently clumsy phrase in itself, but Pound tells us

> how Johnson (Lionel) died
> By falling from a high stool in a pub. . . .
> *(Hugh Selwyn Manberley)*

It seems likely that Pound's poem was written somewhat after that of Yeats, as nearly as I can judge from the dates at my disposal, and that the passage was intended as a comment on Yeats's phrase. At any rate, it would be a fair enough comment. Immediately below 'much falling' we get a very thin reincarnation of Roland's horn. The fourth stanza deals with John Synge. He is described as 'that enquiring man', a phrase to which I do not object in itself. But every time Synge appears by name in Yeats's poems, he is described as 'that . . . man', and we expect the formula as regularly as we come to expect rock, thorn trees, cold light, shaking and trembling, and scarecrows; furthermore, the unnecessary use of the demonstrative adjective is one of Yeats's most obviously mechanical devices for achieving over-emphasis. The remainder of this stanza is undistinguished, but one should consider these details: in line five, *certain* is used as a pronoun instead of an adjective; in line six we have 'a most desolate and stony place'; and in the last we have 'Passionate and simple as his heart', a phrase which is not only one of Yeats's common clichés but one which indicates as clearly as many others the anti-intellectual bent of his work. The fifth stanza deals with Yeats's uncle George Pollexfen, who, it seems, had been a vigorous horseman in his youth, but who had devoted himself to astrology in his later years. The diction is dull, but once again there are strange details. For example, if solid men and pure-bred horses are determined by the stars, then why not other men and horses? The limitation could have been clarified by such a word as *even*, but the writing is slovenly; as Pound said long ago, poetry should be at least as well written as prose. The words *sluggish*, *contemplative*, and *outrageous* indicate that Yeats disapproved of his uncle's later interests because they were, in some sense, intellectual; but Yeats himself was interested, throughout much of his life, in equally pseudo-intellectual studies. Perhaps the stanza is an example of what Cleanth Brooks would call irony; but it is also dull. The sixth stanza is respectably executed except for two details. In the second line, 'as it were' says nothing; it may have been used to fill out the line and achieve a rime, or it may have been used in the interests of colloquial style, although it is not colloquial. It seems to be lazy. The next to the last line, 'Our Sidney and our perfect man' is exorbitant praise. One might accept it as a mere outburst of grief except for the fact that Yeats devotes the rest of the poem to praising Gregory in these terms: he was a great horseman, scholar, and painter; he had the knowledge to give expert advice in architecture, sculpture, and most of the handicrafts. He may well have been a great horseman, but so is many a jockey; the praise in the other departments, however, appears excessive, for if it were not we should have heard of Gregory's accomplishments from other sources. He appears to have been no Sidney, but a charming and admirable young man who dabbled in the arts. We have familiar stereotypes in the last stanzas: cold rock and thorn, stern colour, delicate line, secret discipline, none of them really described or defined; we have the facile commonplaces of the final lines of stanzas eight and nine and the somewhat comical example of misplaced particularity in the final line of stanza eleven. In the twelfth and final stanza, Yeats tells us that he had hoped in this poem to comment on everyone whom he had ever loved or admired but that Gregory's death took all his heart for speech. He had managed to write twelve stanzas of eight lines each, however, before he stopped, but this remark serves as a kind of apology for the loose structure of the poem – a structure which remains loose in spite of the apology.

Coole Park, 1929 (p. 238) is a poem in honour of Lady Gregory and her home, Coole Park, which she had been forced to sell to the Forestry Department, although she was permitted to live there until her death. The poem is a typical meditation on the virtues of old families and on their patronage of the arts, but especially upon Lady Gregory as a force in bringing distinguished men together and guiding their work. The theme is therefore the intellectual force that Lady Gregory exerted upon these men: Douglas Hyde, a negligible poet who became a distinguished Celtic scholar, whose poetry Yeats apparently admired and whose scholarship he regretted; John Synge, whose plays Yeats greatly admired and vastly overrated; Shawe-Taylor and Hugh Lane, nephews of Lady Gregory and patrons of the arts but scarcely great men; and Yeats himself. Shawe-Taylor and Hugh Lane are described as 'those impetuous men'. This is a Yeatsian formula to describe distinguished gentlemen, and Synge appears in the usual formula for Synge: 'that slow, that meditative man'. The unfortunate Hyde is buried in the worst pseudo-poeticism of all, and Yeats employs a prettily apologetic description of himself. The central figure of speech appears in the third stanza. The first two lines of the first stanza place Lady Gregory and a swallow together in what appears to be an accidental juxtaposition, but in the third stanza the men are compared to swallows, and we are told that Lady Gregory could keep a swallow to its first intent, could control the flight of swallows. Obviously, she could do nothing of the sort; she may suppose that she could control talented men in some fashion, but we are not told how. The movement of the swallows is charming; Lady Gregory's influence on the men, presumably an intellectual influence, is never given us. What we have is a fairly good vehicle with almost no tenor, or fairly good decoration of an undefined theme. In the last two lines, however, the third stanza collapses almost completely. Line seven reads: 'The intellectual sweetness of those lines'. At the level of the vehicle, the lines are those of the swallows' flight; at the level of the tenor we have nothing, for 'intellectual sweetness' is merely a sentimental phrase with no conceptual support. The last line of this stanza, 'That cut through time or cross it withershins', is especially unclear. As to *withershins* the *Shorter Oxford English Dictionary* gives this account of it:

1. In a direction contrary to the usual; the wrong way – 1721.
2. In a direction contrary to the apparent course of the sun (considered as unlucky or causing disaster) – 1545.

The last line of the first stanza is pseudo-poetic. The third and fourth lines of the last stanza are commonplace, and the sixth and seventh are baffling: why should the mourners stand with backs to the sun and shade alike, and why is the shade sensual? This is verbiage for the sake of verbiage.

The best poem of this kind, I believe, is a late one, *The Municipal Gallery Revisited* (p. 316). There are a good many characteristic defects. In his attempt to achieve a conversational tone (or perhaps out of inadvertence) Yeats wrote a fair number of lines which are awkward in movement. The poem is predominantly iambic pentameter, but if we are to read it in this meter, we encounter problems, some more serious than others. Line four can be read only as three trochees followed by two anapests. In line eight of the same stanza we get this:

A revolutionary soldier kneeling to be blessed.

That is, we have four syllables in the first foot and either three or four in the second, depending on our pronunciation of *revolutionary*. It is hard to read the first line of the second stanza as anything but an alexandrine. In line three of the second stanza, we have a trochee in the last position if we pronounce *Ireland* correctly, but this is the only line in the poem in which this awkward variation occurs, and we are not prepared for it and are tempted to mispronounce the word for the sake of the rime. Line five in the same stanza is an alexandrine and the first lines of four, five, and six are alexandrines. We have such formulae as 'terrible and gay' and 'John Synge . . . that rooted man'. At the opening of the fourth stanza we have rhetorical exaggeration:

Mancini's portrait of Augusta Gregory,
'Greatest since Rembrandt', according to John Synge;

But this is followed immediately by the almost weary qualification:

A great ebullient portrait, certainly.

At the opening of the third stanza we have the expression of emotion through physical action:

Heart-smitten with emotion, I sink down,
My heart recovering with covered eyes.

But this is an account of an old man looking at the portraits of his dead friends and is understandable in a measure; it seems a somewhat unscrupulous and undignified play for our sympathy, but it has not the empty violence of comparable passages from earlier poems. The transition from five to six is awkward. Yeats apparently thought that the line at the end of five needed a footnote, and I dare say it does; but he puts his footnote in parentheses at the beginning of six, and it is unimpressive as poetry, and it detracts from the unity of six. Except for this defect, six is well enough written, but its effect depends upon Yeats's view of the ideal society, 'dream of the noble and the beggarman', a view by which I find myself unmoved. The last stanza overrates Yeats's friends but is the moving statement of an old man who held them in high esteem and who now reviews them all in the official portraits, all of them being dead. Perhaps the best apology for this poem is to be found in a poem by Robert Bridges, written a good many years earlier, his *Elegy among the Tombs*:

Read the worn names of the forgotten dead,
Their pompous legends will no smile awake;

Even the vainglorious title o'er the head
Wins its pride pardon for its sorrow's sake;
And carven Loves scorn not their dusty prize,
Though fallen so far from tender sympathies.

The best of the political poems, I suspect, is *Easter, 1916*. The worst
fault in the poem is the refrain, 'A terrible beauty is born'. One can
understand the sentiment, but the diction is pure Yeatsian fustian. In
the first stanza I regret the repetition of 'polite meaningless words',
but the defect is minor. In the line 'To please a companion', however,
we have an unrhythmical prose, if we pronounce *companion* correctly; to save the rhythm, we have to say 'companee*un*'. In the first
seven lines of the next stanza, lines which are passably written, we
have Yeats's view of what women should not do. In the next two
lines,

This man had kept a school
And rode our winged horse,

we have a pseudo-poeticism as bad as Hyde's sword or Roland's
horn. A little farther on we have this:

So sensitive his nature seemed.

The line is written in a rapid tetrameter, and it occurs in a poem
which otherwise is written in heavily accented trimeter, and for the
moment it ruins the movement. To save the meter, we should have
to read *sens'tive*, but the *Shorter Oxford English Dictionary* does not
give this pronunciation, and it seems an unlikely one. In the third
stanza the stream and the other details of momentary change are the
main part of the vehicle; the unchanging stone is the rest. The vehicle,
as mere description, is very well handled. The tenor, however, is
this: the truly spiritual life consists of momentary change; fixity of
purpose turns one to an imperceptive stone. This is familiar Romantic
doctrine, but I see no reason to take it seriously. In the last stanza, he
tells us that the Easter martyrs turned themselves to stone and perhaps in a poor cause, but he praises them for their heroism and laments
their deaths. The poem is marred by certain faults of style and by
more serious faults of thinking, which we must regard as virtues if
we are to be greatly moved.

I will turn now to a few poems which seem to me the most nearly successful.

The Wild Swans at Coole (p. 129) is perhaps the best of these. The line 'And now my heart is sore' is unfortunate, but otherwise the poem is excellently written. There are two unobtrusive but brilliant details, the effect of which seems to permeate the entire poem. In the first stanza we are given a quiet but excellent description of the dry autumn at twilight. The fifth line reads: 'Upon the brimming water among the stones'. The word *brimming* separates the world of water from the world of dryness with an almost absolute precision, and this separation is of the essence of the poem. In the fourth stanza we find a similar detail:

They paddle in the cold
Companionable streams. . . .

The cold streams are companionable to the swans but not to the aging human observer. Richard Ellmann gives us an interesting fact about the poem:

When the poem was first published in *The Little Review* in June 1917, the fifth and fourth stanzas were reversed. By putting the fourth stanza at the end Yeats made it possible to read it symbolically so that his awakening would be his death, a paradox well within his intellectual boundaries. Unfortunately, the word 'but' was now superfluous at the beginning of the last stanza: he nevertheless allowed it to remain.

(The Identity of Yeats)

One could employ this incident to illustrate Yeats's carelessness, a carelessness which can easily be documented elsewhere; but the word is not superfluous. In the third line of the fourth stanza the swans are either on the water or in the air, and at the end of the stanza they are in the air. 'But now', the last stanza tells us, they are on the water. This seems reasonable. And what is Mr Ellmann's authority for believing that Yeats's awakening would be his death? If the authority is to be found in Yeats, I have never seen it or a citation of it. The question with which the poem ends would be troublesome if it could not be understood or if it left the final meaning in doubt. Mr Unter-

ecker (*A Reader's Guide*), a disarmingly naive seeker for richness of
ambiguity, has this to say of it:

This complex question (and many others Yeats will soon be
asking) suggests its own mysteries: like that of the swans the
pattern of man survives; yet 'I', awakening some day (into
death?) will find the pattern of immortality 'flown away'
(and myself immortal?).

Why should the swans be a pattern of immortality? Yeats implies
clearly enough that they are an immortal pattern, but that is another
matter. As Wordsworth said, 'The Form remains, the Function
never dies'. Alice Meynell made this distinction between the poet
(a mortal individual) and the birds (an immortal form):

Hereditary Song,
　　Illyrian lark and Paduan nightingale,
Is yours, unchangeable the ages long;
　　Assyria heard your tale.

Therefore you do not die.
　　But single, local, lonely, mortal, new,
Unlike, and thus like all my race am I,
　　Preluding my adieu.
　　　　(*The Poet to the Birds*)

The idea is easy to grasp, whatever one may think of the style. And
why should Yeats's awakening signify his death? Let us remember
that the poem was written when Yeats was nearing the age of fifty,
and that he saw himself as a man of declining powers. His theories of
the phases of the moon and of the gyres were merely a rationalization
of opinions which he had long held, and the poem entitled *The
Phases of the Moon* appears in the same volume with this poem.
Yeats at this time is about to enter upon the fourth period, the period
of 'wisdom', in which creativity is lost; he is departing from subjectivity, which makes creation possible. The swan, moreover, has
been traditionally a symbol for beauty, and in Yeats's system water
and water-birds represent subjectivity. I would judge, then, that in
this poem Yeats sees in the swans a symbol of his creative power, still
present, but soon to be lost. The question then means: 'On whom will
this talent light when it has left me?' The poem in these terms is clear
and a fine poem. The word *companionable*, as I have accounted for it,

may seem to offer a difficulty if the talent is understood to be still present; but the talent seems to be on the point of departure, and the water (subjectivity), though companionable to the talent, is about to be uncompanionable to the poet.

I Am of Ireland (p. 262) appears to be a dialogue between Cathleen ni Houlihan (Maude Gonne) and W. B. Yeats. The lady seems to be inviting the poet to enter into Irish politics, and he finds the idea little to his liking. The poem is not a great poem, for the subject is too slight, but the movement and diction are masterly. Its chief weakness resides in the fact that it has to be paraphrased so baldly with reference to Yeats's life and prejudices. More information ought to be contained within the poem: more information might have led to a poem of greater intellectual richness or it might have led to a flat didactic poem. It is likely that Yeats chose the best method in the light of his own limitations, but the method is a makeshift.

Long-legged Fly (p. 327) is one of the most interesting poems, but as usual there are difficulties. The first stanza describes Caesar planning a battle to save civilization, and the third gives us Michelangelo painting the Pope's chapel, that is, creating civilization; but the second stanza describes Helen practising a tinker's shuffle on the empty streets of Troy. The refrain indicates that all three persons are engaged in deep thought over important action, but Helen is not depicted as thinking – she is depicted as unthinking; and, although Helen brought about the fall of Troy, she did not plan the fall but was merely an accidental cause. Although the detail of the second stanza is exceptionally fine, the theme collapses. Furthermore, in the opening lines of the third stanza, Yeats says that Michelangelo is painting his Adam in order to provide a sexual awakening for girls at puberty (for documentation of this obsession see *Under Ben Bulben IV*, p. 341) and this strikes me as so trivial (and so wrong) an aim for the painter's work that the poem is badly damaged by it: it is an example of Yeats's pseudo-religious glorification of sexuality. Then there are the two versions of the refrain in the second stanza. In the edition which I am using, the refrain at the end of the second stanza reads '*His* mind'. This cannot refer to Helen, and if it is correct, then we have some kind of supernal mind working through all three of the figures; this concept would be very vague, and the first stanza, in this event, would be misleading. The editors of the variorum edition, however, point out that this reading occurs only in my edition, and they give 'Her mind' as the correct reading. They are almost certainly right, but the bad proof-reading in almost all of Yeats's books would seem to indicate at least a possibility that they are wrong. If they are right, then the refrain at the end of the second stanza is meaningless. The descriptive detail throughout the poem and the movement of the lines are about equally beautiful.

I would like to mention a few minor efforts for one reason or another. *For Anne Gregory* (p. 240) is a charming and witty poem. *Crazy Jane Grown Old Looks at the Dancers* (p. 255) is beautifully done as regards diction, syntax, and every aspect of rhythm. One can say, perhaps, that the subject is melodramatic, or, in any event, that it is certainly of small importance. I admire the execution but seldom reread the poem. *Lullaby* (p. 259) is almost equally graceful and is equally slight. *After Long Silence* (p. 260) has often been highly praised. The first six lines are excellent, but at the end we are told that this is 'The supreme theme of Art and Song':

Bodily decrepitude is wisdom; young
We loved each other and were ignorant.

This is not, of course, the supreme theme of Art and Song, but we ought to consider what the lines mean. Bodily decrepitude and wisdom (a contemptible quality, according to Yeats) are the same thing; both are reached in old age (in the fourth period of the moon). Youth, love, and ignorance are the best things in life, according to the doctrine. Now I shall not speak in favor of bodily decrepitude, for I am beginning to experience it and know what it is; and I have nothing against youth and love, for I observe them about me daily and find them charming. But as a simple matter of fact, wisdom (in the normal sense of the word) is highly desirable and ignorance is not. In the world as we find it, we cannot have everything at once, but we must take things as they come and pay for what we get. However, my interpretation of the sixth line may be wrong. Yeats may have meant that the two friends were discoursing upon the supreme theme for discourse; namely, Art and Song. In this event, the two final lines would mean: *faute de mieux*. Because of the syntax and punctuation, it is impossible to be sure, although the first of my two readings strikes me as the more likely; either way the meaning of the two last lines in themselves remains the same. *The Cat and the Moon* (p. 164) gives us a cat which is beautifully described and a moon which is merely a stage property. *The Gyres* (p. 291) is very badly written: the first stanza in particular is pure Pistol. But the poem is also revealing, for Yeats is welcoming the destruction of civilization with enthusiasm, and is predicting the return of the kind of civilization which he admires and believes once to have existed. The reader of *The Second Coming* should study this poem as a companion-piece. The six poems entitled *Under Ben Bulben* (p. 341) give a clear summary of his ideas and attitudes, and are obviously offered as a final statement. One reads a succinct summary of the social ideas, for example, in the fifth of these, and of Yeats's attitude toward himself in the sixth. Mr Unterecker believes that the horseman of the epitaph is one of the wild horsemen of the mountains, who descend upon the world in times of disaster; this may be so, but I have always supposed him to be one of Yeats's ideal aristocrats. The wild horsemen appear in the first poem, the mortal horsemen in the fifth (as well as in *The Gyres*).

First of all we should discard the idea that Yeats was in any real sense a Mallarméan Symbolist. There is not, so far as my limited knowledge goes, any extensive translation of Mallarmé's criticism. The original prose is extremely difficult, and I do not believe that Yeats ever had sufficient command of French to read it; he certainly had not in the years when he was forming his style. And Mallarmé's verse is more difficult than his prose. The simple fact of the matter is that Yeats (from *Responsibilities* onward, at least, and often before) was usually trying to say something clearly. His obscurity results from his private symbols (which resemble the medieval symbols in their intention), from the confusion of his thought, and from the frequent ineptitude of his style. From *Responsibilities* onward, in fact, he became more and more openly didactic. He quite obviously was deeply moved by his ideas and expected us to be moved by them. But unfortunately his ideas were contemptible. I do not wish to say that I believe that Yeats should be discarded, for there are a few minor poems which are successful, or nearly successful, and there are many fine lines and passages in the more ambitious pieces. But in the long run it is impossible to believe that foolishness is greatness, and Yeats was not a great poet, nor was he by a wide margin the best poet of our time. There are greater poems in Bridges, Hardy, Robinson, and Stevens, to mention no others, and in at least half a dozen later poets as well. His reputation is easily accounted for. In the first place, there is real talent scattered throughout his work; in the second place, our time does not recognize any relationship between motive and emotion, but is looking merely for emotion; in the third place, Yeats's power of self-assertion, his bardic tone, has overwhelmed his readers thus far. The bardic tone is common in Romantic poetry: it sometimes occurs in talented (but confused) poets such as Blake and Yeats; more often it appears in poets of little or no talent, such as Shelley, Whitman, and Robinson Jeffers. For most readers the bardic tone is synonymous with greatness, for through this tone the poet asserts that he is great, in the absence of any (or sufficient) supporting intelligence. If the poet asserts his own greatness long enough and in the same tone of voice, the effect is hypnotic; we have seen the same thing on the political platform in the persons of such speakers as Mussolini, Father Coughlin, and Adolf Hitler. But in time the effect wears off, and of course (among poets, anyway) such mountebanks have been following each other in rapid succession and tend to replace each other, whereas the relatively scarce poet of real talent remains, even though under-estimated. While the tone is effective, however, a good deal of damage is done. In our time Yeats has been regarded as the great poet in person, the poet of the impeccable style. He has thus become a standard for critics, with the result that the work of better poets has been obscured or minimized; and he has become a model for imitation, with the result that the work of a good many talented poets has been damaged beyond repair.

William Empson

'Mr Wilson on the Byzantium Poems', *Review of English Literature*, vol. 1, no. 3   July 1960

The analysis[1] by Mr Wilson of the two poems about Byzantium has raised no objection that I have seen, and I suppose is thoroughly in the modern movement, but seems to me very strange. Surely, at

1 F. A. C. Wilson, *W. B. Yeats and Tradition*, Gollancz.

least, not all critics would agree with his statement that 'Byzantium, then, is Elysium, the "country of the young"'. In *Sailing to Byzantium* the country of the young is Ireland, and that is why the ageing Yeats has sailed away from it. He calls it *That* because he is looking back at it; 'therefore (because it is no country for old men) I have sailed to Byzantium' ends the second verse of *Sailing to Byzantium*. I do not believe that the Bosphorus has either salmon-falls or mackerel-crowded seas; it is a basic trouble about critics who revere 'Symbolism' that they will not allow the literal meaning any weight at all. Mr Wilson gives an interesting quotation from the first draft, which would prove that Ireland is meant if any proof were needed:

Here all is young . . .
Weary with toil Teigue sleeps till break of day

An Irish pet name for the Irish is not a thing an Irish Nationalist could use for the population of Byzantium, and Mr Wilson gives no reason for supposing he did.

The effect of the mistake is that Mr Wilson ignores the 'story', the actual human situation which the poet is describing with much humour and good sense; hence he is deaf to the changes of tone which are a major beauty of the poem. He contentedly says, of both poems as I understand, 'the action takes place in the heavenly world', and thereafter any symbolism used by any mystic can be piled on to the words so long as it makes them imply disgust for all human experience. But the real action is rather saltily in this world; Yeats is planning his strategy as a Grand Old Man. 'Obviously I shall get jeered at in Dublin if I act young any longer; I shall have to find how to turn myself into a monument of intellect'. It is a libel on Yeats to suppose he could write down that phrase about himself without intending it to be rather funny.

The third verse, I readily agree, is entirely serious; he feels the need to prepare his soul for death, he reverences the saints who have done so, also he reverences the other-worldly art of Byzantium; a very specific historical style which he connects with a current movement of taste, the Cubists and T. E. Hulme and Boris Anrep (he did the floor of the entrance to the National Gallery, but there he was anxious not to compete with the paintings; Yeats would think of him as the one man who was actually making for churches mosaics which felt as spiritually thrilling as the Byzantine ones by the same occasional use of jagged stone) and so forth. Also he seriously believed that Europe was entering a new Dark Age, and may have been right; the chief point about Byzantium was that it survived for a thousand years which included the Dark Ages, so that it, or its destruction, could help to start the Renaissance at the other end. This pickled culture was obviously what a wise old poet ought now to make a spiritual migration to. But in the fourth and last verse, when he describes himself as succeeding at this line of effort, he shows exquisite good taste in making himself funny; it is one sentence of continually delicious hesitating rhythm, full of the lilting flipness of the comic prose of Oscar Wilde. Nobody who had once experienced the beauty of the poem could be induced to turn back and read into it Mr Wilson's interpretation.

It is as well for me to insist that this internal literary ground is what seems to me decisive, and not some ideological one, because Mr Wilson produced rather alarming evidence, from Yeats' letters to Sturge Moore, that he took a solemn view of the bird which ends the poem. I recognize of course that he felt it as a rich inclusive symbol, and he was accustomed to treat his work with due solemnity; also he might think it rather indecent to explain the exact tone he had intended to Sturge Moore, and anyhow keeping his tongue in his cheek was one of his dearest pleasures. One could see plenty of these mechanical singing birds in the Forbidden City at Peking, though I think the Communists have got tired of showing them; Queen Victoria used to send them to the Empress Dowager. These ones were heavily jewelled, but I was shown a less expensive one working when I was a child, and I expect Yeats was too. No great reverence can be felt for them; what Yeats is saying is 'I tell you what I'll do; I'll turn myself into one of those clockwork dickey-birds, in a gilt cage'.

Consider, few poets have cared to write down 'When I die I shall go to Heaven'. They would feel it bad luck as well as bad taste, and Yeats was not at all the man to feel otherwise. Then, as to symbolism, the more you think of birds as able to take messages up to Heaven, intensely spontaneous in their lyrics, and so forth, the more a clockwork bird with a built-in tweet-tweet is bound to seem pathetically ludicrous. Just the thing to please children, on the other hand, and there the poet does retain a firm contact with the world of the young which he must now school himself to leave. No doubt he felt sure that the Byzantines, if they too could make this machine as he says he has read somewhere, would make it an impressive piece of sculpture; so there is a genuine boast about himself, but it is wry enough to be sweet. Perhaps some readers will deny that the toy is meant to 'work'; but it is said to sing, that is how it will keep a drowsy emperor awake. Yeats, with his distaste for the machine age, cannot be supposed to give himself hearty praise in his incarnation as such a thing.

A similar point urgently needs to be made about the first four lines of the second poem, *Byzantium*. Mr Wilson says about them: 'Since Yeats did not write long stretches of mere imagery, all this has to be assigned some meaning beyond the merely literal.' I find here a breath-taking assumption that language can never be used to tell a story; that the only 'literal' meaning it can have is the pictures it makes in your head. Surely it is enough to point out that the lines have a perfectly straightforward meaning, one which is greatly to the credit of Yeats' good sense. To begin with, he would know that the actual life of the holy city was monotonously shocking, or at any rate appears so in Gibbon, the obvious place for him to look. The emperors regularly murdered and tortured their relations, while the mass of the population was locked in an entirely fatuous struggle between the Green and Blue factions of the circus, a canalization of their inherent brutality which might have been invented for 1984. Yeats made clear enough that he knew this in the lyrical prose sentence about Byzantium which set the stage for both poems; if he were offered a magical choice, he said:

I would choose to spend my month in Byzantium, a little before Justinian opened St Sophia and closed the Academy of Plato. I think I could find in some little wine-shop some philosophical worker in mosaic who could answer all my questions, the supernatural descending nearer to him than to Plotinus even, for the pride of his delicate skill would make what was an instrument of power in princes and clerics, a murderous madness in the mob, show as a lovely flexible presence like that of a perfect human body.

(A Vision)

This rigid mummified type of society, with its fierce suppression of natural impulse and its immensely exalted anti-natural art, is precisely where all experience outside the art is reduced to 'the fury and the mire of human veins'; that is why Yeats makes so much of the contrast here. He has been accused of fascism, but he seems to have regarded the totalitarian state as merely a dismal necessity of the coming stage of history, as of some previous ones. Not at all surprisingly, then, the spiritual tourist is found at the beginning of the poem disillusioned by what he has seen of Byzantium in the daytime; what he has come there for can only be found after dark, in the dreams of the city's ghosts. It is hard on Yeats, as a political thinker at any rate, that his interpreters are so determined to love religious tyranny that they positively cannot imagine his meaning when he says he doesn't love it.

The first two lines of the poem, then, dismiss the life of the holy city with curt contempt. The rest of the first verse, very sensitive and imaginative, is direct description of it at night:

The unpurged images of day recede;
The Emperor's drunken soldiery are abed.
Night's resonance recedes, night-walker's song
After great cathedral gong.
A starlit or a moonlit dome disdains
All that man is;
All mere complexities;
The fury and the mire of human veins.

Presumably midnight tolls out, and belated revellers going home can be heard surprisingly far off; in the ensuing peace, the superb architecture despises the people of the city. One therefore listens to the silence, and is prepared to meet what is apparently the ghost of a statue. This is very fine, and there is no occasion to explain it away as 'symbolic'; though certainly the literal details come to be felt to carry extra meanings. Such is the normal process; Dante took for granted that his allegory must be accepted as a story before its extra meanings could grow in the mind, and why may not poor Yeats write an allegory too?

Throughout the third verse of *Byzantium*, and only there, the clockwork dickey-bird reappears, in an even more rippingly aristocratic frame of mind, scolding like Donald Duck. That it 'can like the cocks of Hades crow' is a splendid riddle, and Mr Wilson may be right in saying that this process could call a soul to 'the necessity of reincarnation'. I do not think he need go on to take for granted that Hades is Heaven, and that the toy is 'perched at the very summit of the Kabbalistic Tree of Life'. If the poet meant that, he failed to express it; and he does on the other hand convey strongly though mysteriously that tart sense of the paradoxes of life with which he has already made us familiar. 'Or', says the verse, meaning perhaps 'if not imposing an unwelcome reincarnation', the bird can simply 'scorn' with a raucous cry all 'common', that is, real, birds and flowers. The poor toy is described as embittered by the moon, usually expected to recall tender memories, so it seems to have got mixed up with one of the holy palace eunuchs. Here again it is a libel on Yeats to assume he greatly admired the frame of mind he describes. He could indeed mean to present himself, and Dean Swift too, as this scolding toy, but neither his good taste nor his Irish bitterness would have let him feel it as a simple dreamy deification.

Neo-Christian critics should recognize, surely, that Yeats still refused to become a Christian even while his final plays were showing a rather horrible interest in the mysticism of sacrifice. He is not as other-worldly as Mr Wilson makes him. Mysteriously enormous as the short poem contrives to feel, chiefly I think by the sharp changes of tone which make each verse seem a separate jagged block in the mosaic, thus taking even further the technique of the first Byzantium poem, it does not rise out of the world but presents at the end the forces in conflict as eternal, and presents the conflict with exaltation. The word *break*, used twice in the last verse, is I think more ambiguous than Yeats intended; or rather, when he introduced it with the phrase 'break the flood', he thought that that would define the second use, because he expected his readers to know how a breakwater acts. It is built out into the sea, and prevents the waves from harming the land not by simply rebuffing them but by a more artful process of distracting them and in a sense yielding to them. A Symbolist critic like Mr Wilson despises the world far too much even to want to know any such thing; and yet it is only by this more humane interpretation that I can find any sense in saying that the marbles of the dancing floor break the passions. A veto upon dancing would be the way to disrupt them, but the dancing floor is a place where they can work out their energies harmoniously. The last word of Mr Wilson on the poem is that *gong-tormented* sea means 'man's life . . . is endlessly tormented by the idea of death', and this seems to me merely cynical; the way the cathedral bell really torments the people is by giving them difficult aspirations to engage in more noble activity.

I find I get this reaction again and again; what our present commentators offer proudly as a specially high-minded interpretation seems to me, morally speaking, a nasty-minded one, so that it is a hopelessly wrong account of the poem in view.

C. K. Stead

from *The New Poetic* 1964

Easter 1916, written to commemorate the 1916 rising against the British occupation of Ireland, is one of the finest of Yeats' public poems. It is a complex poem which, more than illustrating Yeats' achievement of objectivity by means of the dramatic 'mask', uses the terms of drama in order to stylize and objectify the world of political fact which is its subject. In the writing of this poem literary problems have become, for Yeats, analogues for the problems of living: 'Life' and 'Art' interact and merge into a single image.

The first three sections of the poem look backward to a 'comic' world that has been left behind – a world of restless individuality, of mutability, subject to death and regeneration. The fourth section points forward to a world of tragic stasis, achieved by those killed in the rising. Thus the movement of the poem – from the temporal to the timeless – and the intermediate position of Yeats' *persona* in that movement, make the poem a forerunner of the more famous *Sailing to Byzantium*.

The opening lines of the poem present the 'comic' Dublin scene before the Easter rising:

I have met them at close of day
Coming with vivid faces
From counter or desk among grey

Eighteenth century houses.
I have passed with a nod of the head
Or polite meaningless words,
Or have lingered awhile and said
Polite meaningless words. . . .
  (*Easter 1916*)

These, whom Yeats met 'at close of day', are the Irish patriots, shaped in the world of modern commerce ('from counter or desk') which came into being with 'grey eighteenth century' reason. Dublin is part of the civilization that followed when 'the merchant and the clerk,/Breathed on the world with timid breath' – a fragmented society, where 'polite meaningless words' serve in place of collective spiritual enterprise. 'Doubtless because fragments broke into ever smaller fragments' Yeats writes in his *Autobiographies*, 'we saw one another in the light of bitter comedy'. The 'vivid faces' of the patriots could never, it seemed, assume the static mask of tragedy. So the *persona* of this poem recalls his certainty

> that they and I
But lived where motley is worn.

But we are warned:

> All changed, changed utterly:
> A terrible beauty is born.

Comedy, Yeats suggests in an essay, accentuates personality, individual character; tragedy eliminates it in favour of something universal: 'tragedy must always be a drowning and breaking of the dykes that separate man from man, and . . . it is upon these dykes comedy keeps house. . . .'

The second section of the poem sketches the personalities of some of the nationalists before their destruction in the Easter rising. One, beautiful when young, had spoiled her beauty in the fervour of political agitation; another was a poet and schoolteacher; a third had shown sensitivity and intellectual daring; a fourth had seemed only 'a drunken vainglorious lout'. But the 'dykes that separate man from man' have now been broken. Each has

> resigned his part
In the casual comedy . . .

Transformed utterly:
A terrible beauty is born.[1]

So far the change seems all achievement: the petty modern comedy
has given way to tragic beauty. But this is also a '*terrible* beauty',
beauty bought only at the expense of life:

Hearts with one purpose alone
Through summer and winter seem
Enchanted to a stone
To trouble the living stream,
The horse that comes from the road,
The rider, the birds that range
From cloud to tumbling cloud,
Minute by minute they change;
A shadow of cloud on the stream
Changes minute by minute;
A horse hoof slides on the brim,
And a horse plashes within it;
The long-legged moor-hens dive,
And hens to moor-cocks call;
Minute by minute they live:
The stone's in the midst of all.

This third section is a general image of the world subject to time and
death ('minute by minute they live') – an image which implies
another, kindlier way of seeing the Dublin street before the rising.
The nationalists have transcended the mutable word, but only by the
destruction of normal human values, by a single-mindedness that
turns the heart to stone. The movement of this section imparts the
joy of life, which throws a new light on the 'terrible beauty',
emphasizing terror over beauty. The events are thus presented with
an ambiguity which does justice to their complexity.

'Nations, races, and individual men', Yeats tells us,

are unified by an image, or bundle or related images,
symbolical or evocative of the state of mind which is, of all

1 Cf. *Autobiographies*: 'I had seen Ireland in my own time turn from the
bragging rhetoric and gregarious humour of O'Connell's generation and
school, and offer herself to the solitary and proud Parnell as to her anti-self,
buskin followed hard on sock . . .'

states of mind not impossible, the most difficult to that man,
race or nation; because only the greatest obstacle which can
be contemplated without despair rouses the will to full
intensity.

(*Autobiographies*)

The 'most difficult' image which the nationalists have contemplated
'without despair' is that of a united, independent Ireland. But there
is another way of looking at their aspirations:

We had fed the heart on fantasies,
The heart's grown brutal from the fare;

Approval and disapproval, delight and disappointment, lie behind
the poem. Out of the tensions in Yeats's own mind a complex
image is generated. We know from what Maud Gonne has written
that Yeats hated in her the passionate intensity that turned the heart
to stone.

Standing by the seashore in Normandy in September 1916
he read me that poem *Easter 1916*; he had worked on it all
the night before, and he implored me to forget the stone and
its inner fire for the flashing, changing joy of life.[1]

But it was Yeats as a man who urged her to abandon her patriotic
intensity. As a poet his task was more difficult: to make an image that
would encompass the event, transcending mere 'opinion' – his own,
and that of others. To achieve this he must transcend himself, giving
up his personality as the revolutionaries gave up life, in order to
achieve the Mask of tragedy. At this level the writing of the poem
becomes an analogue for the event which is its subject. Yeats is
caught up in the play, and must move with it. He can no longer take
pleasure in 'a mocking tale or a gibe' at the nationalists' expense, for
he is no longer 'where motley is worn'. Nor can he pass judgement:
'That is heaven's part'. 'Our part' is only that of chorus –

                  our part
To murmur name upon name,
As a mother names her child

1 *Scattering Branches, Tributes to the Memory of W. B. Yeats,* ed. Stephen
Gwynn, 1940, pp. 31-2.

When sleep at last has come
On limbs that had run wild.

At whatever human expense, a new symbol of heroism has been created. For good or ill

MacDonagh and MacBride
And Connolly and Pearse
Now and in time to be,
Wherever green is worn,
Are changed, changed utterly.

　　The Irish mind carries a new symbol, and Irish literature a new poem: there is a new stone resisting the flow of the stream. Such an achievement constitutes a defeat over the mutable world. The personalities of principal actors and chorus – of all those whose interaction created the play – are irrelevant to the effect. The world is, for the moment in which the event is contemplated, 'transformed utterly'.

　　Yeats stands alone among English speaking poets of this century in his ability to assimilate a complex political event into the framework of a poem without distortion of the event or loss of its human character in abstraction. It will be worth keeping *Easter 1916* in mind when we come to consider the English poets of the First World War. Of them, the patriots are absurdly partisan, abstract and rhetorical; while the disillusioned soldier poets – though more admirable than the patriots because their poems come from honest feeling and particular experience – are too closely involved in the destruction to be capable of transforming these things, as Yeats transforms them, into a universal image. It is . . . a matter of establishing a correct distance between the poet and his subject. The soldier poets stand too close to their subject, the patriots at too great a distance. Yeats' dramatic Mask is a means of holding himself at a correct distance.[1] He had

1 Cf. Yeats writing of two of his contemporary poets in *The Boston Pilot*, 23 April 1892. 'The din and glitter one feels were far too near the writer [John Davidson]. He has not been able to cast them back into imaginative dimness and distance. Of Mr Symons' method . . . I have but seen stray poems and judge from them that, despite most manifest triumphs from time to time, he will sometimes fail through gaining too easily that very dimness and distance I have spoken of. He will, perhaps, prove to be too far from, as Mr Davidson is too near to, his subject.' (*Letters to The New Island*.)

pored long enough over the slow fires of his own and others' art, to know that death in itself is a commonplace; but that particular death, transformed in poetry to an object of contemplation, becomes a symbol – a way of understanding and expressing the human condition.

In *Easter 1916* Yeats has already achieved a solution – one solution – to a problem which had bedevilled poetry for many years: the problem of how a poem could enter the public world without losing itself in temporal 'opinion'. *Easter 1916* is not a pure Symbolist poem, for it is capable of discursive paraphrase; but no paraphrase can use up the poem's life. The event which is its subject is not described, but re-fashioned. There is no question of simply praising heroism or blaming folly. The men of the poem are all dead – 'all changed, changed utterly' – no longer men at all but symbols that take life in the mind. Yeats leaves his personality, his opinions, behind. He puts on the Mask of tragic chorus, and out of the slow impersonal contemplation of a particular event in which idealism, folly, heroism, and destructiveness were intermixed, fashions an image which stands for all such events in human history.

Donald Davie

'Yeats, The Master of a Trade', in D. Donoghue (ed.),
The Integrity of Yeats 1964

On April the 21st, 1930, Robert Bridges, the Poet Laureate, died. On May the 7th, Yeats wrote a letter of condolence to Mrs Bridges. This is what he wrote:

Dear Mrs Bridges
May I, despite the slightness of our acquaintance, tell
how much I feel your great loss. I think I remember your
husband most clearly as I saw him at some great house
near you where there were some Servian delegates. He
came through the undistinguished crowd, an image of
mental and physical perfection, and one of the Servians
turned to me in obvious excitement to ask his name. He
has always seemed the only poet, whose influence has

always heightened and purified the art of others, and all
who write with deliberation are his debtors.

My wife joins with me in sending you our sympathy.

Yours,   W. B. Yeats.

It's entirely characteristic that, wanting to pay a tribute to a man
he had known, Yeats should dwell upon his physical presence as
something arresting or commanding in itself. For Yeats this was a
matter of principle; it shows him trusting the image just as fearlessly
outside the world of poetry as inside that world. This way of standing
by the image through thick and thin is one of the most striking things
about Yeats, and it's something that has been noticed time and again.
But there's something else in the letter which is just as characteristic,
though this is noticed much less often – I mean, the last sentence:
'He has always seemed the only poet, whose influence has always
heightened and purified the art of others, and all who write with
deliberation are his debtors.' I can conceive that to someone who is
not a poet or not a practising artist or craftsman of some sort, it may
appear that, in saying this about Robert Bridges, Yeats is not saying
very much. He's saying that Bridges was never anything but a good
influence on other poets. And 'influence', we may think, is something
that interests critics and commentators but doesn't interest or concern
the poet himself. And so we might even suppose that Yeats is 'damning with faint praise', tactfully getting round the difficulty that he
doesn't think much of Bridges' poetry in itself, by saying that all the
same it was always a good influence on others. But I'm sure that this
isn't at all what Yeats intended; he meant this as very high praise of
Bridges indeed, almost the noblest tribute that one poet can pay to
another.

For if there are indeed some kinds of 'influence' that excite
commentators very much and poets hardly at all, there are other
sorts of influence by which a poet sets much greater store than any of
the critics do. And this sort is the one that Yeats points to when he
appeals to 'all who write *with deliberation*'. It's the sort of influence
which we describe (not very happily) as *technical* influence; a matter
of quite cold-blooded 'know-how', having to do with tricks of the
trade and rules of thumb – such as a note on how it's usually better
to rhyme verb with noun than verb with verb. This is the sort of

practical tip which a poet has in mind when he talks about 'influence', and this is what Yeats means when he talks about the influence of Bridges. 'Tricks of the trade' – that's what I said. And in fact 'trade' is the word that Yeats uses himself:

Irish poets, learn your trade,
Sing whatever is well made, . . .
   (*Under Ben Bulben*)

Or if it isn't 'trade', it's 'craft':

All things can tempt me from this craft of verse:
One time it was a woman's face, or worse –
The seeming needs of my fool-driven land;
Now nothing but comes readier to the hand
Than this accustomed toil.
   (*All Things Can Tempt Me*)

'Accustomed toil' – there the point is even clearer. Yeats gave himself all sorts of airs, claimed special privileges and access to special sources of wisdom – and all in the name of poetry; but equally, whenever he speaks narrowly of the act of composition, he talks of it in terms which are quite disconcertingly matter-of-fact, as a skill or a body of skills to be learned and practised, to be learned *through* practice, except (and here we come back to 'influence') – except for such skills as can be learned through following good models, inherited as it were from accomplished masters, from masters such as Bridges.

Yeats, in a word, was very thoroughly and completely a *professional* poet. And it's because of this that we know he intended his tribute in the letter about Bridges to be a very noble tribute indeed. He must have hoped that such a tribute might be paid to him after he too was dead. And so I ask if the tribute that Yeats paid Robert Bridges thirty years ago can now be paid to Yeats himself.

At first blush, it may seem that the question has only to be asked, to be answered with a resounding affirmative. Yeats, surely, is a much greater poet than Robert Bridges; and so it must follow that poets of today have far more to learn from him, that he is a far more accomplished master for them to follow. But in fact an artistic tradition doesn't work in this way, not at all. The greatest poets are hardly ever the best models to follow, the best influences on those who come after them. The tradition – the tradition in the sense of a body of transferable skills, of heritable 'know-how' – is carried far more by poets of the second rank than by the first rank. And a very little thought will show how this must be so. For it's precisely a sign of the greatest talents, that they can take risks which would be suicidal for the less abundantly gifted. This is one of the reasons for keeping, to describe such really great talents, the now unfashionable term, 'genius'. The genius is almost by definition the man who breaks the rules, the man who can get away with murder. And so, obviously, to try to follow such a model is disastrous. Even in the unlikely case that you, as a beginning poet, are yourself as great a genius as John Milton, you will still be asking for trouble in modelling yourself on Milton; because your genius, though equal to his, will be different – you will break as many rules, but they will need to be different rules. For this is the second thing about genius – that it is (not quite always, but very nearly) above all *distinctive*. What the great genius does is to twist the language to suit what he is and what he has to say. To adopt his style is to have to adopt his personality and his standpoint; and the greater he is, the more likely it is that his personality will be idiosyncratic, his standpoint highly individual. This must be so, just because the personality and the standpoint which emerge from his style are so indelibly, so magnificently *his*, and no one else's. What one wants as a model is almost the exact opposite of this – the sort of poet (so much more precious to other poets than to any one else) whose personality is expunged almost completely from what he writes, so that one has the peculiarly winning and rare effect of the language speaking through the poet as medium, not the other way round. This effect of anonymity, an extreme of impersonality in poetry, *can* be associated with truly great poets (Ben Jonson, I would say, is the unique example of this in English), but this is a very rare occurrence; it's much more common to find this, or something like it, in poets of the second rank such as Bridges. And it's from poets like these that one can learn to use the language poetically without at the same time having to adopt a false personality and a foreign standpoint. It's for these reasons (and many others like them) that there is nothing in the least paradoxical about saying that the worst disaster which befell English verse drama was Shakespeare, the worst disaster which befell the English epic was Milton.

And so you have anticipated, of course, the point which I must make: no, we *cannot* say of Yeats, what Yeats said of Bridges, that his influence 'has always heightened and purified the art of others'. We cannot say this of Yeats precisely because Yeats was a greater poet than Bridges; because Yeats was a genius, whereas Bridges wasn't.

I have laboured this point a little because in England at any rate (much more, I think, than in Ireland or the United States), there is a very general reluctance to face up to this fact about Yeats; there is a general assumption that with Yeats we can both have our cake and eat it, can declare him a great poet and yet a 'central' poet, a highly individual voice and yet a model to be generally followed. We have him proposed to us as exemplary because he expresses a twentieth-century sensibility as faithfully as his great contemporary, T. S. Eliot, yet without having to throw over as many of the traditional skills as Eliot did. What we are asked to believe in fact is that Yeats is like Ben Jonson, one of those very rare great poets whose influence is in no way vitiated by the very fact of their greatness. I do not believe this. And to justify my not believing it, I need only point to any one of the very numerous poems I seem to come across, in which it is all too clear that the authors have lately been reading Yeats. These are poems in which the master's voice quite drowns out the pupil's. I don't want to inflict poor poetry upon you, and so I'm not reading any poem like this. Any one who reads the current magazines, anthologies and slim collections will have come across such poems for himself; they are very common, and indeed you will find the reviewers noting them.

But in any case, it would surely be very strange if Yeats *were* a poet like Ben Jonson, in this respect. It would be very strange if an Irish poet, a poet so consciously and deliberately Irish as Yeats was, should have that sort of centrality in the English tradition which some of Yeats' English admirers claim for him. I will name only one feature of Yeats' poetry which seems to me indelibly Irish; and this is its very marked *histrionic* element. Yeats was very conscious of this, and quite deliberate about it. He wrote:

Every now and then, when something has stirred my
imagination, I begin talking to myself. I speak in my own
person and dramatize myself, very much as I have seen a
mad old woman do upon the Dublin quays, and sometimes

detect myself speaking and moving as if I were still young,
or walking perhaps like an old man with fumbling steps.
Occasionally, I write out what I have said in verse, and
generally for no better reason than because I remember that
I have written no verse for a long time.

This catches exactly what I mean by the histrionic quality of Yeats'
imagination. And it may or may not be a naturally Irish way of
composing poems; I am sure it is not an English way. I am not aware
of any English poet who by his own account went to work in anything like this way. Certainly I cannot conceive that Ben Jonson thus
dramatized himself in order to write his poems.

All the same, it's not for nothing that I keep coming back to Ben
Jonson's name. For while I believe that Yeats' poetry as a whole
isn't of the sort that always or often has a good influence on the art of
others, yet it is true, I think, that there is one body of poetry by Yeats
which comes near to this, one phase in Yeats' career when he wrote
poems which *can* profitably be taken as models by other writers.
And this phase of Yeats' writing life is announced when the poet
invokes, specifically, Ben Jonson's name:

While I, from that reed-throated whisperer
Who comes at need, although not now as once
A clear articulation in the air,
But inwardly, surmise companions
Beyond the fling of the dull ass's hoof
– Ben Jonson's phrase – and find when June is come
At Kyle-na-no under that ancient roof
A sterner conscience and a friendlier home,
I can forgive even that wrong of wrongs,
Those undreamt accidents that have made me
– Seeing that Fame has perished this long while,
Being but a part of ancient ceremony –
Notorious, till all my priceless things
Are but a post the passing dogs defile.

These verses – the lines I've just read – are the tailpiece to a collection which Yeats published in 1914, called *Responsibilities*. And it's
generally agreed that this collection marks an important stage in

Yeats' development. In fact you still find people who believe they can pin-point the stage at which Yeats grew from a good poet into a great one, or at least (to use their own vocabulary) the 'mature' Yeats takes over from the immature; and it's in *Responsibilities* that some of these critics claim to find this turning-point, a turning away from the use of a special literary language for poetry to the use of a common, a colloquial language. For my part I believe that no such turning-points are to be found in Yeats, that on the contrary it's one of his glories to have moved so far and changed so continually *always in an unbroken and gradual process*. All the same *Responsibilities* does announce a sort of new departure for Yeats, and I'd like to give you my sense of this.

I'd do so by pointing not after all to the explicit invocation of Ben Jonson, not to that in the first place, but to the line, 'Being but a part of ancient ceremony'. For the next few years 'ceremony' is a word that recurs constantly in Yeats' poems. I need remind you only of *The Second Coming*:

Things fall apart; the centre cannot hold;
Mere anarchy is loosed upon the world,
The blood-dimmed tide is loosed, and everywhere
The ceremony of innocence is drowned: ...

'The ceremony of innocence ...' And then there is the last stanza of *A Prayer for My Daughter*, the poem which follows *The Second Coming* in the collection of 1921:

And may her bridegroom bring her to a house
Where all's accustomed, ceremonious;
For arrogance and hatred are the wares
Peddled in the thoroughfares.
How but in custom and in ceremony
Are innocence and beauty born?
Ceremony's a name for the rich horn,
And custom for the spreading laurel tree.

As those last lines in particular make clear, 'ceremony' is the word that Yeats uses for what he finds most valuable, at this stage of his life, in the aristocratic way of life. He recognized that way of life in the household of Lady Gregory at Coole; and he envisaged himself at this time as a specially privileged retainer of such a noble house, the poet maintained by the family to serve them by his poetry just as their grooms and chambermaids served them in humbler ways. This was the relationship between poet and patron which Ben Jonson celebrated in many of his verse-epistles, and which he preferred to being patronized by the public at large, just as Yeats preferred it after his disappointment with the Abbey Theatre audiences. In fact of course, as Yeats realized, this sort of poet-patron relationship was common all over Europe at the time of the Renaissance, as much in the Italian city-state of Urbino as in Elizabethan England. And Yeats at this time in his life tries to impose this Renaissance relationship, and the valuable things in that relationship, upon the quite different and as he thinks inferior relationship between poet and reader which rises out of twentieth-century society.

Accordingly, it's at this time, when Yeats sees himself, not as an isolated individual dramatizing himself and his personal predicaments, but as a professional hired to serve a patron; when he sees himself above all as in the lineage of Ben Jonson and the poets of Renaissance Europe – it's at this time that Yeats strives for and sometimes attains that impersonality, that effect of anonymity, which alone can make a poet the best sort of model for others to follow. Consider only the last two lines of *A Prayer for My Daughter*:

Ceremony's a name for the rich horn,
And custom for the spreading laurel tree.

The images here – of the cornucopia, the horn of plenty, and of the laurel tree – are the most hackneyed images imaginable. And that is only to say, the most traditional. These lines could have been written by any good poet writing in any Western European language at any time from the sixteenth century to the present day. That at least is the effect that Yeats was striving for; and I think he attains it. This *had to be* the effect. For what the poet is saying is that 'ceremony' in the sense of time-hallowed precedent, immemorial unwritten usage, is supremely important in life; and so he's in duty bound to conform to his own prescription, and in that part of his life which is his writing to use no devices but those which are authenticated by precedent, taken out of common stock, traditional.

And this is the first lesson which a poet of today can most profitably learn from this body of Yeats' poetry: that hackneyed, conventional images are in themselves no worse, and in fact are probably better for most purposes, than unprecedented images. The young poet can learn, in fact, that all his efforts to be above all original, distinctive, himself and no one else – all these exertions are probably wasted labour.

He can learn something else. He can notice, in this last stanza of *A Prayer for My Daughter*, how many of the words are abstract words – 'arrogance', 'hatred', 'custom', 'ceremony', 'innocence', 'beauty'. To be sure, it's no accident that this cluster of abstractions comes in the last stanza out of ten: the preceding nine stanzas have given these words the meaning that the poet can now take for granted; he's earned the right to use them. All the same the 'prentice-poet can learn from this that he almost certainly has an excessive fear of abstract words; that his efforts to be always concrete, always specific, never to state a thing but always to embody it in an image – these efforts too, like his efforts to be original at all costs, are largely superfluous.

This is related, I think, to the point about how Yeats came to use common speech in his poetry, the speech of the street-corner instead of the speech of the library. By and large this is no doubt true. And by and large it is also true that the young poet has to learn this, how there is no special language for poetry, no specially poetical words as against others that are unpoetical. But Irish speech-usage differs from British and American usage; and so British and American poets, at any rate, can model themselves in this respect more easily and surely on some of Yeats' British and American contemporaries than on Yeats himself. But there *is* one sort of speech which they can learn about from Yeats better than from any other master. This isn't the language of the street-corner; it's the language of the political hustings and the leading article in the newspaper. Padraic Colum recalled how Yeats in his younger days used to tell young poets never to use a word that a journalist might use. But John Synge said to Colum, 'Words have a cycle; when they become too worn for the journalists the poets can use them again.' And writing in 1947 Padraic Colum could see that Synge had been right, and that Yeats' own practice proved it. For by the end of Yeats' life, as Colum rightly observed, Yeats was using to superb poetic effect the words of the journalists. The instance Colum gave was the line, 'The Roman

Empire stood appalled'; and there could hardly be a better example. What shows up in this, I tend to think, is the Irish tradition of oratory. At any rate it's in Yeats' use of this range of vocabulary, in what I'm inclined to call *civic* speech, that he has most to teach a young poet about poetic diction.

And I limit myself to this aspect of poetry, its *diction*, because it's here that I think Yeats' practice is most instructive for us later poets. Fifteen or twenty years ago this would not have been true. At that time it was Yeats' use of metre which was most instructive, and if this is instructive no longer it's because the lesson has been very thoroughly learned already. For nothing is more striking about poems in English over the last twenty years than the way in which the poets have turned away from 'free verse', to using again the traditional metres. In fact poets today mostly adhere to these traditional forms more strictly than Yeats did; yet there seems to be no doubt that no one has been so influential as Yeats in bringing about this most marked reversion to metre. And this is a point that I should have made earlier perhaps. Yeats has already been, for good or ill, more influential than any other poet writing in English in the present century.

'For good or ill', I say. And this brings us back where we started. Yeats' influence has not been universally beneficial. His greatest poems – *Sailing to Byzantium, The Tower, Among School Children* – these poems, which come later than those I've been talking about, have tended to lead later poets astray. For these are poems in which Yeats takes liberties which hardly anyone else can afford to take; this is what makes these poems glorious, it is also what makes them dangerous. It's the slightly earlier collections – above all, *The Wild Swans at Coole* and *Michael Robartes and the Dancer* – which contain the poems which are models of poetic diction. And of these at least I believe we *can* say that their influence 'has always heightened and purified the art of others'. And it's for the sake of these poems by Yeats that all of us who write with deliberation are now his debtors.

Donald Davie

from '*Michael Robartes and the Dancer*', in D. Donoghue and
J. R. Mulryne (eds.), *An Honoured Guest* 1965

In *The Death of Synge* ('Extracts from a Diary Kept in 1909'), Yeats
wrote:

F— is learning Gaelic. I would sooner see her in the Gaelic
movement than in any Irish movement I can think of. I fear
some new absorption in political opinion. Women, because
the main event of their lives has been a giving themselves
and giving birth, give all to an opinion as if it were some
terrible stone doll. Men take up an opinion lightly and are
easily false to it, and when faithful keep the habit of many
interests. We still see the world, if we are of strong mind
and body, with considerate eyes, but to women opinions
become as their children or their sweethearts, and the
greater their emotional capacity the more do they forget all
other things. They grow cruel, as if in defence of lover or
child, and all this is done for 'something other than human
life'. At last the opinion is so much identified with their
nature that it seems a part of their flesh becomes stone and
passes out of life. *(Autobiographies)*

This obviously is saying what *A Prayer for My Daughter* was to say
about Maud Gonne:

An intellectual hatred is the worst,
So let her think opinions are accursed.
Have I not seen the loveliest woman born
Out of the mouth of Plenty's horn,
Because of her opinionated mind
Barter that horn and every good
By quiet natures understood
For an old bellows full of angry wind?

But it chimes also, because of the imagery of stone, with lines from
Easter 1916:

Too long a sacrifice
Can make a stone of the heart.

However, it is only in *Michael Robartes and the Dancer*, where Con
Markievicz takes her station among so many other women, that this
chime can be heard. Moreover, the assertion is made in *Easter 1916*
altogether more hesitantly and self-doubtingly than in either *A
Prayer for My Daughter* or *The Death of Synge*. For it comes only after
the stone has been much discussed and much imaged in earlier lines:

Hearts with one purpose alone
Through summer and winter seem
Enchanted to a stone
To trouble the living stream.
The horse that comes from the road,
The rider, the birds that range
From cloud to tumbling cloud,
Minute by minute they change;
A shadow of cloud on the stream
Changes minute by minute;
A horse-hoof slides on the brim,
And a horse plashes within it;
The long-legged moor-hens dive,
And hens to moor-cocks call;
Minute by minute they live:
The stone's in the midst of all.

And here, although it is certainly the stream that is called 'living', and
is associated with the lively and life-giving activities of sexual pairing
('hens to moor-cocks call'), yet the stone troubles the stream in a way
which goes beyond the literal fact that it makes the running water
eddy and popple. Moreover, the stream, with its unseizable mutability, the sliding and plashing which it induces, is clearly a much less
stable and certain image to set against petrifaction than is the rooted
and hidden tree which is set against it in *A Prayer for My Daughter*.
And the waterfowl which haunt the stream are no more like the
linnet which haunts the tree than they are like the ducks of *Demon
and Beast* which are called 'absurd' and 'portly' and 'stupid'. They
are called 'happy' also; but *Demon and Beast* makes it plain that their

happiness was bought on terms that were too easy, by a lax and passive abandonment to the course of nature. At this point, in fact, *Easter 1916* goes past the point where exegesis can track its meaning. The imagery of stone and birds, rider and horse and stream, has a multi-valency which discursive language cannot compass – and this accrues to these images simply because of the beams which fall upon this poem out of the other poems in the same collection. Because Yeats holds and keeps faith in the discursive language, for instance by the sinewiness of his syntax, as his contemporaries Eliot and Pound do not, a moment like this when perceptions pass beyond the discursive reason is poignant in his poetry as it cannot be in theirs, and we do not dream of grudging him the right to acknowledge his defeat and to retire baffled before it; as he does in the last section of the poem.

On the other hand, up to 'Hearts with one purpose alone', the poem has been, though profound, straightforward. In a letter written to Lady Gregory on 11 May 1916, which shows Yeats already at work on the poem ('I am trying to write a poem on the men executed – "terrible beauty has been born again" ' (*Letters*), Yeats reports what Maud Gonne thought of the Easter Rising: 'Her main thought seems to be "tragic dignity has returned to Ireland".' And through the first two sections of the poem this is the meaning which Yeats, too, is reading out of the event. In the refrain 'A terrible beauty is born', 'terrible' must surely point to Aristotle's definition of the tragic emotion as compounded of terror and pity; and so it strikes off against 'the casual comedy' and 'lived where motley is worn'. It is doubtless true that in the months before the Rising the Republican army was, in fact, a joke to the Dublin clubmen. But more than accurate reportage was involved for Yeats. It is a fact of literary history that the Anglo-Irish literary tradition since the seventeenth century, up to and including Synge, had scored all its most brilliant successes in comedy, even in stage-comedy; whereas Yeats, from the days of his youthful campaigning for the National Literary Society, had hoped and worked for an Irish literature that should be, on the contrary, heroic. That hope he had abandoned in 1912. The events of 1916, which proved that Irishmen were capable of a tragic gesture, seemed to show Yeats that he had abandoned hope too soon, and in the poem he seems to reproach himself for this. Yet does he, in fact, reproach himself? Certainly there is no evidence from elsewhere that the Rising made Yeats embrace with renewed enthusiasm the hopes he had entertained for Irish national culture in his youth. The truth is that the poem is an expression of self-reproach only so far as 'Hearts with one purpose alone'. At that point Yeats' reflections on the Rising move beyond Maud Gonne's, and only at that point does Yeats ask himself if the Rising makes him revise all his schemes of values. He decides that it does not; or rather, since the pity of the subject rules out any decisions being taken, he does not decide that it does. And this is perhaps the most impressive thing about the whole poem, with the impressiveness of a human utterance rather than a fashioned artifact – that the 1916 leaders are mourned most poignantly, and the sublimity of their gesture is celebrated most memorably, not when the poet is abasing himself before them, but when he implies that, all things considered, they were, not just in politic but in human terms, probably wrong.

John Holloway

from 'Style and World in *The Tower*', in D. Donoghue and J. R. Mulryne (eds.), *An Honoured Guest* 1965

The ostensibly modest purpose of this essay is to discuss, as it appears in *The Tower* (a representative later collection), Yeats' style. 'Modest' not only because the subject is limited in a way which precludes full discussion of the book, but also because much has been written about Yeats' style already, and one might think that another discussion must necessarily be jejune. 'Ostensibly' implied dissent from this: on two counts. The more far-reaching is that examination of style which goes to the roots of style, finds itself dealing with more than style. The expression 'style *and world*' is far from self-explanatory, but it hints at where the argument will go. The more obvious reason for employing the word 'ostensibly' is that what has been said hitherto about Yeats' later style required not mere recapitulation, but correction and expansion: not modest tasks, but perhaps excessively ambitious ones.

T. R. Henn was one of the earlier critics to note that a major part of Yeats' achievement in his later poems was an 'achievement of style'; the expression is, in fact, one of his chapter headings in *The Lonely*

Tower (the chapter deals with poems mainly from the 1930s). But clearly, 'the achievement of style is precisely this swift flashing of the images' or 'there is the certainty of control, grammar and idiom continuing to give each word its full value' leave room for later critics. Richard Ellmann's remark that when Yeats wrote *The Tower* he 'put the full weight of his heroic personality behind it' seems to me at best uninformative. Margaret Rudd speaks of 'odd phrasing' and giving concreteness to the abstract. The author of the Yeats chapter in the *Pelican Guide* refers to the poet's 'consistently public tone' and 'lofty rhythms', adding that the style of the later work is 'formal, elaborate, yet easy and humane': a paraphrase of what F. R. Leavis wrote in 1933: 'the verse ... is idiomatic and has the run of free speech, being at the same time proud, bare and subtle'.

Altogether it seems a not very informative catalogue: especially since the belief that 'language of common speech' (the 'easy', the 'idiomatic') serves as a guiding idea for Yeats' later style is extremely misleading. That this is so will be disputed: one hopes, on the apparent authority of Yeats himself:

My own verse has more and more adopted ... the syntax
and vocabulary of common personal speech. (to H. J. C.
Grierson, *Letters*)
I believe more strongly every day that the element of
strength in poetic language is common idiom. (to John
Quinn, *Letters*)

The quotations come pat enough; but when Yeats spoke of common idiom as the fit medium of the poet, he had distinctions in mind which are remote from 'common speech' as a current slogan indicates:

Let us get back in everything to the spoken word ... but ...
the idiom of those who have rejected, or of those who have
never learned, the base idiom of the newspapers. (*Samhain*,
1902)

In the present context it is unnecessary to take up exactly how 'common idiom' had for him its link with the Western Irish peasantry; and their speech, its link in turn with the 'vocabulary from the time of Malory'. Yeats' general position is clear from his 'General Introduction for My Work' (1937):

I hated and still hate . . . the literature of the point of view.
I wanted . . . to get back to Homer, to those that fed at his
table. I wanted to cry as all men cried, to laugh as all men
laughed, . . . the Young Ireland poets . . . did not know that
the common and its befitting language is the research of a
lifetime. (Essays and Introductions, 511)

How little Yeats by 'common' meant 'colloquial' can be seen in any
later passage taken at random:

Having inherited a vigorous mind
From my old fathers, I must nourish dreams
And leave a woman and a man behind
As vigorous of mind, and yet it seems
Life scarce can cast a fragrance on the wind,
Scarce spread a glory to the morning beams,
But the torn petals strew the garden plot;
And there's but common greenness after that.
     (Meditations in Time of Civil War)

Leaving aside such a phrase as 'spread a glory', which (it might be
conceded) is a thought, not an idiom, remote from common speech,
I find eight indisputable deviations from standard English idiom in
these eight lines ('old fathers' for ancestors, 'scarce' for scarcely, 'but'
for only are the most obvious); and the time has come to recognize
that the staple of Yeats' later verse is not common idiom at all, but
the relinquishment of one deviation from common idiom (that
which strikes us, to speak very loosely, as the worn-out poetic diction
of the nineteenth century, and especially the nineties) and its replacement by another deviation; one more original, calculated and
expressive, but a deviation none the less.

   Yeats' own remarks in prose offer guidance to a concept of style
much more considered and articulated than merely 'common speech'.
The 1926 letter to Grierson, quoted above, goes straight on to say that
'natural momentum in the *syntax*' is 'far more important than
simplicity of vocabulary'. The letter to Quinn, quoted more fully,
reads, 'the element of strength in poetic language is common idiom,
just as the element of strength in poetic structure is common passion' (my

italics in both cases). Looking back in 1937, Yeats underlines this once more:

It was a long time before I made a language to my liking; I began to make it when I discovered some twenty years ago that I must seek, not as Wordsworth thought, words in common use, but a powerful and passionate syntax, and a complete coincidence between period and stanza. . . . I need a passionate syntax for passionate subject-matter.

    (Essays and Introductions, 521–2)

The idea of 'everyday speech' recedes farther and farther. In a letter to Olivia Shakespear (April 1921) Yeats writes that *Nineteen Hundred and Nineteen* is 'not philosophical but simple and passionate' (*Letters*, 668): the echo of Milton is worth a note. So is 'I like a strong driving force' (*Letters*). So is his comment in *A Vision* on the poems now to be discussed: 'I put *The Tower* and *The Winding Stair* into evidence to show that my poetry has gained in *self-possession and power*' (my italics). So, again, is a particularly interesting letter which Yeats wrote to his father in March 1916, noticing the element of pattern in art as the subjective and non-imitative one, and calling it 'an intensity of pattern' (*Letters*).

Power, passion, intensity, energy – the last word is recurrent in Yeats' discussions – these are the terms which weight his own references to 'common speech' and give them a highly distinctive turn. An exact register of the language that Yeats 'made to his liking' will bring out, in fact, how the constant deviation from what he called 'common personal speech' is always in the direction of speech in the sense of the poet's own most personal voice and presence: of an engagement of his own subjectivity and energy as the continuing focus of the poems and everything in them.

That this may be traced in the thought of Yeats' later poems is not, of course, in dispute; and to establish this no more need be quoted than the opening lines of *The Tower*. But those who know that poetry lies less in thought than in language will be willing to trace the controlling attitudes of the verse down into the smaller details of language. They will be willing to notice, for example, that when Yeats writes:

Two men have *founded* here
    (*Meditations in Time of Civil War*)

. . . ancestral night that can . . .
Deliver from the crime of death and birth
    (*A Dialogue of Self and Soul*)

or

I *summon* to the winding ancient stair
    (ibid.)

he is not perpetrating an arbitrary and resultless deviation from
common idiom. In transforming these normally transitive verbs into
intransitive, and thus leaving the reader to sense their objects for himself, he is employing a syntax which both adds speed to his verse and
contributes something to the *persona* of the author: his stance of
emphatic terseness, his demand that the reader shall submit to the
demands of the verse and recognize for himself what the writer
declines to pause over. The 'strength' lies in a deviation from
'common idiom', because this is a deviation of a particular kind and
in a particular direction.

    Consider another example of the same syntactical irregularity:

What if those things the greatest of mankind
Consider most *to magnify, or to bless,*
But take our greatness with our bitterness?
    (*Meditations in Time of Civil War*)

Here the oracularly unidiomatic verbs are linked with another
deviation from common idiom. 'What if . . .?' is not common idiom
as a question, either in standard or Irish English. Once again, the
deviation is in the direction of the terse and passionate: for although
the standard form in 1960s English might be 'Suppose . . .' Yeats'
question must be seen as an emphatic and elided version of 'What
would happen if . . .?' or some question taking that form. It is wrong
to dismiss the point as trifling. Not only does Yeats use this form of
interrogation repeatedly:

And what if my descendants lost the flower
Through natural declension of the soul?
    (ibid.)

... what if mind seem changed ...
And I grow half contented to be blind!
   (All Souls' Night)

But names are nothing. What matter who it be ...
   (ibid.)

What matter if the ditches are impure?
   (A Dialogue of Self and Soul)

'What then?' sang Plato's ghost
   (What Then?)

What matter though numb nightmare ride on top ...?
   (The Gyres)

Not only is there this recurrence, but in *Ancestral Houses* the interrogative, and the curt and authoritative form of it, sustain and indeed
create the whole second half of the section. The whole closing passage
is a defiant confrontation of the possibility envisaged in the question
and left resolutely unresolved by the poet.

   Consider, in the light of Yeats' 'made a language to my liking',
the phrase 'crime of death and birth' in the passage just quoted from
A Dialogue of Self and Soul. A literate reader can no doubt accept the
life, death = crime metaphor by half-conscious reference to the *de
contemptu mundi* tradition, or more exactly, indeed, to the *Phaedo*. But
Yeats does not leave him to rely on this reference. 'Death and birth'
link back to 'love and war' earlier in the stanza; and the quality of
both of these are already determined by the 'razor-keen' edge of
Sato's sword, and its embroidery wrapping '*torn* from some court-
lady's dress'. A stanza later, when Yeats claims 'a charter to commit
the crime once more', it is clear by now that the poem is not merely
giving meaning to its own metaphors, but doing this with a force and
brevity which come from something indeed like 'making a language':
a process of cumulative word-manipulation which means that the
words are farther from 'common idiom' at the end of the poem than
they were at the beginning.

   One can by no means say that this occurs in all poetry, though it is
not, of course, confined to Yeats'. Nevertheless, this aspect of his
later verse contributes much to energy and creativity, not only be-

cause it helps actually to make possible Yeats' emphatic terseness, but also because it is itself an example of plastic energy: of the poet's beginning to make something which might be called a self-contained world of language within the poem. *A Dialogue of Self and Soul* has more of this language-creation in it. This is perhaps most easily seen by working backwards from its closing image:

> When such as I cast out remorse
> So great a sweetness flows into the breast
> We must laugh and we must sing,
> We are blest by everything,
> Everything we look upon is blest.

The image is exactly that which closes *Friends* (in *Responsibilities*, 1914); and the mood of exaltation and delight is one which Yeats recurrently felt in varying forms: reference might be made to the opening page of *Anima Hominis* ('all my thoughts have ease and joy, I am all virtue and confidence'), or to a passage in *Anima Mundi* ('everything fills me with affection, I have no longer any fears or any needs'). But in the *Dialogue*, one of Yeats' more richly esoteric poems, the force of the flowing sweetness is more explicit (and almost the opposite of its force in *Friends*); and it acquires that force from the language-creation of the poem. Yeats is, in fact, conducting a rehearsal, in meditation during this life, of the stages of the Dreaming Back (part 2, stanzas 1–3) and the Return (the closing stanza) which are explained more fully in *A Vision*. 'In the *Return* . . . the *Spirit* . . . is compelled . . . to trace every passionate event to its cause until all are related and understood' (*A Vision*). It was for a good reason that 'Trace to its cause' in the prose text became 'follow to its source' in the poem. 'Source', giving the sense of a spring of fresh water to the sweet flow, itself gains this concreteness of idea from the 'fecund ditch' of the immediately preceding lines:

> Or into that most fecund ditch of all,
> The folly that man does
> Or must suffer, if he woos
> A proud woman not kindred of his soul.

Other associations we might find for 'fecund ditch' are either (if present at all in a sound reading) wholly inept, or else no more than a sarcastic irrelevancy on Yeats' part. Here, 'fecund' has associations with squalor and worthlessness; and these come from the

>   if it be life to pitch
> Into the frog-spawn of a blind man's ditch

of the preceding lines. This point of reference itself takes shape from the opening lines of the whole second part:

> A living man is blind and *drinks his drop*.
> What matter if the ditches are impure?

Ditch as source of drink, ditch as home of life, may be seen branching their way through the whole poem; and it is this which gives the final transition its power; for the transition from ditch to source is no transition from an event merely back to its cause, but one from the whole life of the sensual world, back to its origin in the world of the soul. The supramundane meaning of the poem is written into the very grain of its imagery, and written there by this cumulative 'making of a language' through the poem itself.

Since I have trespassed three pages forward into *The Winding Stair* for a clear and manageable specimen of this side of Yeats' style, perhaps I may trespass a lesser distance backward into *Michael Robartes and the Dancer*, as far as *A Prayer for My Daughter*, for a simpler example, perhaps, and an even clearer one. This poem ends with an act of language-creation, of naming, which is perfectly explicit:

> Ceremony's a *name* for the rich horn,
> And custom for the spreading laurel tree.

But the identity created in this act of naming works backwards at least as much as forward; and if we ask, for example, why it is a 'spreading' laurel tree, we find the answer by no means in realism, in a reference to the habit of growth of that plant; but in something entirely different. 'Spreading' already has a special sense given it by the development of the poem:

> May she become a flourishing hidden tree
> That all her thoughts may like the linnet be,
> And have *no business but dispensing round*
> *Their magnanimities* of sound.

In turn it is 'magnanimities', and 'merriment' in the lines which
follow, that give the appropriate associations for 'laurel' at the end of
the stanza:

O may she live like some green laurel
Rooted in one *dear perpetual* place.

Why, it may be asked, does the reader accept that 'dear' without
qualm? Because the poem has already, through contrast, given to
'rooted' meanings which go beyond the tree itself:

    many a poor man that has *roved* . . .
From a *glad kindness* cannot take his eyes.

It is 'glad kindness', in fact, which means that the reader need not
recall the cheerful unassumingness of the linnet's song (if he knows of
it); and then, when we call to mind the opening situation of the
poem, where Yeats likens the destructive forces of the future to a
storm coming in from the sea, and calls the storm a '*roof*-levelling
wind' (line 5) we can see how by the time he writes:

Assault and battery of the wind
Can never tear the linnet from the leaf

Yeats has in effect created for himself a private language. All the
important words of his sentence take their meanings from a progressive charging which they receive from the developing poem.

It is a cumulative enrichment, quite different from the enrichment
so often to be found in Shakespeare's verse. Most characteristically,
Shakespeare's enrichment of meaning consists in eliciting a series of
ideas from a single metaphor; or in yoking of metaphors together, or
moving from one through a second and so on, in such a way that they
illuminate each other at the same time as they explore the main topic.
In Yeats' verse it is rather the realities marking out the very substance
of the poem – its opening situation, its main line of thought and
meditation – which are progressively charged with richer and fuller
meanings. In respect, for example, of *King Lear*, it would not be to the
gilded fly and the vex'd sea that comparison would turn, but to the
knights or the stocks, the heath or the cliff – fixed and established
realities in the whole play. And as soon as it is recognized that this

comparison would be the appropriate one, it becomes clear that there is little real comparison to be made.

If the question is of those realities which mark out and punctuate the landscape of Yeats' poems one by one, the next step is to take stock of how these objects, initially, find their places in the verse; remembering always that the purpose of doing so is to explore further and comprehend better how the ultimate focus of the later poems is what Yeats himself saw his vocabulary and syntax as *for*: self-possession and power, passionate subjectivity. To begin with, the richness is emphatically no richness of concrete describing. Yeats' nodal objects, if they may be so termed, arrive starkly and as it seems arbitrarily in his poems. The richness lies not in how they are delineated in detail, but in their interrelation, their use. Yet in this very starkness of arrival lies the key to their quality; the service they render to Yeats' most central intent:

> There is no obstacle
> But Gregory's wood and one bare hill.
>   (*Prayer for My Daughter*)

> I pace upon the battlements and stare
> On the foundations of a house, or where
> Tree, like a sooty finger, starts from the earth.
>   (*The Tower*)

There is no doubt of the stark arrival, but the next lines bring out what should perhaps be called its essential mode:

> ... *and call*

> Images and memories
> From ruin or from ancient trees,
> For I would ask a question of them all.

This mode is nothing less than an establishing of the most characteristic and recurrent relation between poet and what enters the world of his poems:

> O sages standing in God's holy fire ...
> Come from the holy fire ...
> And be the singing-masters of my soul.
>   (*Sailing to Byzantium*)

It seems that I must bid the Muse go pack,
Choose Plato and Plotinus for a friend
> (*The Tower*)

And I myself created Hanrahan. . . .
> (ibid.)

As I would question all, come all who can. . . .
> (ibid.)

It is time that I wrote my will;
I chose upstanding men
> (ibid.)

Bid a strong ghost stand at the head
That my Michael may sleep sound . . .
> (*Prayer for My Son*)

I dream of a Ledaean body . . .
> (*Among School Children*)

Horton's the first I call . . .
> (*All Souls' Night*)

I summon to the winding ancient stair
> (*A Dialogue of Self and Soul*)

I declare this tower is my symbol
> (*Blood and the Moon*)

I meditate upon a swallow's flight
> (*Coole Park*)

The gyres! the gyres! Old Rocky Face, look forth;
> (*The Gyres*)

I call on those that call me son,
Grandson, or great-grandson. . . .
> (*Are You Content?*)

It must be noticed, first, that these lines are not drawn at random from the poems in which they appear. They are either the opening lines of the poems from which they come, or something not far short of that: the words from *Among School Children*, for example, mark the point at which the deeper meaning of the simple opening scene begins to be unfolded. In effect, they generate, or in one or two cases illustrate, the radical organization of the poems where they appear.

The *forming ritual* of these poems, one may say, is the solemnized calling-up of objects by the poet to people the world of his imagination. I hesitate to use the correct word, because it has become a favourite, in recent critical discussions, of writers who admit that they are uncertain of its meaning; but these ritual phrases reveal the *ontology* of what constitutes Yeats's world: the kind of reality, the status of reality, which is possessed by the objects in it. It is part of the nature of these poems that they do not offer to depict and describe things which the reader is invited to envisage as having prior, independent existence. On the contrary, the reader is invited to see them as called into being by the *fiat* of the poet, peopling a world *ab initio* as part of the creative act. This is the radical form. Yeats reverts to it again and again. Its indirect presence may be traced even in passages where the act of 'summoning' is not overt:

Around me the images of thirty years . . .
  (*The Municipal Gallery Revisited*)

Another example, for the implied analogy with Yeats himself seems inescapable, is the passage in *Ancestral Houses*:

Some violent bitter man, some powerful man
Called architect and artist in, that they,
Bitter and violent men, might rear in stone
The sweetness that all longed for night and day,
The gentleness none there had ever known . . .

and it is in this way that all the other sections of *Meditations in Time of Civil War* ought to be seen: if one is in doubt, for example, about the opening lines of *My Table*:

Two heavy trestles, and a board
Where Sato's gift, a changeless sword,
By pen and paper lies,
That it may moralise
My days out of their aimlessness . . .

the clue may be found in the *Letters*: 'I make my Japanese sword and its silk covering *my symbol of life* . . .' (*Letters*, 729).

  Once more, it is to passion, to energy, to 'self-possession and power' that the discussion returns; for what I am arguing is that the inner-most structure of poem after poem, of, in fact, the larger part of the major poems, is what ultimately gives incarnation to energized subjectivity, to passionate and powerful self-possession: and this innermost form is nothing other than the creation, by a series of as if vatic acts, of a whole world of objects ordered as their creator desires. Hence the initial starkness and simplicity; hence, as the energizing and creative act proceeds, the cumulative interrelation and enrichment. One of the finest passages anywhere in *The Tower* seems to symbolize Yeats' own creativity in his later poems:

Surely among a rich man's flowering lawns,
Amid the rustle of his planted hills,
Life overflows without ambitious pains;
And rains down life until the basin spills. . . .

This landscape, too, is the work of a single creator; the lines in fact express in verse the same sense of what makes a work of art as Yeats had expressed twenty years before – in a note which he entitled *First Principles*:

. . . a farce and a tragedy are alike in this, that they are a
moment of intense life . . . reduced to its simplest form . . .
an energy, an eddy of life purified from everything but
itself.

Taken as a whole, the stanza from which those *Ancestral Houses* lines were taken is an example, decisive in its clarity, of the 'complete coincidence between *period* and *stanza*' mentioned in a passage already quoted above. This coincidence is not, of course, something necessary to all poetry that can move the reader. Horace is one of many who cultivated the sensitive felicity of its exact opposite. But 'period' is the key word. Yeats does not mean merely sentence. He means that unit of expression, complex not compound merely, where the thought seems to have no organization and contour until the very instant of its completion. And 'thought' is a key, too; for just as syntax has little meaning save through the line of argument beneath it, so there is no complexity and control of syntax save what emerges from the unfolding and conclusion of that process of thinking which the syntax expresses and models. Yeats' 'intensity of pattern' is created for him by another aspect of his all-pervading energy: energy of argument.

With these points in mind, I propose now to examine *Meditations in Time of Civil War*, section 4, and consider in particular what 'intensity of pattern' may be seen in it from argument that creates coincidence of period and stanza; and more generally, how far the points which have emerged so far can account for what may be taken as 'style' in the verse, and how far there is something they leave unexplained.

It is easy to see in this poem the congeries of realities that, characteristically, Yeats assembles. That congeries comprises his daughter, his son, his house and its owls ('this laborious stair', 'this dark tower'), the friendly neighbour, the girl he married. Clearly (though there is here no ritual of summoning) the poem does not explore these as independent realities, but assembles them for its own sake. Clearly again, an intensifying pattern of argument runs from end to end of the poem. The first stanza argues that because one thing is so, a second must also be so in spite of something which argues to the contrary. The second stanza also has a clear logical form: if one thing happens, something else ought to follow. The third and closing stanza states an analogy which is no chance resemblance, but a systematic one (that is, the second part of it is indirectly entailed by the first).

So much for argument. In addition, there is a good deal of that progressive enrichment of ideas which was discussed earlier. The love and friendship of wife and neighbour are seen to make a 'circle', because of what is said about the owls (their lowliest counterpart under the greatest of all Circles); and the 'desolation' which the owls cry to the desolate sky is no arbitrary sentimentality, but an exact reflection of the 'torn petals' and 'common greenness' which the first stanza gave as the inevitable consequence of the flower that spread to the sun.

Yet it is both superficial and incomplete to rest in the idea of 'logic' as an adequate analysis of this 'intensity of pattern'. Part of the pattern lies in the thought-forms of the poet, but these are following relations of cause and effect as much as of logic; and in the end it becomes clear that the powers of logic at work in the poem are no more than one aspect of something more generic and comprehensive: an always-expanding network of transferring energies, of active interrelatings, among the individual realities which comprise the poem's 'world'. It is a world, in the first place, of vigorous action, of process and event, of emphatically transitive verbs.

Consider some details. It is the poet's ancestors (his 'old fathers') who impose his present nature on him; and that in turn, the birth and nature of his son and daughter. The flower of life casts its fragrance on the wind, spreads its colour before the sun; the torn petals, the common greenness, vigorously follow. If the children degenerate, it will be a 'natural declension', effect of determined causes. It shall ruin the Tower, and therefore it is that the owls shall nest in it and reach the sky with their calling. The ultimate law of the world, which determines men's life as birds', relates the poet to his circle of friendship and affection, to wife and to neighbour; and fixes in a circle the past and a future sometimes flourishing, sometimes in decline.

'The owls *shall* nest in it'. The idiom was deliberately chosen. At that point in his poem, Yeats was not expressing a natural necessity so much as laying one down as a pure act of his own will. So, once more, in the last stanza. The Tower may flourish or go to ruin through the forces of nature; but it was chosen, decked and altered by decision of the poet. In fact, when Yeats is writing in this style, *three* kinds of necessity and constraining interrelation are at work between the items of his thought. First, the implications of logic (of which the only clear example in *My Descendants* is how the circles of the owls relate to the circle of human life); second, the necessities of cause and effect; and third, the connections which the poet announces as imposed by himself. Logic, reality and *fiat* make a unity: no mere mirror of the physical cosmos, but a newly made one. Yeats's 'world' in the major later poems comprises not simply the objects which he promulgates, but also and along with them the acts of thought by which these are promulgated and manipulated. This is what follows from – or creates, depending on how one looks at it – the passionate subjectivity of the poem: an ever-present continuity in them of their vehemently feeling, thinking, willing creator.

Conor Cruise O'Brien

from 'Passion and Cunning: Notes on the Politics of Yeats',
in N. Jeffares and K. G. W. Cross (eds.), *In Excited Reverie* 1965

Comment on the question of Yeats' attitude to fascism has been
bedevilled by the assumption that a great poet must be, even in
politics, 'a nice guy'. If this be assumed then it follows that, as Yeats
obviously was a great poet, he cannot *really* have favoured fascism,
which is obviously not a nice cause. Thus the critic or biographer is
led to postulate a 'true Yeats', so that Yeats' recorded words and
actions of fascist character must have been perpetrated by some
bogus person with the same name and outward appearance.[1]

If one drops the assumption, about poets having always to be nice
in politics, then, the puzzle disappears, and we see, I believe, that Yeats
the man was as near to being a fascist as his situation and the conditions of his own country permitted. His unstinted admiration had
gone to Kevin O'Higgins, the most ruthless 'strong man' of his
time in Ireland, and he linked his admiration explicitly to his rejoicing
at the rise of fascism in Europe – and this at the very beginning,
within a few weeks of the March on Rome. Ten years later, after
Hitler had moved to the centre of the political stage in Europe,
Yeats was trying to create a movement in Ireland which would be
overtly fascist in language, costume, behaviour and intent. He turned
his back on this movement when it began to fail, not before. Would
the irony and detachment of this phase of disillusion have lasted if a
more effective fascist leader and movement had later emerged? One
may doubt it. Many in Germany who were 'disillusioned' by the
failure of the Kapp *putsch* and the beer-cellar *putsch* were speedily
'reillusioned' when Hitler succeeded – and 'disillusioned' again
when he lost the war.

Post-war writers, touching with embarrassment on Yeats' pro-
fascist opinions, have tended to treat these as a curious aberration of
an idealistic but ill-informed poet. In fact such opinions were quite
usual in the Irish Protestant middle-class to which Yeats belonged (as

---

1 There is a sense of course in which the poet, actually engaged in writing his
poetry, is 'the true Yeats', but that is another matter.

well as in other middle-classes), in the twenties and thirties. The *Irish
Times*, spokesman of that class, aroused no protest from its readers
when it hailed Hitler (4 March 1933) as 'Europe's standard bearer
against Muscovite terrorism' and its references to Mussolini were as
consistently admiring as those to Soviet Russia were consistently
damning. But the limiting factor on the pro-fascist tendencies of the
Irish Times and of the Irish Protestant middle-class generally was the
pull of loyalty to Britain – a factor which did not apply – or applied
only with great ambivalence – in the case of Yeats. Mr T. R. Henn is
quite right when he says that Yeats was 'not alone in believing at that
moment of history, that the discipline of fascist theory might impose
order upon a disintegrating world'. I cannot follow Mr Henn, however, to his conclusion that 'nothing could be further from Yeats'
mind than [fascism's] violent and suppressive practice' (*The Lonely
Tower*, p. 467). 'Force, marching men' and 'the victory [in civil war]
of the skilful, riding their machines as did the feudal knights their
armoured horses' (*On the Boiler*), surely belong to the domain of
violent and suppressive practice.

Just as one school is led to claim that the pro-fascist Yeats was not
the 'true' Yeats, so another tries to believe that the fascism to which
Yeats was drawn was not a 'true' fascism.

Several critics have assured us that he was drawn not really to
fascism, but to some idealized aristocracy of eighteenth-century
stamp. 'In all fairness', writes Dr Vivian Mercier, 'we should allow
that his views were closer to Hamilton's or even to Jefferson's than
they were to Mussolini's.[1] As far as political theory is concerned
this is probably correct – although the name of Swift would seem
more relevant than that of Hamilton or of Jefferson. But it ignores
one important reality: that Yeats was interested in contemporary
politics and that he was a contemporary, not of Swift's or Jefferson's,
but of Mussolini's.[2]

1 'To pierce the dark mind', *Nation* (10 December 1960). My friend Dr
Mercier, like almost all scholars from Ireland who have written on Yeats,
finds his aristocratism, as an Anglo-Irish attitude, more congenial than the
aboriginal writer of the present essay can find it.
2 He had, in any case, the assurance of his friend Ezra Pound (*Jefferson and/or
Mussolini*) that the Duce was translating Jeffersonian ideas into twentieth-
century terms.

He would certainly have preferred something more strictly aristocratic than fascism, but since he was living in the twentieth century he was attracted to fascism as the best available form of anti-democratic theory and practice. Mr Frank O'Connor, who knew him well in his last years and – politics apart – greatly admired and liked him, has told us plainly that 'he was a fascist and authoritarian, seeing in world crises only the break-up of the "damned liberalism" he hated'.[1]

George Orwell, though critical, and up to a point percipient, about Yeats' tendencies, thought that Yeats misunderstood what an authoritarian society would be like. Such a society, Orwell pointed out, 'will not be ruled by noblemen with Van Dyck faces, but by anonymous millionaires, shiny-bottomed bureaucrats and murderous gangsters'. This implies a degree of innocence in Yeats which cannot reasonably be postulated. O'Higgins and O'Duffy were not 'Duke Ercole and Guidobaldo', and Yeats had considerable experience of practical politics, both in the nineties and in the early twenties. 'In the last forty years,' wrote J. M. Hone in the year of Yeats' death, 'there was never a period in which his countrymen did not regard him as a public figure.'[2] When he thought of rule by an elite, it was a possible elite, resembling in many ways the nominated members of the Senate in which he had sat.[3] Its membership – bankers, organizers, ex-officers – would correspond roughly to what

1 'The Old Age of a Poet', *The Bell* (February 1941). He also mentions an Abbey dispute over an attempt by Yeats to stage *Coriolanus* for purposes of 'fascist propaganda'. Mr Sean O'Faoláin, a more cautious observer, who also knew Yeats at this time, speaks of his 'fascist tendencies' ('Yeats and the Younger Generation', *Horizon*, vol. 5, January 1942).

2 'Yeats as a Political Philosopher', *London Mercury*, April 1939. Hone adds that, among Yeats' fellow Senators, a banker thought the poet would have made 'an admirable banker' and a lawyer thought that 'a great lawyer' was lost in him.

3 'In its early days,' Yeats wrote of the Senate, 'some old banker or lawyer would dominate the House, leaning upon the back of the chair in front, always speaking with undisturbed self-possession as at some table in a board-room. My imagination sets up against him some typical elected man, emotional as a youthful chimpanzee, hot and vague, always disturbed, always hating something or other.' (*On the Boiler.*) In another mood, however, he wrote about these oligarchs in a more disparaging vein. (*A Packet for Ezra Pound.*)

Orwell, in more emotive language, describes. Nor should it be assumed – as Orwell with his 'murderous gangsters' seems to imply – that the sensitive nature of the poet would necessarily be revolted by the methods of rule of an authoritarian state.[1] Yeats – unlike, say, his brother, or Lady Gregory – was not, in politics, a very squeamish person. Seventy-seven executions did not repel him; on the contrary, they made him admire O'Higgins all the more. At least one of his associates of the early thirties might have been described as a 'murderous gangster'. And when, in 1936, Ethel Mannin appealed to him for a gesture which would have helped the German writer, Ossietzki, then in a Nazi concentration camp, Yeats refused. 'Do not,' he said, 'try to make a politician of me . . .'[2]

It is true that neither Yeats nor anyone else during Yeats' lifetime knew what horrors fascism would be capable of. But the many who, like Yeats, were drawn to fascism at this time knew, and seemed to have little difficulty in accepting, or at least making allowances for, much of what had already been done and continued to be done. 'The Prussian police,' wrote the *Irish Times* in an editorial of February 1933, 'have been authorized by Herr Hitler's Minister to shoot Communists – a term which in Germany has a wide political connotation – on sight.' The same editorial which contained this information ended with the words: 'Naturally the earlier phases of this

---

1 The late Louis MacNeice in *The Poetry of W. B. Yeats* seems to have been the first to lay much stress on Yeats' relation to fascism, but could not quite make up his mind what that relation was. He refers to Yeats at one point as 'the man who nearly became a fascist', having spoken of him earlier as having arrived at 'his own elegant brand of fascism'.

2 To Ethel Mannin, April 1936. In fairness to Yeats it must be noted, however, that in order to help Ossietzki he would have had to recommend him to the Nobel Committee for consideration for the Nobel Prize – something which, on artistic grounds, he may well have been unwilling to do. His degree of 'toughness' on political matters, minimized as it has been by some of his admirers, should not be exaggerated either. In the Senate he supported an amendment to the Government's Public Safety Bill intended to secure independent inspection of prisons (Senate Debates, I. cols. 1440–41; 1638–9). He also sent 'warm blankets' to Maud Gonne when his government put her in jail (*Letters*, p. 696). But in all essentials he supported the Government's policy of firmness. 'Even the gentle Yeats,' wrote Sean O'Casey, 'voted for the Flogging Bill' (i.e. the Public Safety Bill which introduced flogging as a punishment for arson and armed robbery). Yeats voted for the Second Reading (26 July 1923). This was in the aftermath of the Civil War.

renascence are crude, but Germany is finding her feet after a long period of political ineptitude.'[1]

Yeats read the newspapers; he also read, as Hone records, several books on fascist Italy and Nazi Germany.[2] If, then, he was attracted to the dominant movements in these countries, and if he supported a movement in his own country whose resemblances to these Continental movements he liked to stress, it cannot be contended that he did so in ignorance of such 'crude' practices as the *Irish Times* described.[3]

Some writers – notably Professor Donald Torchiana in his well-documented study *W. B. Yeats, Jonathan Swift and Liberty*[4] – have insisted that, in spite of Yeats' authoritarian and fascist leanings, he was essentially a friend of liberty. 'Both Swift and Yeats,' Torchiana concludes, 'served human liberty.' The senses in which this is true for Yeats are important but clearly limited. He defended the liberty of the artist, consistently. In politics, true to his duality, he defended the liberty of Ireland against English domination, and the liberty of his own caste – and sometimes, by extension, of others – against clerical domination. Often these liberties overlapped, and the cause of artist and aristocrat became the same; often his resistance to 'clerical' authoritarianism (his position on the Lock-out, on divorce, on censorship) makes him appear a liberal. But his objection to clerical authoritarianism is not the liberal's objection to *all* authoritarianism. On the contrary he favours 'a despotism of the educated classes' and in the search for this, is drawn towards fascism. It is true that fascism was not in reality a despotism of the educated classes, but it was a form of

1 The *Irish Times* was in no way exceptional in this kind of comment. I cite it only because it was the journal of the class to which Yeats belonged, and he read it.

2 Hone tells us (*W. B. Yeats*) that Yeats had learned with 'great satisfaction' of a law of the Third Reich 'whereby ancient and impoverished families can recover their hereditary properties'. Professor T. Desmond Williams of University College, Dublin, tells me that 'to benefit from the hereditary law [of September 1933] you had to trace your ancestry back to 1760 and you had to be purely Aryan. There was provision for the return of land that had passed into "impure" hands as a result of mortgages.'

3 It is true that the Blueshirts did not even try to go to anything like the lengths of their Continental models. It is also true that, unlike the case of their models, the Communists whom the Blueshirts were fighting were, in Ireland, largely imaginary.

4 *Modern Philosophy* (August 1963).

despotism which the educated classes in the twenties and thirties showed a disposition to settle for – a disposition proportionate to the apparent threat, in their country, of communism or 'anarchy'. In assessing Yeats' pro-fascist opinions, there is no need to regard these as so extraordinary that he must either not have been himself, or not have known what he was about.

A. D. Hope

'William Butler Yeats' from *Collected Poems*   1968

To have found at last that noble, candid speech
In which all things worth saying may be said,
Which, whether the mind asks, or the heart bids, to each
Affords its daily bread;

To have been afraid neither of lust nor hate,
To have shown the dance, and when the dancer ceased,
The bloody head of prophecy on a plate
Borne in at Herod's feast;

To have loved the bitter, lucid mind of Swift,
Bred passion against the times, made wisdom strong;
To have sweetened with your pride's instinctive gift
The brutal mouth of song;

To have shared with Blake uncompromising scorn
For art grown smug and clever, shown your age
The virgin leading home the unicorn
And loosed his sacred rage –

But more than all, when from my arms she went
That blessed my body all night, naked and near,
And all was done, and order and content
Closed the Platonic Year,

Was it *not* chance alone that made us look
Into the glass of the Great Memory
And know the eternal moments, in your book,
That we had grown to be?

Harold Bloom

from *Yeats* 1970

Sailing to Byzantium was written in August–September 1926, four years before the writing of *Byzantium*. F. L. Gwynn was the first, I believe, to indicate a crucial difference between the historical vision of the two poems.[1] The first Byzantium is that praised in *A Vision*, the city of Justinian, about AD 550, while the city of the second poem is as it was 'towards the end of the first Christian millennium'. The cities are both of the mind, but they are not quite the same city, the second being at a still further remove from nature than the first.

Melchiori, in an intricate study of the poem, showed that *Sailing to Byzantium* recalls Yeats's early story, *Rosa Alchemica*, and so there is no reason to doubt that the poem is a finished version of Yeats's kind of alchemical quest. The highest claim yet made for *Sailing to Byzantium* is that of Whitaker, who says of this poem and *Among School Children* that 'in them is created a new species of man who – unbeknownst to himself, as it were – *is* his contrary.' Yeats would have delighted in this claim, but that the poem justifies it is open to some question.

Yeats's first intention in *Sailing to Byzantium* was not to speak in his own proper person, but as 'a poet of the Middle Ages'. A medieval Irish poet, seeking to make his soul, sets sail for the center of European civilization. But, as Curtis Bradford demonstrates, this *persona* gradually is eliminated from successive drafts of the poem, and the speaker in the final version may be taken as Yeats himself, a Yeats seeking his *daimon* at the center of Unity of Being, a city where the spiritual life and the creation of art merge as one.[2]

The great example of such a visionary city in English poetry is of course Blake's version of the New Jerusalem, Golgonooza, the city of Los the artificer. There are Blakean elements in both Byzantium poems, but Yeats's city is emphatically not Blake's, and Blake would have disliked birds (however artificial) and dolphins as final emblems

1 F. L. Gwynn, 'Yeats's *Byzantium* and Its Sources', *Philological Quarterly*, vol. 32, no 1, January 1953.
2 Curtis Bradford, 'Yeats's Byzantium Poems: A Study of Their Development', in John Unterecker (ed.), *Yeats*, Prentice-Hall.

of imaginative salvation. The forms walking the streets of Yeats's city are images, but they are not the Divine Image or Human Form Divine that Blake insisted upon in his vision of last things. The vision of both Byzantium poems is more Shelleyan than Blakean, and the repudiation of nature in both poems has a Shelleyan rather than Blakean twist.

I would guess the ultimate literary source of Yeats's Byzantium to be in Shelley's longest poem, the allegorical epic, *The Revolt of Islam*, a poem that Yeats read early, and remembered often. It is not today among the more admired of Shelley's longer poems, and rightly stands below *Alastor*, which preceded it, and *Prometheus Unbound*, which came after. But it has considerable though uneven power, and it is a worthy companion to *Endymion*, having been composed in competition to Keats's longest poem. Most of the poem is an idealized account of left-wing revolution, not likely to move Yeats at any time in his life. But the first and final cantos are almost purely visionary, and they had considerable effect upon Yeats, who cites them in his major essay upon Shelley.

In canto I of Shelley's poem, there is a voyage to an immortal Temple:

... likest Heaven, ere yet day's purple stream
Ebbs o'er the western forest, while the gleam

Of the unrisen moon among the clouds
  Is gathering. ...

Shelley's starlit dome is surrounded by 'marmoreal floods', and reveals itself to us only through the arts, and then only in part:

Like what may be conceived of this vast dome,
  When from the depths which thought can seldom pierce
Genius beholds it rise, his native home,
  Girt by the deserts of the Universe;
  Yet, nor in painting's light, or mightier verse,
Or sculpture's marble language, can invest
  That shape to mortal sense –

Within the Temple, which is lit by its own radiance, brighter than day's, are paintings wrought by Genii in a winged dance, and also the forms of departed sages, set against the background of fire. It seems only a step from this to Byzantium.

'I fly from nature to Byzantium', reads one cancelled line of Yeats's poem, and another cancelled phrase salutes the city as the place 'where nothing changes'. The poet is asking for transfiguration, though at the expense of being made 'rigid, abstracted, and fanatical/ Unwavering, indifferent'. For his need is great, his function as poet being done:

All that men know, or think they know, being young
Cry that my tale is told my story sung. . . .[1]

Yeats seeks the Condition of Fire, as Blake sought it in Golgonooza, or as Shelley's Adonais attained it, but his motive here is very different from Blake's or even Shelley's. Byzantium is not attained after:

Mystery's tyrants are cut off and not one left on Earth,
And when all Tyranny was cut off from the face of
   Earth. . . .

Nor does the soul of Yeats, after reaching the Holy City, serve as a beacon, 'burning through the inmost veil of heaven', guiding others to the Eternal. Yeats's Condition of Fire is neither a criticism of life, as Blake's and Shelley's are, nor is it a manifestation of a freedom open to all who would find it, nor indeed is it a state of imaginative liberty at all. It is 'extreme, fortuitous, personal', like the moments of visionary awakening in Wallace Stevens, though it does not present itself honestly as being such. It is also a state, ironically like the 'sweet golden clime' sought by Blake's Sun-Flower, in which the human image must subside into the mechanical or merely repetitively natural, unless it is willing to start out upon its quest again. For Byzantium is no country for men, young *or* old, and the monuments it contains testify to aspects of the soul's magnificence that do not support humanistic claims of any kind whatsoever. Keats, standing in the shrine of Saturn, stands in Byzantium, and is told by the scornful Moneta that those to whom the miseries of the world *are* misery do not come into that shrine. Yeats would have found this irrelevant, for his Byzantium does not admit the 'senti-

[1] Curtis Bradford, *Yeats at Work*, p. 98.

mentalist', the *primary* man, at all. We need not find this excessively relevant, but we might hold it in mind as we read *Sailing to Byzantium*, for the limitations of the poem's ideal ought to be our concern also.

'God's holy fire', in this poem, is not a state where the creator and his creation are one, as in Blake, but rather a state where the creator has been absorbed into his creation, where the art work or 'artifice of eternity' draws all reality into itself. Yeats's too-palpable ironies in the last stanza of the poem are redundant and, as Sturge Moore remarked, the poet is unjustified in asserting that he is 'out of nature'.[1] He is where he always was, poised before his own artifact, and so less accurate than the Keats who contemplated the Grecian urn, knowing always his own separation from the world wrought upon it.

I am suggesting that *Sailing to Byzantium* belies its title, and is a rather static poem, and a peculiarly evasive one. The poem that did not get written is, in this case, more impressive than the final text. If Mrs Yeats and Jon Stallworthy were right, then the poem began as a prose fragment exploring again that tragedy of sexual intercourse which is the perpetual virginity of the soul.[2] A man past sixty, in early autumn, broods on the loves of his lifetime, and decides that 'now I will take off my body' even as 'for many loves have I taken off my clothes'. As once his loves 'longed to see' but could not be enfolded by his soul, perhaps his soul now can cease to be virgin. The line of a later verse draft, 'I fly from nature to Byzantium', would then be a wholly dualistic sentiment, abandoning sexual for spiritual love. That is hardly characteristic of Yeats, early or late, and shows only a mood, however powerful. The prose fragment says 'I live on love', which is not very characteristic either. In the drafts of the opening stanza a significant change from the simplistic dualism, and the tense concern for love, is quickly manifested. The contrast presented is between the Christ child, smiling upon his mother's knee, and the old gods in the Irish hills, with whom the poet identifies.

1 Ursula Bridge (ed.) *W. B. Yeats and T. Sturge Moore, Their Correspondence* 1901–37.
2 Stallworthy, 89–90.

He is Oisin again, finding no place in the Ireland of St Patrick, and so he sails to Byzantium.[1]

The flight then is not so much from nature as from a new dispensation of the young. The old poet of the old faith is doubly alienated, and this complex estrangement is the double root of the poem. As a poet, Yeats voyages to find a new faith; as a man, his quest is away – not from the body so much as from the decrepitude of the body. Byzantium is the state of being of 'the thing become', as one of the drafts puts it, 'and ageless beauty where age is living'. In the final draft of the poem's first stanza, much of this richness of the quest-motive is gone, and age alone seems to impel the poet on his journey.[2]

Much else dropped out of the final poem, including both a prophetic and a purgatorial element. The final line – 'Of what is past, or passing, or to come' – is severely qualified by the rest of the last stanza, but in the drafts it is presented without irony:

And set in golden leaves to sing
Of present past and future to come
For the instruction of Byzantium. . . . [3]

There is an echo of Blake here, not of the voice of the Bard of Experience, but of the purged prophet Los in *Jerusalem*, crying out in triumph that he beholds all reality in a single imagining:

I see the Past, Present and Future, existing all at once
Before me; O Divine Spirit sustain me on thy wings!
That I may awake Albion from his long and cold repose.

Blake-Los affirms his mission in the context of experience, the 'long and cold repose' of man, while Yeats seeks his function in the context of a reality beyond experience, but the affinity is clear nevertheless. So is the necessity of purgation, of being made free of

1 A fuller study than this book can be, of Yeats's place in the tradition of displaced or internalized quest-romance, would relate the 'sailing' of this lyric not only to *The Wanderings of Oisin*, and *The Shadowy Waters*, and their source in *Alastor*, but to the many versions of sea-quest in later nineteenth-century poetry. Yeats had read many more minor poets of the generation just before his own than most of his scholars have.
2 Curtis Bradford, *Yeats at Work*, p. 111.
3 Ibid., 102.

the Spectre or Selfhood, if the prophetic role is to be assumed, evident both in Blake and the Yeats of the drafts, but not of the final text, where only the heart, natural passion, is to be consumed away. Yeats, in one draft, attempts to mount the purgatorial stairs as Dante does, or Keats in *The Fall of Hyperion*, but fails:

When prostrate on the marble step I fall
And cry amid my tears –
And cry aloud – 'I sicken with desire
Though/and fastened to a dying animal
Cannot endure my life – O gather me
Into the artifice of eternity.'[1]

This does not match the incisiveness gained when Yeats says of his heart: 'It knows not what it is,' in the final text, but something valuable is lost also, the consciousness that an experiential purgatory must still be borne if a humanizing prophecy is to be uttered. Yeats, as always, knew very well what he was doing as a reviser, and he finds intensity through simplification in the final text. What *Sailing to Byzantium* lacks is just the reverse, the simplification through intensity that sometimes does take Yeats into the Condition of Fire.

Helen Vendler

'Sacred and Profane Perfection in Yeats', unpublished essay   1971

At the serious height of his career, and after an early preoccupation with the supernatural, Yeats banished his sacred mythologies from his verse:

The holy centaurs of the hills are vanished;
I have nothing but the embittered sun;
Banished heroic mother moon and vanished.
    (Lines Written in Dejection (1919))

The mythologies stayed banished for about ten years, while Yeats found 'more enterprise in walking naked' – from 1910 to 1919, roughly speaking. They had to resort to the extraordinary means of

1 Curtis Bradford, *Yeats at Work*, p.101.

mediumship to re-insert themselves into Yeats's work, since his conscious mind was clearly set on resisting them. He could only let his mythologies back into his poetry by pretending that their reappearance had nothing to do with his will, that all these visions were dictated by outside forces. The absolute necessity of mythologies to Yeats's verse is proved by the contortions he underwent to re-admit them, but once they resurfaced they were never again the rather simple creations beckoning the human child away from a world too full of weeping. In *Under Ben Bulben* he gives us a deathbed summary of his mythological sages, witches, and immortal ghosts, saying, 'Here's the gist of what they mean.' Their gist is that 'There's a purpose set/Before the secret working mind:/Profane perfection of mankind.' In that phrase – 'profane perfection' – the Platonic sacred is violently matched with the incarnate human, and the history of Yeats's mythologies is recapitulated in brief. The 'purer' sacred perfection of his early work leads to a thicket of alternative perfections later on, and it is those later perfections which establish Yeats's unique stature among modern poets.

In the early verse, the sacred supernatural which Oisin's Niamh and all the Sidhe represent is ostensibly a hedonistic element, explicitly opposed (in *The Countess Cathleen* and *The Unappeasable Host*, for instance) to the Christian supernatural. Nevertheless, the function of the pagan sacred supernatural – to remove the soul of man from this vale of tears – is indistinguishable from that of the Christian supernatural, and in *The Secret Rose* (1899), the visionary experience under whatever guise is metaphysically the same, since Christians, Bacchantes, lovers, and Magi all share the same otherworldly quest whose end is not glory but passivity – to be enfolded in the sacred perfection of the Rose:

Surely thine hour has come, thy great wind blows,
Far off, most secret, and inviolate Rose?

'Surely thine hour has come,' breathes Yeats in 1899: but when that hour comes round at last, in 1921, it will not be the enfolding Secret Rose that will appear but a hulking creature entirely different:

And what Rough Beast, its hour come round at last,
Slouches toward Bethlehem to be born?
    (*The Second Coming*)

Both the Secret Rose and the Rough Beast are recastings of Yeats: Yeats created his gods in his own image, and in rewriting his verses, he remade himself. His whole career, including the evolution of the mythologies from Rose to Beast, is a long reshaping and reprojection of his changing self and soul.

In the bad time, spiritually speaking, between 1910 and 1919, Yeats sank often into a state of ironic apathy, exhausted and unable to attach himself permanently to anything: 'Those that I fight, I do not hate,/Those that I guard I do not love' (1919). The Sidhe, who once beckoned with their living voices to a sacred Faeryland, have stiffened into a repetitive iconic unsatisfied and unsatisfying ancient-ness, as we can tell from the single mythological poem of this period, *The Magi* (1919). In this great poem (which precedes by one page in the *Collected Poems* Yeats's disavowal of mythologies in *A Coat*), the central word, twice repeated, is 'unsatisfied'. Sacred perfection, in both of its Christian manifestations – the Incarnation and the Cruci-fixion – has been tried and found wanting; the Magi, unsatisfied by their original view of Bethlehem, waited for Calvary: now, unsatis-fied by that, they vainly hope that this time Bethlehem can satisfy them. But it is clearly their own hapless fixed yearning which pre-vents their participation in the uncontrollable or the turbulent. They are ghostly figures, ever the same, ever fixed, ever hovering, ever appearing and disappearing, ever impotent. These sacred figures are no guide to the perplexed; these drifting animated dissatisfactions are of no use to their poet-son, and he gives up on them though they continue, 'now, as at all times', to haunt him. The poem marks a dead end.

Art, at this point, offers no repose. Like the apparitional Magi, drifting in and out of sight, art 'disappears' the instant we stop looking at it; and Yeats's 'discontent' is a version of the Magi's 'unsatisfied' response:

> I bade
> My discontented heart to draw content
> From beauty that is cast out of a mould
> In bronze, or that in dazzling marble appears,
> Appears, but when we have gone is gone again,
> Being more indifferent to our solitude
> Than 'twere an apparition.

From now on, Yeats vows, he will have no exterior sacred apparitional guiding image – a faery Mistress, a processional Magus, an immortal statue – but will have only an image drawn from himself – 'the mysterious one . . . most like me, being indeed my double', and yet 'the most unlike, being my anti-self' (1919). It would seem an end to mythology.

But, somewhere under ground, the mythologies are preparing to reassert themselves, though in a far more problematic manner. In their first appearance before the eyes of Michael Robartes they seem indeed merely static allegorized elements of the self – the sphinx-like intellect, the Buddha-like heart, and the dancer-like creative soul (1919). The extreme relief at the end of the poem, where Yeats says that he, 'ignorant for so long', has at last been rewarded by a vision of his true self and its chief principles, comes I think from the resurgence of mythologies, even in this semi-allegorical form. There is a beast, there is a Buddha, there is a dancer – what matter if, under their guises, they are also head, heart, and soul?

This vision remains for some time, however, a private one. The isolation of the Irish airman continues, reinforced by Yeats's confusions of feeling over the Easter Rising. His new world of profane perfection of the faculties of the self admits no others but himself. It may be true that 'a terrible beauty is born', but Yeats patronizes the Irish heroes, who lacked that 'marble or . . . bronze repose' Yeats identified with ideal presences. The Irish patriots are regarded not so much with admiration as with pity and commiseration, a forbearance from a harsher judgement:

And what if excess of love
Bewildered them till they died?

They died, in short, not of English bullets but of their own bewilderment of passion, confused and excessive, resembling nothing so much as Yeats's own young self, 'that sea-rider Oisin led by the nose' to 'vain battles'. To win Yeats's praise now required something much more bitter than young enthusiasm (however unfair to the 1916 patriots such a judgement may seem). Yeats had become 'certain as can be/That every natural victory/Belongs to beast or demon' (1921). This statement, immediately preceding The Second Coming, authorizes us to see the demonic beast of that poem as a symbol, strange as it may seem, of 'natural victory'. Yeats's starving gaze into Faeryland, starved for the bosom of the faery bride, has become a gaze blank and pitiless as the sun. His past is still alive in him, of course, and is represented by the disorientated falcon and the indignant desert birds, but they are powerless in their retrospective flutterings, and Yeats's Sphinx, with its massive slow approach, moves into the ascendant. This Beast is now Yeats's tutelary spirit, and its appearance marks, along with Yeats's rejection of the ineffectual Magi, a signal and brutal reversion to a mythology no longer a weak conceptualization of Aristotelian faculties, but wholly on the way to the profane, enunciating itself in a harsh poetry.

The liberation, if we may call it such, marked by the acknowledgement of hatred and desire, lust and rage, produced a flood of images of profane perfection, first and most beautifully in *Sailing to Byzantium* (1928) where for once the sacred and profane perfections, versions of the Magi and the Beast, exist in perfect equilibrium. In fear that the sensual mode will desert him, Yeats decides to forsake it first, and his salvation from the sensual world is to come about via the 'Sages standing in God's holy fire', or so it seems; and we wonder whether this poem is not a regression to Faeryland after all, in which, after his voyage to Byzantium, a passive Yeats will nevertheless have to depend on the intervention of the all-powerful Sages to take him out of the realm of nature into their own realm of sacred perfection. Are the sages only a superior version of the ancient faery-mistresses? After all, everything, it would seem, is to be done by *them* – they must *come* from the holy fire, *perne* in a gyre, *be* the singing masters of Yeats's soul, *consume* his heart away, and *gather* him into the artifice of eternity. If the poem ended there it would be another version of 'Come away, O human child'. But of course this great and famous poem ends with a gratuitous and stunning reversal – a change from the sacred to a civilized profane, from anguish to urbanity. Now, in the last tableau, it is Yeats who acts. The poem has led us to expect that Yeats, once out of nature, would become a sublime sage like his sacred 'fathers' and 'masters'. Not at all. On the contrary, he almost impudently rejects their sacred Hebraism and chooses instead the elegant Hellenism of the social world of the Emperor and his lords and ladies. This unforeseen gleam of humour and buoyancy in Yeats is nevertheless by itself too light to end a poem with such grave beginnings, and so the nightingale becomes an oracle – the Hellenic equivalent, after all, of the Hebraic prophets. In that city where 'nature' – the lords and ladies – and the realm out of nature – sages and hammered bird – meet, sacred perfection and profane perfection breathe the same air. But even 'sacred perfection' by the end of the poem has been subtly re-defined. The realm of 'God's holy fire' where the sages really live is forsaken for 'the artifice of eternity' where the sages live in mosaic and the bird in hammered gold.

Yeats's later and far more physical male image of profane perfection, as we know from *Long-Legged Fly* and *Under Ben Bulben*, is Michelangelo's Adam in the Sistine Chapel, the beautiful mute aspiring animal about to be touched by sacred perfection and thereby given a soul. Leda is the corresponding female image, and the question asked by *Leda and the Swan* is whether profane perfection, once touched or animated, can any longer be said to be only profane: in short, is there any living profane perfection which does not finally include what we mean by the divine or the sacred? In *Leda and the Swan*, as in *The Second Coming*, a profane fleshliness in the sacred itself – in Jove's 'brute blood' and in the 'slow thighs' of the Beast – makes the division ever more equivocal, and complicates our ideas of both the sacred and the profane. What is emphasized is the perennial necessity of Jove for Leda, of Leda for Jove, the Beast for Bethlehem, Bethlehem (wakened and waiting with its cradle set rocking in expectation) for the Beast.

However, the mutual attraction of the profane and the sacred comes, in human terms at least, to a heartbreaking end. Our worshipping, whether sacred or profane, is at once our exaltation and our undoing, since we ourselves, Yeats tells us, as for the first time since *The Secret Rose* he once again subsumes sacred and profane perfections under one rubric, imagine and fabricate those presences whose perfections we worship. With a new epistemological certainty, Yeats tells us that what we adore (and what we loathe as well) we ourselves create: passion creates the image of the beloved, piety creates the image of the god, maternal affection creates the image of the destined child – but lovers, mothers, and devotees experience the same heartbreak in the end:

Both nuns and mothers worship images,
But those the candles light are not as those

That animate a mother's reveries,
But keep a marble or a bronze repose,
And yet they too break hearts.
    (*Among School Children*)

In a metaphysical bleakness, Yeats begins an invocation:

                O Presences
That passion, piety, or affection knows,
And that all heavenly glory symbolize –
O self-born mockers of man's enterprise –
    (ibid.)

But Yeats breaks off, to see whether, out of this wreckage, he can summon up an image of perfection which will not end by destroying its worshipper. In terms of his own life, he can find none: as he knows life, body is always bruised to pleasure soul, wisdom is won only at the cost of being wanly bleary-eyed from study, poetic beauty in verse is born only out of sexual despair. And yet, remembering perhaps Keats's remark that poetry should come as naturally as leaves to a tree, and remembering the perfect spontaneity of a dancer's dance (as well as the aesthetic distance of its devotees) he concludes that some perfection, at least in the realm of the profane, is not arduous but efflorescent and immediate:

O chestnut-tree, great-rooted blossomer,
Are you the leaf, the blossom, or the bole?
O body swayed to music, O brightening glance,
How can we know the dancer from the dance?
    (ibid.)

But these perfections – the tree, the dancer – are alien to him, summoned up from outside his own nature and his own passions. To a tree and a dancer we give assent as they give us pleasure; but love (which animates nuns, mothers, and lovers) or, to give it a worse name, self-projection, bears no part in our relation, however visual and pleasurable, to trees and dancers. The tree and the dancer are questioned, as Yeats will later question Old Rocky Face, for an answer which never comes. And yet, these unattainable perfections of blossom and dance remain, in the lyric domain, as vividly realized as any of Yeats's more passionate creations: his wishes, even though translated out of passion into aesthetics, continue to match poetic strength with his despairs. Though these final wistful sublimities, the tree and the dancer, are only virtually and not actually present, who will say that *Among School Children* ends in dejection? On the contrary, the heroic effort in the last four lines to pull the poem out of its pitiless reflexive despondency is a mark of the hold that the idea of perfection had on Yeats's imagination, however difficult he found it to say anything about its actual existence.

As Yeats comes to believe that we create the perfections we worship, and that it matters very little whether they be sacred or profane since the humanly tragic end of each is identical, he begins to think differently about the Irish patriots. The sacred perfections of wisdom, beauty, and art are no longer opposed in Yeats's mind to the profane perfection of heroism, and so the Irish nationalists can become, like his sages, revelatory personages. Though he at first addresses the ghosts of Eva and Constance Gore-Booth in the old tender patronizing tone of 1916, he soon finds that he cannot act at all without the help of these his ghostly contemporaries. Helpless himself, he entreats them to begin the holocaust which will consume their common folly and guilt, and his entreaty reminds us of his earlier plea to the sages of Byzantium:

Arise and bid me strike a match,
And strike another till time catch;
Should the conflagration climb,
Run till all the sages know.
We the great gazebo built,
They convicted us of guilt,
Bid me strike a match and blow.
(*In Memory of Eva Gore-Booth and Con Markiewicz*)

More and more, retrospectively, Yeats begins to see his friends as sacred or profane sages, mediums 'as though a sterner eye looked through [their] eye'. Maud Gonne's bronze head later becomes such a medium, but the human creature who was the model for the oracular head has vanished in this grim sublimation, the flesh suppressed in the need for a fixed mask through which tragedy can speak. This total disjunction – between the girl all full of magnanimity of light and the dark tomb-haunting soul of the head – will mark Yeats's cruellest separation between life and sage-like perfection. The game – given the savage judgement of the head, wondering what is left for massacre to save – seems not worth the candle, the sacrifice of a beautiful form. Yeats is again tempted to forsake life entirely, to join forces with the Soul; but its seductive promises of eternity and deliverance from the crime of death and birth (so like the promises of the sages in *Sailing to Byzantium*) are answered finally by the brutal patience of the Self: 'I am content to live it all again' (1933).

But Yeats was not to be rid of the heartbreaking ideal Presences, at least not by any mere fleshly defiance, however nobly and violently spoken. His truer position, at this point in his life, appears in *Byzantium* (1933), where the immortal golden sages of *Sailing to Byzantium* have faded to a mysterious and silent mummy. The realm of perfection is no longer greeted with longing frustration as 'the artifice of eternity', but rather is hailed as 'death-in-life and life-in-death'. Byzantium now seems entirely chillier and more deathlike. Where we once saw fiery sages and an Emperor's courtly society, we now see a darkened empire from which everything human and sociable has been ruthlessly suppressed. Only the artifacts, in cold disdain and bitterness, appear, and they scorn the human and the natural. Only art, not life, can exist in this vivified museum of mummies, and Yeats, in the poem, will not journey into the land but will remain astraddle on the dolphin's mire and blood. When Plotinus does get to the Elysian Fields, on the other hand, he finds, rather as Yeats had in *Sailing to Byzantium*, not the sacred perfection he had expected but instead a profane scene of elemental coupling:

> But Thetis' belly listens.
> Down the mountain walls
> From where Pan's cavern is
> Intolerable music falls.
> Foul goat-head, brutal arm appear,
> Belly, shoulder, bum,
> Flash fishlike; nymphs and satyrs
> Copulate in the foam.
>   *(News for the Delphic Oracle)*

This excerpt comes from the *Last Poems*, and is their grossest image of profane perfection, phrased as a retrospective irony on Yeats himself. Peleus, like Oisin, is 'led by the nose', but will eventually discover, as Yeats did, the primal activity around him.

The most famous summary statement of Yeats's continuing relation to his images of perfection comes of course in *The Circus Animals' Desertion*, with its lament for vanished ladders. We have seen almost every possible relation with the perfect envisaged over Yeats's career: the poet can walk side by side with a Presence, following it into Faeryland (or Byzantium); the Presence can descend to the poet, like Jove to Leda; the Presences can hover over the poet, forever inaccessible in a parallel plane, like the sages or the Magi; the Presences are *post hoc*, confirmatory, like those that give dreams their looking glass; the Presences can remain aloof and force us to climb up to their 'proper dark'. When our ladders, in this last formulation, are gone in the depletion of old age, there can be no more encounters with heavenly perfection or profane perfection, since all such vertical encounters are animated by youth, idealism, hope, or love. Except one: the encounter with art, the one lasting form. It is the visible form preserved of the heartbreaking sacred Presences; but it is as well, because it is man-made, a profane perfection.

The indifference of statues, once so painful to Yeats, now becomes their great virtue. Their stylization, impersonality, and remoteness are those of the Ideal: the Ideal, he now sees (rejecting the cruder and grosser profane perfections which did violence to his own nature, so naturally given to dream and vision) is ever indefinite and abstract as are the nouns we call it by – Hope, Virtue, Love, Piety, Patriotism – and is ever redefined by our individual and yearning participation in it. Statues carved to mathematical calculations of harmony give a concrete sexual object to adolescent dreams of perfection; the Pythagorean numbers, impersonally incarnate in marble or in bronze, might seem to lack character,

But boys and girls, pale from the imagined love
Of solitary beds, knew what they were,
That passion could bring character enough,
And pressed at midnight in some public place,
Live lips upon a plummet-measured face.
    (*The Statues*)

The case is generalized; like the boys and girls, all men need the constancy to an ideal object to which they may attach their personal actions. The import of *The Statues* is both comic and tragic: comic in the *success* of the symmetrically exchanged kiss of life and Presence, tragic in its formulation of our perpetual adolescence, forever worshipping a silent and unresponsive Presence. Or is it unresponsive? During the first half of the poem, yes; by its definition it must be, since the Presence is a set of numbers, a blueprint, a ratio of the intellect temporarily given shape by a sculptor. But when the human factor enters, the Presence takes on a living reality, is given, so to speak, a human body instead of a bronze body to wear. When a new hero, Padraic Pearse in the 1916 Post Office siege, acts out an old concept, pressing his 'live lips' to the 'plummet-measured' heroism of Cuchulain defined in the archaic motions of the sagas, he becomes his hero:

> When Pearse summoned Cuchulain to his side,
> What stalked through the Post Office? What intellect,
> What calculation, number, measurement, replied?

This reply from a sacred Presence is what Yeats has been wishing all his life to affirm, through the absurd experiments of his youth, through the comic association with Madame Blavatsky, through the attendance at seances, through the automatic writings of his wife. Yet the wish for an utterance from an oracle is repeatedly defeated, most finally in *The Man and the Echo*, where the illegitimate wish to wrest an answer from the voice of history to an extra-historical question is frustrated by a mocking silence.

It is deeply ironic that Yeats's reply should come, finally, from the patriots whose motives and wisdom he questioned, against whose blunt action and bewilderment of love he set his own solitary study in his tower, his own pursuit of esoteric wisdom. The Presences were all the time in the Post Office, ennobled in his last poem to a hybrid construction with his own Tower, as though Yeats were to say that the Post Office and the Tower are one. At the end of *The Statues*, there is a high and destined common aim:

> We Irish, born into that ancient sect,
> But thrown upon this filthy modern tide

And by its formless spawning fury wrecked,
Climb to our proper dark, that we may trace
The lineaments of a plummet-measured face.

To so trace the lineaments of gratified desire is a fulfillment of
dream. The last poem has no such satisfactions. In *The Black Tower*,
the bitter doctrine of *Under Ben Bulben* – that man makes lock, stock,
and barrel out of his bitter soul – receives its adequate image. *The
Statues* had maintained the illusion of dialogue, of reply, as the resur-
rected Cuchulain stalked through the Post Office, an active interpola-
tion in the landscape, like the Rough Beast. But Yeats's bleaker view
is that images become tireless and tiring projections of an inaccessible
perfection on a constantly self-renewing void. This epistemological
exhaustion is countered by a moral stoicism none the less heroic for
its rational absurdity. Bound by an oath to wait till their king returns,
the besieged soldiers in the black tower wait, knowing their king is
dead and buried and will never return. The sacred perfection of the
kingly presence does not any longer exist, if indeed it ever did, but if
it did it would be the source of allegiance. Therefore the mute oath
and the objectless faith. The last kiss, as Yeats wrote at the end of his
life, is given to the void. Though the poem is written in terms perfectly anonymous, the heroes are recognizably Yeats's Irish nationalists, answering his earlier question, 'O when may it suffice?' with
the reply, 'Never'. Man is bound by a real faith to his unreal Presences, whether sacred or profane, and on that unrelenting truth, of a
human resistance to Fate supported only by a nonexistent Presence,
Yeats ends his life.

William H. Pritchard

'The Uses of Yeats's Poetry' in *Twentieth-Century Literature in Retrospect* (Harvard English Studies, no. 2) 1971

Describing Robert Frost's creation of an official role for himself, Randall Jarrell imagines Yeats saying about him, as Sarah Bernhardt said of Nijinsky, 'I fear, I greatly fear, that I have just seen the greatest actor in the world.' With equal justice the remark could be made about Yeats – and no doubt was by Frost at some time or other.

> Heart-smitten with emotion I sink down,
> My heart recovering with covered eyes;
> Wherever I had looked I had looked upon
> My permanent or impermanent images:[1]

Lines like these from *The Municipal Gallery Revisited* were what first attracted me and I presume other readers to W. B. Yeats. What we heard, we were convinced, was the accent of passionate sincerity – extreme speech from the poet's heart of hearts. Yet it could not be simply the heart speaking because critics agreed that Yeats's poetry was subtle, complex, allusive, and thought through its images; was dramatic, ambiguous, and possessed the requisite amount of lyric tension. In other words, poetry as it used to be in the days of the Metaphysicals before things fell apart, Dryden and Milton were magniloquent, Tennyson and Browning ruminated. I may have owned a copy of *The Permanence of Yeats* (featuring essays by Brooks, Tate, Ransom, and others) before I did the *Collected Poems*; at any rate I had most certainly read the standard critical texts on Yeats's poetry before I was in any sense 'inwards' with it. I knew that the most important poems were *Sailing to Byzantium*, *The Second Coming*, *Among School Children*, and *Byzantium*; knew that there was a lot of magic around you didn't really have to believe in but which was at least preferable to modern science and a materialistic view of things; knew that mainly it was metaphor that counted.

An overall view of the poet's career was also provided: Yeats began by writing dream poetry characterized by lulling rhythms

[1] All quotations of Yeats's verse are from *The Collected Poems of W. B. Yeats*, copyright Macmillan Co. (New York, 1956), by permission of the publisher.

and Irish names (soon spiced with theosophical ones) whose message was that we should leave the unhappy world if possible and go away somewhere apart. These early poems could be condescended to, though a few of them possessed minor virtues and there was the popular *Innisfree* with something of the status of Paderewski's 'Minuet'. Then by a miracle Yeats broke free of these bad habits (though his example constitutes a warning: 'No serious poet could propose to begin again where Mr Yeats began', F. R. Leavis) and proceeded to write harsher, sparer lyrics which confronted the real world, usually in scorn or bitterness. He went on to create a system out of which came the metaphors for some of his greatest poems, published in *The Tower*. The system was a bit maddening but didn't get in your way much once you looked up 'perne in a gyre' and made the decision to pronounce it with a hard 'g'. He wrote some poems about Crazy Jane which were astonishingly sexual; and his *Last Poems* were simple, sensual, passionate, and bitter, though there was disagreement on whether they constituted a step forward or back from the *Tower* Yeats. On the whole his example was very much an inspiring one: along with T. S. Eliot he invented Modern Poetry, but he was a more human figure than Eliot, and certainly a better guide in relation to passionate love since he never did dirt on life. If he couldn't always be trusted on politics we could still forgive him: 'You were silly, like us. Your gift survived it all. . . .'

This version of Yeats is not a pack of lies; if anything more than a private fantasy – and I assume it is familiar to other readers – then doubtless there is truth in it. But a fairly low-grade truth: an easy way of categorizing and understanding a strange writer that for all its good intentions manages to explain away the strangeness and tame a wild, a 'fanatic' heart into the orderly subject of literary essays. And though the library is now filled with sound books on Yeats they will be of little help to a reader trying to feel the life of a particular poem, or asking whether it has any life, rather than studying up on Yeats's aesthetic, or his use of the Hero, or of History, or Tragedy. Scholars are notoriously adept at writing *around* poems by considering them as illustrations of something else; what that something else has to do with anybody sitting down and merely reading a poem is problematic. My concern here is for this mere reader of Yeats: I would like to imagine a more active one who is sometimes puzzled or uncertain, often moved but not always sure what he was moved by. My aim is to create a few difficulties where, well-wadded with stupidity, we walk about with a headful of critical essays that tell us what each line of every poem is supposed to mean or illustrate or import.[1]

Suppose, that is, instead of glossing the 'Heart-smitten with emotion' lines quoted earlier by saying that at this point in the poem Yeats feels overcome, conveys an attitude to us in such and such a tone, reveals his momentary speechlessness in the face of his old friends for whom he finds words later on – suppose instead of saying any of these things we tried to locate the reader by asking how he responds to 'Heart-smitten with emotion . . .' What does he say? Does he say anything? Does he think yes, there I could be too, sinking down on my knees – I am like the speaker? Does he judge the speaker in any tentative way? Does he sympathize with him, admire him, or hold back and wait to see what happens next? Does he hesitatingly whisper a question about the sincerity of the gesture? Is it sincere or stagy, and how is it different from similar gestures in other poems? The moment in my own reading of Yeats when for the first time someone asked a question of this sort occurred in an undergraduate course of Lionel Trilling's which ended with Yeats. During a discussion of *To a Friend Whose Work Has Come to Nothing* Trilling quoted the final lines, 'Be secret and exult,/Because of all things known/That is most difficult,' then commented: 'Of course that's

[1] I am not arrogant enough to suppose myself the first critic to be concerned with how the reader of Yeats behaves. From the great body of critical writing about Yeats after 1940, much of it concentrated on the analysis of individual poems, I would single out essays by Arthur Mizener, L. C. Knights, and Randall Jarrell (all from the *Southern Review*, Winter 1942), as 'overviews' of the poet's career which spring from and always remain in touch with a common reader's responses to the poems. More recently, essays by John Holloway and Donald Davie (in *An Honoured Guest* 1965) are similarly oriented and enlightening, as are the chapters on Yeats in C. K. Stead's excellent book *The New Poetic*, Penguin, 1969.

Two recent books, in whole or in part about Yeats, present the most passionately opinionated readings of the poetry I have encountered and probably constitute the most adverse criticism, though much seasoned with admiration, his poems have received. Though in this essay I will not deal with F. R. Leavis' chapter on Yeats in his *Lectures in America*, nor Harold Bloom's recent *Yeats* my reviews of them can be consulted: see 'Discourses in America', *Essays in Criticism*, July 1969 and 'Mr Bloom in Yeatsville', *Partisan Review* Spring 1971.

not true, is it?' What happened next is lost to me, but I remember being annoyed at the liberty I thought Trilling had taken: *imagine* questioning the terms of a poem in this way and setting yourself up as judge of how much truth it speaks! Though I still feel that Trilling's remark was a (probably deliberate) simplification of Yeats's attitude, it loosened me up to the extent that I must have then determined not to spend the rest of my days explicating *Byzantium* in sound, objective ways, but to throw in my lot with Yeatsian subjectivity. If death and life were not till man made up the whole, 'made lock stock and barrel|Out of his bitter soul,' then neither are poems until they elicit the subjective voice of a reader, a voice with enough responsiveness in it to interest at least one other reader in the world.

This essay proposes to be exemplary of such an approach, insofar as it tries to connect statements about 'Yeats' or 'Yeats's poetry' with what a particular reader (me, or rather my best self) does on a specific poetic occasion. It also assumes that the subjective voice is most likely to be brought into play when one's response is ambiguous in the Empsonian sense – when hitherto uncharted possibilities are discovered in the poems and in oneself. And if talk about the uses of poetry sounds as though it is to be considered as equipment for living, I believe that we do so use it, but in strange ways. Poetry is a criticism of life; the difficulty is, as Paul Goodman says somewhere, in finding out what it's saying.

Some chronological distinctions may be of use at this point: 'Early Yeats' designates the poems up through *The Wind Among the Reeds* and those from *The Green Helmet* and *In the Seven Woods* in which a similar manner predominates. 'Middle Yeats' refers mainly to *Responsibilities* and *The Wild Swans at Coole* but reaches back to poems in the two previous volumes and forward to *Michael Robartes and the Dancer*; the term as used in this essay is little more than a convenient catch-all for attitudes and experiments tried in those poems from the second decade of this century. 'Great Yeats' is *The Tower* and *The Winding Stair*; although I do believe those volumes contain some 'great' poems, the term is employed to designate that period of maximum creativity which most critics agree can be located in the 1920s. And then there is 'Late Yeats' – the *Last Poems*.

Early Yeats is the right place to begin asking questions about the uses of this poetry. Reading through the collected volume the eyes soon glaze over, as too often The Poet Pleads with the Elemental Powers; and the mind is not fully occupied with things like the ballad of Moll Magee, or the Foxhunter. But even apart from the often intrinsically lulling and deadening character of their rhythms – exactly what Yeats said he was trying to achieve in his early verse – it is more than usually hard to focus: what is there to focus *on* if one isn't specially interested in Yeats's use of the occult, or of Irish themes, or Pre-Raphaelite colours and odours? Pure sound and rhythm? A retreat to aesthetic purity might be in order if the rhymer were less of a histrionic and theatrical personality and more like the speaker of, say, Lionel Johnson's poems; with Yeats the presence of a personality, of an attractive and compelling poetic voice, makes impossible a retreat into admiration of 'pure' anything. Years ago Leavis referred to the 'paradoxical energy' informing many of these early dream-poems and first met in the introductory *Song of the Happy Shepherd*:

The woods of Arcady are dead,
And over is their antique joy;
Of old the world on dreaming fed;
Grey Truth is now her painted toy;
Yet still she turns her restless head:
But O, sick children of the world,
Of all the many changing things
In dreary dancing past us whirled,
To the cracked tune that Chronos sings,
Words alone are certain good.

On it runs, telling us the same thing over and over again: to dream, to scorn action and deeds, to look over history and see how nothing has survived but stories made of words, to gather some 'echo-harbouring' shell and speak fretful words to it so that they may be reworded melodiously and thereby somehow comfort us – as this very poem seeks to, by rewording melodiously sad truths. If not so calculatingly arresting in its movement, nor hushedly portentous in its sentiment as the familiar *Innisfree*, the poem still sounds un-abashedly theatrical when put next to a comparable 'escapist' lyric by Robert Frost like *Into My Own*, the opening poem in his first volume: 'I should not be witheld but that some day/Into their vastness I should steal away ...' Unlike Frost's quiet confession, the histrionic lecturer who announces that 'I will arise and go now' or tells us not to hunger fiercely after truth is continuous with the grand, to some readers shrill, Yeatsian voice of *The Tower* or *Under Ben Bulben* that pontificates about Man, the Soul, Ireland.

The finest moments in Early Yeats occur when this voice calls out arrestingly and tells us to leave what we're doing and listen to the news of a place where things go in more heart-stirring ways than in the fretful ordinary world. Our acceptance of this voice must be deliberately whole-hearted, naively unqualified by our burden of knowledge. The 'paradoxical energy' of these languid poems is such that in the best of them Yeats never simply says how sad or how weary all things are, but puts an adverb before the adjective: how marvelously weary, how perfectly sad all things are, they exclaim. 'Who will go drive with Fergus now|And pierce the deep wood's woven shade' – the poem is alive only when the reader experiences a simple thrill, abandons qualifications, and swings along with the advice 'And no more turn aside and brood|Upon love's bitter mystery.' Whatever the glories or sorrows of driving with Fergus, you will never be the same afterward; the game is, like that of the Happy Shepherd in the poem quoted earlier, to reword in melodious guile 'Love's bitter mystery' so as to make the world of troubles *marvelous* troubles. If the willing reader is touched it is because certain inexpressible yearnings of which he may be either proud or ashamed or both have been touched. He has allowed himself to be taken in but feels rather exhilarated by the whole business.

By contrast, the typical Middle Yeats poem replaces the imperative mode ('dream thou|For fair are poppies on the brow|Dream dream ...') with a rhetorical interrogative. This change of address is usually described by critics as coincident with Yeats's turning away from the enchantments of unreal dream and settling on the imperfect real world; his playwriting for the Abbey theatre helped him achieve a new spare line, less indulgent diction, and the conversational, sometimes colloquial tone in which the poems are conducted. In other words, Yeats is praised for 'withering into the truth', for 'walking naked' the very way he liked to think of himself as having done.

But it is perhaps a doubtful compliment to accept a poet at no more than his own valuation of himself – as having turned from

Dream to Truth – especially since we have the advantage of hindsight. Undeniably the poems have become craftier; the rhetorical interrogative is exploited with great suppleness.

> Why should I blame her that she filled my days
> With misery, or that she would of late
> Have taught to ignorant men most violent ways,
> Or hurled the little streets upon the great,
> Had they but courage equal to desire?
> What could have made her peaceful with a mind
> That nobleness made simple as a fire,
> With beauty like a tightened bow, a kind
> That is not natural in an age like this,
> Being high and solitary and most stern?
> Why, what could she have done, being what she is?
> Was there another Troy for her to burn?

The title, *No Second Troy*, assures us that there wasn't – an unnecessary assurance, since it is the poem's essence to leave no room for doubt of any sort. Describing the style as colloquial or conversational is just about as useful or accurate as calling one of Hamlet's soliloquies impassioned. Surely these lines are no closer to language as it is 'really used' by men than are the lines of *Who Goes with Fergus* or *Song of the Happy Shepherd*. But a useful comment of Edward Thomas's on Frost's 'colloquial' style may help with Yeats. Thomas is defending Frost against the strictures of Sturge Moore:

> All he [Frost] insists on is what he believes he finds in all
> poets – absolute fidelity to the postures which the voice
> assumes in the most expressive intimate speech. So long as
> these tones and postures are there he has not the least
> objection to any vocabulary whatever or any inversion or
> variation from the customary grammatical forms of talk. In
> fact I think he would agree that if these tones and postures
> survive in a complicated and learned and subtle
> vocabulary and structure the result is likely to be better
> than if they survive in the easiest form that is in the very
> words and structures of common speech.[1]

1 *Letters from Edward Thomas to Gordon Bottomley*, Oxford University Press, 1968.

As opposed to the weakly connected flow of 'ands' (surely the most significant word in Early Yeats) in the Fergus or Innisfree or Shepherd poems, the complicated and subtle structure of No Second Troy is strongly syntactical. Its strength will brook no oppositions, no qualifications, no perhapses.

All energies stand in the service of a style of triumph. Whoever or whatever the poem seems to be about (in this one it is Maud Gonne, a heroic Helen mocked by clown and knave) the ultimate hero is the 'I', supreme in his capacities for bringing all to mind and disposing of it in a striking way – 'Why, what could she have done, being what she is?' The beauty of this poem, and of the best Middle Yeats, is indeed like a tightened bow, on the surface for all to inspect; it doesn't yield any more than does one of Ben Jonson's epigrams (Yeats was reading him at the time) to critical probings after complex feelings and significances. The style of triumph cannot afford such complexities; or rather, they must be wholly contained by the lyric voice which impressively details them ('Why should I blame her ... What could have made her peaceful ... Why, what could she have done') only to place them firmly in the last line. For all 'her' nobleness, the 'I' is finally superior to her, as he is in more obvious ways to the citizens of 'an age like this' who cannot appreciate her.

So where does this take us? To the conclusion, I think, that the celebrated turn toward reality in Yeats's poetry from roughly 1903 to 1915 is rather the substitution of one dream for another. Instead of imagining an isle to which he and a beloved would fly when or if things become other than they are, the poet creates tightened structures of rhetoric which protect and exalt him (or, in the case of To a Friend ...' appropriate a worthy other like Lady Gregory to Yeatsian lonely rectitude) even as they frequently say that he has been vanquished, is harassed and worn out: No Second Troy, The Fascination of What's Difficult, the prologue to Responsibilities, To a Wealthy Man ... To a Friend Whose Work ..., To a Shade – these are some familiar examples. Put another way: if in these middle poems Yeats often achieves the 'passionate syntax' he once spoke of, it is to the exclusion of the subjective exploration he later undertook. His very difficult and pregnant motto 'In Dreams Begins Responsibility', when read in the light of Responsibilities and those poems beginning with *The Fisherman* and *Ego Dominus Tuus* which soon followed it, suggest less a rejection of dream in favour of reality than a felt necessity to ask harder and less rhetorical questions about the self which spins out the dream. How is responsibility incurred? What does it have to do with the kind of poem most worth writing, most subjectively (even more than syntactically) passionate, most sincere? These questions, and the search for answering qualities of truth, passion, sincerity, kept Yeats productively busy in the remaining twenty-five years of his life.

Ego Dominus Tuus, written in 1915 and published as part of *Per Amica Silentia Lunae* – Yeats's first full formulation of the anti-self theory – is usually condescended to as a poem, then plundered for utterances that demonstrate what the poet was thinking in 1915. Admittedly, the dialogue form looks precious and the dice are loaded (remember Pound's reference to the one speaker, *Ille*, as really Willie) but it is an extraordinarily engaging poem nonetheless, and its bold, extravagant formulations – like those which later mark *A Vision* at its best – signal an audacious widening of Yeats's horizons. Because it is longer and more unwieldy and leisurely in its development than the tensely compressed lyric verse of Middle Yeats, it manages to stay changing and fresh, not quite assimilated into our ears even after many readings. Its point of maximum depth comes after *Ille* has demonstrated, brilliantly and movingly, that the chief imagination of Christendom, Dante Alighieri, did not 'find himself', but rather an image that was most unlike his own poor self; *Hic* replies in a sensible you-go-too-far-old-fellow tone:

Yet surely there are men who have made their art
Out of no tragic war, lovers of life,
Impulsive men that look for happiness
And sing when they have found it.

Robert Browning perhaps? But *Ille* will allow no exceptions:

                                No, not sing,
For those that love the world serve it in action,
Grow rich, popular and full of influence,
And should they paint or write, still it is action:

The struggle of the fly in marmalade.
The rhetorician would deceive his neighbours,
The sentimentalist himself; while art
Is but a vision of reality.
What portion in the world can the artist have
Who has awakened from the common dream
But dissipation and despair?

Ille uses the same words – dream, reality, the world, singing –
made familiar by Yeats's poetry since it announced that the woods
of Arcady were dead; but if still exclusive, the analysis is now more
interesting. When glossed, the lines say that an artist, a true singer,
can have no truck with the world, no 'portion . . . But dissipation and
despair' since 'art|Is but a vision of reality'. This is a very sad or very
promising situation, depending on how you look at it, so the poem
looks at it in both ways: dissipation and despair are not just what
morbid aesthetes from the Rhymers' club specialized in but what any
man in his necessary dealings with life suffers – 'while art|Is but a
vision of reality'. The phrase can be read with many different stresses,
on art or vision or reality or even 'Is but', or on all of them alike. A
vision of reality, then, both less and more than reality – 'Is but'.
Yeats went on in his autobiography to name this awakening from the
common dream with terms like 'ecstasy' or 'tragedy' or 'the quarrel
with ourselves'. The terms are less important than is the challenge
laid down by these lines: namely, how to embody a vision of reality
in poetry that is also humanly interesting – in fact, since his terms are
so extreme, of supreme human interest – without succumbing to the
world, the 'common dream' from which bad poets never awaken
and by which merely sensitive poets are ruined. Yeats refuses to be, in
the words of a famous *New Yorker* cartoon, a very sick little poet.

Taking *Ego Dominus Tuus* as a prolegomenon to any future
healthy poetry makes sense in the context of four gravely impressive
poems which followed it in the next few years: *Easter 1916, In
Memory of Major Robert Gregory, A Prayer for My Daughter*, and *The
Second Coming*. Each presents an awakening from a dream, common
or otherwise, in the interests of a vision of reality; each focuses
intently on some person or event outside the lyric speaker; each
presumes to speak in public, though not propagandistic, ways. They

have in common the central presence of an unhappy mind – dried up, distracted, unfeeling or in despair – which is touched by something outside itself and changed thereby. An argument could be made that these poems represent the peak of Yeats's achievement, especially for readers dissatisfied with what they see as the self-absorption, aestheticism, or inhumanity of Great and Late Yeats. The first three (*The Second Coming* less so) require that human feelings and responses be brought into play as Yeats's previous verse has seldom demanded; there is nothing esoteric in their concerns and little in the language that embodies them. They succeed in being intensely personal, subjective (in Yeats's phrase from the *Autobiography*) in that they recreate all that exterior fate snatches away. If in dreams begins responsibility, these are preeminently the poems where those dreams are given their most imaginative, balanced exploration and where their costs – to life – are most vividly set forth.

Frank Kermode's term 'romantic image' is still the best for pointing at what is coherent, unified, powerful – at whatever the poet is not – which can only be approximated by the language of a particular poem. But of course merely applying the term to the 'image' of a poem is no indicator of quality or value. Some images, as it were, are more 'romantic' than others: a simpler-minded Yeats could have worked a good vein and written poem after poem exclaiming about a Fisherman or some comparable anti-self – how admirable, how unlike my own poor self! Instead he discovered that a romantic image need not be merely consolatory, a wistful gesture at something you are not (as if one should improve his shy personality by becoming talkative and outgoing), but something to be literally admired, wondered at, shocked by, not to be contemplated without a tinge of fear or dread. Take the elegy to Robert Gregory. If it consisted only of endless variations on what a splendid portmanteau fellow Gregory was ('Soldier, scholar, horseman, he,|And all he did done perfectly') the poem would, and to some extent does, have the limitations of conventional special pleading. It moves rather towards a conclusion where Gregory becomes an image, a pure spirit who understood 'all' – 'All lovely intricacies of a house', 'All work in metal or in wood' – in his undivided, unified being 'As though he had but that one trade alone'. So it is with something like self-consummation – for reader and poet – that this spirit's apotheosis is evoked:

Some burn damp faggots, others may consume
The entire combustible world in one small room
As though dried straw, and if we turn about
The bare chimney is gone black out
Because the work had finished in that flare.
Soldier, scholar, horseman, he,
As 'twere all life's epitome.
What made us dream that he could comb grey hair?

What indeed! The question is not quite so loaded as 'Was there another Troy for her to burn?' nor so simply inviting as 'Who will go drive with Fergus now'. The poet has been awakened from one of those 'common dreams' – of the loved hero's living to comb grey hair – and the alternative is not dissipation or despair; rather, the sudden, glamorous, and passionate extinction of life. A passage from Yeats's autobiography tells us about violent energy, like a fire of straw, being useless in the arts. But we don't need it here to see that the poet, burning damp faggots like the rest of us, has nevertheless preserved himself, has made something out of experience maybe less glamorous but surely more enduring than any 'flare' set off by Gregory. Yet this self-preservation isn't presented as a triumph, and more is asked of the reader here than in earlier poems: while he must give his admiration to Gregory – the image – he must also imagine experience through the complex, depressed, and extraordinarily *tonal* world of the man who remains behind: 'I had thought, seeing how bitter is that wind|That shakes the shutter . . .' Nobody gets a cheer at the end of the poem. There is no convenient outlet for one's mixed feelings about heroic life, the art that celebrates it, and the artist who suffers, with whatever discretion, to create it.

It is *Easter 1916* that most movingly depicts how responsibility begins in dreams. After the flexible tone of the first two sections places the Irish revolutionaries, as well as the speaker's social – indeed tonal – judgements of them ('What voice more sweet than hers|When, young and beautiful|She rode to harriers?'), an anonymous voice sings out:

Hearts with one purpose alone
Through summer and winter seem
Enchanted to a stone

To trouble the living stream.
The horse that comes from the road,
The rider, the birds that range
From cloud to tumbling cloud,
Minute by minute they change . . .
The stone's in the midst of all.

Efforts to paraphrase this moment are even less satisfactory than usual; we know by section four when Yeats points the moral ('Too long a sacrifice | Can make a stone of the heart') that the revolutionaries have been transformed utterly, beyond the language of social judgement; also that they have been enchanted to a stone, a fixed idea which turned their hearts to stone. But as, in the flux of section three, 'the long-legged moor-hens dive, | And hens to moor-cocks call', it's not clear that we hold *any* distinct idea. Enchanted by events beyond our discourse we wake only to confront the painful questions which end the poem, finally and most unbearably – 'And what if excess of love/Bewildered them till they died?'

After these questions the salute to MacDonagh and MacBride and the repetition of 'A terrible beauty is born' are ways of using words that recognize their formulaic character, thus their limitations. Even in using them one has looked beyond them. To write, in the language of *The Fisherman*, a poem cold and passionate as the dawn, which is what Yeats did in *Easter 1916*, demands a full exploitation of the tone and syntax through which ordinary life – 'the casual comedy' – is set forth. Then beyond that, springing out from it and against it, is the momentary presence of a toneless voice singing of a realm beyond comedy or bitterness or society, where horses plash and moor-cocks call and where things do not yield up their meanings to the words that would summarize them. The result is a muted and impersonal poem which remains with us and is not easy to live with; its 'responsibility' involves no clear course of action but rather a fitful seeing-around of all action.

Compared to this truly ambiguous poem, *The Second Coming* is single-minded, visionary, even optimistic in its bearing as it uses and transforms the public situation of *Easter 1916* – 'The best lack all conviction, while the worst | Are full of passionate intensity' – into striking private capital. The visionary motive hints of things to come:

of *Sailing to Byzantium*, *Two Songs from a Play*, *Leda and the Swan*; of *Byzantium*, *The Gyres*, and *Lapis Lazuli*. Such poems are informed with a voice by turns hushed and exultant: neglecting the middle range of speech, relatively uninterested in cultivating nuance and shade of tone, it is at home only in extremes of pitch, it brooks no obstacles nor is it concerned with posing unanswerable questions to itself. Leavis called Shakespeare's verse 'exploratory-creative' of experience; though some of Yeats's poems could be so termed, they are not the ones in the list above, whose prevailing gesture towards experience is imperious or dismissive or brilliantly exploitive of it. As with Early Yeats the favored mood is imperative; as with Middle Yeats the style of triumph is in vogue, though bolstered now by systematic mythical-historical 'truths' of character and epoch.

For all their invocations of gyres, the *Magnus Annus*, a vast image out of *Spiritus Mundi* – the difficulties of these poems are superficial, mainly disappearing once one finds the way around their surfaces; they change and deepen less upon re-reading than do the poems I term ambiguous. One recites, declaims, gestures his way through *The Second Coming* or *Byzantium* (what pleasure there is, say, in intoning 'At midnight on the emperor's pavement flit|Flames no faggot feeds nor steel has lit') and finds himself close to an experience in pure declamatory rhythms. So too the outcome of these poems seems predestined, somehow made up in the poet's mind before he wrote the first line – though of course the revisions tell us this was not in fact the case. As for their personal reference, the presence of an 'I' in *The Second Coming* ('The darkness drops again; but now I know . . .') or in *Byzantium* ('I hail the superhuman|I call it birth in life . . .') is but a convenience, a register for visionary supersensations from which knowledge is ecstatically gained.

In other words, little or no complex penetration of a mind occurs in these poems, with the result that the reader, too, escapes unscathed, changed not utterly but only theatrically, very much for the nonce. Yeats's famous remark about beginning to live when we conceive life as tragedy is anterior to these poems, which, though they can be *about* tragedy – as in *Lapis Lazuli* – about the 'fury and the mire of human veins' (*Byzantium*), are by that token outside of it, detached from it. And the reader is occupied with watching a performance by a magnificently skilled conjurer (what will he think of next? where will he move?) rather than with bearing witness to tragic experience undergone through the sequence of the poem.

But Yeats knew very well that if conceiving life as tragedy is the beginning of living, then poems would transcend the fury and mire of human veins only at their peril. Not uncritical of his own romantic image, he attempted, increasingly in the poems from *The Tower* and beyond, to put difficulties in the way of the would-be transcender. So in a poem like *Dialogue of Self and Soul* the enraptured Soul affirms the virtues of silence to the degree that he fades right out of the poem, conveniently leaving Self three stanzas in which to proclaim his commitment to the 'frog-spawn of a blind man's ditch', then, having converted life to its lowest terms, to forgive himself and affirm the lot:

We must laugh and we must sing,
We are blest by everything.
Everything we look upon is blest.

Very well, and undeniably thrilling, but as much of a brag as the corresponding movement upward towards becoming a golden bird set on a bow, and no more the occasion for complex feelings on the reader's part. For all its stylistic nobility this sudden casting out of remorse is a bit glib.

I want now to argue that the deepest poetic alternative to the arrogant single-mindedness with which a romantic image disdains and rejects the world is not a corresponding single-mindedness in the other direction, saying Yes rather than No to life. Yeats's problem, which he came to grips with superbly in a number of poems, was to get the rival claims of the image and of life – as he often called it, the Heart – stated in all their fullness and exclusiveness; then to end the poem in such a way that neither he nor the reader could say exactly where triumph was, or if it were properly a triumph at all. Not to give in to misery, to the passive suffering of which he accused Wilfred Owen's poetry, nor loudly to affirm 'What matter'; but, in Jarrell's marvellous phrase about Frost's best work, to write poems which make either optimism or pessimism a hopeful evasion.

Heart-mysteries there, and yet when all is said
It was the dream itself enchanted me. . . .

The poems to be considered from Great and Late Yeats I first selected by impulse as particularly compelling, only to see on re-flection their common concern with those matters of the heart experienced before 'all is said'. 'What shall I do with this absurdity – O heart, O troubled heart' begins *The Tower*; and though the ques-tion refers to the 'caricature' of 'decrepit age', the poem proceeds to locate the heart's trouble in a less facile way. *The Tower*, along with *Meditations in Time of Civil War*, *Among School Children*, *Her Vision in the Wood*, *Parnell's Funeral*, *The Circus Animals' Desertion*, and others, are evidence of a human fineness of response that has been ignored by those who accuse Yeats of ending where he began, in but a fancier version of aestheticism. Their pleasures and difficulties are many; I shall select from them only a few crucial moments where the engaged reader's life is fullest.

Part 1 of *The Tower* asks what to do with decrepit age, then part 2 takes thirteen winding stanzas to prepare for the closing affirmation of part 3. The final stanza of part 2 is my interest, coming as it does after the poet has sent imagination forth to call up all sorts of people from history, legend, his own writings as aids and witnesses to his dilemma. This calling up is often broken in upon by the caller's impatience with his own game ('And followed up those baying creatures towards – |O towards I have forgotten what – enough!'); only Hanrahan is finally allowed to remain, on the purely fictional grounds that he has 'reckoned up every unforeknown, unseeing| Plunge . . . into the labyrinth of another's being'. At this point Yeats poses the question all this rambling has led up to:

Does the imagination dwell the most
Upon a woman won or a woman lost?
If on the lost, admit you turned aside
From a great labyrinth out of pride,
Cowardice, some silly over-subtle thought
Or anything called conscience once;
And that if memory recur, the sun's
Under eclipse and the day blotted out.

At which point the day is blotted out and the 'I' proceeds to write his will, choosing 'upstanding men' who, like the Fisherman of an earlier poem, do not exist, are but a dream. Yet this resolution, grand as it is, is also somewhat diversionary: the poignancy brought into the poem by asking shrewdly whether the imagination dwells the most on a woman lost (and clearly suggesting that it does) cannot be blotted out. 'Too long a sacrifice can make a stone of the heart' ran the line from *Easter 1916*. In terms of *The Tower* one should read: too long a dwelling on the romantic image of what you don't have, be it Maud Gonne or another, has its own costs to the heart. And though the third section of the poem boldly sets out to make these human costs 'Seem but the clouds of the sky|When the horizon fades', the very beautiful 'bird's sleepy cry' which ends the poem only too hauntingly reminds us of them.

The costs of homage to the romantic image are resonantly generalized in the penultimate stanza of *Among School Children*:

Both nuns and mothers worship images,
But those the candles light are not as those
That animate a mother's reveries,
But keep a marble or a bronze repose.
And yet they too break hearts – O Presences
That passion, piety or affection knows,
And that all heavenly glory symbolize –
O self-born mockers of man's enterprise;

These heartbreakers and mockers of man's enterprise live in the 'where' of the final stanza, that mythical realm where art is not a vision of reality but indistinguishable from it: an unironic paradise where leaf, blossom, or bole, dancer and dance, are one. Yeats's paradise is not treated with the condescending wit Wallace Stevens employs in *Sunday Morning* to set forth his boringly perfect realm, because it is evoked out of less firm acceptance of our mortal lot than is felt when Stevens intones 'Death is the mother of beauty'. To call, as Yeats does, the images 'self-born mockers of man's enterprise' is to speak painfully from *here*, where sons give mothers pains and nuns can't live up to their aspirations, where the extravagance of lyric invention and its grandeur of apostrophe ('O chestnut-tree, great-rooted blossomer') is a measure of how much deprivation a man can feel because he is what he is, alas, and not another thing.

Among School Children seems to me Yeats's finest poem because it is inclusive, ultimately impersonal but also modest, as the old scarecrow fades out into the guise of any and all of us. I can't imagine, that is, a reader who would not want to be spoken for by the last two stanzas of the poem, stanzas which elevate and ennoble life rather than transcend it or puff it up or sweep it out of the way. They are in addition an antidote to over-zealous iconographers who would focus excitedly only on the meanings of chestnut-tree or dancer, forgetting that 'And yet they too break hearts'. Yeats went on to write a wonderful poem about an old woman, bitter in her bodily misery, who thought she was watching a ritual grieving for the fatal wounding of Adonis ('It seemed a Quattrocento painter's throng,|A thoughtless image of Mantegna's thought') when all the time it was her own suffering lover, who suddenly – a 'beast-torn wreck' – fixes an eye on the woman, and she proceeds to fall senseless among the crowd, unaware 'That they had brought no fabulous symbol there|But my heart's victim and its torturer'. The imagination does dwell the most upon a woman (or a man) lost; no fabulous symbol there, but a heart's victim and torturer. If a reader doesn't feel the tug at his own heart no critic should try to argue him into it. But *Her Vision in the Wood* is, like *Among School Children*, both humanizing and tragic in the peculiarly ecstatic way Yeats conceived of tragedy; all arrogant self-congratulation has been purged, leaving only the best poetic self.

These late poems speak most movingly about the paradox of being a poet: how a heightened capacity for the imaginative entertaining of images, dreams, 'presences' seems to involve waverings, dissatisfactions, guilt about matters of the heart – the human condition – and attendant self-lacerations ('Admit that you turned aside from a great labyrinth'). Wordsworth's fine lines from *Resolution and Independence* are about all men – 'As high as we have mounted in delight/ In our dejection do we sink as low'. But since the poet mounts highest in delight and it is his obligation to share this delight with other men, then it seems hard that 'We poets in our youth begin in gladness/But thereof come in the end despondency and madness'. Out of this discovery, and out of his own poems about the heart as victim and torturer, came the heroic stock-taking of what has good imaginative reason to be thought of as Yeats's final poem, *The Circus Animals' Desertion*. It is a bona fide modernist poem in that, like so

much of Eliot or Stevens or Williams, it is about itself and about
Poetry, extraordinarily self-absorbed even as it mounts a criticism of
certain aggrandizing and inhuman tendencies in the poet's omnivorous
self. It also manages to be – and this in distinction to many modernist
poems – boldly though not crassly unrepentant, and it ends in exultation, not prayer. In the first of its three parts (a single stanza) the
'broken man' says he may have to be satisfied with his heart now in
dried-up age, though he remembers how his circus animals, winter
and summer, have been on show. He then goes on, in part 2, to name
some of them – old performers and figures like Oisin or the prota-
gonist of *The Countess Cathleen* – and tells how these dreams and
images usurped the thought and love usually devoted to human
affairs. The final stanza of part 2:

And when the Fool and Blind Man stole the bread
Cuchulain fought the ungovernable sea;
Heart-mysteries there, and yet when all is said
It was the dream itself enchanted me;
Character isolated by a deed
To engross the present and dominate memory.
Players and painted stage took all my love,
And not those things that they were emblems of.

The beautifully pointed economy and accuracy of these lines,
lordly in their cool analysis of how it was, won't stand to be con-
tradicted; and it has seemed to some readers that the famous single
stanza which ends the poem in part 3 comes down unequivocally,
and at long last, on the side of the heart and opposed to the 'masterful
images' that grew in pure mind. Those who want Yeats to emerge as
a last-minute humanist, saved in the nick of time from his own
players and painted stage, tend to salute this final stanza as a very good
thing to have said. But what in fact *is* said? How is the heart affirmed
and accepted?

These masterful images because complete
Grew in pure mind, but out of what began?
A mound of refuse or the sweepings of a street,
Old kettles, old bottles, and a broken can,
Old iron, old bones, old rags, that raving slut

Who keeps the till. Now that my ladder's gone,
I must lie down where all the ladders start,
In the foul rag-and-bone shop of the heart.

This poetry says, when all the poetry is taken away from it, that with the circus animals, the ladder gone, the poet will settle at last for his heart in all its sordidness and poverty. Yet with the poetry left in, as it were, the effect is to substitute a whole new array of circus animals for the old departed ones, the difference being that the new ones are called by sensationally low names like 'that raving slut|Who keeps the till'. Who will go drive with Fergus now? Yeats never ceases to issue invitations to himself; if the place of lying down is to be the heart rather than the dream, he will make sure it's no ordinary heart, but one never seen before on sea or land – a foul rag-and-bone shop of a heart. When all is said it was the dream itself that enchanted him: but this final poem says that 'all' most fully and eloquently.

   Triumph or defeat, then? Optimistic or pessimistic? A reader confronted with this poem can't use it to improve his own life as a shot in the arm to further endeavours of a particular sort. If he accepts it he must live with a strange imagination whose intransigence is supreme, whose reference to human life is as ambiguous as the acceptance of the heart in *The Circus Animals' Desertion*. And perhaps the main or only use of Yeats's poetry is that it teaches us to extend our notions of what it is to accept the heart, to be enchanted by a dream; that – as 'Character' is 'isolated by a deed|To engross the present and dominate memory' – his poetry so engrosses and dominates us as to make it unclear and unimportant whether we use it or are used by it.

Select Bibliography

Editions

The Collected Poems of W.B. Yeats, Macmillan, 1950.
The Collected Plays of W.B. Yeats, Macmillan, 1952.
Autobiographies, Macmillan, 1955.
A Vision, rev. edn, Macmillan, 1956.
Mythologies, Macmillan, 1959 (includes *Per Amica Silentia Lunae*).
Essays and Introductions, Macmillan, 1961.
Explorations, Macmillan, 1962 (contains further essays).
The Variorum Edition of the Poems of W.B. Yeats, ed. Peter Allt and Russell K. Alspach, Macmillan, 1957.
The Variorum Edition of the Plays of W.B. Yeats, ed. Russell K. Alspach, Macmillan, 1966.
Uncollected Prose by W.B. Yeats, vol. 1, ed. J. P. Frayne, Columbia University Press and Macmillian, 1970.

Bibliography and Reference

A Bibliography of the Writings of W.B. Yeats, ed. Allan Wade, Rupert Hart-Davis, 1958.
A Concordance to the Poems of W.B. Yeats, ed. Stephen Parrish, Cornell University Press, 1963.

Correspondence

Letters, ed. Allan Wade, Rupert Hart-Davis, 1954.
Letters on Poetry from W.B. Yeats to Dorothy Wellesley, Oxford University Press, 1940.
Letters to Katharine Tynan, ed. Roger McHugh, Clonmore and Reynolds, 1953.
W.B. Yeats and T. Sturge Moore. Their Correspondence 1901–1937, ed. Ursula Bridge, Routledge & Kegan Paul, 1953.

Biographies

Richard Ellmann, *Yeats: The Man and the Masks*, Macmillan, 1948.

Joseph Hone, *W.B. Yeats*, Macmillan, 1943.

A. Norman Jeffares, *W.B. Yeats: Man and Poet*, Yale University Press, 1949; rev. edn, Routledge & Kegan Paul, 1962.

Criticism

R.P. Blackmur, 'W.B. Yeats: Between Myth and Philosophy', *Form and Value in Modern Poetry*, Doubleday, 1957.

Harold Bloom, *Yeats*, Oxford University Press, 1970.

Curtis Bradford, *Yeats at Work*, Southern Illinois University Press, 1965 (Yeats' revisions).

Cleanth Brooks, 'Yeats's Great Rooted Blossomer', *The Well Wrought Urn*, Reynal and Hitchcock, 1947, pp. 163–75 (*Among School Children*).

Cleanth Brooks, 'Yeats: The Poet as Myth-Maker', *Modern Poetry and the Tradition*, University of North Carolina Press, 1939 (*A Vision*).

Reuben A. Brower, 'Yeats', in *Major British Writers*, Harcourt Brace & World, 1954.

Denis Donoghue (ed.), *The Integrity of Yeats*, Mercier Press, 1964.

Denis Donoghue, *The Ordinary Universe*, Macmillan, 1968.

Denis Donoghue and J.R. Mulryne (eds.), *An Honoured Guest*, Arnold, 1965 (essays on Yeats by recent critics).

Denis Donoghue, *Yeats* (Modern Masters), Collins, Viking Press, 1971.

Richard Ellmann, *The Identity of Yeats*, Oxford University Press, 1954. *Eminent Domain*, Oxford University Press, 1967.

Northrop Frye, 'Yeats and the Language of Symbolism', in *Fables of Identity*, Harcourt, Brace & World, 1963.

James Hall and Martin Steinmann (eds.), *The Permanence of Yeats*, Macmillan, 1950, Macmillan Co., 1961.

A. Norman Jeffares, *A Commentary on the Collected Poems of W.B. Yeats*, Macmillan, Stanford University Press, 1968.

Frank Kermode, *Romantic Image*, Routledge & Kegan Paul, 1957.

Louis MacNeice, *The Poetry of W.B. Yeats*, Oxford University Press, 1941.

Graham Martin, 'The Later Poetry of W.B. Yeats', in *Pelican Guide to English Literature*, vol. 7 (ed. Boris Ford), *The Modern Age*.

Thomas Parkinson, *W.B. Yeats: The Later Poetry*, University of California Press, 1964.

J. Stallworthy, *Between the Lines*, Oxford University Press, 1963 (Yeats' revisions).

C.K. Stead, *The New Poetic*, Penguin, 1969.

Southern Review, Yeats issue. Winter 1942.

John Unterecker, *A Reader's Guide to W.B. Yeats*, The Noonday Press, 1959.

Helen Vendler, *Yeats's Vision and the Later Plays*, Harvard University Press, 1964.

J.B. Yeats, *Letters to his son W.B. Yeats and others*, Faber, 1944.

Acknowledgements

For permission to use copyright material acknowledgement is
made to the following:

For 'The Moods', 'The Autumn of the Body' and 'The Symbolism of
Poetry' by W. B. Yeats from *Essays and Introductions* to Mrs W. B.
Yeats, the Macmillan Company of London and Basingstoke and the
Macmillan Company Inc. of New York; for 'Reveries Over Child-
hood' and 'The Trembling of the Veil' by W. B. Yeats from *Autobiog-
raphies*, to Mrs W. B. Yeats, M. B. Yeats, the Macmillan Company of
London and Basingstoke and the Macmillan Company Inc. of New
York; for 'Per Amica Silentia Lunae' by W. B. Yeats from *Mythologies*
to Mrs W. B. Yeats, M. B. Yeats, the Macmillan Company of London
and Basingstoke and the Macmillan Company Inc. of New York; for
'Nationality and Literature' by W. B. Yeats from *Uncollected Prose of
W. B. Yeats* edited by John P. Frayne to Columbia University Press and
the Estate of W. B. Yeats; for 'The Later Yeats' by Ezra Pound from
Literary Essays of Ezra Pound copyright Ezra Pound 1918, 1920, and 1935
reprinted by permission of New Directions Publishing Corporation
and Faber & Faber Ltd; for letters from John Butler Yeats to W. B.
Yeats to Faber & Faber Ltd, M. B. Yeats and Anne Yeats; for *W. B.
Yeats: A Critical Study* by Forrest Reid to Folcroft Press Inc.; for 'Mr
Yeats Swan Song' by John Middleton Murray from the *Athenaeum*
1919 to the *New Statesman*; for 'The Tower' by Theodore Spencer to
the *New Republic*; for 'Axel's Castle' by Edmund Wilson to the author;
for 'T. Sturge Moore' by Yvor Winters from *Hound and Horn*, also
forthcoming *Uncollected Essays of Ivor Winters* ed. Francis Murphy, and
to Swallow Press, 1972 to Mrs Janet L. Winters; for 'The Later Poetry
of W. B. Yeats' by Theodore Spencer from *Literary Opinion in America*
edited by Morton Zabel, to Mrs W. J. Bender; for 'The Later Poetry
of W. B. Yeats' by R. P. Blackmur from *Southern Review*, reprinted in
Language as Gesture, copyright R. P. Blackmur 1940 and Allen & Unwin
to Harcourt, Brace Jovanovich Inc., for 'The Public v. the late Mr
William Butler Yeats' by W. H. Auden to the *Partisan Review* and the
author; for 'In Memory of W. B. Yeats' by W. H. Auden from
Collected Shorter Poems to Faber & Faber Ltd and Random House Inc.;
for 'Yeats' by T. S. Eliot from *On Poetry and Poems* to Faber & Faber
Ltd and Farrar, Strauss & Giroux Inc.; for 'Yeats: Master of Diction' by
W. H. Auden, review of last poems and plays to *Saturday Review* and the
author; for 'Yeats Epitaph' by Louis MacNeice to *New Republic*; for

'The Development of Yeats's Sense of Reality' by Randall Jarrell from *Southern Review* to Mrs Mary Jarrell; for 'The Romanticism of W. B. Yeats' by Arthur Mizener from *Southern Review* to the author; for 'The Assertion of Values' by L. C. Knights from *Southern Review*, reprinted as 'Poetry and Social Criticism: The Work of W. B. Yeats' in *Explorations* to Chatto & Windus Ltd and the author; for 'W. B. Yeats' by George Orwell reprinted in *Collected Essays, Journalism and Letters* to Harcourt, Brace Jovanovich Inc.; for *The Personal Principle* by D. S. Savage to Kennikat Press Inc.; for 'The Severity of Mr Savage' by John Crowe Ransom to *Kenyon Review* and the author; for 'The Sacred Book of the Arts' by Hugh Kenner to *Gnomon*; for '*Among School Children*' by John Wain from *Interpretations* to Routledge & Kegan Paul Ltd and the author; for 'At Hawk's Well' by Hugh Kenner to *Gnomon*; for *Romantic Image* by Frank Kermode to Chilmark Press Inc.; for 'The Poetry of W. B. Yeats' from *Forms of Discovery* by Yvor Winters, *Critical and Historical Essays on the Forms of the Short Poem in English*, to the Swallow Press, Chicago; for 'Mr Wilson on the Byzantium Poems' by William Empson from *Ariel* (*A Review of International English Literature*) to the author; for *The New Poetic* by C. K. Stead to Hutchinson Publishing Group Ltd and Harper & Row Inc.; for 'Yeats the Master of a Trade' by Donald Davis from *The Integrity of Yeats* edited by Denis Donoghue to the author and Mercier Press; for *Michael Robartes and the Dancer* by Donald Davie from *An Honoured Guest* edited by D. Donoghue and J. R. Mulryne to Edward Arnold Ltd; for 'Style and World in *The Tower*' by John Holloway from *An Honoured Guest* edited by D. Donoghue and J. R. Molryne to Edward Arnold Ltd; for 'Passions and Cunning' by Conor Cruise O'Brian from *In Excited Reverie: A Centenary Tribute to W. B. Yeats* edited by A. N. Jeffares and K. G. W. Cross to the Macmillan Company of London and Basingstoke and the Macmillan Company of New York; for *Yeats* by Harold Bloom copyright 1970 by Oxford University Press Inc. reprinted by permission; for 'Sarced and Profane Perfection in Yeats' by Helen Vendler to the author; for 'The Uses of Yeats Poetry' by William H. Pritchard from *Twentieth Century Literature in Retrospect*, *Harvard English Studies* 2, to the department of English, Harvard University and the author.

Index

Index

Extracts included in this anthology are indicated by bold page references
References to individual works by Yeats are listed together under his name.